MYKHAILO HRUSHEVSKY

THE POLITICS OF NATIONAL CULTURE

Ukraine's foremost historian and one of its most prominent national leaders, Mykhailo Hrushevsky was at the turn of the century a leading figure in the transformation of the Ukrainian national revival into a major political movement. His pivotal role in Ukraine's drive toward national autonomy earned him both the admiration of his countrymen and the vilification of his critics.

The first scholarly biography of Hrushevsky, Thomas Prymak's study focuses on three major periods in the historian's life and in Ukraine's modern history. The first, from 1894 to 1917, was one of intensive scholarly and community activity for Hrushevsky and the advancement of his notion of federalism. The second, from 1917 to 1924, features Hrushevsky in the principal role in the Ukrainian revolution, and ends with his promotion of the Ukrainian cause abroad. The third period deals with his controversial return home to Soviet Ukraine, his uneasy yet productive relations with the regime whose ideology he steadfastly refused to endorse, and his mysterious death in 1934.

Hrushevsky is still a target of attacks by the Soviet government. This biography presents a balanced and judicious evaluation of a figure who remains a villain in the eyes of the Kremlin and a hero to Ukrainian émigrés.

THOMAS PRYMAK is Research Associate, Chair of Ukrainian Studies at the University of Toronto.

THOMAS M. PRYMAK

Mykhailo Hrushevsky: The Politics of National Culture

UNIVERSITY OF TORONTO PRESS
Toronto Buffalo London

© University of Toronto Press 1987
Toronto Buffalo London
Printed in Canada

ISBN 0-8020-5737-3

Canadian Cataloguing in Publication Data

Prymak, Thomas M., 1948–

Mykhailo Hrushevsky

(University of Toronto Ukrainian studies; 3)
Bibliography: p.
Includes index.
ISBN 0-8020-5737-3

1. Hrushevśkyĭ, Mykhaĭlo, 1866–1934. 2. Historians
– Ukraine – Biography. 3. Ukraine – Politics and
government – 1917–   . 4. Ukraine – Intellectual
life. 5. Nationalism – Ukraine. I. Title. II. Series.

DK508.47.H7P79 1987   947'.71084'0924   C87-094046-5

This book has been published with the help of a grant from the Canadian Federation for
the Humanities, using funds provided by the Social Sciences and Humanities Research
Council of Canada.

For Yassy

Obviously, the cooling of raw emotion and substitution of tepid intellectual discourse for the language of attack and defense tends to immerse any historical subject in ambivalent complexities. The most vital history is likely to be written during the period when emotion remains strong enough to be recollected in tranquillity (Wordsworth's definition of the well-spring of true poetry) and before anger or love have been completely obscured by intellectual constructs.

William H. McNeill 1980

Contents

Acknowledgments

It is fitting to acknowledge the encouragement and help that I have received from various quarters. A number of learned men read the manuscript of my book and suggested improvements. These include my former doctoral program supervisor, Professor Peter Brock of the University of Toronto, and also Professors Paul Magocsi, John Keep, and Bohdan Budurowycz of the same institution, and Professor Ivo Lambi of the University of Saskatchewan. For several years, I also corresponded with Professor Lubomyr Wynar of Kent State University and with the late Ivan L. Rudnytsky of the University of Alberta, each of whom, in his own way, contributed to the formation of my ideas about Hrushevsky. Several institutions, including the Canadian Institute of Ukrainian Studies, provided financial assistance during the earlier, thesis, phase of my studies of Hrushevsky, and the Chair of Ukrainian Studies at the University of Toronto awarded me an Edward Schreyer Post-doctoral Fellowship and provided me with stenographic help which assisted in turning the work into a book. The Shevchenko Scientific Society of New York City also provided me with a research grant. It has been a long and adventurous journey, and to all those who contributed to the enterprise, especially those who accompanied me for some part of the way, I offer my sincere thanks.

THOMAS M. PRYMAK

Abbreviations

AN URSR	Akademiia Nauk Ukrainskoi Radianskoi Sotsiialistychnoi Respubliky. Academy of Sciences of the Ukrainian Soviet Socialist Republic
CPbU	Komunistychna Partiia (bilshovykiv) Ukrainy. Communist Party (Bolsheviks) of Ukraine
NTSh	Naukove Tovarystvo im. Shevchenka. Shevchenko Scientific Society
RUP	Revoliutsiina Ukrainska Partiia. Revolutionary Ukrainian Party
SVU	Soiuz Vyzvolennia Ukrainy. Union for the Liberation of Ukraine
SVU	Spilka Vyzvolennia Ukrainy. League for the Liberation of Ukraine
TUP	Tovarystvo Ukrainskykh Postupovtsiv. Society of Ukrainian Progressives
UNS	Ukrainskyi Narodnyi Soiuz. Ukrainian National Union
UNT	Ukrainske Naukove Tovarystvo. Ukrainian Scientific Society
UPSR or Ukrainian SRs	Ukrainska Partiia Sotsiialistiv-revoliutsioneriv. Ukrainian Party of Socialist Revolutionaries
USDLP or Ukrainian Social Democrats	Ukrainska Sotsiial-demokratychna Robitnychna Partiia. Ukrainian Social Democratic Labour Party
VUAN	Vse-Ukrainska Akademiia Nauk. The (All-) Ukrainian Academy of Sciences
VUTsVK	Vse-Ukrainskyi Tsentralnyi Vykonavchyi Komitet. All-Ukrainian Central Executive Committee

Note: For abbreviations of the titles of journals and newspapers, see the bibliography.

While still a student at Saint Vladimir University in Kiev (c. 1890), Hrushevsky stood out from his fellows and attracted the attention of his superiors. His long beard, high forehead, and receding hairline gave him a mature, intelligent look that caused young friends and colleagues to dub him 'the beard of Saint Onufry.' The dignity and intelligence remained lifelong characteristics; the saintly calm disappeared in the maelstrom of Galician public life.

From an undated photograph first printed in M. Hrushevsky, *Pro ukrainsku movu i ukrainsku shkolu,* 2nd edition (Kiev, 1913), introduction.

Saint Vladimir University was founded in 1834 with the purpose of reducing Polish influences in Kiev. The large red-coloured building looked like this in Hrushevsky's time, but remains little changed to the present. In the 1920s, it was reorganized into the Kiev Institute of Popular Education and in 1939 was renamed the Kiev Taras Shevchenko State University.

Ivan Nechui-Levytsky promoted the pure Ukrainian language as it was spoken among the countryfolk of central Ukraine. He helped the schoolboy Hrushevsky to publish his first literary efforts but fiercely criticized him after 1905 when the historian promoted Galician linguistic influences on new Dnieper Ukrainian literary production.
Portrait by Opanas Slastion, 1890s.

The historian Volodymyr Antonovych exercised a powerful influence upon Hrushevsky's scholarship and arranged for his appointment to the new chair of Ukrainian History at the University of Lviv. Just as Antonovych personified cultural activism in the 1890s, so Hrushevsky personified the politicization of the post-1905 Ukrainian national movement. From O. Lototsky, *Storinky mynuloho*, II, 199.

The combination of formal morning-coat and embroidered peasant shirt (*sorochka*) might seem unusual to a West European, but aptly characterized the progressive and popular-educational theme of the Ukrainian national movement of the early twentieth century when this picture of Hrushevsky as Professor of History in Lviv was taken in 1911. From *Vistnyk SVU*, no. 128 (Vienna, 1916). Courtesy of the Ukrainian Cultural and Educational Centre, Winnipeg.

Hrushevsky's 1896 marriage to the modest schoolteacher Mariia Voiakovska caused a minor scandal in Galician Ukrainian society, which considered this daughter of a Greek Catholic (Uniate) village priest a poor match for the wealthy young professor from Kiev. But the marriage was a happy one and helped to make possible Hrushevsky's enormous scholarly and literary production and solid contribution to public life. In this photograph (c. 1900), Hrushevsky sits on one side and Mariia, who is dressed in white, on the other, and they are surrounded by Mariia's family.
From *Vistnyk SVU*, no. 128 (Vienna, 1916). Courtesy of the Ukrainian Cultural and Educational Centre, Winnipeg.

In 1900, Hrushevsky's daughter, Kateryna, was born, and within a few years she could play on the grass in front of her father's impressive new house in Lviv. The writer Ivan Franko built a smaller home next door to his friend Hrushevsky and, with official approval of the Franko cult in the Soviet Union, it has become a national shrine. But contemporary visitors to the Franko Museum are not told that the stately mansion next door was once the home of the greatest of modern Ukrainian historians and the first president of the Ukrainian People's Republic.

From I. Krypiakevych, *Mykhailo Hrushevsky*, p. 33. Courtesy of the British Library, London.

Hrushevsky inherited a large library from his father and steadily added to it in Lviv. Ukrainian artifacts and rugs decorated the interior of his Lviv house. This photograph was taken before 1914.

From Symon Narizhnyi, *Ukrainska emigratsiia*, p. lxxxv.

Hrushevsky and Franko amidst the representatives of the western Ukrainian intelligentsia who gathered in Lviv in 1898 to celebrate the centenary of the rebirth of Ukrainian literature. Sitting: Mykhailo Pavlyk, Ievheniia Ievrotynsky, Nataliia Kobrynska, Olha Kobylianska, Danylo Lepky (Marko Murava), Andrii Chaikovsky, Kost Penkivsky. Standing in the first row: Ivan Kopach, Volodymyr Hnatiuk, Iosef Makovei, Mykhailo Hrushevsky, Ivan Franko, Oleksander Kolessa, Bohdan Lepky. Standing in the second row: Ivan Petrushevych, Filaret Kolessa, Iosef Kyshakevch, Ivan Trush, Denys Lukiianovych, Mykola Ivasiuk.
From *Naukovyi zbirnyk III Prysviachenyi pam'iati Volodymyra Hnatiuka* (Priashiv, 1967), p. 56.

In 1898, Hrushevsky spent a great sum to acquire a spacious and dignified new building for the Shevchenko Scientific Society (NTSh) in Lviv. The Society functioned as an unofficial Academy of Sciences for the entire Ukrainian people until 1914, but lost government support after the incorporation of eastern Galicia into the new Polish Republic. With the Soviet occupation of eastern Galicia during the Second World War, the Society was dissolved in the homeland and its facilities were incorporated into the Academy of Sciences of the Ukrainian Soviet Socialist Republic. In the 1940s and the 1950s, émigré scholars reconstituted the Shevchenko Scientific Society as a federation of scholarly organizations operating throughout the Western world.

T. LXXXIII.   P. 1908 кн. III.   Рік XVII.

ЗАПИСКИ

НАУКОВОГО ТОВАРИСТВА ІМЕНИ ШЕВЧЕНКА

НАУКОВА ЧАСОПИСЬ,

ПРИСЬВЯЧЕНА ПЕРЕДОВСЇМ УКРАЇНСЬКІЙ ІСТОРІЇ, ФІЛЬОЛЬОҐІЇ Й ЕТНОҐРАФІЇ,

виходить у Львові що два місяці під редакцією

МИХАЙЛА ГРУШЕВСЬКОГО.

———+▪+———

MITTEILUNGEN

DER ŠEVČENKO-GESELLSCHAFT DER WISSENSCHAFTEN IN LEMBERG.

WISSENSCHAFTLICHE ZEITSCHRIFT, GEWIDMET VORZUGSWEISE
DER UKRAINISCHEN GESCHICHTE, PHILOLOGIE UND ETHNOGRAPHIE.

REDIGIERT VON

MICHAEL HRUŠEVŚKYJ.

B. LXXXIII.   1908, III B.   XVII Jahrgang.

———+●+———

Накладом Наукового Товариства імени Шевченка.

З друкарнї Наукового Товариства імени Шевченка
під зарядом К. Беднарского.

———+ Вийшло 30/VI с. с. +———

Hrushevsky edited over 120 volumes of the *Zapysky NTSh* and contributed articles and reviews to almost every issue before 1914. The journal continued to exist under the Polish Republic, and then in the emigration, but never again achieved the quality and volume of the Hrushevsky era.

Title page of the *Zapysky NTSh*, 1908.

Russian monarchists claimed that German money was behind the Ukrainian movement in
south Russia, but the reverse was more true. Money from Dnieper Ukraine supported
the growth of the Ukrainian literary and scholarly movement in Austrian Galicia, as the
donations of Ievhen Chykalenko, the wealthy scion of an old Cossack family, clearly
show. Moreover, after 1905 he published Kiev's Ukrainian-language daily newspaper,
Rada, in which many articles by Hrushevsky appeared.
From Narizhnyi, *Ukrainska emigratsiia*, p. cxiv.

It is unclear whether Maxim Kovalevsky's Free Russian University in Paris, or some other institution, provided the inspiration for the 1904 free summer school on Ukrainian culture, which was a true example of the influence of the 'Galician Piedmont' upon Dnieper Ukraine. In this photo, the ethnographer Fedir Vovk, Hrushevsky, and Ivan Franko are flanked by other teachers and students of the school. Standing at the very back (from the left): 1 / Iu. Sytny, 2 / O. Skoropys, 3 / D. Rozov, 4 / V. Zahaikevych, 5 / T. Iermy (Mrs Bodnarova), 6 / Mykhailo Mochulsky. Second row: 7 / Volodymyr Lavrivsky, 8 / E. Holytsynsky, 9 / Iulian Bachynsky, 10 / M. Krushelnytska (Drozdovska), 11 / Dmytro Doroshenko (the future historian) 12 / Ia. Hrushkevych, 13 / L. Chykalenko (son of the publisher), 14 / D. Shukhevychivna-Starosolska, 15 / Mykhailo Hrushkevych, 16 / S. Dolnytsky, 17 / A. Khomyk, 18 / M. Rostkovych. Third row: 19 / Volodymyr Doroshenko (the NTSh librarian), 20 / M. Pidlisetska (Mudrakova), 21 / H. Chykalenkivna (daughter of the publisher), 22 / Ko. Holytsynska, 23 / O. Andriievska, 24 / M. Lypa, 25 / I. Lypa, 26 / F. Sholudko, 27 / V. Paneiko, 28 / L. Smishchuk, 29 / L. Harmatii. Sitting in the first row: 30 / P. Riabkov, 31 / T. Revakovych, 32 / I. Bryk, 33 / M. Hankevych, 34 / Fedir Vovk, 35 / M. Hrushevsky, 36 / Ivan Franko, 37 / Hrushevsky's wife, Mariia, 38 / the ethnographer Volodymyr Hnatiuk. Sitting on cushions at the front: 39 / M. Dvernytska, 40 / V. Chykalenkivna, 41 / A. Trusheva, 42 / Ivan Trush (the painter).

After the Russian revolution of 1905, the ban on printing books and newspapers in the Little Russian, that is, the Ukrainian language, was not strictly enforced, and Hrushevsky was finally able to found a new Ukrainian Scientific Society to publish Ukrainian-language scholarship in Kiev. The foremost Ukrainian artist of the day, Vasyl Krychevsky, designed bookcovers for Hrushevsky's mass-circulation histories. The illustrations were always based on historical examples from the period in question. Shown here are the covers for *Kulturno-natsionalnyi rukh na Ukraini XVI–XVIIv.* (*The Cultural-National Movement in Ukraine in the Sixteenth and Seventeenth Centuries*) (Kiev–Lviv, 1912), and for *Iliustruvana istoriia Ukrainy* (*Illustrated History of Ukraine*) Kiev–Lviv, 1912; reprinted Winnipeg, n.d.).

ВИДАВНИЦТВО
ВІДРОДЖЕННЄ

ПРОФ. МИХАЙЛО ГРУШЕВСЬКИЙ

ПРО УКРАЇНСЬКУ МОВУ
І УКРАЇНСЬКУ ШКОЛУ

ДРУГЕ ВИДАННЄ.

N. 11.   ЦІНА 12 КОП.

Between 1905 and 1914, Hrushevsky repeatedly called for the expansion of the primary school system in Dnieper Ukraine with instruction in the Ukrainian vernacular. This is the title page from his pamphlet *Pro ukrainsku movu i ukrainsku shkolu* (*About the Ukrainian Language and Ukrainian Schools*) (Kiev, 1913), which was put out by 'Renaissance Publishers.'
Courtesy of the Ukrainian Cultural and Educational Centre, Winnipeg.

The Serhii Hrushevsky School in Kiev was named after the historian's father, who was a well-known pedagogue. Rebuilt by Vasyl Krychevsky in 'the Ukrainian national style,' it was an irritation to Russian nationalists in Kiev, who in 1913 tried to replace the Hrushevsky name with another that smacked less of 'Mazepist' separatism.

Premier Peter Stolypin was a close ally of the Russian Nationalist Club, which was strongest in the western borderlands of the Empire. The Club had its principal centre in Kiev, where in 1911 Stolypin was assassinated in the Opera House in the presence of Tsar Nicholas II. A monument was erected in the city in memory of this faithful servant of the Tsar, but in February 1917 it was one of the first casualties of the revolution.

After the collapse of the imperial order, supporters of the new Provisional Government, the Soviets, and the Ukrainian movement all organized demonstrations in support of their respective positions. This photo shows a great Ukrainian demonstration in Saint Sophia square in Kiev in the spring of 1917. Several dozen blue and yellow flags are clearly visible in the centre with the famous statue of Bohdan Khmelnytsky on the left. From *Istorychnyi kalendar-almanakh Chervonoi Kalyny na 1937 rik* (Lviv), p. 17.

After the outbreak of revolution, Hrushevsky was immediately elected president of the Ukrainian Central Rada and returned to Kiev, where he was greeted as 'a martyr for the sake of Ukraine.' He joined in the great Ukrainian demonstration of 19 March (Old Style) and addressed a crowd of over a hundred thousand people from the balcony of the City Hall.

The origin of this picture is unknown.

The Ukrainian Central Rada began as a lobby group to represent Ukrainian interests before the Provisional Government, but over the course of several months evolved into the revolutionary parliament of a new Ukrainian state. Hrushevsky presided over its meetings in the recently completed building of the Pedagogical Museum, which had been used by the military during the war. The building was designed by the architect P.F. Aloshyn with classical features and an exterior frieze depicting the progress of knowledge and education. In the 1920s, the building housed the Museum of the Revolution and included a section on the Central Rada. In 1938, it became the Kiev branch of the V.I. Lenin Central Museum, reflecting the general centralization process of the Stalin era. The domed building on Volodymyrsky Street remains a symbol of national independence and democracy among Ukrainian émigrés.
Private collection, Toronto.

Hrushevsky at the Third Ukrainian Military Congress in Kiev, end of October 1917. Hrushevsky and Petliura, who would soon go different ways politically, are standing in the middle on a slightly raised platform. The platform gives Hrushevsky some extra height, but his grey-white beard and heavy black coat and hat clearly mark him off from the soldiers around him. On the right side are the representatives of the French, Belgian, and Romanian military missions. Some old copies of this photo bear an inscription stating that it was taken on the occasion of the Third Universal, which proclaimed the autonomous Ukrainian People's Republic.
Origin unknown.

Professor M. Hrushevsky as President of the Ukrainian Central Rada, 1917–18, and President of the Ukrainian People's Republic, 1918. This picture is of unknown origin but appears to be an official portrait of the Head of State.

Coat of Arms of the Ukrainian People's Republic, 1918. Hrushevsky was inclined toward designs which reflected the progressive commitment of the new Ukrainian state, but he loyally supported the Trident of Saint Volodymyr (Vladimir) the Great, proposed by Dmytro Antonovych and confirmed by the Mala Rada. Hrushevsky's principal contribution was the encompassing olive wreath, which symbolized peace and prosperity.

An Academy of Arts was established under the Central Rada; an Academy of Sciences
under the Hetman. This photo shows the professors and founders of the Ukrainian
State Academy of Arts, Kiev, 5 December 1917. Standing (from the left): G. Narbut, V.
Krychevsky, M. Boychuk, Sitting: A. Manievich, O. Murashko, F. Krychevsky, M.
Hrushevsky (Head of State), I. Steshenko (secretary of education), M. Burachek. Works
by Vasyl Krychevsky are visible in the background.

Hrushevsky in a crowd of Ukrainian soldiers and political activists near the exit of the Church of Saint Sophia, Kiev, late 1917. At the time of the Treaty of Brest-Litovsk, the Ukrainian People's Republic made international headlines in western Europe. This picture appeared in *L'Illustration* (Paris), 1918, 2 March 1918, and in the *London Illustrated News* (London), 9 March 1918. The former carried the banner 'An Independent Ukraine!' In the latter the caption read: 'President of the Rada, and called 'Father of the Ukraine': Professor Grushefsky with his ministers.'
Courtesy of the Metropolitan Toronto Library Board.

The burnt-out shell of Hrushevsky's great seven-storey house in Kiev, 1918. The ornamental designs and balconies added by Vasyl Krychevsky are still clearly visible along the front and side.

From *Istorychnyi kalendar-almanakh Chervonoi Kalyny na 1938 rik* (Lviv), p. 64.

Ignored at the Paris Peace conference, Hrushevsky enjoyed some success at the International Socialist Conference in Lucerne, 1919. From the left: D. Isaievych, B. Matiu-shenko, M. Hrushevsky, P. Didushok.
From Narizhny, *Ukrainska emigratsiia*, p. clxxx.

Hrushevsky's rivals on the Right. The Hetman, Pavlo Skoropadsky, with his most important Ukrainian supporters, the historians Dmytro Doroshenko (left) and Viacheslav Lypynsky (right). This photo probably dates from the 1920s when all three lived in emigration.
From Narizhnyi, *Ukrainska emigratsiia*, p. clx.

Hrushevsky's SR rivals, the leaders of the Prague group, Nykyfor Hryhoriiv and Mykyta Shapoval with Mykyta Halahan, Prague, 1923.
From Narizhnyi, *Ukrainska emigratsiia*.

[?]61 (47.711 Київ) Укр. Акад. Наук 1 : 9 (47.71)

ВСЕУКРАЇНСЬКА АКАДЕМІЯ НАУК
ACADÉMIE DES SCIENCES d'UKRAINE—SECTION HISTORIQUE
„L'Ukraine", revue bimestrielle des études de l'Ukraine,
sous la direction de M. Hrushevsky, président de la Section

УКРАЇНА

НАУКОВИЙ ДВОХМІСЯЧНИК УКРАЇНОЗНАВСТВА

ОРҐАН ІСТОРИЧНОЇ СЕКЦІЇ АКАДЕМІЇ
(б. Українського Наукового Товариства в Київі)
ПІД ЗАГАЛЬНОЮ РЕДАКЦІЄЮ ГОЛОВИ СЕКЦІЇ
акад. МИХАЙЛА ГРУШЕВСЬКОГО

при ближчій участі академиків, професорів і співробітників академії:
Д. Багалія, С. Веселовського, М. Возняка, О. Гермайзе, О. Грушевського, В. Данилевича, С. Єфремова, А. Кримського, М. Макаренка, В. Міяковського, О. Новицького, В. Перетца, М. Птухи, С. Семковського, О. Синявського, К. Студинського, Є. Тимченка, П. Тутковського, В. Щербини та инших.

1925
книга 3

КИЇВ
Закінчено книгу 15 березня

Загального числа
книга 12

ДЕРЖАВНЕ ВИДАВНИЦТВО УКРАЇНИ

Hrushevsky considered his work at the All-Ukrainian Academy of Sciences (VUAN) to be a continuation of his activities at the pre-revolution Ukrainian Scientific Society in Kiev and at the Shevchenko Scientific Society in Lviv, as this title page from the journal *Ukraina* plainly states. The term 'All-Ukrainian' (*Vse-Ukrainska*) was used because the Academy claimed to serve all the Ukrainian lands and not just those within the Soviet Union.
Title page of *Ukraina*, no. 12 (Kiev: Derzhavne vydavnytstvo Ukrainy, 1925).

Academician Hrushevsky in 1926. The 'Hrushevsky cursive,' which helped to make possible the historian's phenomenally productive scholarly career, showed in his handwriting as well as in his relations with colleagues, as the autograph below this semi-official portrait reveals.
From a portrait taken in connection with Hrushevsky's jubilee in 1926.

Hrushevsky's office in the Historical Section of the All-Ukrainian Academy of Sciences (VUAN). Interior design by Vasyl Krychevsky, 1929.

The orientalist A. Iu. Krymsky was the permanent secretary of the Ukrainian Academy of
Sciences and one of Hrushevsky's chief rivals within it. He is shown here in early 1941
as holder of the Order of the Toiling Red Banner, but he disappeared without trace a few
weeks later.

From A.Iu. Krymsky, *Tvory v p'iaty tomakh*, vol. v, pt. 1 (Kiev, 1973), frontispiece.

By 1931, Hrushevsky was almost blind and for a second time exiled from his native Kiev, but he continued to study and write profusely in spite of the fact that few of his works could still be published. This photo is undated and of unknown origin.

Hrushevsky died under mysterious circumstances but was given a state funeral and buried in Kiev. The Soviet Ukrainian government commissioned Vasy Krychevsky to design the gravestone. It was completed in 1935 and stands about twelve feet tall. Fresh flowers are still often found before it.

MYKHAILO HRUSHEVSKY

Introduction

Mykhailo Hrushevsky (1866–1934) is one of the better-known Ukrainian figures of modern times. He was the greatest of Ukrainian historians, the organizer of an unofficial Ukrainian Academy of Sciences in Austrian Galicia, the most celebrated spokesman for federalism in the pre-revolutionary Russian Empire, the first president of the modern Ukrainian state (1917–18), and the single most important cultural figure in the early days of the Ukrainian Soviet Socialist Republic.

In spite of Hrushevsky's enormous importance in the history of modern Ukraine, and, indeed, of Russia and all Eastern Europe, controversy, propaganda, and legend have surrounded his person and his career has long remained shrouded in mystery. True scholarship about him is rare indeed, and the bulk of writing treating his role in the political history of Eastern Europe consists of a polemical literature in which Hrushevsky is either savagely attacked as a heretical 'separatist,' a weak-hearted autonomist, and a 'bourgeois nationalist,' or lavishly praised as a devoted patriot, a heroic intellectual, and a wise political leader.

In contrast to Ukrainian scholars, who, whether they are sympathetic to Hrushevsky or not, generally stand in awe of their greatest historian, Russian and Polish authors tend to fall into the camp of Hrushevsky's most vocal critics. This process began as early as the turn of the last century, when conservative Russian publicists and patriotic Russian reformers attempted to ignore the emerging 'Ukrainian question' and labelled Hrushevsky a 'separatist' who was endangering the unity of the Russian people and the Russian state. (Poles disliked his social radicalism and his insistence that Eastern Galicia and Right Bank Ukraine were essentially Ukrainian lands.) The criticism has been continued by scholars and propagandists now writing in the Soviet Union, who, whether they like it or not, are compelled to label Hrushevsky a 'bourgeois nationalist' and an enemy of the

Ukrainian and Russian peoples. Thus, while the wording has changed, the intensity of the criticism has not.[1]

European and American students of the history of Eastern Europe, and especially of Russia, have not escaped the influence of this steady attack on Hrushevsky. In general, Western scholars tend to see the Ukrainian historian as little more than another intellectual 'awakener' pounding the tribal drum of ethnic nationalism in a remote corner of Eastern Europe. His historical terminology is rejected, and his radical revision of what he called 'the traditional scheme of Russian history' is ignored. No western student of Russian history has ever attempted to outline his career in public life or his contributions to the history of either Russian or Ukrainian political thought. Thus, fruitful discussion of Hrushevsky's role in modern history has been limited to a relatively small circle of Ukrainian-language publications appearing in the West.[2]

Within non-Soviet Ukrainian historiography, there are two major schools of thought concerning Hrushevsky. According to the first school, Hrushevsky was the far-sighted scholar who criticized the Russian bureaucratic-police state and the moribund Habsburg monarchy and spread European learning and a modern sense of national consciousness among the impoverished and oppressed Ukrainian people. He saw that the era of the landlords and capitalists was coming to an end and he bound the fortunes of the national movement to the Ukrainian peasantry and the newly emerging Ukrainian working class. He symbolized in his person the most honourable phase of the democratic and socialist revolution of 1917, and he was the principal architect of the independent Ukrainian People's Republic, which forced the Bolsheviks to take cognizance of the existence of Ukrainian national aspirations and create a rival Ukrainian Soviet Socialist Republic. According to this point of view, which is generally upheld by left-wing but liberal-democratic Ukrainian scholars, especially veterans of the events of

1 For some general remarks on the formation of the Hrushevsky legend, see my historiographical survey: 'Mykhailo Hrushevsky: Populist or Statist?' *Journal of Ukrainian Studies*, no. 10 (Toronto, 1981), 65–78. On the Hrushevsky myth in the Soviet Union, see M. Halii, 'M. Hrushevsky i "Ukrainska radianska entsyklopediia,"' *Vilna Ukraina*, no. 42 (New York, 1964), 29–38.
2 There is currently an effort underway to remedy this problem by translating Hrushevsky's major work, his ten-volume *History of Ukraine-Rus'*, into English. For details of the project, which reflects Hrushevsky's enormous prestige among the Ukrainian public in the West, see Petro Stercho, 'Vydannia velykoi istorii Ukrainy Mykhaila Hrushevskoho nevidkladne zavdannia ukrainskoi vilnoi nauky i usoho hromadianstva,' *Samostiina Ukraina*, nos. 5–6 (Chicago, 1977), 15–22. For some critical remarks, see Oleksander Dombrovsky, 'Do pytannia anhliiskoho perekladu istorii Ukrainy-Rusy M. Hrushevskoho,' *Ukrainskyi istoryk*, nos. 1–4 (1968), 138–41.

1917–20, Hrushevsky was a great scholar, a wise civic leader, and a formidable politician.[3]

The second interpretation of Hrushevsky's career is far more critical. According to this school of thought, Hrushevsky's populist (*narodnyk*) approach to history and politics and his critical attitude toward bureaucracy and statehood were nothing more than outdated and narrow-minded prejudices. As a historian, he ignored the cultural achievements and the traditions of the educated, landowning classes; as a politician, he was more a theoretician of anarchy than a statesman concerned with the construction of a sovereign national state. Moreover, in 1917–18, he was the leader of a nation at war who, preferring to rely on the unorganized masses and vague talk of federalism and liberty, foolishly disbanded his army at the critical moment. He overestimated the creative capacities of the common people and, instead of providing wise leadership when it counted, merely followed the illiterate and confused masses down the path of anarchy and destruction. According to this point of view, which is espoused both by more conservative and by more radically nationalist Ukrainian scholars, Hrushevsky was not the statesmanlike father of the modern Ukrainian republic, but rather a naïve and short-sighted *narodnyk*, and his mission had failed because of it.[4]

This study does not fully accept either of these two positions. It is not intended to be either the hagiography of a great patriot or a criticism of Hrushevsky's ideas about history or of his political tactics in 1917–20. It is, rather, an attempt to discard the emotional baggage of Hrushevsky's most avid supporters and fierce critics of 1917, when he became a symbol of the Ukrainian revolution, and of 1924, when he finally returned from emigration to Soviet Ukraine. At the same time, it is an attempt to sidestep Western indifference, to cut through crude Russian monarchist and Soviet propaganda, and to dispel some of the more absurd ideas and most elementary fallacies surrounding this very controversial figure.[5]

3 This is the point of view of M. Halii, who in 1960 published a small collection of Hrushevsky's political polemics, and of the editors of the American-based democratic socialist journal, *Vilna Ukraina*, which flourished during the 1950s and 1960s. It is shared by Matvii Stakhiv, Dmytro Solovei, V. Dubrovsky, Panas Fedenko, and others cited in the present work.

4 For a statement of the conservative Ukrainian position, see Omeljan Pritsak, 'U stolittia narodyn M. Hrushevskoho,' in *Idei i liudy vyzvolnykh zmahan* (New York, 1968), pp. 187–230. This point of view is generally shared by the widely respected historian Dmytro Doroshenko, the intensely nationalist journalist Petro Mirchuk, and others cited in the present work.

5 As late as the 1960s, émigré Russian nationalists like Andrei Dikii, *Neizvrashchennaia istoriia Ukrainy-Rusi*, 2 vols. (New York, 1961), and Nikolai Ulianov(?), *Proiskhozhedenie Ukrainskogo separatizma* (New York, 1966), continued to paint Hrushevsky as a Germanophile traitor to Russia. The latter (pp. 238–40) even linked his name to the Polish/Ukrainian racial theorist

This work is biographical in nature. It seeks to outline the most important events of Hrushevsky's public life and to paint a picture of how he dealt with the cultural and political dilemmas of his time. Though Hrushevsky was certainly a great historian, this book is not a historiographical study, but rather a kind of political biography with an emphasis upon the interaction between broadly political and fundamentally cultural questions. It describes Hrushevsky as a scholar and a university professor, as an organizer of cultural life and institutions, as a polemical writer and a critic and advisor to politicians in the Austrian parliament and in the Russian State Duma. It outlines his experience as a public figure during the First World War and as a political actor during the revolution. Finally, it deals with Hrushevsky's return to Soviet Ukraine and its cultural and political implications. It is a first synthesis of a long and stormy career.[6]

I make use of certain concepts and terms that have a specific meaning within the context of Ukrainian history, but are little known or differently understood by scholars who are not adepts of this somewhat esoteric science. For example, the terms 'nationalism' and 'nationalist' deserve some elucidation. On the one hand, Hrushevsky and most of his closest collaborators accepted and propagated the idea of modern nationalism, which, it is generally agreed, was born in the rhetoric of popular sovereignty during the French revolution, gained new cultural and linguistic content during German resistance to Napoleon, and, in eastern Europe, was mobilized with the spread of literacy and accelerated social and economic change. On the other hand, Hrushevsky, who for many years led the Ukrainian national movement, seldom talked about sovereign statehood, rejected the idea of race as a basis for political organization, and never called himself a 'nationalist.' In fact, he made a clear distinction between national/popular (*natsionalnyi/narodnyi*) and nationalistic (*natsionalystychnyi*), seemed to recognize the pejorative origin of the term 'nationalist' and, as the reader of this book will quickly discern, consistently used it in a negative sense.[7]

Franciszek Duchiński, and the Nazi official Alfred Rosenberg, and concluded: 'Everything that happened in Ukraine during the years of revolution had its source in Hrushevsky's Lviv classroom.'

6 The only previous attempt at such a synthesis is the unpublished study by Jaroslaw Pelenski, 'Der ukrainische Nationalgedanke im Lichte der Werke M. Hruševskyjs und V. Lipinskys,' Ph D thesis, Ludwig-Maximilians-Universität (Munich, 1956). Pelenski's work concentrates more on analysis of historiography and ideology than on public life and biography.

7 On the origin of the word 'nationalism' and its negative connotations see Philip L. White, 'What Is a Nationality?' *Canadian Review of Studies in Nationalism,* XII, 1 (Charlottetown, 1985), 1–24. On the history of nationalism as an idea, see the classic works of C.J.H. Hayes, *The Historical Evolution of Modern Nationalism* (New York, 1968), and Hans Kohn, *Nationalism: Its Meaning and History* (Princeton, 1965). For a highly respected sociological treatment, which emphasizes 'mobilization' and 'communication,' see Karl W. Deutsch, *Nationalism and Social Communication* (Cambridge, Mass., 1966).

The next generation took things one step further. During the 1920s and 1930s, defeated Ukrainian ideologues and politicians, émigrés who were involved with the rise of 'integral' nationalism in central and eastern Europe, transformed earlier distinctions into one between socialism and 'socialists,' who dallied with humanitarian ideals and federalist cooperation, and nationalism and 'nationalists,' who were willing to sacrifice all before the altar of national unity and independence. Within this narrower Ukrainian émigré context, of course, Hrushevsky was placed squarely in the socialist rather than in the nationalist camp.[8]

The stormy events of the mid-twentieth century changed the situation once again. The rise and fall of fascism completely discredited nationalist extremism and a new generation of Ukrainian émigré historians began to discard the vocabulary of their fathers. During the 1960s and the 1970s, for example, some of the historians gathered together in the European- and American-based Ukrainian Historical Association partly, at least, reverted to the earlier distinction between 'national,' which was generally seen as positive and was applied to Hrushevsky, and 'nationalist' which was more extreme and was not. Thus while the general student of east European or Soviet affairs might well label as a 'nationalist' any politically active Ukrainian who did not or does not accept a Russian national identity, it is important to note that this term has a much more restricted meaning within modern Ukrainian historiography and is seldom, if ever, applied to autonomists or federalists who are not committed to sovereign Ukrainian statehood, or even to those supporting independence who never had anything to do with integral nationalism.[9]

The word 'populism' also deserves to be examined. In general, it has been used to describe political theories or social movements which have a special rural and anti-urban character, mistrust the outside world, and see life in simple dualist terms, the rulers and the ruled, the oppressors and the oppressed. In the Russian case, populism (*narodnichestvo*) refers to the specific intellectual and political

8 For the situation in the 1920s, see Alexander J. Motyl, *The Turn to the Right, The Ideological Origins and Development of Ukrainian Nationalism 1919–1929* (Boulder, Colorado, 1980).

9 The publication during the war of W.E.D. Allen's *The Ukraine: A History* (Cambridge, 1941) did much to discredit Hrushevsky in the eyes of an English public that already suspected the Ukrainian national movement of pro-German sympathies. The subsequent publication of an English translation of Hrushevsky's popular-style *Iliustrovana istoriia Ukrainy* – under the title *A History of Ukraine* (New Haven, 1941) – was not sufficient to clear his name completely. For a critical review of the literature see B. Budurovych, 'Mykhailo Hrushevsky v otsintsi zakhidno-evropeiskoi i amerykanskoi istoriohrafii,' *Vyzvolnyi shliakh,* xx (London, 1967), 171–81. For the current distinction between 'national' and 'nationalist,' see for example, the editorials and articles by Lubomyr Wynar in the Ukrainian Historical Association journal *Ukrainskyi istoryk* (New York–Toronto–Munich), 1963ff.

movement, initiated by the journalist Alexander Herzen, which planned to avoid the perils of western European capitalism and urban factory life by using the traditional Russian village commune as the basis for a future socialist reorganization of society. This theory of a 'separate path' to socialism, propagated by a revolutionary élite, formed the essence of the Russian populist movement and did not lack adherents in the southern provinces of the Russian Empire where many ethnic Ukrainians, or 'Little Russians' as they were then usually called, became its supporters.[10]

Ukrainian populism (*narodnytstvo/narodoliubstvo*) was also oriented toward the village and was dualist in character. It did not, however, idealize the traditional Russian village commune, which did not exist in ethnic Ukrainian territories; nor did it evolve into a tightly knit revolutionary and conspiratorial organization determined to overthrow the government by force. Rather, it was a much more diffuse phenomenon that was closely linked to the history of the Ukrainian national movement in the nineteenth century.

The Ukrainian national movement was populist to its very roots. The fiery and melancholic poems of the former serf Taras Shevchenko (1814–61) had elevated the Ukrainian vernacular into a literary language and had become the hymns of the national movement. These powerful verses, with themes borrowed from the folksongs and lore of the local peasantry, helped to transform the name 'Ukraine' from a vague geographic into a dynamic national concept. The historian Mykola (Nicholas) Kostomarov (1817–85) drew up a program for the secret Panslav Brotherhood of Saints Cyril and Methodius (1846) which stressed that the ruling classes had deserted the common Ukrainian people for the sake of the privileges of landowning Pole or Muscovite; federal reorganization of the Slavic lands was the only way to restored harmony and justice. A younger historian, Volodymyr Antonovych (1834–1908), repeated Kostomarov's condemnation of oppressive states, while the political émigré Mykhailo Drahomanov (1841–95) developed Kostomarov's federal ideas into a concrete political program embodied in a liberal-style written constitution (1884). The two men disagreed on tactics – Antonovych preferring cautious cultural work, Drahomanov political action abroad – both continued to invoke the image of the poet Shevchenko. Thus, by Hrushevsky's time, the mainstream of the Ukrainian national movement was traditionally 'populist' and federalist, but in a way that was considerably at odds with the more famous Russian populist movement.[11]

10 For an outline of the literature on Russian populism with special reference to national questions, see my 'Herzen on Poland and Ukraine,' *Journal of Ukrainian Studies*, no. 12 (Toronto, 1982), 41–9. More generally, see Ghita Ionescu and Ernest Gellner, eds., *Populism* (London, 1969), and Margaret Canovan, *Populism* (New York, 1981).

11 There is no adequate history of the Ukrainian national movement in the nineteenth century. For an

This book is based primarily upon the writings and speeches of Hrushevsky himself. These writings – essays, polemics, public addresses, letters – provide the basic chronology of the study and answer some fundamental questions about Hrushevsky's real concerns and how he dealt with them. Hrushevsky was the author of a number of brief autobiographical essays which are especially valuable in this regard. All of this material is listed in the bibliography.

The second most important source is the large body of literature produced by Hrushevsky's friends, students, colleagues, rivals, and enemies. This includes contemporary polemics, correspondence, and diaries, as well as reflective literature such as memoirs and general histories produced by participants in the events. Among the diaries and memoir literature, the reflections of Oleksander Lototsky are especially valuable for Hrushevsky's early career, those of Ievhen Chykalenko and Dmytro Doroshenko are valuable for the period preceding the revolution, those of Mykola Kovalevsky and Mykyta Shapoval deal with the period from 1917 to 1924, and those of N. Polonska-Vasylenko and others are fullest for the Soviet period. Each of these authors is of about equal value for the period that he or she describes, though some, like Kovalevsky, are obviously admirers of Hrushevsky, while others, like Doroshenko and Polonska-Vasylenko, are clearly unfriendly to him.[12]

The final class of materials I have used are monographs and histories written by scholars less directly connected with the actual events described. These include a great variety of materials ranging from general histories of the revolution like that of John Reshetar to specialist studies of certain aspects of Hrushevsky's career by scholars such as V.V. Miiakovsky.

Special mention must be made of the work of Lubomyr Wynar and his colleagues of the Ukrainian Historical Association. For over twenty years, Wynar and his associates have made a special point of collecting and analysing Hrushevsky materials, and of publishing them in their journal, *Ukrainskyi istoryk*. The materials gathered and published by Wynar include Hrushevsky's autobiographical writings, his letters to individuals and institutions in North America, correspondence concerning him, and memoir material especially devoted to him. *Ukrainskyi istoryk* is the single most frequently cited title in the present study and

---

outline of developments in Dnieper Ukraine, see E. Borschak, 'Ukraine in the Russian Empire in the Nineteenth and the Early Twentieth Centuries (1800–1917),' in *Ukraine: A Concise Encyclopaedia,* vol. 1 (Toronto, 1963), 667–89. Also see Iu. Boiko, 'Narodnytstvo,' *Entsyklopediia ukrainoznavstva,* vol. v (Paris–New York, 1966), 1700–1, and V. Markus, 'Federalism,' *Encyclopaedia of Ukraine,* vol. 1 (Toronto, 1984), 866–9.

12 For some critical remarks on the memoirs of Doroshenko and Polonska-Vasylenko, and an examination of Hrushevsky as revealed to readers of Soviet Ukrainian historical fiction, see Dmytro Solovei, 'U spravi zhyttiepysu M.S. Hrushevskoho,' *Vilna Ukraina,* no. 17 (1958), 9–21.

though my interpretations often differ from those expressed in this journal, I readily acknowledge that my task would have been made much more difficult without the significant and often irreplaceable work of its contributors.

Transliteration is always a problem for historians writing about a country that uses a non-Latin script. I have used a simplified version of the American Library of Congress system, a version which omits the soft-sign and in adjectival masculine personal names omits the final iot; thus we write Hrushevsky, not Hrushevs'kyi. My only departure from this system is the use of the apostrophe (') to signify a soft-sign in words that have a special meaning for political historians. For example, *PYCb* is rendered Rus', not Rus.

All Ukrainian personal names are given according to the original Ukrainian spelling and not in the English equivalent; thus Mykhailo Hrushevsky, not Michael Hrushevsky, and Oleksander Lototsky, not Alexander Lototsky. On the other hand, better-known Russian personal names are left in their commonly accepted English equivalent; thus Paul Miliukov, and Alexander Kerensky.

Geographical names pose a more difficult problem. The foremost city of present-day western Ukraine is still known variously as Lviv, Lwów, Lemberg, and Lvov, and all of these names can be found on maps. In general, I use Ukrainian names for places located in the Ukrainian SSR, Russian names for those in Russia, and Polish names for those within present day Poland. Alternate forms have been relegated to square brackets; thus Gdańsk [Danzig], and Lviv [Lwów]. Occasionally, a commonly accepted historical or English form is retained; thus Kiev, Galicia, and Volhynia; and occasionally a Ukrainian form is used first in order to stress the Ukrainian ethnic claims discussed in the text; thus Kholm [Chełm] and Pidliashshia [Podlasie].

For a story which takes place in both the Russian Empire, where the Old Style Julian calendar was in common use until the revolution, and also in Austrian Galicia, where the Western Gregorian calendar was more frequently used, exact dating of events becomes a problem. I have left events occurring in old Russia in the Old Style, although, on occasion, when an event has some international connection, a reference to the New Style follows. For example, when I. Nechui-Levytsky in the Russian Empire writes to Hrushevsky in Galicia, the form given in the note is Nechui-Levytsky, letter of 10 (22) March 1899. During the revolution, when exact dating becomes more important, events are again given in both the Old and New Style.

I

Youth and Education 1866–1894

Mykhailo Serhiiovych Hrushevsky was born into a family that came from the class of married clergy permitted by the Eastern Orthodox Church. In a brief *Autobiography* Hrushevsky relates that by the eighteenth century his family was settled in the Chyhyryn district of the Kiev region in central Ukraine.[1] His father, Serhii Fedorovych Hrushevsky (1833–1901), had gained renown as a scholar of slavistics and was the author of an official textbook of Church Slavonic that came to be widely used throughout the Russian Empire. Serhii spent most of his life, however, as a schoolteacher and administrator in some of the more remote provinces of the empire. Mykhailo Hrushevsky's mother, Hlafira Opotskevych, was similarly of priestly lineage from the Kiev area, and it is this district that the Hrushevsky family considered to be their ancestral home.[2]

On 17 September 1866, in Kholm [Chełm], a mixed Ukrainian-Polish district near the frontier with Austrian Galicia, the Hrushevskys were blessed with their first son, whom they named Mykhailo. Serhii Hrushevsky was at that time teaching at a Greek Catholic or 'Uniate' gymnasium. The director of the Kholm school district was Teofan Lebedyntsev (1828–88), a well-known pedagogue and historian, and first publisher of the early journal of Ukrainian studies *Kievskaia starina* (1882–1907). Lebedyntsev seems to have drawn Serhii into a circle of scholars, antiquarians, and cultural enthusiasts who were imbued with a local

1 Hrushevsky, *Avtobiohrafiia*, ed. A. Gregorovich (Toronto, 1965), p.1. This edition is a reprint of the Lviv, 1906 edition which appeared in connection with Hrushevsky's first jubilee and of which only fifty copies were printed. It is referred to below as *Avtobiohrafiia–1906*.

2 Ibid. For a description of the Hrushevsky family background, based on materials provided by the Hrushevsky family itself, see V. Miiakovsky, 'Do biohrafii M. Hrushevskoho,' in *Krakivski visti*, nos. 69–70 (Cracow, 1944), and reprinted in *Ukrainskyi istoryk*, nos. 1–4 (1976), 114–20.

patriotism that formed one element in what later came to be called Ukrainian national consciousness.[3]

In 1869, when his son was only three, Serhii was transferred to the Caucasus. News from Ukraine was infrequent. 'However,' the younger Hrushevsky later wrote, 'under the influence of my father's stories, which cultivated in me a warm sympathy to everything Ukrainian – language, song, and tradition – I soon awoke and became conscious of my Ukrainian national feeling. This was strengthened by reading and by those rare trips to Ukraine which at that time took on the glow of a distant "fatherland." '[4]

Since the elder Hrushevsky was a school inspector and was moved from district to district, the family lived first in Kutais (1869), then in Stavropol (1870–8), and finally in Vladikavkaz. Of his father, the younger Hrushevsky writes further: 'He was not an active Ukrainian in the present [1928] sense of the term, but was distinguished by poetic feeling and vividly felt the beauty of Ukrainian life and tradition which he passed on to me. But what in his quiet, clear, even-tempered nature lived more passively in the sphere of his internal experiences, almost not influencing his activity, in my intense, nervous personality took on the character of a dominating stimulus to thought, expression, and feeling.'[5]

Such an intense dedication did not show at first. While he was away from his parents at gymnasium in Tiflis (1880–6), Hrushevsky became, in his own words, a 'lonely, dreamy youth' who devoted much of his time to reading.[6] This did not mean, however, that he was insensitive to his surroundings. Tiflis had been the capital of ancient Georgia and was still a city where different peoples lived side by

3 Such persons generally referred to themselves as 'svidomi ukraintsi'; that is conscious Ukrainians. Lebedyntsev tried to find places in his administration for his former classmates, the alumni of the Kiev Theological Seminary which had inherited the traditions of the famous Mohyla Academy. The writer Ivan Nechui-Levytsky (1838–1918) and Serhii Hrushevsky are listed among his friends. See M. Korduba, *Diialnist Teofana Lebedyntseva v Kholmshchyni* (Lviv–Cracow, 1943), p. 32, and the quotation in L. Wynar, 'Zhyttia i naukova diialnist M. Hrushevskoho,' *Ukrainskyi istoryk,* nos. 1–2 (1966), 18–19.

4 *Avtobiohrafiia–1906,* p. 1. L. Wynar, 'Avtobiohrafiia Mykhaila Hrushevskoho z 1906 i 1926 iak dzherelo dlia vyvchennia ioho zhyttia i tvorchosty,' *Ukrainskyi istoryk,* nos. 1–3 (1974), 108, writes that 'there is no doubt that Serhii Hrushevsky was a typical representative of Ukrainian ethnographic patriotism which he transferred to his son.' See Wynar's description of Serhii's career (pp. 107–8) and the necrology upon which it is based in *Literaturno-naukovyi vistnyk,* XIII (1901). 220.

5 M. Hrushevsky, 'Iak ia buv kolys beletrystom,' preface to his collection of short stories *Pid zoriamy* (Kiev, 1928); reprinted in *Vybrani pratsi,* ed. M. Halii (New York, 1960), pp. 170–7, esp. p. 171, and again in *Ukrainskyi istoryk,* nos. 1–4 (1980), 89–94. All citations from this work are from the Halii edition.

6 Ibid.

side. This situation had a strong influence upon the formation of Hrushevsky's character and he was aware of it. He later wrote:

The extraordinarily varied colour and national composition of the population swirled about me. The atmosphere, thick with national questions and the conflict of the various local cultures with Russian centralism, exalted my national feelings and made them the centre of my thoughts and emotions. The goal, content, and happiness of life for me was to serve the Ukrainian national renaissance. I was acquainted with the history of the rebirth of the Slavic nations ... The incompleteness of the Ukrainian renaissance, the dispersion of the Ukrainian intelligentsia, its disregard of its duty toward the voiceless and ignorant [*bezsovistnoiu*] popular mass, the rejection of a glorious past, of the treasures of [our] native nationality, seemed to be a terrible shame and dishonor upon me and my generation. It was our responsibility to cleanse ourselves of this dishonour.[7]

The young Hrushevsky read all of the materials related to Ukraine that he could obtain. He was impressed by the history of the Slavic literatures by A.N. Pypin and V.D. Spasovich and he eagerly awaited each new issue of the historical journal in which M.I. Petrov's series on modern Ukrainian literature appeared. The young bibliophile was delighted when his father bought him a subscription to *Kievskaia starina*,[8] and he buried himself in Kostomarov's splendid histories and in the various works of Panteleimon Kulish, Mykhailo Maksymovych, and Apolon Skalkovsky.[9] A part-time position as school librarian assured him access to other books and other fields as well.[10]

It seems that Kostomarov, in particular, had a powerful influence on the young Hrushevsky. A brilliant writer, an imaginative populist historian, and a famous 'Ukrainophile,' Kostomarov was committed to a decentralization of the Russian Empire; together with the poet Shevchenko, he had been a leading member of the Brotherhood of Saints Cyril and Methodius (1846), which had translated inchoate federalist and Panslavic feelings into the ideal of a Ukrainian national awakening. In a vague and youthful way, Hrushevsky adopted the Cyril-Methodian ideals. He was saddened, however, by the fact that even Kostomarov's modest program

---

7 Ibid., p. 172.

8 Ibid.

9 M. Hrushevsky, 'Avtobiohrafiia–1926,' ed. L. Wynar, *Ukrainskyi istoryk,* nos. 1–4 (1979), 79–85, esp. 83. This brief autobiography was first published in 1926 in connection with Hrushevsky's sixtieth birthday. In the 1930s the booklet was removed from Soviet libraries and became a bibliographic rarity.

10 'Iak ia buv kolys beletrystom,' pp. 170–1; L. Wynar, *Molodist Mykhaila Hrushevskoho* (Munich–New York, 1967), p.8.

concerning non-political cultural action remained unfulfilled. When so much remained to be done, there could simply be no question of taking the idea of national liberation beyond the cultural movement. Federalism had to be relegated to the future, and national independence was out of the question. 'And so,' the Ukrainian enthusiast concluded, 'my program of activity was considerably simplified.'[11]

The summer vacation of 1884 saw Hrushevsky try his hand at writing in Ukrainian. He wrote both verse and short stories; it was the prose that developed more quickly. In his first efforts, Hrushevsky wrote simple romances and made use of traditional themes and a Ukrainian folk setting. One of the gymnasium teachers encouraged and helped the boy. This gave Hrushevsky enough confidence to write to his father's old friend I.S. Nechui-Levytsky, one of the central figures of the Ukrainian literary movement of the time. From reading Petrov's articles, Hrushevsky had found out that Nechui-Levytsky was a schoolteacher in Kishinev, and, signing his work with a pseudonym and enclosing return postage, he mailed it off to him.

The young writer did not have to wait long for a reply. 'You have talent,' Nechui-Levytsky assured him, 'anyone who has read your efforts through will tell you this. Moreover your letter is written in a very good, clear, and easy Ukrainian at which I am amazed.' Nechui-Levytsky went on to suggest that for the present the youth put aside his dreams about far-off Ukraine. 'In the meantime, look around you at life in the Caucasus. Write about the life of the Georgian or Armenian people. Write in Ukrainian, and ... all this will be interesting.' Nechui-Levytsky further encouraged Hrushevsky by telling him that he would pass on such manuscripts to a publisher, perhaps the Galician *Dilo* or *Zoria*.[12]

There was further correspondence between the two. Hrushevsky sent Nechui-Levytsky more material and Nechui repeated his advice about turning to Caucasian life. He cautiously suggested that Hrushevsky concentrate on prose, as it was much better than his attempts at poetry.[13] The young writer took his

11 In 'Iak ia buv kolys beletrystom,' p. 172, Hrushevsky recalls that he had been completely ignorant of the dispute between the Kievan Ukrainophiles, who were primarily concerned with cultural revival, and the émigrés, who were more political. He noted that the national liberation, democratic, and somewhat socialist ideals of the Cyril-Methodians were adopted by Ukrainians, just as the ideas of Belinsky and Shchedrin had once formed the integral creed of the Russian *narodniki* or populists of the 1840s and 1860s.

12 Letter of 25 September 1884, in I.S. Nechui-Levytsky, *Zibrannia tvoriv u desiaty tomakh*, vol. X (Kiev, 1968), 295–6. Nechui-Levytsky added as a postcript: 'Don't send stamps!'

13 See Nechui-Levytsky's letters of 18 November 1884 and 27 February 1885. Also see his letter of 11 May 1885 to Oleksander Konysky, in which he notes that Hrushevsky is only seventeen years old and nonetheless 'a new and talented man of letters.' These are all in ibid. pp. 296–9.

mentor's advice and went on to try his hand at social satire. In 'Sublieutenant Skavuchak' Hrushevsky described, as he later put it, 'that Little Russian Sublieutenant type who carries to an extreme his satisfaction over his talents and successes.' One of the officials in charge of the school residence served as his model.[14] By the middle of the school term, he was working on a theme that had caught the attention of all Russia. *Bekh al-Jugur* told the story of the English occupation of the Sudan and the rising of the Mahdi. Hrushevsky made use of his practical knowledge of the Moslem world (gleaned from life in Tiflis) to describe the struggle of the Sudanese Moslems against the British. In this story, the British appear as aggressive, brutal, and arrogant imperialists whose hypocrisy is only matched by greed. The Sudanese are simple village people, believers who will resist to the last man and will die happily in the knowledge that paradise is not far away. After describing the efficient massacre of a defenceless Sudanese village, Hrushevsky puts the following words into the mouth of the English chaplain:

We have the consolation that we are not going to such trouble here for ourselves. We are acting here as the bearers of culture and enlightenment for all humanity. We are carrying the light of science into this desert for these savages. And they will not forget it! Perhaps these very people who hate us so today, or at least their descendants, will remember us, and our names will be the most beloved of all for them![15]

There is no subtlety in the young Hrushevsky's mockery of the theory of the 'white man's burden'; there is no equivocation in his description of the British colonial army. Indeed, distance was irrelevant. Hrushevsky lived among the Moslem population of the Caucasus, where the massacres of the famous Russian general, Ermolov, were recent history. The battle scenes in *Bekh al-Jugur* bear a striking resemblance to Baddeley's description of the Ermolov campaigns, and Tolstoy's reflections upon military life in the Caucasus. The young Hrushevsky must have felt considerable kinship to the region. Many years later, he recalled: 'I set forth in this tale all the liberationist and anti-imperialist feelings of that time. I wrote as a Ukrainian patriot and an opponent of violence and the exploitation of the colonial peoples ... I made fun of tottering morals and religious hypocrisy.'[16]

Hrushevsky sent off his new material to Nechui-Levytsky. It was not long before he received a favourable reply; a few months later *Bekh al-Jugur* appeared

14 'Iak ia buv kolys beletrystom,' pp. 172–3.
15 M. Hrushevsky, 'Bekh al-Dzhugur,' in his collected fiction published under the title *Pid zoriamy* (Kiev, 1928), p. 29.
16 'Iak ia buv kolys beletrystom,' p. 173.

in the Galician newspaper, *Dilo* (nos. 66–8, 1885). 'I had found myself,' the young writer concluded, 'and I had found my calling.'[17]

Throughout the school year 1885–6 Hrushevsky prepared feverishly for the matriculation exams. Being the school's best student, he hoped to win its highest distinction, the gold medal. But fate intervened. Hrushevsky lost the medal and suffered a crushing psychological blow as well. This crisis was caused by events related to the theft of official theme of the examination questions from the office of the school's principal. It was an annual custom among the Tiflis students to try to steal this theme from their school office and then distribute it to all the other gymnasium students in the city. The school that was able to do this first won special honour. As it turned out, Hrushevsky's school got hold of the themes, but the plotters were discovered. Instead of the expected prestige, the school was officially dishonoured and Hrushevsky lost his gold medal. 'It is true,' he recalls, 'that the themes were replaced by new ones and we did quite well on them.'

But all the same our gymnasium, the best school of the district, was scandalized. Instead of triumph, what shame! They took away our medals and treated us like good-for-nothings . . . This catastrophe deeply affected me and I felt all the moral degradation connected with it. What is the good of ambition! To hell with ambition! To hell with ambitious plans! If they are built on literature, on writing, then to hell with literature and writing! Such is the gluttony of ambition! You must get hold of yourself. Scrupulous execution of duty and nothing more.[18]

Hrushevsky gave up the idea of becoming a great writer.

He was left with the somewhat less glorious fields of history and slavistics. Hrushevsky assures us that the various polemics about the origins of Rus' and of the Cossacks, the polemics between the Ukrainophiles and the centralists, and finally the ban on the Ukrainian language all made a great impression on him.[19] The boy was drawn ever more to historical questions. On 18 July 1886, he wrote to

17 Ibid., p. 173. For Nechui-Levytsky's comments, see his letters of 28 May and 5 August 1885 to Hrushevsky in his *Tvory*, x, 300–3. A second short story, *Bidna divchyna*, also dated 1885, appeared in *Step: Khersonskyi beletristychnyi sbirnyk* (Saint Petersburg, 1886). This was also achieved through the mediation of Nechui-Levytsky. See his *Tvory*, x,' 304, and Hrushevsky, 'Iak ia buv kolys beletrystom,' p. 170. The Western Ukrainian writer and critic Ivan Franko did not think much of the second story and compared it unfavourably with Hrushevsky's earlier work. In a Polish-language review published in *Prawda* (Warsaw), no. 49 (1887) and reprinted in Ukrainian translation in his *Zibrannia tvoriv u piatdesiaty tomakh*, vol. xxvii (Kiev, 1980). 114–16, Franko wrote of *Bekh al-Jugur:* 'This very lively tale testified to the young writer's extraordinary talent. Unfortunately, the work which he has printed subsequently . . . has not lived up to expectations.'
18 'Iak ia buv kolys beletrystom,' p. 170.
19 *Avtobiohrafiia–1926*, p. 83.

the rector of Saint Vladimir University in Kiev and asked to be admitted to the history department in the historical-philological faculty.[20]

Hrushevsky's father was well aware of his son's enthusiasm for things Ukrainian. He also knew of the dangers awaiting him in Kiev. The old schoolteacher extracted a promise from the boy that he would not participate in any secret student circles during his course of study. Satisfied with this pledge, Serhii (who had by this time acquired quite a fortune from the royalties on his textbook of Church Slavonic, which was being used in the Russian school system) decided to finance his son's university education.[21]

Serhii Hrushevsky did not misjudge the situation in Kiev. Two years before his son's arrival, there had been large demonstrations at the university. These had resulted in mass expulsions from the institution and the banishment of many students from the city. [22] The minister of education, Count Dmitry Tolstoy, as part of his general reform of education took away the university's autonomy, and a new curriculum based on the intensive study of classical languages was imposed on all students. Undergraduates were expected to translate lengthy Russian texts into fluent Latin and Greek. This left very little time for specialities in other, more political subjects, and only a few general courses were offered. 'These lectures,' remarks Hrushevsky, 'could not do much for a student who was developed and well read in any kind of speciality.'[23]

The repressions weighed heavily upon both students and faculty. But in spite of the depressing atmosphere, Hrushevsky applied himself to university study with his usual stamina and asceticism. He accepted his father's advice and eschewed the company of his fellow students. During the first year or two, some of them resented this strange behaviour and began to think of him as a 'careerist.'[24] But he did well in his studies and by the second year had met the man who was to have more influence upon his basic intellectual formation than any other single person. This man was the historian Volodymyr Antonovych.[25]

Although Antonovych had been born into a Polish gentry family from Right Bank Ukraine, an early interest in social questions had led him to sympathize with the impoverished Ukrainian peasantry. By the eve of the Polish insurrection of 1863, he had broken with the Polish national movement and taken a clearly

---

20 Text in Miiakovsky, p. 116.
21 *Avtobiohrafiia–1906*, p. 2.
22 *Miiakovsky*, p. 117.
23 *Avtobiohrafiia–1906*, p. 3.
24 'Iak ia buv kolys beletrystom,' 176.
25 On Antonovych see the biography by D. Doroshenko, *Volodymyr Antonovych* (Prague, 1942), and my outline, 'Mysterious Historian: The Life of Volodymyr Antonovych,' *Forum,* no. 51 (Scranton, Pennsylvania, 1982), 26-7.

Ukrainian position. All of Antonovych's historical writings came to breathe a special sympathy for the Ukrainian common folk. As well, his opposition to the Poles had bought him some respect in government circles, and eventually he was appointed professor of Russian history at Saint Vladimir's University. It was not long, however, before the government had turned against the 'Ukrainophiles,' and Antonovych and his colleagues were themselves under increasing pressure. Their secret *Hromada* or society cautiously restricted itself to cultural work, and Antonovych himself had to be very careful. While his natural modesty and reserve enabled him to survive these difficulties, they had nevertheless left their mark.'The greatest ornament of Ukrainian scholarship of the time,' writes Hrushevsky, 'Professor Antonovych gave us the impression of a man worn out by these persecutions. In those bad times, he avoided close contact with the students and ever more withdrew from history into the "more tranquil" spheres of archaeology, historical geography and numismatics.'[26]

Antonovych quickly saw Hrushevsky's potential and during these first years put him to work on unusually advanced and specialized historical subjects. Soon the young scholar was doing brief articles and reviews for a number of journals and newspapers. But his first real historical 'work,' as he put it, grew out of the seminar essay that he did for Antonovych in 1887. After a few revisions, Hrushevsky's detailed account of 'South Russian Grand Ducal State Castles of the Mid-Sixteenth Century' appeared in the university's scholarly journal.[27]

There were also other historians at the University of Kiev who may have influenced Hrushevsky's early development. In his autobiography, Hrushevsky notes that, from lectures and private reading during these years, he had acquired an interest in economic and legal history. The Kievan historico-legal school was then flourishing under the inspiration of Mikhail Vladimirsky-Budanov (1838–1916), and Ivan Luchytsky (1845–1918) was teaching economic history. It is possible that these two men had some influence upon Hrushevsky's intellectual formation. But on the whole, it was not the legal-statist or even economic approach that was to form the main current in Hrushevsky's writings; rather it was the democractic *narodnyk* or 'populist' approach that he had learned from Antonovych.[28]

---

26 *Avtobiohrafiia–1906*, p. 3.

27 'Iuzhnorusskie gospodarskie zamki v polovine XVI veka,' *Universitetskie izvestiia*, no. 2 (Kiev, 1890), 1–33. P. Golubovsky reviewed this work favorably in *Kievskaia starina*, August (Kiev, 1890), 333–4. There is a full bibliography of Hrushevsky's early works in the *Naukovyi zbirnyk prysviachenyi profesorovi M. Hrushevskomu* (Lviv, 1906), pp. 1–4, which was issued on his fortieth birthday and commemorated the first decade of his work in Galicia. (See chapter 3, note 61.)

28 See the brief comments in *Avtobiohrafiia–1926*, p. 84. I. Vytanovych 'Uvahy do metodolohii i istoriosofii M. Hrushevskoho,' *Ukrainskyi istoryk*, nos. 1–2 (1966), 48, suggests the influence of

This came out very clearly in Hrushevsky's next major publication. In his third year at the university (1888–9), Hrushevsky was assigned work on the history of the Kiev area. This was in keeping with the general plan worked out by Antonovych in which Ukraine was divided into regions and each advanced student was assigned to do a detailed history of a particular region. Once this project was completed, a full general history of Ukraine could be written.[29] Hrushevsky's work on the history of the Kiev area took two years to complete. But when it was finished, his *History of the Kievan Land from the Death of Iaroslav to the End of the Fourteenth Century* had ensured his graduation, won him a gold medal, and earned him international recognition in the world of scholarship. Furthermore, he was granted a stipend and invited to continue his research.[30]

Hrushevsky's monograph on the Kiev area reflected certain basic populist ideas of the late nineteenth century. It divided ancient Kievan society into two distinct classes. On the one hand there was the leading stratum, that of the prince and his retainers. Supported by the boyars, this class held the political and cultural life of the state within its hands. Military matters, trade, civil life, literature, and religion were the patrimony of this element. On the other hand, the masses lived their own life apart from the princely entourage. The literate culture of the princes did not penetrate into the village. This led to a continuous tension and conflict between the two. It was this basic internal conflict, Hrushevsky suggested, which, with the advent of the Mongol invasions, was the most important reason for the collapse of the princely state.[31] Thus a simple dualism characterized Hrushevsky's early work. This dualism consisted of the juxtaposition of the rulers and the ruled. It was a feature integral to the thinking of Antonovych, and common to nineteenth-century populist historiography as a whole.

Vladimirsky-Budanov and Luchytsky, but Miiakovsky, p. 118, has established that neither Luchytsky nor Golubovsky, nor the famous historiographer V. Ikonnikov gave a seminar during Hrushevsky's first years in Kiev. Both Miiakovsky and Vytanovych admit the primary importance of Antonovych.

29 D. Doroshenko, 'Survey of Ukrainian Historiography,' *Annals of the Ukrainian Academy in the US*, v–vi (New York, 1957), 172–88, and *Volodymyr Antonovych*, pp. 161–3. Also see N. Polonska-Vasylenko, *Istoriia Ukrainy*, 2 vols. (Munich, 1972–6), I, 20–3, which puts things in a more general context.

30 M. Hrushevsky, *Ocherk istorii kievskoi zemli ot smerti Iaroslava do kontsa XIV veka* (Kiev, 1891), 520 pp. This work first appeared in the Kiev *Universitetskie izvestiia* in various numbers for 1891. The book's reception is discussed in L. Wynar, 'Ranni istorychni pratsi Mykhaila Hrushevskoho i kyivska shkola Antonovycha,' *Ukrainskyi istoryk*, nos. 3–4 (1966), 28–9. Hrushevsky completed the necessary exams in Greek and Latin and graduated on 24 September 1890. See the relevant documents in Miiakovsky, pp. 119–20.

31 Summary in Wynar, 'Rani istorychni pratsi,' p. 29. Hrushevsky was to develop this thesis further in the first volumes of his *Istoriia Ukrainy-Rusy*.

Hrushevsky's populist approach is evident as well in his other publications of this period. In 1891, he published an article on the history of Volhynia in which princely rivalry is shown in its worst light; and in the next year, Hrushevsky published two more articles which drew a sympathetic picture of the efforts of what the called the 'popular masses' to rid themselves of princely rule.[32] Hrushevsky's thesis is most fully developed in the article titled 'Social Movements in Ukraine-Rus' in the Thirteenth Century.' In this article, which he published in Austrian Galicia – where the Ukrainian language could be freely used – Hrushevsky spelled out a positive role for what he called the 'Tatar people'; that is, those ancestors of the modern Ukrainians who, in the darkest days of the Tatar ascendancy, had abandoned their despotic princes and submitted directly to the more distant Tatar rulers. They did this, Hrushevsky claimed, in order to preserve the traditions of their Orthodox faith and national culture and to obtain more political, economic, and cultural freedom than would be possible under the oppressive princely state. In a discussion of historical 'progress' and historical 'regress,' Hrushevsky listed the negative features of the old princely state and concluded: 'We cannot value the state as a cultural and progressive form except when it provides an opportunity for the spiritual-moral , economic, and political development of society.'[33]

This typically *narodnyk* concentration upon people rather than polity was not universally accepted. In a critical review of Hrushevsky's work which appeared in the Galician journal *Narod* (1893), the Ukrainian political émigré Mykhailo Drahomanov (1841– 95), who had earlier drafted a federal constitutional project and criticized Antonovych and the Kieven circle for restricting themselves to cautious cultural activities, again broke ranks with his fellow Ukrainian activists and criticized Hrushevsky for borrowing from German sociology, or for independently dreaming up, a clear distinction between 'society' (*Gesellschaft/ Hromada*) and the 'state' (*Staat/Derzhava*). Within the Russian Empire, oppositional thought gave the former a positive and the latter a negative connotation. Drahomanov, however, did not agree. Instead, he pointed out that while some state forms were despotisms, others – from the renaissance Italian commune to the medieval English kingdom – had given birth to liberty and parliamentary government. Thus the distinction between 'good' society and 'bad'

---

32 'Volynskii vopros 1077–1102,' *Kievskaia starina*, XXXIII (Kiev, 1891), 32–55, 259–72; 'Barskaia okolichnaia shlakhta do XVIII veka,' ibid., XXVI (1892), 260–77, and especially M. Serhiienko (pseud.), 'Hromadskyi rukh na Ukraini-Rusy v XIII vitsi' *ZNTSh*, I (Lviv, 1892), 1–28.

33 Parts of Hrushevsky's article are reprinted in M. Stakhiv, ed., 'Materiialy pro svitohliad Hrushevskoho,' *Mykhailo Hrushevsky u 110 rokovyny narodzhenia, ZNTSh*, vol. CXXVII (New York, 1978), p. 223.

state is put in question. 'In reality,' Drahomanov concludes, 'there is no qualitative distinction between these two categories, although there might be some kind of quantitative one.'[34] Hrushevsky, one presumes, took note.

In the meantime, he had begun preparation for the exams and dissertation required for the *magister* degree. He had completed the exams by 1893, but work on the dissertation – *The Province of Bar: Historical Sketches* – continued into 1894. Antonovych had suggested a topic that required intensive archival work and Hrushevsky was compelled to make extensive use of the archives in Kiev, Warsaw, and Moscow. It was a tough assignment, and the historian was never to forget its difficulties. He later recalled:

The theme that Antonovych assigned me was an unhappy enough choice. A great deal of work was required in order to fill the order and although a valuable enough book (though also very specialized) in a very little worked field of social-national history of Podillia from the fourteenth to the eighteenth centuries, together with two volumes of documentary materials, was the result, nevertheless, the fruits of the work were not great in comparison to the labour that had been put into it, and a great deal of courage was required in order to avoid giving up somewhere along the way. All the same, this very difficult schooling in archival work which I had to undergo – hundreds of books of legal documents, work in the archives of Kiev, Warsaw, and Moscow – did not go in vain and were of service to me later.[35]

About this time, Antonovych had also conscripted Hrushevsky into work on a multi-volume Dictionary of Ukrainian National Biography which was in preparation. This was a widely conceived work in which scores of people were involved. Under each letter some two to three hundred articles would appear. By 1894, work was completed up to the letter 'O,' and arrangements were made to have the dictionary published, first in Ukrainian by the Shevchenko Scientific Society in Austrian Galicia and then in Russian in Dnieper Ukraine (if the censors would

34 Much of Drahomanov's review is reprinted in the collection of documents edited by Stakhiv, ibid., pp. 223–6. Drahomanov further notes that the Zaporozhians who had fled to the Danube to lead a free Cossack life under the formal but distant suzerainty of the Ottoman Sultan had produced nothing to compare with the poetry of Shevchenko which was the product of a Ukraine burdened by the oppressions of the Russian tsarist state.

35 *Avtobiohrafiia–1926*, p.86. Antonovych's grandson, Dr Marko Antonovych, writes: 'The remarks about Hrushevsky that my father told me and that came from the mouth of my grandfather were that Hrushevsky took the work of the historian out of the archives and into the library.' Thus, it seems, he especially chose a theme for Hrushevsky on which he could not work in a library. And this turned out for the good although Hrushevsky was not satisfied.' See L. Wynar, 'Zhyttia i naukova diialnist M. Hrushevskoho,' *Ukrainskyi istoryk*, nos. 1–2 (1966), 29, note 57.

allow it). Unfortunately, editorial and translation problems delayed publication, the material became dated, and the project was never carried out.[36]

Ascetic devotion to scholarship was not the sole outlet for Hrushevsky's manifold energies. After his first years in Kiev, the promise that he had solemnly made to his father could no longer hold him and the young historian mixed more with his fellow students and began to take part in matters with more of a social or political character. 'At first,' explains a friend from these days, a theological student by the name of Oleksander Lototsky, 'he was mainly involved in the organization of scholarly work, but this work increasingly acquired a political character as well.' In fact, he seemed to have some kind of natural charisma. Lototsky continues:

I clearly remember the Mykhailo Serhiiovych of those days. His deep pensive visage made a sad and even a rather severe impression: because of his deeply set eyes and his beard, which was at that time already quite long, we used to refer to him as 'the beard of Saint Onufry.' But as soon as he mixed with people, his lively nature came out: his characteristic smile lit up his face. It was humorous and ironic and at the same time warm and welcoming. The smile, together with his sparkling eyes, made his half-jocular way of discussing things entirely natural, and in this way the boredom of a discussion which often had a dry content was unconsciously dissipated.

Of Hrushevsky's relations with his fellow students, Lototsky writes that 'there was no trace of a doctoral tone, of any kind of *magister dixit* about him.'

Being the oldest among us (he was about twenty-five years old) and of incomparably greater talent, social consciousness, and scholarly erudition than we, he was in actual fact a *magister* for us. He filled our spirits with consciousness and knowledge; he inspired us with enthusiasm and taught us how to work. But at the same time, he was a sincere comrade and behaved as an equal to us all. The most naive thought did not cause him to lose patience.[37]

Lototsky adds that Hrushevsky's logic and skills at discussion were such that he could always lead an opponent out of the intellectual wilderness into the light, and cap it off with a delightful smile while at the same time allowing this same opponent to think that he had done it all on his own.[38] Thus it was natural that Hrushevsky soon took the lead in several student and semi-academic organiza-

36 O. Lototsky *Storinky mynuloho*, 4 vols. (Warsaw, 1932–9), I, 170–1. Also see the brief remarks of P. Magocsi, 'Nationalism and National Bibliography: Ivan E. Levyts'kyi and Nineteenth Century Galicia,' *Harvard Library Bulletin*, XXVIII (Cambridge, Mass., 1980), 99, note 58.
37 Lototsky, I, 181.
38 Ibid.

tions. His home became the frequent meeting place of a circle of students from the Kiev Theological Seminary and his personal collection of Ukrainian books soon developed into a private leading library.[39] The practical experience in the organization of student and academic life gained during these early years was to serve him well in the very near future.

Even at this early stage, politics could not be entirely excluded from academic life. The 1880s and 1890s were the years of the so-called 'dark reaction,' and, as political parties were still little known in the Russian Empire, political life usually centred in more or less informal and secret discussion groups. This was especially true of the hard-pressed Ukrainian circles in Kiev. In the 1890s, there already existed a fairly radical Ukrainian grouping that was committed to the overthrow of bureaucratic tsardom. This group mirrored the émigré federal constitutionalist Drahomanov, the Galicians Ivan Franko and Mykhailo Pavlyk, and the Ukrainian Radical Party in Galicia which was inspired by them and which precariously engaged in open party politics under the conservative Austrian constitution.[40] Hrushevsky, however, naturally fell in with the more moderate political and social circle which was a continuation or offshoot of the secret cultural organization called the *Stara hromada* or Old Community. This informal circle gathered around Antonovych, O. Konysky, T. Rylsky, and M. Lysenko. The latter figures had close contact with the other major Ukrainian political grouping in Galicia, the 'populists' or *narodovtsi,* who were more influential than the Radicals and who were playing an important role in the Galician provincial assembly. The *narodovtsi* also had representation in the central parliament (*Reichsrat*) in Vienna. Through the united efforts of the Galician *narodovtsi* and Antonovych's Kievan circle, negotiations began toward a political compromise with dominant Polish bureaucracy in Galicia.[41]

By late 1890, an agreement was reached. The Ukrainians were to receive concessions in the educational sphere: official recognition and use of the phonetic 'Ukrainian-Rus'' script, more schools, financial support for the Shevchenko Literary Society, and the creation of new Ukrainian chairs at the University of

39 Ibid., p. 225.
40 Ibid., pp. 165–6. At the centre of this Kievan radical grouping stood Mykola Kovalevsky (1841–97), a former military school instructor who had spent ten years in exile (1879–89) for his Ukrainian activism.
41 See Doroshenko, *Volodymyr Antonovych,* pp. 79–85. Lototsky, I, 166, 181, calls Antonovych, Konysky, and Hrushevsky 'the active trio of political action of the time.' The Radicals took note when, at the funeral of a certain Karachevsky, Hrushevsky, who had not been known for his piety, read aloud (presumably in Ukrainian) a passage from the New Testament and made the customary ritual prostrations (*poklony*). Drahomanov's circle was at that time involved in the publication of a vernacular Ukrainian Bible. See the summary of his letter to Lesia Ukrainka in Olha Kosach-Kryvuniuk, *Lesia-Ukrainka: Khronolohiia zhyttia i tvorchosty* (New York, 1970), p. 266.

Lviv. The Polish-controlled Galician administration of Count Kazimierz Badeni obtained parliamentary cooperation from the Ukrainians, and the Austrian government in Vienna was pleased at the restoration of internal accord at a time of uncertain international relations. The agreement was supposed to initiate a 'new era' in Ukrainian-Polish relations.[42]

Antonovych and his friend Konysky had played an important role in arranging the 'compromise' as the agreement was called. With the pressures of political reaction in Russia so great, it made sense to support the expansion of education, the establishment of scholarly institutions, and a general Galician cultural flowering which, it was hoped, would provide the base for a kind of Galician Piedmont. 'In the Ukrainian circles of Kiev in which I moved,' writes Hrushevsky, 'great significance was attached to the reform of the Shevchenko Society.'

It was expected that the Poles would give aid to the Ukrainian cultural and educational movement according to the so-called 'agreement' of the Ukrainian *narodovtsi* of Galicia and the government. At the beginning of 1891, Professor Antonovych, returning from a journey to Galicia, told me about the plan for a chair of Ukrainian history at Lviv University. This chair was offered to Professor Antonovych, but he did not wish to take this burden upon his old shoulders and recommended me. In view of the significance that the Kievan Ukrainians were then giving to the Galician movement, I enthusiastically accepted this plan: the Kievans hoped to create a pan-Ukrainian cultural, literary, and scholarly beacon in Galicia which through the work and achievements of the writers and scholars of all Ukraine would be able to break through the system that banned the Ukrainian language and nationality in Russia.[43]

On 31 March 1892, the Austrian emperor, Franz Josef, published a decree announcing the foundation of the new chair; on 11 April 1894, Hrushevsky was officially confirmed as its holder.[44]

Almost exactly one month later, on a clear spring day, Hrushevsky defended

42 See I.L. Rudnytsky, 'The Ukrainians in Galicia under Austrian Rule,' in *Nationbuilding and the Politics of Nationalism: Essays on Austrian Galicia,* ed. A. Markovits and F. Sysyn (Cambridge, Mass., 1982), pp. 23–67, especially pp. 57–8, which gives full references. It is likely that the central Austrian government and military authorities pushed the Poles into the agreement. In their anxiety to reduce internal tensions, court and military officials even approached Pavlyk and the Radicals with whom there was little chance of lasting cooperation. See M. Lozynsky, *Mykhailo Pavlyk: ioho zhyttia i diialnist* (Vienna, 1917), pp. 15–16.
43 *Avtobiohrafiia–1906,* 3–4; *Avtobiohrafiia–1926,* pp. 85–6.
44 *Akten Osterreichisches Haus Hof und Staatsarchiv Kabinetskanzlei,* 1894, no. 1544, cited in Pelenski, 'Der ukrainische Nationalgedanke,' p. 15. See the discussion in L. Wynar, 'Halytska doba zhyttia Mykhaila Hrushevskoho,' *Ukrainskyi istoryk,* nos. 1–2 (1967), 5–22, esp. p. 6.

his *magister* dissertation in the Great Hall of Saint Vladimir's University. The élite of Kievan Ukrainian society was present, as were many of their Russian counterparts. A multitude of younger students also attended. The dean, Professor T.D. Florinsky, who was a 'Slavophile' and long-time enemy of the Ukrainian movement, read the *curriculum vitae* of the candidate. 'I remember,' writes Lototsky, 'that feeling of moral satisfaction (which, as it turned out, was not peculiar to me) when this voice that was hostile to everything Ukrainian while reading the *curriculum* could not omit the facts about the collaboration of Mykhailo Serhiiovych in the *Zapysky* of the Shevchenko Scientific Society, and his nomination as professor holding the Ukrainian chair at Lviv University.'[45]

The candidate himself was the next to step forward; he was greeted with warm applause. Although Hrushevsky's first words were a little hesitant, he soon gained his composure and ended well. Then his 'official opponent,' Professor Antonovych, took the podium. The quiet warmth of his address moved the audience: 'We are with you,' he began. 'We have worked together; we have sought scholarly truth together. If mistakes have been made, then this too we have done together. We are people of the same views, of the same scholarly conclusions. Thus in essential matters, I cannot be your opponent.' Antonovych then described the scholarly *credo* of the young man, asked for clarification of a few minor points concerning the dissertation, and ended his address. The questions and evaluation of the other official opponent, Professor V.S. Ikonnikov, led to an equally happy conclusion. Finally, Florinsky counted the votes of the faculty who were present and officially declared Hrushevsky a Master of History. Applause and greetings followed and Florinsky too congratulated Hrushevsky. A bystander heard him remark: 'I hope that you will also defend your doctoral thesis here in such a way. But then, on the other hand, perhaps you will write your doctorate in the Ukrainian language.'[46]

Hrushevsky's graduation was a triumphal event for the Kievan Ukrainians. That same evening, at a large reception held in Hrushevsky's home, both Antonovych and Konysky delivered speeches which revealed the hopes that they placed in the young professor and the new venture in Galicia.[47] Hrushevsky himself looked

---

45 Lototsky, I, 182. Born in Saint Petersburg in 1854, Florinsky distinguished himself as an expert on the South Slavs and Byzantium. He penned several anti-Ukrainian tracts, the most important of which was *Malorusskii iazyk i 'Ukrainsko-Ruskyi' literaturnyi separatizm* (Saint Petersburg, 1900), in which he expressed his discomfort at the thought that a great talent like Hrushevsky had rejected a glorious career as a Russian professor for the narrow opportunities of Ukrainian scholarship (pp. 99–100).

46 Lototsky, I, 182–3. *Kievlianin* (Kiev), no. 137 (1894), carried a report on the occasion of the thesis defence.

47 Lototsky, I, 183.

forward to the opportunities that the uncensored scholarship of the Austrian Empire might provide. During the summer of 1894, he saw his dissertation and archival work sent to press;[48] thereafter, he began to prepare the course of lectures that he was to deliver in the upcoming university term.[49] Armed with a forthright and businesslike character, the vigour and enthusiasm of youth, a clear sense of identity, a brilliant academic record, and a strong feeling of mission, the novice professor set out to do battle with the unknown protagonists of ignorance and injustice. Habsburg Galicia awaited him.

When the young Hrushevsky first stepped into the revered halls of Lviv University, the basic elements of his character had already been formed. From the time of his early youth in the Caucasus, he had displayed a seriousness and industry that were remarkable in one so young. His love of reading and his capacity for planned and prolonged work were first revealed in the gymnasium, but were to remain with him throughout his life. This rich childhood gave him a sense of self-confidence that was reinforced by the financial security that his father was able to provide. In both Tiflis and Kiev, the self-assurance was reflected in the precociousness of the younger Hrushevsky's literary and academic production. Held to the study desk during his early university years, he had a confidence that was eventually translated into an assertiveness that surprised and delighted his comrades and thrust him into the centre of Kievan Ukrainian life. Hrushevsky was not much of a public speaker, but he soon revealed promising abilities as a cultural organizer. By 1894, he was already a leader, a bearded Saint Onufry, and a patriarch among his peers.

The qualities of leadership which are rooted in assertiveness and industry are of little value without a clear sense of direction. But this trait too can be traced back to Hrushevsky's youth and education. At his father's knee, the youngster acquired a love for old Ukraine, its legends and its language. From his childhood reading, he learned of Shevchenko, of Kostomarov, and of the Ukrainian national awakening. He familiarized himself with the experience of the other Slavic nations and realized that the Ukrainian awakening was still incomplete; he was impatient with the limited goals of the Ukrainophiles.

---

48 *Avtobiohrafiia–1906* pp. 4–5; *Avtobiohrafiia–1926*, p. 87. The dissertation, *Barskoe starostvo: istoricheskie ocherki*, was published in Kiev in 1894. The two volumes of new documentation which Hrushevsky had discovered in the course of his research appeared in *Arkhiv iugozapadnoi Rossii*, vol. VIII in 2 parts (Kiev, 1894).

49 In his brief autobiographies, 1906, pp. 4–5, 1926, p. 87, he writes: I threw myself into this work with youthful enthusiasm and with no premonitions of the difficult situation and those disillusionments that awaited me in Galicia.' Also see Paul Magocsi, *National Cultures and University Chairs* (Toronto, 1980), pp. 11–12.

There is little doubt that Hrushevsky's Caucasian upbringing made clear the extent to which the requirements of a regional or local nationality can come into conflict with the centralizing tendencies of a great imperial state. As his first literary efforts show, Hrushevsky's sympathies were entirely on the side of the former. It was the simple folk and not the governing élite that attracted the young man's devotion. Many years later, he explained the matter thus:

I was brought up in the strict tradition of Ukrainian radical populism, which originated in the Brotherhood of Saint Cyril and Methodius, and firmly believed that, in the conflict between the people and the government, blame attaches to the government, since the interests of the working people are the highest good, and if they are flouted, the people are free to change their social system.[50]

University training strengthened these values. In Antonovych, the young Hrushevsky found a mentor who shared his populist-national views. The professor set him to work on his ancestral Kievan area, inspired him, and helped to mould his national consciousness. 'Volodymyr Bonifatiievych,' his student later wrote, 'was just as dear to us as he was suspicious and hateful to all those Ukrainophobe elements that surrounded our Ukrainian movement on all sides, lying in wait and watching for the first favorable moment to stamp it out and destroy it utterly.'[51]

Antonovych was compelled to be cautious. No progress, he believed, could be made through sudden and haphazard revolutionary upheavals or ethereal émigré political programs such as those of Drahomanov; only slow and painful educational and cultural work could bear lasting results. Hrushevsky writes: 'He placed the role of culture extraordinarily high in national life; he considered political work without a cultural base to be building on sand.'[52] This conviction lay

---

50 M. Hrushevsky, 'Ukrainska Partiia Sotsiialistiv-revoliutsioneriv ta ii zavdannia,' *Boritesia-poborete,* no. 1 (Vienna, 1920), 12.

51 M. Hrushevsky, 'Z sotsiialno-natsionalnykh kontseptsii Antonovycha,' *Ukraina,* no. 30 (Kiev, 1928) 3.

52 'Volodymyr Antonovych: osnovni idei ioho tvorchosty i diialnosty,' *Zapysky Ukrainskoho Naukovoho Tovarystva,* III (Kiev, 1909), 5–13, especially 11. Hrushevsky continues: 'He was prepared to acknowledge that the misfortunes experienced by the Ukrainian people were a result of the low cultural level of Ukrainian society ... and he saw in culture, the spread of education, knowledge and [national?] consciousness the single road to correcting the fortune of our people. A deeply convinced evolutionist, not only did he not believe in the success of revolutionary tactics, he did not believe either in the possibility of sharp jumps and upheavals in general. He dreamed of social and national progress in terms of centuries, and even in the most deceiving moments of our life, he did not give way to optimistic hopes. The political viewpoint of Antonovych ... was formed under the powerful influence of the ideas of the Cyril-Methodians ... and with their ideas about federalism and autonomy, they completed his evolution in ideas.'

at the base of the professor's political views and was an element in the agreement of 1890 with the Galician Poles. Hrushevsky inherited his mentor's appreciation for cultural work and brought it with him to Galicia. Coming to Lviv as a protégé of Antonovych and Konysky, Hrushevsky had also inherited their political contacts. The commitment to cultural progress in the homeland was to be a lasting feature of Hrushevsky's life work; it was a permanent value acquired from Antonovych. The political contacts were not. Given Hrushevsky's vigorous and assertive character and the peculiarities of political life in Austrian Galicia, a policy of caution and reserve could not last. The Galician period was to mark the beginning of a new stage in Hrushevsky's development.

2

The Young Professor 1894–1897

It was only with the greatest difficulty that the Galician Ukrainians had obtained a minimum of concessions from the Poles who ruled the province. In Vienna, where the Poles also had considerable influence, there were similar problems with the confirmation of these concessions from the imperial government. The Austrian minister of education, Baron Paul von Gautsch, objected to the Ukrainian claims to a chair of history, declaring that 'Ruthenian history is not real scholarship.' Therefore, the new position was established with the euphemistic title 'The Second Chair of Universal History with special reference to the History of Eastern Europe.'[1] Similarly, there were objections to Hrushevsky's Russian citizenship and his Orthodoxy. But a favourable evaluation by the professors of Lviv University and Austrian government bureaucrats, who pointed out that the young man was neither an enthusiastic Russian Panslav nor any kind of ultranationalist, eventually led to an imperial decree confirming Hrushevsky's appointment to the chair.[2]

Rumours about Hrushevsky preceded his arrival. The young scholar was coming as a protégé of Antonovych and Konysky and their moderate Galician

1 Hrushevsky discusses this in his *Avtobiohrafiia–1906*, p. 4, and he quotes von Gautch: 'Ruthenische Geschichte ist keine konkrete Wissenschaft.' See the remarks of Pelenski, 'Der ukrainische Nationalgedanke,' p. 15, and Wynar, 'Halytska doba,' p. 6. Ukrainian was to be the language of instruction.

2 The report states that Hrushevsky is 'ein Mann von ernster, solider, ehrenhafter Gesinnung, welcher sich lediglich der wissenschaftlichen Forschung widmet. Seiner politischen Gesinnung nachgehort derselbe der jung-ruthenischen-nationalen, sogenanaten ukrainischen Parteirichtung an, huldigt aber ebensowenig panslawistischen, als ultra-nationalen Tendenzen.' *Akten Oster-reichisches Haus-Hof und Staats-Archiv. Kabinetskanzlei*, no. 1544 (1894), quoted in Pelenski, p. 15, and Wynar, 'Halytska doba,' p. 7. Ivan Krypiakevych mentions the objections to Hrushevsky's religion and citizenship in his short biography: *Mykailo Hrushevsky: zhyttia i diialnist* (Lviv, 1935), p. 18.

friends, especially the Ukrainian delegate to the Austrian *Reichsrat,* Oleksander Barvinsky, who had been active in setting up the chair.[3] By 1894, however, it was becoming evident that the Polish administration was loath to cooperate with the Ukrainians and did not desire any real change in a political system that left all real power in Polish hands. Many *narodovtsi* were growing critical of Barvinsky's policy of collaboration, and two mutually hostile factions emerged. Iu. Romanchuk, K. Levytsky, and others broke with Barvinsky. Meanwhile, Franko, Pavlyk, and the Radicals, who had opposed the compromise from the beginning, could feel justified. When Drahomanov wrote to Franko asking for information about Hrushevsky, the latter replied:

I do not know much about Hrushevsky. He is a newcomer to our literature and has produced a few short stories under the pseudonym Mykhailo Zavoloka, and even written a novel 'Ours and the Strangers'.' A very weak thing. As to his political views, it seems that he is a follower of Barvinsky, and so, not long ago, last spring or perhaps the spring of this year when Barvinsky went to Ukraine to gather the signatures of people who approved of his policy and rejected those of Romanchuk, his signature was among those gathered.[4]

By the beginning of September 1894, the young professor had arrived in Lviv and the Galicians got a chance to observe him more closely. On 30 September 1894, Hrushevsky delivered his inaugural lecture at Lviv University. It was a public lecture and most of the leading lights of Galician Ukrainian society as well as the students of the university were present. Many Poles attended too, and the Great Lecture Hall was filled to overflowing.[5] Hrushevsky's lecture was on the ancient history of Rus'. In it he speculated as to the structure of the Rus' state and accepted a limited and modified form of Kostomarov's 'federal' hypothesis; he repeated his own earlier theory about the stratification of society, and about the princely structure and the masses living two separate lives, the factor that led to sudden collapse under Tatar pressure. Society used this opportunity, Hrushevsky

3 On Barvinsky, see I. Sokhotsky, 'Budivnychi novitnoi ukrainskoi derzhavnosty v Halychyni,' in *Istorychi postati Halychyny* (New York–Paris–Sydney–Toronto, 1961), pp. 102–17.

4 Ivan Franko, letter of 9 August 1894 to Drahomanov, in Franko's *Tvory v dvadtsiaty tomakh,* vol. xx (Kiev, 1956), p. 520.

5 See 'Pershii vyklad z davnoy ystoriy Rusy profesora Mykhaila Hrushevskoho,' *Dilo* (Lviv), no. 220, 1(13) October 1894, and Krypiakevych, pp. 18-19. Among the Poles was Leon Wasilewski, a Polish Socialist Party activist and afterwards an adviser to Marshal Pilsudski on the national question. L. Wasilewski, 'Moje wspomnienia ukraińskie,' in *Spohady, Pratsi ukrainskoho naukovoho instytutu,* vol. VII (Warsaw, 1932), p. 29. In his *Kresy wschodnie* (Warsaw–Cracow, 1917), p. 35, Wasilewski writes: 'The arrival of Prof. Hrushevsky in Lviv had results of unexpected importance in the life of Galician Rus', above all in the field of scholarship as equally in politics.' Wasilewski goes on (pp. 36–8) to give an account of Hrushevsky that is unusually dispassionate and, indeed, favorable when compared with other Polish accounts.

assured his audience, to achieve 'autonomy' from the ruling princes. On the other hand, the old state forms survived in a modified form in Western Rus'. Hrushevsky then seemed to be replying to Baron Paul von Gautsch as he turned to the question of the continuity of Ukrainian historical development. 'I have gone beyond the chronological limits of my survey,' he concluded, 'in order to show how all periods of Rus' history are closely and inseparably joined together.'

One and the same popular struggle, one and the same main idea spans the centuries through various political and cultural circumstances. The nation, the popular mass, links them into one whole, and is, and must be, the alpha and the omega of historical discourse. It is – with its ideals and struggles, with its battle, with its successes and its failures – the sole hero of history. The goal of our history is to understand its economic, cultural, and spiritual condition, its adventures, its desires and ideals. In accordance with these principles, we are compelled to make the popular mass our point of reference even in our ancient history. For the most part, the state structure is of interest to us in so far as it influences the condition of people, in so far as it falls itself under the influence of society, and in so far as it answers society's desires and struggles. Culture too as it is developed in the high strata of the nation is, for the most part, interesting to us not for its own sake, but rather because it reflects what is general and national.

Hrushevsky made one last point: 'In my time,' he said, 'I have gone through the philosophical school and with this I strongly affirm the principle: *nemini credere*. One must be always seeking and never be satisfied, never think that one possesses the whole truth ... Science is unceasing scepticism ... All *juratio in verba magistri* is impossible.'[6]

Hrushevsky's words stunned the audience. The local notables, many of them elderly gentlemen, were accustomed to view history in terms of kings, princes, and tsars. To hear that popular uprisings were the stuff of history, and that scepticism was its method, was almost too much for them. 'But what was there to do,' explained a younger observer, 'when such a revolutionary had already come, and when such authorities as Professor Volodymyr Antonovych and Oleksander Konysky had said to honour him. It was necessary to keep quiet and see what would happen.' In the meantime, they clapped.[7]

---

6 Hrushevsky, 'Vstupnyi vyklad z davnoi istorii Rusy vyholoshenyi u lvivskim universyteti 30 veresnia 1894r.,' *ZNTSh*, IV (1894), 140–50. He ends enigmatically: 'Most of all, I should like to see this spirit of inquiry and criticism in my collaborators and listeners and I would sincerely wish that, above all, they do not take my words lightly.'

7 See M. Mochulsky, 'Z ostannikh desiatylit zhyttia Franka 1896–1916,' *Za sto lit,* III (Kiev, 1928), 237–8, and the report in *Dilo*, no. 220 I(13) October 1894. Also see Krypiakevych, p. 19. A few days later, *Dilo* printed Hrushevsky's speech in full. See *Dilo* no. 228 (23), 11 October 1894, and following numbers.

In mid-October, the eminent literary scholar Professor Omeljan Ohonovsky unexpectedly died, and the young historian from Kiev suddenly became the focal point of Galician Ukainian intellectual life. At the cemetery, Hrushevsky delivered a funeral oration in which he assured those present, including Franko – who seemed to have missed his inaugural lecture – that Ohonovsky's name was known and loved as far away as the Caucasus and the Black Sea.[8]

Aside from the occasional public address, such as the Ohonovsky oration, Hrushevsky, like any other professor just taking up his first university appointment, had to spend most of his time preparing his course lectures, delivering them, and meeting with students.[9] One of these students later described his first meeting with the young professor. It occurred shortly after the inaugural lecture and took place in the Barvinsky home. 'The first impression of the person,' writes M. Korduba, 'did not correspond at all to what I had imagined.'

Short, lean, with an unusually thick beard and a nervous way of talking, he did not at all look like that type of university professor that I was accustomed to see around Lviv. I was presented to the professor as his future student and the title *tovarysh,* with which he immediately greeted me, coming as it did from the mouth of a university professor, disconcerted and astonished me.[10]

Hrushevsky's openness and immediacy soon won him the hearts of the youth. Almost every Ukrainian student at the university attended his lectures so that they had to be held in the largest auditorium. At first there were only a few students in his senior seminars, but it was not long before the seminars filled out and slowly, over the years, the graduates who could contribute to the scholarly periodicals of the Shevchenko Scientific Society (which were edited by Hrushevsky) grew into a virtual historical school.[11]

In spite of his popularity, Hrushevsky was not a brilliant lecturer. He spoke quickly and dryly.[12] Possibly he did this out of respect for 'scientific objectivity,'

8 See the reports in *Dilo*, no. 234, 18 (30) October 1894, and no. 235, 19 (31) October 1894. In his *Avtobiohrafiia–1906.* p. 5, Hrushevsky notes: 'Shortly after my arrival in Galicia, Prof. Ohonovsky died, and it fell to me, so to speak, to be the scholarly representative of Galician Ukraine.' Franko wrote to Drahomanov (*Tvory*, xx, 525–6) describing the funeral orations.

9 *Avtobiohrafiia–1906.* p. 5.

10 M. Korduba, 'Pryizd prof. M. Hrushevskoho do Lvova,' *Vistnyk Soiuza Vyzvolenia Ukrainy* (Vienna), no. 128 (1916), 795, and quoted in Wynar, 'Halytska doba,' p. 9.

11 Korduba, p. 795; Krypiakevych, pp. 19–20.

12 Wynar, 'Halytska doba,' p. 13, has collected the testimony of several students to this effect. Hrushevsky retained this characteristic to the end. Mykola Chubaty, 'Dodatkovi spomyny pro Mykhaila Hrushevskoho z 1912–1914 rokiv,' *Ukrainskyi istoryk,* nos. 3–4 (1975), 78–9, reports that Hrushevsky's style of lecturing had not changed much after almost twenty years. V. Dubrovsky (see below, chapter 9, note 6) reports that this same style marked the public lectures that he gave in Soviet Ukraine.

since he was soon to display considerable talent as a public speaker. At any rate, it was in the seminar that he revealed his true qualities as a teacher. He was able to guide his students from various historical sources, through reading and evaluating historical writings to independent conlusions. Gently and progressively, Hrushevsky eased his students from lesser compositions into solid research. Moreover, at no stage was the time or material wasted. Hrushevsky conscripted his hesitant students into the work of the NTSh and its journal, the *Zapysky*. Their work at first appeared in its reviews and bibliographic notes. Later these young scholars were contributing regular articles and could often boast a significant publication record before their graduation.[13]

Hrushevsky tried to provide for the material needs of his students as well. He saw to it that contributors to the NTSh publications received an honorarium, and he expended much effort soliciting funds in Eastern or 'Dnieper' Ukraine for the construction of a subsidized 'Academic Home' which would serve as a student residence.[14] Because Hrushevsky was a man of independent means, this sensitive attitude toward the material needs of his students is all the more remarkable.

In the eyes of its numerous critics, the gains of the Polish-Ukrainian Agreement of 1890, or the New Era as it was known, seemed very small. But the vigorous new professor, being firmly committed to the national rebirth, was to make the fullest possible use of them. His work in the NTSh is especially striking. Hrushevsky quickly replaced Barvinsky as the editor of the *Zapysky* and he worked hard to build up the journal. He also took over the Historical-Philosophical Section from Anatol Vakhnianyn, who had earlier translated from Russian some of the young historian's work for the daily *Dilo*.[15]

---

13 Korduba, p. 795, writes: 'The professor drew us, his students, into the review section. At first, this surprised us, because we felt that we did not have enough training for discussing and criticizing the work of specialist scholars. But Hrushevsky quickly succeeded in destroying these doubts and lack of confidence in our powers. He gave each of us a book from the ones that had to be discussed and commanded us to read it. Later he advised us to compare what we had read with one or another earlier work on the same theme and after this he immediately asked about the result, the comparison, the impression that the new book had made, etc. He listened patiently to the verbal review, made a comment here or there, suggested that we pay more attention to this or that point, and exclaimed: "And now comrade, try to write it all down." In this way, he made us, eighteen to twenty-year-old boys, into reviewers and so the first student reviews appeared in the *Zapysky*.' On Hrushevsky as a seminar leader, see Krypiakevych, p. 21, and Chubaty, pp. 78–9.

14 The wealthy Ukrainian landowner and patron of *Ukrainstvo*, Ievhen Chykalenko, gave twenty-five thousand rubles for this purpose. See his *Spohady (1861–1907)* (New York, 1965), p. 226. Hrushevsky's fund-gathering in Eastern Ukraine was also known outside of the Ukrainian community, as for example to the Pole Wasilewski, *Kresy wschodnie*, p. 36. Also see L. Wynar, *Mykhailo Hrushevsky i Naukove Tovarystvo im. Tarasa Shevchenka 1892–1930* (Munich, 1970), pp. 39–40, 14–15.

15 In 1873, with the help of the Ukrainians living under the Russian government, which had recently banned the use in print of the Ukrainian vernacular (1863, 1876), the Shevchenko Society was

As Hrushevsky gradually took control of the NTSh, the scholarly work of the society took on a regular pattern. The achievements of the Historical Section, so important for the future development of national consciousness, especially stand out. A veteran of these days writes:

The members of the section gathered together for the purpose of scholarship two or three times a month. They would read their papers at these meetings and discuss various scientific matters. Up to 1914, under Hrushevsky's direction, some 320 such meetings took place at which 550 scholarly presentations were made. Both older scholars and young historians who had finished university took part. But Hrushevsky was the soul of all this work: he read his own papers, always took part in the discussions, and always had something new and interesting to say. The breadth of his knowledge was simply amazing; there was no kind of historical question on which Hrushevsky did not have something to say.[16]

Because of the great task ahead, none of the material presented at these meetings was wasted. The papers were usually revised and published later on in the various organs of the society.

Such a careful allocation of intellectual resources was very necessary. The NTSh *Zapysky* had begun rather weakly,[17] and contributions promised by the

---

founded as a literary organization. The reform that turned it into an institution of research and scholarship was carried out in 1892. Oleksander Barvinsky was elected its president. There were three sections: (a) Historical-philosophical, director Anatol Vakhnianyn; (b) Philological, director Omelian Ohonovsky; (c) Mathematic-physical science-medical, director Ivan Verkhratsky. The models for these pioneering founders were the Czech Academy of Sciences in Prague and the Polish Academy in Cracow. Polish opposition and Russian government protest prevented the Austrian government from granting the institution the title 'Academy of Sciences.' There is no doubt that its 'golden age' occurred under Hrushevsky's leadership. Wynar's *Mykhailo Hrushevsky i NTSh* is the most detailed study of the subject. V. Veryha, 'Naukove Tovarystvo im. Shevchenka v dobi Hrushevskoho,' in *Iuvileinyi zbirnyk naukovykh prats v 100-richia NTSh* (Toronto, 1977), pp. 15–32, is a very readable account. In the latter volume, pp. 7–14, there is a brief history by B. Stebelsky, who brings up to date the standard history by V. Doroshenko, *Ohnyshche ukrainskoi nauky* (New York, 1961). There are several essays on the same theme in *Almanakh UNS na rik 1973* (Jersey City, NJ). Also see S. Horak, 'The Shevchenko Scientific Society (1873–1973): Contributor to the birth of a Nation,' *East European Quarterly*, VI (Boulder, Colorado, 1973), 249–64.

16 Krypiakevych, p. 23.

17 This seems to have been the opinion of Ivan Franko, who immediately saw that the article by Serhiienko on 'Social Movements in Ukraine-Rus'' was more or less simply a chapter from Hrushevsky's history of the Kiev area. See his letter of 14 January 1893, to Drahomanov in *Tvory*, XX, 469–72. Drahomanov advised Franko not to collaborate with the conservative Barvinsky and not to contribute to the *ZNTSh*. Both Drahomanov and the Ukrainian orientalist, Ahatanhel Krymsky, singled out Hrushevsky's article as being the most original contribution to the collection. See the discussion in Wynar, *Mykhailo Hrushevsky i NTSh*, pp. 17–18.

Dnieper Ukrainians – Konysky, Antonovych, Luchytsky, and others – failed to materialize. Nevertheless, through the efficient use of seminar materials and by accepting contributions from those oppositional Ukrainian figures who had been previously excluded by the cautious Barvinsky, Hrushevsky quickly expanded the scope of the NTSh publications. 'Taking over as the editor of the *Zapysky*,' the historian recalls, ' ... I turned it from a yearbook into a quarterly, later a bi-monthly. I myself contributed many research articles, notes, and reviews.'[18] By the time of Hrushevsky's retirement on the eve of the First World War, the *Zapysky NTSh* numbered some 110 thick volumes and had become the single most important collection of *Ukrainica* in existence.[19]

The young historian provided the stimulus to other publishing ventures as well. In 1895, a special Archaeographic Commission was founded. The commission began publication of two carefully edited documentary collections: (a) *Sources for the History of Ukraine-Rus'*, and (b) *Monuments of Ukrainian-Rus' Language and Literature*. These expensive volumes, which were so important for documenting the continuous existence of a Ukrainian-Rus' people, appeared in alternate years: *Sources* one year, *Monuments* the next. In the first series alone, Hrushevsky published some eleven volumes of new historical documentation. In the years between 1895 and 1913, many other scholarly serials appeared, including two major collections of ethnographic material. The energetic historian played an important role in all of this activity.[20]

The question of a decent library for the Shevchenko Society was another of Hrushevsky's priorities. Again, it was directly related to the problem of the national renaissance. At the end of 1897, the historian noted that 'we are in a very bad state when it comes to the question of a library.'

On all of our territory from the Sian to the Kuban, there is not a single library that has a well-chosen and more or less full collection of all that which belongs to our people and its territory. There is nothing [good] to say about Lviv itself and Austrian Ukraine-Rus'.

18 *Avtobiohrafiia–1906*, p. 5.
19 Such is the opinion of all the authorities cited in note 15 above. Also see the introduction to M. Boiko, *Index to the Memoirs of the Shevchenko Scientific Society 1892-1982* (Bloomington, Indiana, 1984).
20 Veryha, p. 18, gives a good summary of Hrushevsky's work as editor and publisher. There is a more detailed account in Wynar, *Mykhailo Hrushevsky i NTSh*, pp. 17–27. On pp. 20–1, Wynar discusses the content of *Zherela do istorii Ukrainy-Rusy*. On the *Pamiatky ukrainskoi-ruskoi movy i literatury* see below, note 35. Hrushevsky's student, Krypiakevych, p. 23, writes that the various NTSh publications 'were distributed not only among Ukrainians, but went out to the major foreign libraries and to the universities and academies of all the educated nations, both in Europe and in America and even in Australia. These were the first Ukrainian publications that drew the attention of the whole academic world to Ukraine.'

Sometimes the most elementary publications concerning Ukrainian history, the history of literature, and ethnography cannot be found.[21]

To rectify this situation, Hrushevsky solicited further donations from Dnieper Ukraine and initiated a wide-ranging exchange program with scholarly institutions in other parts of Austria-Hungary, the Russian Empire, and abroad. By 1897, Hrushevsky had recruited a full-time librarian and by 1900, the NTSh was involved in 168 regular exchange programs with institutions as far apart as Saint Petersburg and Philadelphia. Though it never became the largest academic library in Lviv, the NTSh collection was very well chosen and reflected the 'pan-Ukrainian' interests of its founders. It was to serve its users well.[22]

The problem of housing the books and providing research facilites remained. In 1898, which was the fiftieth anniversary of the revolutions and emancipation of 1848, and the one hundredth anniversary of the birth of modern Ukrainian literature, Hrushevsky took the daring step of using a large private donation for the purchase of an expensive new building on Charnetsky Street. The building was a multi-storeyed structure with plenty of space and an impressive façade. It was centrally located in the best part of the city, with the palace of the Galician viceroy on one side and the palace of the Roman Catholic archbishop on the other. A younger contemporary recounts that the ruling 'Polish aristocrats of the city of Lviv were very uncomfortable about the establishment of the Ukrainian scholarly society in this particular place.'[23]

They were not the only ones. At first, many of the older and more conservative members of the NTSh hesitated to endorse the project. The donor had originally earmarked the funds for a medical school in a future Ukrainian university, and there was no point, they thought, in unnecessarily antagonizing the mighty Poles.[24]

21 Quoted by I. Krevetsky in *LNV*, XXXI (1905), 156–157.
22 Hrushevsky served as chief librarian until 1897, when he managed to overcome conservative resistance and hire the radical publicist, Mykhailo Pavlyk, to fill the position. The two men soon quarrelled, but Pavlyk retained his post. For a general history, see V. Doroshenko, *Biblioteka Naukovoho Tovarystva im. Shevchenka* (New York, 1961). As late as 1905, the NTSh possessed only 21,000 volumes in comparison with the university's 200,000 and the 100,000 of the *Narodnyi Dom*, which was much older but was in the hands of the 'Muscophiles.' See I. Krevetsky's note in *LNV*, XXXI (1905), 156–7.
23 K. Pankivsky, 'Spohady pro NTSh,' *Ukrainskyi istoryk*, no. 4 (1978), 94–5.
24 Pankivsky (ibid.) writes that 'many members of the society, the older ones who worked at higher posts in the government administration, hesitated to take responsibility for using 100,000 *karbovantsi* [that is, rubles], which had been designated by the donor for the creation of a medical faculty . . . for another purpose . . . They were mistrustful of the great plans of the young head of the society.'

It was not in Hrushevsky's character to bow to such logic. In fact, it seems that this bold project was the young professor's way of breaking through what he considered to be the stultifying myopia and paralysing inferiority complex of the Galician Ukrainian intelligentsia. The impressive building on Charnetsky Street was meant to confer a sense of dignity upon the Galician Ukrainians and remind them of the cultural unity of all of the Ukrainian lands. It was meant to be the physical symbol of the national renaissance and the role of the Galician Piedmont in it.[25]

Even in his personal life, the young professor's unorthodox manner and new ideas ruffled the feathers of the local notables. At first, Hrushevsky naturally mixed with the Barvinsky circle and the moderate public figures who had worked so hard to achieve the agreement of 1890. It was among the sons and daughters of these people that he met his future wife, the young school teacher Mariia Voiakovska, who was a friend of Barvinsky's daughter Olha.[26] However, Mariia came from a rather poor clerical family and the conservative Galicians did not consider her a good match for the wealthy young professor from Kiev. The cultural élite frowned upon their marriage which took place in 1896, and certain influential gentlemen never forgave Hrushevsky's insult to their eligible daughters.[27] Later on, this was to have serious consequences for Hrushevsky's public activity.

During these first years in Galicia, Hrushevsky was busy with his academic responsibilities and avoided direct involvement in political life. But the cultural flowering that Galicia was then experiencing had obvious political implications, and party divisions among the Ukrainians made themselves felt from the very beginning. The struggle between the peasant-oriented Radical Party and the more legalistic and intelligentsia-oriented populists (*narodovtsi*) could not be entirely excluded from the halls of the NTSh. It fell to Hrushevsky to see that these disputes did not impede the progress of scholarship.

The problem arose immediately after his arrival. Within his first days in Lviv,

25 See the brief discussion in Wynar, *Mykhailo Hrushevsky i NTSh*, p. 33.
26 Pankivsky, 'Spohady,' p. 94. Nykolai Voiakovsky, letter of 2 March 1966, to L. Wynar in L. Wynar, 'Materiialy do biohrafii Mykhaila Hrushevskoho,' *Ukrainskyi istoryk*. nos. 1–2 (1982), 66–8.
27 It was Professor Volodymyr Shukhevych who was most upset about Hrushevsky's indifference to his daughter. See V. Doroshenko, 'Ivan Franko i Mykhailo Hrushevsky,' *Suchasnist,* no. 1 (Munich, 1962), 20–2. I. Rakovsky, 'Prof. M. Hrushevsky u Lvovi,' *Almanakh UNS na 1952 rik* (Jersey City, NJ), pp. 82–3, also discusses these matters. The marriage was a happy one and Mariia was able to provide a warm, quiet, and orderly home life for her famous husband. Besides being a woman of 'good sense,' she also was to contribute to *Literaturno-naukovyi vistnyk* (mostly translations from French literature) and to the organization of Ukrainian theatre in Kiev, and was to sit in Ukraine's revolutionary parliament, the Central Rada. See the brief article in the *Entsyklopediia ukrainoznavstva*, vol. II (Paris–New York, 1957), 453.

the new professor found a note in his mailbox from the most famous of all Galician Radicals, the writer and poet Ivan Franko. The note described a project for the publication by the NTSh of a collection of Ukrainian apocryphal and legendary materials. A few days later, Franko visited the professor and explained his plan more fully.[28] Many years later, Hrushevsky reflected upon the logic of Franko's visit:

Up to this time, he had stood aside from the Shevchenko Society. It had an old reputation for being a very exclusive institution whose positions were filled from the *narodovtsi* public and were inaccessible to 'dissidents' [*ynakomysliashchykh*]: high membership fees and various entrance formalities preserved it from external influences. Its restructuring from such a tightly knit corporation into a 'scientific society,' carried out in 1891–1892, lowered the membership fee and made it more accessible to a wider circle of scholarly workers; but the society still kept its reputation for being a stronghold of right-wing, conservative *narodovstvo* . . . There was no work or no place in it for the more left, radical, and social democratic elements, and when, after the above-mentioned reform, Franko himself declared his desire to sign up as a member of the society, the administration did not accept him. But he was not discouraged by this, and when my arrival in Lviv became known, he decided to make use of it. He correctly surmised that I, as a man not tied down by Galician complications and armed, so to speak, with a pan-Ukrainian mandate, would cross the Galician wattled fences, and especially in the Scientific Society, which was the centre of my work, would not be hemmed in by its traditions.[29]

On 23 October 1894, Hrushevsky wrote a formal letter to Barvinsky asking him whether it would be possible to engage Franko as a co-worker. Barvinsky replied in the negative, saying that men like Franko and his fellow radicals would only cause problems for the society; Barvinsky advised the young professor that it would be best to rely on his own powers and those of other young scholars. This would suffice for the publication of the historical documents in question.[30]

We do not know what Hrushevsky told Franko. Perhaps he informed him of his own appreciation of the writer's achievements and hinted to him that Barvinsky would soon retire from his central administrative position. We do know that on 10 November Franko wrote to Drahomanov, who was still critical of Antonovych's cultural circle: 'I am far removed from the *narodovtsi* and only hear this or that about their activity every now and then . . . After Ohonovsky's death, Barvinsky gives orders at the *Prosvita* society. In the Shevchenko Society, so I hear, they want to make Hrushevsky the head.'[31]

28 M. Hrushevsky, 'Apostolovi pratsi,' *Ukraina*, no. 6 (Kiev, 1926), p. 5.
29 Ibid.
30 Wynar, *Mykhailo Hrushevsky i NTSh*, p. 45, quotes Barvinsky's letter.
31 Ivan Franko, letter of 10 November 1894 to M. Drahomanov, in *Tvory*, xx, 527–8.

Meanwhile Franko, who had recently obtained a doctorate in Slavistics from Vienna, was applying for a lecturing position in Ukrainian literature and ethnography at Lviv University. He had thought that his chances were good, especially following the death of Ohonovsky. However, after the formation of the selection committee, a rumour reached him that for some reason Hrushevsky was opposed to his candidacy.[32] Throughout December 1894, the 'habilitation' or selection process continued, and on New Year's Day, Franko was able to inform Drahomanov that all was going well and that there was a possibility that he would get Ohonovsky's chair. He further told Drahomanov that the Poles on the Habilitation Committee, though favourable to his candidacy, were fearful of how the provincial viceroy, Count Kazimierz Badeni, would react to the appointment of a Radical and a convicted socialist who had been sent to prison on more than one occasion. Some committee members – Hrushevsky among them – wished to solicit the opinions of Professor Tretiak of Cracow and of Franko's doctoral supervisor, Professor Jagić of Vienna. This request was rejected by the rector of the university.[33]

The final habilitation colloquium at which the candidate was examined did not take place until 18 March 1895. During January and February, however, almost certainly with the encouragement of Hrushevsky, Franko had begun to take part in the activities of the NTSh. To begin with, the Galician writer presented a project for the publication of folk-songs and other ethnographic materials. The conservative veterans of the society were not enthusiastic. 'Except for Hrushevsky and some of the young students,' Franko informed Drahomanov, 'no one is interested in these things.'[34] Once again, Hrushevsky, it seems, managed to push the project through. By 20 February, Franko had also presented his plan for the publication of a series of Ukrainian apocrypha and was already preparing the first volume for press. It was this material that filled the first volumes of the *Monuments of Ukrainian-Rus' Language and Literature*.[35] Hrushevsky had accepted Franko's

32 Ivan Franko, letter of 14 November 1894 to Drahomanov, in *Tvory*, xx. 528.
33 Franko was hoping that the university position would free him from financial dependence on his journalistic work for the Polish liberal newspaper *Kurier Lwowski*. See the letter to Drahomanov in *Tvory*, xx, 531–5. Franko's account corresponds to that of the university archives. For the relevant documents, see *Ivan Franko: Dokumenty i materiialy* (Kiev, 1966), pp. 180–1, 184. The stated reason for the request for outside opinions was that two of the Polish professors on the committee did not feel competent to judge Franko on the questions of Ukrainian literature. Perhaps Hrushevsky supported the request because the approval of such eminent scholars as Tretiak and Jagić would strengthen Franko's hand considerably when it came to governmental confirmation of the appointment.
34 Ivan Franko, letter of 25 January 1895 to Drahomanov, in *Tvory*, xx, 539.
35 Ivan Franko, letter of 20 February 1895 to A. Krymsky, in *Tvory*, xx, 543. Some seven volumes of *Pamiatky ukrainskoi movy i literatury* were to appear under Franko's direction. In one of his last letters to Franko, dated 23 February 1895, Drahomanov warned the writer against collaboration

initial proposals and the two men had wasted no time in getting to know one another. It was to be the beginning of a fruitful collaboration that lasted a full decade.

In March, when the time for the habilitation colloquium came, the new professor and the aspiring writer were already well acquainted with each other. For his part, Hrushevsky asked Franko about older Ukrainian hagiographic literature, seventeenth-century drama, and the work of Kotliarevsky. His last question was about nineteenth-century theories of the Cossack epic *Dumy*.[36] Other examiners asked about the definition of nationality and the influence of politics upon the development of Ukrainian literature. Franko handled all these questions well and the committee recommended him for the position of lecturer (*privat-dozent*). The recommendation was sent via the provincial viceroy's office to the minister of education in Vienna. At the advice of Viceroy Badeni, who complained of Franko's political involvement with the Radicals and his suspected socialism, the habilitation was denied.[37]

It is not clear how Hrushevsky reacted to Badeni's action against Franko. Certainly, his faith in the agreement of 1890 must have been somewhat shaken. Moreover, Franko himself blamed Barvinsky and the other Ukrainians who were collaborating with the Polish administration just as much as he blamed Count Badeni.[38] Hrushevsky knew that Franko was the best man for the position, and this must have put some additional strain upon his relations with Barvinsky. On the other hand, Franko's loss of the university position, when combined with the difficulties that he had in maintaining his independent literary and scholarly journal *Zhytie i slovo* – it was plagued by financial problems and a lack of new contributors – caused him to become more involved with and publish much more frequently in the various NTSh organs. In accordance with Hrushevsky's plan for contributors, Franko began to receive honoraria for his contributions; it was not long before his activity had a real impact upon the scholarly production of the society.[39]

---

with the NTSh. Franko did not heed the warning. See M. Vozniak, ed. *Lystuvannia I. Franka i M. Drahomanova* (Kiev, 1928) pp. 495–6.

36 The habilitation protocol is printed in *Ivan Franko: dokumenty i materiialy*, pp. 185–6. It is almost certain that Hrushevsky already knew how well Franko could handle these questions.

37 See the police report, Badeni's report to the minister, and the latter's reply in ibid., pp. 188–91. For Franko's account, which describes an audience with Badeni, see 'Istoriia moiei habilitatsii,' which appears as 'Meine Habilitation' in his *Beiträge zur Geschichte und Kultur der Ukraine* (Berlin, 1963), pp. 68–71.

38 On 30 June 1895 he wrote to Krymsky: 'Because of the viceroy's report the ministry has not confirmed my appointment as lecturer of Ukrainian-Rus' literature. There is no doubt that for this I must thank our New Era men, mainly Barvinsky and Vakhnianyn, who have blackened my name in every possible way in order to prevent my appointment to a chair.' *(Tvory*, XX, 552).

39 Ivan Franko, letter of 17 November 1895, to Krymsky, in *Tvory*, XX, 557–9, gives a good idea of

About this same time, the New Era was clearly shown to be at an end. The famous 'bloody elections' of 1895 and 1897 were manipulated by Badeni to emasculate the Ukrainian opposition parties. Mass arrests, political trials, beatings, and intimidation were the rule. Franko and most of the other opposition candidates did not stand a chance; there were very few oppositional Ukrainians elected to either the provincial legislature or the central Austrian parliament. Most of those Ukrainians who did get elected belonged to Barvinsky's loyalist Catholic Union Party. The emperor ignored the complaints of a mass delegation sent to Vienna by the Ukrainians.[40]

All of this had been totally unexpected by Hrushevsky. It came to him as somewhat of a revelation that the Galician Ukrainians had not been granted more opportunity for unhindered national development. The young professor felt that the Poles had deceived the Kievans with 'false assurances.' How could the hoped-for Galician Piedmont flourish under such conditions? 'I quickly came to be convinced,' he concluded, 'that my Kievan friends had made a serious mistake in their sympathies towards the "compromise" and the "compromisers," that the Poles did not want to give up their dominion and did not understand any relationship to the Ruthenians other than that of a ruling nationality to a servile one.' In consequence, 'even relations with my very closest friends were more or less sharply cut off.'[41] Thus at the same time that Franko was becoming involved in the work of the NTSh, which provided him with a source of material and moral support, Hrushevsky was breaking out of the conservative circles in which he had been moving. A realistic assessment of the unfavourable political situation, a common impatience with the policies of the leading Ukrainian politicians, and a commonality of scholarly gifts and interests were coming to bind the two men together.

This concordance of views was quickly put to the test. In 1895 and 1896, the NTSh was going through a general reappraisal of its activities and a special commission was set up to review the constitution of the society and to propose amendments. The populist (*narodovets*) leader, Kost Levytsky, a certain S. Fedak, and Ivan Franko were appointed to this commission. In December 1896, at an extraordinary session of the NTSh general meeting, this commission proposed a

the writer's new interest in the NTSh. Franko's contributions to NTSh publications are listed in M.O. Moroz, *Ivan Franko: bibliohrafiia tvoriv 1874–1964* (Kiev, 1966), pp. 271ff.

40 On Franko's candidacy see his letter to Krymsky (ibid.) and article on 'Die jungste galizische Wahl,' in *Beiträge*, pp. 299–309. More generally, see M. Stakhiv's introduction to Ivan Makukh, *Na narodnii sluzhbi* (Detroit, 1958), pp. 45–7.

41 *Avtobiohrafiia–1906*. p. 5. Also see Hrushevsky's letter to the editor of *Dilo*, in which he explains that his dissatisfaction began as early as the 1894/5 session of the provincial legislative assembly, when the conservative Polish majority did not make suitable reforms in the matter of local school councils. See M. Hrushevsky, 'Iak mene sprovadzheno do Lvova,' *Dilo*, no. 137 (1898), and reprinted in *Ukrainskyi istoryk*, nos. 1–4 (1984), 230–7.

new constitution that would create a kind of two-tier system of administration. According to this plan, a new category of 'active members' would have real control over the society's affairs; patrons, dilettantes, and other non-scholars would retain some advisory powers, but would be deprived of their right to vote on matters of pure scholarship. The whole idea was to strengthen the professional-scholarly character of the institution, and both Hrushevsky and Franko were strong supporters of the move.

They did not win the war with the first battle. A two-thirds vote in favour was required at the general meeting, and Franko and Hrushevsky could only gather a simple majority. The proposition for a reformed constitution was turned down. A second issue of similar import was also discussed at this meeting. In the past, the *narodovtsi* party newspaper *Dilo* had been printed in the NTSh printshop. But with the growth of political life among the Galician Ukrainians, this arrangement became increasingly partisan. The entry of Franko and the Radicals into the society's work further increased the tensions. Thus Franko and Hrushevsky attempted to neutralize the partisan political contacts of the NTSh by proposing that *Dilo* be printed elsewhere. Once again, however, they were voted down. The meeting ended in a complete stalemate when Hrushevsky, the main initiator of most of the scholarship, resigned both his administrative and editorial positions. Franko, who was still relatively new at the society, resigned his post at the Philological Section and others followed. The NTSh was paralysed, and all scholarly activities temporarily ground to a halt.[42] The issues raised in December 1896 were not resolved until early the following year. This year turned out to be a crucial one in the history of the NTSh.[43]

On 2 February 1897, at the next NTSh general meeting, Hrushevsky was elected the new president of the society. It seems that he was the only man who was really trusted by all parties. Both Radicals and *narodovtsi* favoured his candidacy, and he was elected unanimously. The conservative Verkhratsky resumed his post at the head of the Mathematical Section; Franko resumed his post at the Philological Section, and Hrushevsky did the same in the Historical.[44] Over the course of the year, the constitutional question was again reviewed, and by 1898 a new constitution, which roughly parallelled the earlier one espoused by Hrushevsky and Franko, was confirmed at the general meeting. The 'opposition,' now composed of the conservative politicians, who wished to retain some control over the society, the Radical leader, Pavlyk, who wished to see the NTSh more active in

42 'Zahalni zbory NTSh,' *ZNTSh*, XXII, 4 (1896), 6; Mochulsky, 'Z ostannikh desiatylit zhyttia Franka 1896–1916,' pp. 234–5; Wynar, *Mykhailo Hrushevsky i NTSh*, pp. 15–16.
43 Ibid.
44 See the various reports in *ZNTSh* for 1897 and 1898. Wynar, ibid., pp. 28–30, discusses the matter at length.

popular education and propaganda work, and Hrushevsky's personal enemies, all stood in temporary disarray. The scholarly and 'scientific' character of the institution was affirmed.[45]

The election of Hrushevsky to the presidency of the NTSh ended the first phase of his Galician activity. In general, this first period was an introductory one. It was the first task of the young historian to establish himself firmly as a university professor and the inspirer of university youth. He was able to achieve this in a very short time.

Hrushevsky's second task was to ensure that the NTSh succeeded in creating and making known to the world a respectable body of scholarship in the Ukrainian language. It was a matter of raising the prestige and importance of the vernacular and encouraging its proper development. Without the promised help from Dnieper Ukraine, the young scholar was thrown back upon his own meagre resources and had to rely upon the impoverished Galicians. Nevertheless, with confidence and energy, Hrushevsky dealt a firm blow to that inferiority complex that held the Galician Ukrainians in its iron grip. In a relatively short time, he had turned young students into daring critics and aspiring scholars. The quality of the NTSh publications steadily rose and the physical extent of Ukrainian scholarship rose proportionately.

One of the main obstacles hindering achievement of the above goals lay in the conservative attitudes of Galician Ukrainian society. A complex web of local political and social taboos had to be broken if various factions were to be united and non-partisan scholarship placed on a firm basis. Somehow both the *narodovtsi* of various persuasions and their impatient critics in the Radical Party had to be made to cooperate. The young professor was compelled to walk a tightrope between the conservatives, to whom he owed his position, and the Radicals, with whom he was philosophically more comfortable.

It was the latter who held the real strings to his conscience. Although he had conservative references, Hrushevsky came from the land of extremes, the Russian Empire; he was, in fact, a revolutionary in spirit who did not hide his theoretical commitment to the masses or to the nation as a whole. Unlike many a rebellious ideologue, from the very beginning Hrushevsky found himself in a position of responsibility and power. Thus his theoretical radicalism was not worked out mainly in critical or destructive activity, but rather in practical solutions to

45 The opposition was composed of the following: the future historian of Galician Ukrainian politics Kost Levytsky, who emerged as a main *narodovets* leader; the Radical publicist M. Pavlyk, whom Hrushevsky had appointed to the library and who was already turning against his benefactor; and V. Shukhevych, the Lviv notable whose daughter Hrushevsky had slighted. Wynar, *Mykhailo Hrushevsky i NTSh*, note 6.

pressing issues. He was given an opportunity to use his iron will and gift for organization in the nourishment of a veritable cultural renaissance. Given this opportunity, Hrushevsky felt that it was his duty to collaborate with both conservative and oppositional elements in the attainment of his goal.

The writer and political and social activist Ivan Franko was the foremost among the talented Radicals whom Hrushevsky coopted into his scholarly projects. Unlike the committed historian from the east, Franko was a European through and through. He did not proceed from theory to duty, but rather just the opposite. It was a deep sense of duty that bound him to his oppressed people and it was their practical needs that dictated his political behaviour. This pragmatic sense governed the way he understood Hrushevsky's work. It might be said that the two men proceeded from different directions, but arrived at similar conclusions. Thus, in 1897, Franko penned the following practical evaluation of Hrushevsky's first years in Galicia:

Aside from the enlightenment and political organization of the popular masses, of all that which is now being done in Galicia, in my opinion, most important are those beginnings of scholarly work which Prof. M. Hrushevsky has organized at the Shevchenko Scientific Society and which have now won recognition for the society and for our whole people. This has been done, it is true, not at home, not among the broad Ruthenian population, but beyond the borders of our land in places where people are concerned with scholarship and put a value on scientific work. From Prof. Jagić himself, I have heard warm [*hariache*] acknowledgment and words of wonder at how, from such modest beginnings and miserly funding, this society has contrived to print so much . . . Only in this way, reshaping these scientific achievements, can we go from the era of dilettantism and fruitless politicking and enter the era of maturity and practical politics.[46]

The era of maturity, it was hoped, was not too far off. A sure sign of these expectations was Hrushevsky's deliberate entry onto the political stage. This was done in the closest collaboration with Franko, and it highlights the next phase of Hrushevsky's Galician experience.

46 I. Franko, 'Z novym rokom,' *Zhytie i slovo,* XI (Lviv, 1897), 5–6, and quoted in full by Iu. Lavrinenko, 'Deshcho do evoliutsii svitohliadu Ivana Franka,' *Zbirnyk 'Ukrainskoi literaturnoi hazety' 1956* (Munich), pp. 20–1, who is perceptive enough to pick out the following evaluation of Franko by the theoretician Hrushevsky: 'Franko was a genius of a Galician peasant [*heniialnym halytskym khlopom*], not impulsive, but endlessly enduring and given to work. The heritage of generations of labourers was realized in his work; for them work was not a categorical imperative, but a philosophical function.' Ibid., p. 4, from 'Apostolovi pratsi,' pp. 16–17.

3

Galician Piedmont 1897–1905

Scholarly collaboration between Hrushevsky and Franko had a stimulating effect upon both men. Franko had long studied the literatures of Western Europe and had also experienced 'modern' political life at first hand; there is little doubt that he was happy to share his knowledge and experience with Hrushevsky, who, though some ten years his junior, was probably one of the few intellects among the Galician Ukrainians who could match the brilliant writer. Hrushevsky was also quite impressed by Franko.[1]

On the other hand, the presence in Galicia of the vigorous young historian was bound to have some kind of influence upon Franko. Though Franko protested that he was not impressed by Hrushevsky's talents as a writer of fiction, in the years after the historian's arrival, friends wondered about Hrushevsky's influence upon Franko; the writer revealed a growing interest in historical questions and in 1894 began publishing studies devoted to history.[2] Moreover, by opening the doors of the NTSh to Franko, Hrushevsky provided him with both a scholarly forum in his native Ukrainian language, and considerable – and much needed – financial support for his family. No longer did he have to depend upon his work at the

1 In a long review of Franko's novel *Dlia domashnioho ohnyshcha* published in the first volume of *Literaturno-naukovyi vistnyk* (1898), pp. 27–35, Hrushevsky's opening words are: 'Ivan Franko is one of the most extraordinary creative powers in our contemporary *belles lettres,* and this alone gives every creation that comes from his pen the right to enjoy the special attention of the public.'
2 His first historical studies were devoted to the Galician peasant in the seventeenth century and the Union of Brest (1596). Many of Franko's studies took the form of critical observations upon the synthetic works of Hrushevsky. Although Franko agreed with Hrushevsky's general approach, he had independent ideas about many questions. For a bibliography of Franko's historical works see L. Wynar's 'Istorychni pratsi Ivana Franka,' *Zbirnyk 'Ukrainskoi literaturnoi hazety' 1956* (Munich), pp. 48–63, which is probably the best work on the subject. A. Krymsky was interested in the relationship between the two men and asked Franko about it in his letter of 17 August 1898 in *Tvory v piaty tomakh,* vol. v, part 1 (Kiev, 1973), pp. 322–3. He put it thus: 'Your letter to me was very

various Polish newspapers. 'So from the end of the 1890s,' writes Hrushevsky of Franko, 'a fairly wide circle of work in his own Ukrainian field opened up for him and this consciousness gave him the moral strength for the memorable revolt against that which had kept him bound.'[3]

Hrushevsky was referring to Franko's famous public 'confessions' of 1897. In this year, breaking with his former collaborators and allies, Franko publicly confessed his dislike of both what he considered to be short-sighted Ukrainian 'hurrah-patriotism' and of what he considered to be narrow-minded Polish chauvinism. In a Polish-language article – the use of Polish was anything but diplomatic – he charged his fellow Ukrainians (*Rusini*) with myopia, egoism, and duplicity and said that he felt his patriotism to be not so much a sentiment as 'a great yoke placed upon my back by fate.' When *Dilo* and the *narodovtsi* leaders in turn criticized these statements, Franko stood his ground in the poem: 'You brother, love Rus'!' and as a result, found himself ostracized from the most influential part of Galician Ukrainian society.[4]

The break with Poles occurred about the same time. By referring in a German-language article – the use of German again anything but diplomatic – to the revered author of *Konrad Wallenrod*, Adam Mickiewicz, as 'the poet of treason,' Franko incurred the wrath of his former colleagues on the *Kurier Lwowski* and found himself expelled from the learned Polish societies of which he had been an esteemed member. 'This was the unforgettable moment,' recalls Hrushevsky, 'when Franko, suddenly "eliminated" from Ukrainian and Polish society (and having been replaced quietly and gradually in Radical circles by his

---

short and did not satisfy me. I would like to know a lot more, as for example ... what are your relations with Hrushevsky (because in any case it is clear that Hrushevsky in Galicia is not the same Hrushevsky who was once in Kiev). Certainly your relations have not been without an effect upon him; and it would be interesting to know what role he has played in your literary activity.' In his letter of 26 August (*Tvory*, XX, 580–1), Franko replied in the negative: 'I can say nothing about Hrushevsky's influence upon my literary activity. Neither have his creative works been a model for me, nor is his knowledge of literature such that I could use anything from it.'

3 'Apostolovi pratsi,' p. 6. See the discussion in Volodymyr Doroshenko. 'Ivan Franko i Mykhailo Hrushevsky, *Suchasnist*, no. 1 (Munich 1969), 16–36, especially 28-9.

4 These events are fully described in the standard biographies of Franko by Antin Krushelnytsky, *Ivan Franko* (Kolomyia, n.d.) pp. 130–9, and L. Luciw, *Borets za natsionalnu i sotsiialnu spravedlyvist* (New York, 1969), pp. 431–42. That Hrushevsky shared Franko's opinions is fairly clear from his review of the latter's *Mii izmarahd* (Lviv, 1898), which reprinted Franko's poetry from the preceding years. In this review, Hrushevsky quotes in full Franko's poem 'Ty brate liubysh Rus',' and explains: 'These last verses seem to me to be the best and most appropriate reply of the author [to his Ukrainian critics]. For the rest, the author was found at fault not only for his confession, but also because it appeared in a popular Polish book among Polish chauvinist snipes against the Ruthenians. In general, the quoted verses are a mournful expression of resignation and unhappiness with contemporary *Ukrainstvo*.' *LNV*, II (1898), 173–9, especially 177.

old antagonist, Pavlyk), revealed to me that, at this point, the single source of subsistence for him and his family was his work at the [Shevchenko] Scientific Society.'[5] Stressing the dignity and significance of Franko as a national figure, one with whom he closely identified, Hrushevsky continues:

We his sympathizers made it a point of honour not to allow him to fall into poverty or to humble himself before people who, it seems, wished to humiliate him. It was necessary that Franko not go to them on his knees. On the contrary, from this time until his death, he had the opportunity to work exclusively for the Ukrainian people and in the Ukrainian language . . . Such was the moral strength of that tiny but sincere and determined group which at that time gathered about the scholarly publications of the Scientific Society, the *Literaturno-naukovyi vistnyk,* and the Publishing Society, and which took Franko 'under its wing' in his conflict with 'his own foreigners,' and protested against opportunism and servility in 'high politics,' against 'consolidation' (with the Muscophiles) in national relations, against reactionary 'Ruthenianism' in ideology, and having on its side all of Ukrainian youth – its moral strength was so great, I say, that the *narodovtsi* centre came to reckon it as a thing to be taken very seriously.[6]

These words were written many years later and describe principles that Hrushevsky as well as Franko was to personify. But in 1897, in spite of fully agreeing with Franko's critique of Galician society, the historian still kept his distance from open party politics and restricted himself to the cultural movement. Indeed, at this early stage he could hardly do otherwise, for, as Franko himself explains, to side with one faction or another would certainly have ruined the modest but very real progress that had been made in the work of the NTSh.[7] When

---

5 'Apostolovi pratsi,' p. 14. In this memoir, Hrushevsky goes into Franko's break with the Poles and *narodovtsi* in great detail and again quotes Franko at length. He also reprints in full (pp. 12–13) *Dilo*'s unsigned attack on Franko: 'Smutna poiava.' The *narodovtsi* leader, Iuliian Romanchuk, was its author.

6 Ibid., pp. 14–15. According to the standard Soviet account by I.I. Bass, *Ivan Franko: biohrafiia* (Kiev, 1966), pp. 199–200, Franko was only supported by the young students who collected two hundred gulden for the publication of *Mii izmarahd*; no mention of Hrushevsky or the NTSh is made. Bass even claims that soon afterward the *narodovtsi* came begging Franko to help them with 'their' new publishing venture – *Literaturno-naukovyi vistnyk.* The fact that *LNV* was published by the NTSh and not by conservative *narodovtsi* party circles is not mentioned. Moreover, documents published by the Soviets discredit their own thesis: there were conservative protests against Franko's proposed acceptance into the editorial staff. See below, note 13.

7 In his 'Z ostatnikh desiatylit xix v.,' *Moloda Ukraina* (Lviv, 1912), pp. 73–4, Franko describes Hrushevsky's difficult situation and paints a very positive picture of his activity. In what appears to be a rebuttal to claims advanced by the Barvinsky circle – the essay was written in late 1900 or early 1901 – he writes: 'Whoever might ascribe to himself the service of reforming this society, this one thing must be said: the service of organizing its scholarly work fully belongs to Prof. M.

Hrushevsky finally did enter the political arena, it was to be under completely different circumstances. In the meantime, he continued to prepare the ground by energetic scholarly and cultural activities. These were tied in with a general national-cultural movement which steadily approached a climax, expected to occur in the year 1898.

In this particular year, the Ukrainians of Eastern Galicia planned to celebrate the centenary of the birth of modern Ukrainian literature, the fiftieth anniversary of the 1848 emancipation of the Galician peasantry with the rebirth of Galician-Ukrainian public life, and the twenty-fifth anniversary of Franko's literary activity. The plans were laid well ahead. As early as 1893, Hrushevsky had made suggestions concerning the commemoration of Ivan Kotliarevsky's *Eneida,* the poetic epic written in Dnieper Ukraine that marked the rebirth of the national literature.[8] Thereafter, the Galician Ukrainians began increasingly to stress the

---

Hrushevsky. A man of wide learning, unbreakable will, and inexhaustible energy, he unites in himself the seriousness and criticism of a scholarly historian, a youthful enthusiasm for the cause of the elevation of his native people, and a love of labour and forbearance that can only be truly valued by those who know in all its fullness that Galician quagmire [*shliendriian*] into which the young professor, who had just arrived from Ukraine, was headed, and with which he had to fight with all the means of intelligent pedagogy ... In the course of this, he had to survive thousands of unpleasantries and neutralize formal battles which on one occasion even led to a crisis that threatened to destroy the whole venture. He was able to put himself above all petty intrigues, party and factional antagonisms. Without looking at their party position, he was to introduce into the Society all persons inspired with the idea of the Ukrainian renaissance and enthusiastic about important work; and this benefited the common cause and was the reason for the growth of that maturity and tolerance which ... makes possible the concentration of powers of different types and different shades of opinion in a common task.' For another defence of Hrushevsky's scholarship by Franko, see his 'Za chto starika obideli?' *LNV,* XIII (1901), 39–41. In this brief article, Franko rebuts the remarks of the Galician Russophile P. Svistun: 'Kto bolshii: M. Grushevskii ili A. Petrushevich?' *Galichanin* (Lviv), nos. 216–8 (1900). Svistun had attacked Hrushevsky's critical review of a book by the Old Ruthenian historian, A. Petrushevich (1821–1913). These defences of Hrushevsky by Franko are cited here at length, not so much to beatify the young historian – he was to prove rather good at this himself – as to dispel the carefully cultivated Soviet myth that the two men were at loggerheads throughout their careers because they were the ideological representatives of mutually hostile social classes; that is, that Franko was a 'revolutionary democrat,' while Hrushevsky was a 'bourgeois nationalist.' This thesis is most fully developed in the polemical tract directed against Ukrainian émigré scholarship, V.L. Mykytas, *Ideolohichna borotba navkolo spadshchyny Ivana Franka* (Kiev, 1978), pp. 155–8.

8 M. Serhiienko (pseud.), 'Dlia iuvileiu Ivana Kotliarevskoho,' *ZNTSh,* II (1893), 146–61. On pp. 157–8, he writes: 'The centennial of modern Ukrainian writing is such an occasion, that in truth it deserves a solemn celebration; such a celebration would demonstrate that over the past hundred years, Ukrainian society has significantly grown with regard to national self-consciousness and cultural development.' He goes on to suggest that new luxury and scholarly editions of Kotliarevsky's works be published and that various biographical and literary studies be done for this occasion. Hrushevsky admits, however, that Kotliarevsky's work did not grow out of a vacuum, but rested on the published and unpublished literary efforts of numerous predecessors.

ethnographic and cultural unity of all the Ukrainian lands. In 1898, the Galician Ukrainian cultural leaders consciously made the change of name from 'Ruthenian' to 'Ukrainian'; their traditionalist Ruthenian competitors, who were generally known as 'Muscophiles,' retained control over some key cultural institutions, but had lost the youth and would fall increasingly into the background. The Ukrainian cause was to be egalitarian, liberating, and national in tone.[9]

As one of the main instruments for carrying out these goals, Hrushevsky initiated the publication of a new literary journal. It was to appear under the auspices of the Shevchenko Society. 'At the end of 1897,' he writes, 'I undertook to reform the illustrated weekly *Zoria* and turn it into a scholarly-literary monthly in the style of a European review.'[10] Franko and Osyp Makovei (and later Volodymyr Hnatiuk) joined in as coeditors and in 1898, *Literaturno-naukovyi vistnyk* began to appear.

The establishment of the new journal was to be a landmark in the history of Ukrainian literature; Franko was to place some of his best poetry, prose, and social and political criticism in it; the leading lights of the Ukrainian literary explosion of the turn of the century – Lesia Ukrainka, Mykhailo Kotsiubynsky, Nechui-Levytsky, Olha Kobylianska, and Volodymyr Vynnychenko – all published a good part of their work in it. Hrushevsky himself was to use this forum to air some of his most important social commentaries and polemical works.[11]

The first years were difficult ones and found Hrushevsky contributing literary criticism and fiction as well as acting as editor-in-chief.[12] There were all manner of

9 Kost Levytsky, *Istoriia politychnoi dumky halytskykh Ukraintsiv*, 2 vols. (Lviv, 1926), I, 306–10. The mood of these celebrations is very ably captured in the account of I. Borshchak, 'Le mouvement national ukrainien au XIXe siècle,' *Le monde slave*, nos. 7–12 (Paris, 1930), especially 377–80.

10 *Avtobiohrafiia–1906*, p. 7. Also see V. Hnatiuk, 'Naukove Tovarystvo im. Shevchenka u Lvovi,' *LNV*, XXXVI (1925), 1–11, 176–7; Wynar, *Mykhailo Hrushevsky i NTSh*, pp. 22–4. A few years later, Hrushevsky explained: 'I wanted to enliven the quiet and passive tone of "The Magazine for the Ukrainian Family," which the journal *Zoria* had been, by means of the radical ferment of *Zhytie i slovo*, and to take it beyond the bounds of purely literary-scholarly Ukrainian cultural interests to which it had been devoted, into the whirlpool of worldly social and cultural life and struggle.' Of course, Hrushevsky tried to coopt as many Dnieper Ukrainians as possible into the venture and thus stress its pan-Ukrainian significance. See his 'Do nashysh chytachiv v Rosii,' *LNV*, XXXVII (1907), 1.

11 See the summary in V. Doroshenko, 'Literaturno-naukovyi vistnyk,' *LNV*, book 1 na chuzhyni (Regensburg, 1948), pp. 47–55. After a long and illustrious history, a change in name to *Visnyk*, and a complete change in editorial policy, the journal ceased publication at the time of the Second World War. The volume cited here was the last attempt to revive it. Only a few numbers appeared.

12 *Avtobiohrafiia–1906*, pp. 7–8. Volume I, number 1, page 1 begins with Hrushevsky's short story: 'Iasnovelmozhnyi svat,' which was a Christmas story. Many reviews and articles followed, including the reviews of Franko's works cited in notes 1 and 4 above. Volume II also begins with a short story by Hrushevsky. 'Nerobochyi Hrytsko Kryvyi' was a historical romance set in the eighteenth century.

problems: conservatives in the NTSh, especially members from the clergy, objected to the introduction of Franko onto the editorial board;[13] in Galicia, the public was at first apathetic, while in Russia, there was a question whether the censors and border officials would allow the journal to be distributed. On another level, the journal's critical reviews soon aroused the ire of prospective contributors: Hrushevsky in particular was accused of having too much say in the running of the journal, of placing too much of his own work in it, and of attempting literary criticism when he had no competence in it. He was advised to stick to history.[14]

On the other hand, not all first impressions were negative. In spite of severe reservations about the literary quality of the first few numbers, the Chernyhiv writer, Mykhailo Kotsiubynsky, welcomed the appearance of the new journal and did his best to publicize it in Russian Ukraine.[15] '*Literaturno-naukovyi vistnyk* is a beautiful and substantial journal,' Nechui-Levytsky assured his former protégé, 'and it appeals to my taste. Osyp Makovei and "Spectator" are attractive publicists, interesting, and read with great pleasure.'[16] Elsewhere, Nechui-Levytsky informed Hrushevsky that 'your journal is good, scholarly. There is nothing else to say.'[17] In fact, by the end of the first year of publication, Hrushevsky

13 The Greek Catholic clergy first protested that 'Doctor Franko will place in this *Vistnyk* the same kind of anti-religious articles that he has published in the periodical *Zhytie i slovo*.' See the ecclesiastical newsletter *Dushpastyr* (Lviv), nos. 20–1 (1897) 488, reprinted in *Ivan Franko: dokumenty i materiialy*, pp. 215–16. Thereafter protests spread to Barvinsky's paper *Ruslan*, and to the general meetings of the NTSh. See Mochulsky, 'Z ostannikh desiatylit zhyttia Franka,' p. 241.

14 One of these potential contributors, the Bukovinian writer Olha Kobylianska, was simply furious with Hrushevsky's review of one of her works. 'There is nothing that I like about Hrushevsky's way of writing a critique,' she informed her friend, the *LNV* coeditor Osyp Makovei. See her letter of 13 September 1898 to Makovei in her *Tvory v piaty tomakh*, vol. v (Kiev, 1963), 357–8. Earlier she had written Makovei that a Ukrainian from the east, the lawyer and conservative Ukrainian nationalist Mykola Mikhnovsky, 'is simply furious that Hrushevsky has such a voice in *Vistnyk*, because he is merely a historian and nothing else. He says that the Dnieper Ukrainians are dissatisfied with the *Vistnyk* ... The whole fault lies with Hrushevsky, who has taken too many rights and too great a voice in it – and especially when everything that he writes, he writes badly. (He abstracts from his professional works.) I am letting you know all this in confidence as a good friend' (ibid., pp. 329–335). On 23 March 1898, Kobylianska informed Makovei that Mikhnovsky had published his criticisms of Hrushevsky and *LNV* in the paper *Bukovyna*. 8 (20) March (ibid., 335, 697. Compare Mochulsky, 'Z ostanníkh desiatylit').

15 See his letters to Vira Kotsiubynska in his *Tvory v shesty tomakh*, vol. v (Kiev, 1962), 24–3, 248–9.

16 Nechui-Levytsky, letter of 10 (22) March 1899 (the printed text gives 1889, but this is obviously an error) to Hrushevsky, in *Tvory*, x, 358–9. 'Spectator,' a pseudonym for O. Lototsky, usually dealt with events in the Russian Empire.

17 Letter of 19 February (3 March) 1898, in ibid., p. 349. The question of the reaction of the Russian censors is discussed in an earlier letter to Hrushevsky (ibid., pp. 348–9), and elsewhere.

was able to claim that he had united various literary elements, both young and old, in the creation of a broad-ranging literary adventure.[18] *Literaturno-naukovyi vistnyk* survived, and the program of 1898 was underway.

While literary life and public affairs were increasingly attracting Hrushevsky's attention, he did not neglect his speciality. This same year of anniversaries saw the appearance of the first volume of Hrushevsky's monumental *History of Ukraine-Rus'*. It was not the chance product of an enthusiastic whim.

While he was still in Kiev, Hrushevsky had considered the writing of some kind of substantial synthetic history of Ukraine to be the duty of his generation. When he began teaching in Lviv, he played with the idea of using his university lectures as the basis for a detailed three-volume history: the first volume would be devoted to the oldest period, the second to Ukraine under Lithuania and Poland, and the last to the modern period. By 1897, however, he had decided to expand this into a much more detailed 'scientific' history. He worked hard to see it published in 1898. By the end of the year, the first volume, which was devoted to Slavic antiquity, did in fact appear. Hrushevsky consciously connected the publication of this volume with the centennial celebrations of the Ukrainian renaissance, and he noted that 'in Galicia the *History's* appearance was greeted with great interest, one could even say enthusiasm.'[19] On the other hand, the book was banned in Russia and Polish scholars did not give it the attention that it probably deserved.[20]

In May, the celebrations in connection with the abolition of serfdom reached a climax. The various Ukrainian organizations, in cooperation with the traditionalist Ruthenians, made arrangements for a great public assembly (*velyke vsenarodne viche*) that took place at the High Castle overlooking the city of Lviv. At this mass gathering the national program of 1848 was reaffirmed and the cultural independence of the 'Ukrainian-Rus'' people proclaimed. The general tone of the affair was one of loyalty to the Habsburg dynasty.[21]

Hrushevsky played no part in these events, and, in fact, together with Franko,

18 See the unsigned editorial in the last number of *LNV* for 1898, pp. 3–5. In its first year, *LNV* published forty-one Ukrainian writers, male and female, and translations from the works of twenty-seven foreign writers. Galicia, Bukovina, and Dnieper Ukraine are all represented. Nechui-Levytsky thought the translations from German particularly useful. (See the letters cited in notes 16 and 17 above.)

19 *Avtobiohrafiia–1906*, pp. 9–10, *Avtobiohrafiia–1926*, pp. 76–7.

20 Hrushevsky (ibid.) and most Ukrainian observers believed that the work was consciously boycotted. The first major review, it seems, was by the Polish Slavist, Alexander Brückner, in *Archiv für slavische Philologie*, XXII (1900), 293–4. Brückner was quite severe, rejecting Hrushevsky's strong 'anti-Normanist' position and maintaining that the Ukrainian scholar was 'no linguist.'

21 Levytsky, *Istoriia politychnoi dumky*. I, 306–7. The organizers of this mass meeting sent greetings to Emperor Franz Josef on the occasion of the fiftieth anniversary of his reign. Enclosed was a request for the administrative division of Galicia into an eastern, Ukrainian province and a western, Polish one.

Pavlyk, and Ostap Terletsky, objected to them. The youthful followers of these men even demonstrated against the assembly. They disliked what they thought was its servile attitude toward the monarchy and they disdained collaboration with those whom they scornfully termed 'Muscophiles.' Instead, that evening the youth held a counter-rally 'at which,' Hrushevsky informs us, 'they gave ovations in favour of their ideological leaders.'[22] A much greater counter-demonstration came later in the year.

The Kotliarevsky and Franko jubilees were to be celebrated in October. The organizers faced many problems as the Galician public had still not forgiven Franko for his recent criticism. Of course, the Polish authorities were completely uncooperative. As one of the young organizers later recalled: 'Many people were afraid of appearing in public at the [Franko] jubilee. All the speeches were censored beforehand by the police, who struck out some parts and sent an official to oversee the function; he threatened to close it down on the slightest pretext.'[23]

The jubilee ceremonies took place at the end of the month. In Franko's honour, a multitude from all the Ukrainian parties – including Franko's principal Ukrainian critic, Iuliian Romanchuk – gathered in the Grand Theatre of Lviv's Hotel George. Hnatiuk, Hrushevsky, Pavlyk, and Franko himself gave the major speeches.[24] After Hnatiuk had opened the ceremonies, the young professor spoke: 'The last three decades of our time,' he began, 'will be written into the history of our culture as an extraordinary, memorable, and very happy time. It will be considered the heroic age of the Ukrainian-Rus' national, cultural, and progressive idea.' He continued:

Now we can boldly say that our language will not die and will not perish. When future Ukrainians see that our nation is taking its rightful place among the Slavic nations, when they compare its achievements with those of other peoples and feel that they have their own place in the general march of human progress, when they approach the ideals of liberty and justice without abandoning their national heritage, they will see that the last three decades have been of service in this.

After describing the national awakening and the difficult problems of the nineteenth century, Hrushevsky outlined Franko's part in the struggle and concluded:

22 Hrushevsky, 'Apostolovi pratsi,' p. 15.
23 Vozniak, 'Ivan Franko v dobi radykalizmu,' p. 154.
24 Ibid. The program for the day's events, together with the major speeches, is reproduced in the Soviet source collection *Ivan Franko: dokumenty i materiialy,* pp. 218–25. In spite of the importance that contemporaries accorded to it, Hrushevsky's speech is not reprinted here. Also, the order is reversed so that Pavlyk's speech is accorded greater prominence than was, in fact, the case.

We have come here to thank him for the fact that he has always defended the idea of universal human progress on our national ground. We remember that the Ukrainian national idea is not bounded by formal nationalism itself. It is not only a matter of language and race, but must be progressive and sincerely democratic and cannot be otherwise. With this in mind, we remember that he has always oriented himself according to the real needs of our people and has always based his actions upon vital facts, free from the excessive fabrication of doctrine.

In his contemporary description of the Franko jubilee, Osyp Makovei does not tell us how the audience reacted to Hrushevsky's words. Makovei only notes that they were of special importance and deserved quotation in full.[25]

Several other speakers followed; Franko was the last to address the audience. In an eloquent and forceful speech, he told the assembly of his peasant origins, his sense of duty, and belief in hard work.[26] The audience responded with enthusiasm and Franko was deeply moved. 'It was the happiest moment of his life,' observed one of the younger well-wishers.[27]

There were further festivities the next day. Drama, poetry, public lectures, and more speeches marked the anniversary of Kotliarevsky's *Eneida*; Franko's militant hymn, 'Great Anniversary,' which ended with the cry 'Ukraine has not passed away and will not pass away!,' made an especially great impression.

Taking advantage of the newly aroused enthusiasm of the Ukrainian public, Hrushevsky used the occasion to launch a new Ukrainian-Rus' Publishing Society which was to be devoted to the publication of books for the general population as well as for the intelligentsia. This organization was to be a great success, and eventually the Shevchenko Society turned over the publication of *Literaturno-naukovyi vistnyk* to the new organization.[28]

When the celebrations were over, the entire intelligentsia, it seems, was infused with a new confidence and a new energy. Word of the events spread quickly beyond the borders of Galicia. 'It is a shame that you were not there,' the Bukovinian writer Olha Kobylianska chided her Galician colleague Vasyl

25 Hrushevsky's speech (along with those of the other speakers) is given in full in Makovei's 'Iuvylei 25-litnoi literaturnoi diialnosty Ivana Franka,' *LNV*, IV (1898), 119-22. A large part of it is reprinted in Krushelnytsky, *Ivan Franko*, pp. 5–8, and it is briefly summarized by Vozniak, 'Ivan Franko v dobi radikalizmu,' p. 155.

26 Makovei gives Franko's speech on pp. 128–30; it is reprinted in *Ivan Franko: dokumenty i materiialy*, pp. 223–5.

27 Vozniak, 'Ivan Franko v dobi radikdlizmu,' p. 155.

28 Hrushevsky's public appeal for financial support was published in *Dilo* and reprinted in *LNV*, IV (1898), 101–3. Also see Wynar, *Mykhailo Hrushevsky i NTSh*, pp. 31–3, who gives full references to the contemporary descriptions of these events. There are, as well, good descriptions in Luciw, *Borets*, pp. 456–61, and Borshchak, 'Le movement ukrainien,' p. 378–80.

Stefanyk, 'Franko and Hrushevsky really spoke beautifully . . . It all seems like a dream to me now.'[29] In Dnieper Ukraine too, people heard or read of the events in Galicia.[30] All this augured well for the cultural unity of the various Ukrainian lands.

It was Hrushevsky's firm intention to foster this unity and penetrate the legal boundaries that divided Austrian Galicia and Russian Ukraine. In 1899, another opportunity to do so arose when the Galicians and other Slavs were invited to a large Archaeological Congress in Kiev. The NTSh announced that it was willing to present some thirty scholarly papers in the Ukrainian language. But in Kiev, the conservative Russian monarchists led by T.D. Florinsky objected; eventually the government moved to restrict the use of Ukrainian at the congress. In reply, Hrushevsky and the Galicians refused to attend and, instead, printed their papers separately in NTSh *Zapysky*. Ukrainian scholars in Kiev also boycotted the congress. There was one important consequence: for the first time in many years, the controversy surrounding these events brought the Ukrainian question to the attention of the general Russian public. As a result, Hrushevsky very quickly acquired notariety throughout the Russian Empire as a champion of the Ukrainian cause.[31] 'From this time,' writes one of the students of the Lviv professor, 'Hrushevsky began a planned struggle against the restrictions placed on Ukrainian culture. This was carried on principally in progressive Russian society.'[32] Of course, the Ukrainian movement in Galicia was to be a major weapon in this struggle.

Hrushevsky began to take a direct interest in Galician politics when the various opposition factions started to seek common ground in their struggle against the Polish administration and attempted to form a new political party that was more clearly devoted to general Ukrainian rather than local Galician interests. The failure of the 'compromise' with the Poles and the 'bloody elections' of 1897 were the main driving forces behind the efforts toward such unification. The *narodovtsi* politicians, who had broken with Barvinsky and then were routed in the elections of 1897, were beginning to find that their alliance with the traditionalist Ruthenians (that is, the so-called Muscophiles) was of little profit to them. The *narodovtsi* leaders, Iulian Romanchuk and Kost Levytsky, now sought collabora-

---

29 See Kobylianska's description of the Lviv events in her letter of 12 November 1898, to Vasyl Stefanyk in her *Tvory v piaty tomakh*, v, 369–71.

30 Nechui-Levytsky, letter of 2 (14) January 1899 to Hrushevsky in his *Zibrannia tvoriv u desiaty tomakh*, x, 353–5, informed Hrushevsky that he liked his speech and encouraged him in his project of writing a multi-volume *Istoriia Ukrainy-Rusy*.

31 *Avtobiohrafiia–1906*. p. 10. Lototsky, I, 247–51, summarizes the attacks on Hrushevsky. Also see Wynar *Mykhailo Hrushevsky i NTSh*, pp. 33–4.

32 Krypiakevych, p. 32.

tion with the other opposition elements, especially the Radicals, who had succeeded in electing two members in spite of the 'government terror' of 1897.[33] For its part, the peasant-oriented Radical Party was torn with dissensions. In 1895, the death of its ideological mentor, Mykhailo Drahomanov, had deprived the party of the one man with enough authority to hold it together. In 1896, some members defected to Marxism, while others (Trush, Okhrymovych) left to found an independent and less peasant-oriented grouping that published its own newspaper. Franko and his followers, who were similarly abandoning Drahomanov's international federalism in favour of a more national approach and a more open attitude toward the other classes of Ukrainian society, were left to fight it out with Mykhailo Pavlyk and those who stuck to the idea of a purely peasant-based, Drahomanovite organization.[34] The stage was set for the foundation of a new political party.

The celebrations of 1898 speeded the march of events. Hrushevsky later took pride – and perhaps rather too much credit – in noting: 'Those present at the jubilee celebrations received my speech with enthusiasm and adopted the notes for a concrete Ukrainian program and the actions toward national rights that it entailed.' Franko's eloquent address and fiery poetry, it seems, had also made an impression. Hrushevsky continues: 'One year later, the *narodovets* centre approached Franko and myself with a proposition for the unification of the left *narodovets* elements with our group and the Radicals on the basis of a socialist program. We met this request for the socialization of the program of the Galician intelligentsia half-way and entered a reform committee.'[35]

At the same time, however, there was no talk of socialism. What happened, it seems, was that Romanchuk and Hrushevsky had come to some kind of agreement that would unite the oppositional forces on the basis of wide national and democratic principles. Hrushevsky and Franko were very close at that time and the

33 See Stakhiv's introduction to Makukh, *Na narodnii sluzhbi,* pp. 49–55. A few years later, the conservative Russian adversary of the Ukrainians, the Kiev censor S.N. Shchegolev, observed: 'The circle of Hrushevsky, all of whose anti-Russian activity in Galicia was based upon planting the "Ukrainian-Rus'" language and the phonetic system in the public schools, well understood that the union of the Russian party with the *narodovtsi* endangered both the Ukrainian-Rus' language and phonetic orthography in the schools – the two big fish lying at the base of the program of Hrushevsky and his fellow-travellers. Consequently, the question of disrupting the union of the *narodovtsi* and the Russian party was a question of life and death for Hrushevsky's cause.' See Shchegolev's 'police handbook' on the Ukrainian movement: *Ukrainskoe dvizhenie kak sovremennyi etap iuzhnorusskogo separatizma* (Kiev, 1912), p. 121.

34 M. Stakhiv, *Proty Khvyl: istorychnyi rozvytok ukraniskoho sotsiialistychnoho rukhu na zakhidnykh ukrainskykh zemliakh* (Lviv, 1934), pp. 88–93; John-Paul Himka, 'Ukrainskyi sotsiializm u Halychyni,' *Journal of Ukrainian Graduate Studies,* no. 7 (Toronto, 1979), 33–51.

35 Hrushevsky, 'Apostolovi pratsi,' p. 15.

historian may have had some influence upon the program that Franko then worked out: it approximated the old Radical program, but did not explicitly use the word 'socialism.' Most of this program was then approved by a much-heralded National Congress arranged by the *narodovtsi* politicians and their supporters. The congress elected both Franko and Hrushevsky to the executive committee of the new party and on 28 December 1899 the 'national program' was proclaimed in *Dilo.*[36]

The most striking point in the platform of the new party was the call for a future independent Ukraine. The basic goal of the party, the national program reads, 'is to act so that the entire Ukrainian-Rus' people shall achieve cultural, economic and political independence and be united in time into a single national organism in which for its own benefit the nation as a whole would manage all its own affairs: cultural, economic, and political.[37] In the meantime, the party would aim at unification of and autonomy for the Ukrainian lands within the Austrian Empire; it would also support those Dnieper Ukrainians whose goal was a federal,

36 A description of the congress is given in a leading article titled 'Narodnyi z'izd,' *Dilo,* no. 280, 27 December 1899. In his *Avtobiohrafiia–1906,* p. 6, Hrushevsky mentions that he was elected vice-chairman of the executive committee. Franko states that he and Volodymyr Okhrymovych were primarily responsible for the composition of the program. (See Franko's letter to the editor of *Dilo* in Vozniak. 'Ivan Franko v dobi radikalizmu,' p. 163). Stakhiv, *Proty khvyl,* p. 92, writes thus of Romanchuk's efforts at unification: 'The business became important when Romanchuk succeeded in attracting to it the new professor of Ukrainian history at the University of Lviv ... Mykhailo Hrushevsky, who had not yet had enough time to become well acquainted with affairs in Galicia. He was inspired by the idea of uniting *all progressive and radical elements* into one party and succeeded in drawing Ivan Franko into this as well.' K. Trylovsky, 'Ivan Franko iak poet-hromadianyn,' *LNV,* xci (1926), 42–3, takes the point even further: 'Franko's transference to the "new" party certainly occurred under the influence of Hrushevsky and would have been impossible if Drahomanov had still been alive.' But Mochulsky, 'Z ostannikh desiatylit zhyttia Franka,' pp. 242–3, objected that Franko was no puppet and had long been dissatisfied with affairs in the Radical Party. Lavrynenko, *passim,* and Himka, pp. 45–51, seem to take a similar position.

To Polish observers like Wasilewski, *Kresy wschodniè,* p. 37, and Ludwik Kulczycki, *Ugoda polsko-ruska* (Lviv, 1912), p. 41, as well as Russian foes of the Ukrainians like Shchegolev, *Ukrainskoe dvizhenie,* pp. 99, 120–3, Hrushevsky was the real organizer of the new party. There is considerable speculation as to the historian's exact plans. According to the editors of Makukh, *Na narodnii sluzhbi,* p. 79 (who, however, cite no source for their information): 'At first Mykhailo Hrushevsky was convinced that he would succeed in creating a new scheme of political organization in Galicia. He formulated this scheme thus: (1) Unite the entire Ukrainian Radical Party with the progressive and democratic leaning part of the old body of *narodovtsi.* This would result in the creation of a large new independent Democratic Party with a socialist program as a minimum, but without the socialist name. (2) The conservative and compromising elements from the *narodovtsi* (the New Course men, Barvinsky or his sympathizers among Romanchuk's *narodovtsi* would create a compromise-conservative party).'

37 Narodna programa, '*Dilo,* no. 281, 28 December 1899.

constitutional restructuring of the Russian Empire.[38] Such were the national elements of the party program.

The democratic elements were just as strong. There were calls for universal suffrage and abolition of the curial system by which the Polish gentry maintained its political control of Galicia. 'Our nationalism,' the platform reads, 'must be democratic through and through ... Our ideal is a Ukraine-Rus' without subservient countryfolk and without landlords [*bez khlopa i bez pana*] ... The working masses should be liberated from economic want and slavery and assured the means of production'; and finally, 'all the achievements of the human spirit should be for the benefit of all the people.'[39] In accordance with these principles, the new party was to be called the National Democratic Party.

The founding of the new party was greeted with considerable fanfare. There were articles in all the newspapers discussing its prospects.[40] On Christmas Eve, 1899, Hrushevsky, Franko, Romanchuk, and the rest of the executive 'national committee' addressed an 'Appeal' to the general population. This appeal repeated the main points of the national program and explained that the National Democratic Party was to rest upon the cooperation of the intelligentsia and the wide masses of the population, especially the peasantry.[41] It was an expression of hope at the beginning of the new century.

For Hrushevsky and Franko, at least, the hopes were misplaced. The Radical Party continued to exist as a separate organization. On the other hand, large numbers of clerics and other conservative elements were attracted to the National Democrats and soon began to water down the original democratic postulates. In fact, no one seemed to take the party program very seriously. On the other hand, Romanchuk and his colleagues tried to maintain control over the party through their own appointees. 'Thanks to the party's centralized organization,' wrote Franko, 'I had no opportunity to take part in the discussions of its meetings.'[42]

38 Ibid.
39 Ibid. Also see Stakhiv, *Proty khvyl,* pp. 92–4, who stresses the similarities to the Radical program of 1895.
40 'Holosy presy o novii partii ruskoi,'*Dilo,* no. 286, January 1900. The reaction of the Polish press, for example *Nowa Reforma* (Cracow) and *Czas* (Cracow), was, of course, generally hostile, as was that of the anti-Semitic daily *Deutsches Volksblatt* (Vienna).
41 'Vidozva,' *Dilo,* no. 288, 5 January 1900. With regard to the other nationalities, the appeal reads: 'We cannot envision agreement with the Poles and peaceful work for high cultural goals as long as they are trying to maintain their hegemony over us and Polonize our people. Moreover, we must decisively and energetically fight all Polish parties that oppose our struggle for an independent national life.' As for the Jews, the appeal reads: 'All race and ethnic hatred, as for example anti-Semitism, is foreign to us. But all the same, we must overcome those Jews who exploit our people economically or harm our national cause by supporting our civil political adversaries.'
42 In Vozniak, 'Ivan Franko v dobi radykalizmu,' p. 163.

Both Hrushevsky and Franko, it seems, were being brushed aside. Their plans were not working and they had little choice but to leave. 'Being rapidly convinced that the reform which was carried out had not freed the *narodovets* party from its old habits,' writes Hrushevsky, 'together with Doctor Franko, I left the committee after a few months, ceased to take part in the party activity of the *narodovsti,* and often criticized the error of their ways. I stood together with Doctor Franko and the younger comrade-representatives of the left wing who ran the journal *Literaturno-naukovyi vistnyk.*'[43]

Hrushevsky's departure from the National Democratic Party did not save him from the attacks of the conservative and reactionary Russian press. Simultaneously, he later assured his readers, Galician 'Muscophiles' and Kievan 'Slavophiles' accused him of being the spiritual leader of Ukrainian separatism. For proof, he writes, such people would point to the program of the National Democratic Party and the public appeal that he had signed.[44] Combined with the controversy that had surrounded the Archaeological Congress of 1899, these attacks served to spread Hrushevsky's fame throughout the Russian Empire. In fact, given the strict censorship within Russia, it might be said that the enemies of the Ukrainian national movement were actually putting Hrushevsky at its head. This was to be of considerable significance for the professor's later career. In the meantime, Hrushevsky faced several pressing difficulties in Galicia itself.

Foremost among these was the growing national strife at Lviv University. As the new century opened, Ukrainians and Poles fought for possession of an institution that had originally done its teaching in German and Latin. The Poles, of course, were dominant, but, as their secular intelligentsia grew, the resistance of

---

43 In a note to *Avtobiohrafiia–1926,* pp. 72–3, Wynar writes that Hrushevsky left the National Democrats because he did not agree with their pro-Austrian policy. But his public conflict with the pro-Austrian *Halychanstvo* did not begin until 1904, as Hrushevsky admits in his autobiography. (This is probably the reason why the Kiev censor Shchegolev, *Ukrainskoe dvizhenie,* p. 123, was under the impression that the historian remained 'president of the party bureau until 1904.') Stakhiv, *Proty khvyl,* pp. 94–5, believes that the *narodovtsi* desire to absorb conservative Old Ruthenians into a single 'national party' (symbolized by the dropping of the word 'Democratic' and the adoption of a new name, *Narodne Storonytstvo*) was the principal reason for the disaffection of Franko and Hrushevsky. There is little doubt, however, that the foundation of the National Democratic Party marked a real break with traditional Old Ruthenian sentiment, as both Levytsky, *Istoriia politychnoi dumky,* 1, 307ff., and the outsider Wasilewski, *Kresy wschodnie,* p. 37, and *Ukraina i sprawa ukraińska* (Cracow, n.d.), p. 153, point out.

44 *Avtobiohrafiia–1906,* p. 6, specifically names 'Florinsky and company' as being typical of his detractors. Florinsky, who was a regular contributor to the Russian nationalist paper *Kievlianin,* published his most famous attack on the Ukrainian movement in 1900 (See chapter 1, note 45 above), but continued to engage in such polemics for the next seventeen years.

the Ukrainians steadily increased. It was given a great psychological boost by the celebrations of 1898.[45]

As early as 1897, Hrushevsky had publicly called for the establishment of a new Ukrainian university. A plan was developed to gradually establish parallel chairs at the University of Lviv until the Ukrainian faculty felt strong enough to set up on its own. The public responded enthusiastically and funds were collected from patriotic benefactors as far away as Saint Petersburg.[46]

On the other hand, administrative pressure upon the remaining centres of Ukrainian strength grew. In 1901, for the first time, the Polish dean did not allow the Ukrainian theological students to fill out their registration books in their own language. In July 1901, the dean, again for the first time, would not allow Hrushevsky to speak Ukrainian at the meetings of the Philosophical-Historical Faculty. This resulted in a quarrel between the two men, and the dean demanded that Hrushevsky's words be translated into Polish. A translation was done, but the Ukrainian professor felt that he was being misrepresented and left the meeting in protest. Afterwards there was a dispute as to what had actually happened and letters to both the Polish and Ukrainian press followed.[47]

The next term began in an atmosphere of considerable excitement. The rector's opening address was that of a Polish patriot and there were moves behind the scenes to have Hrushevsky dismissed and brought before the civil courts. On 19 November 1901, some six hundred Ukrainian students held a protest meeting at which a motion calling for the establishment of a Ukrainian university was passed. In consequence, several students were expelled and the situation became more tense than ever. Soon there were interpellations in the Austrian *Reichsrat* with Barvinsky and Romanchuk uniting in defence of the students. The newly elected Greek Catholic metropolitan, Andrii Sheptytsky, also spoke out in favour of the students, and in December, all six hundred withdrew from the university and proceeded to enrol in other Austrian centres of learning. In the parliamentary debates that followed, the conservative Polish politicians claimed that, being 'barbarians' by nature, the Ukrainians did not have the academic manpower to

45 Vasyl Mudryi, *Borotba za ohnyshche ukrainskoi nauky na zakhidnykh zemliakh Ukrainy* (Lviv, 1923). Hrushevsky, *Iz polsko-ukrainskikh otnoshenii Galitsii* (Saint Petersburg, 1907), pp. 22–3, writes: 'To 1870, the university had a German character, but there is no doubt that it was meant to serve the cultural needs of the Ukrainian population of Eastern Galicia.'

46 See Hrushevsky's unsigned article in *Dilo*, nos. 145–7 (1897). Also see Pankivsky, 'Spohady,' pp. 94–5; Wynar, 'Halytska doba,' p. 9–11.

47 The relevant materials were reprinted in V. Hnatiuk, 'Uvahy na suchasni temy: sprava ukrainsko-ruskoho universitetu u Lvovi, *LNV*, XVII (1902), 49–72. Also see Wynar, 'Halytska doba,' pp. 16–17.

staff a separate university. In response, the Ukrainians presented a detailed memorandum, drawn up by Hrushevsky, which listed a large number of Ukrainian scholars teaching at various Austrian, Russian, and even West European universities. Barvinsky, Romanchuk, and a special delegation of Galician public figures presented Hrushevsky's memorandum to the Austrian cabinet.[48]

All of these efforts brought very little relief. It was to take much more student militancy and many years yet before the ministry gave any firm undertakings as to a Ukrainian university. Nevertheless, the Ukrainian public had united around their cause, and Polish administrative pressures did let up somewhat. Moreover, the affair brought the Ukrainian-Polish conflict to the attention of the foreign press.[49]

In spite of these problems at the university, Hrushevsky's personal life remained well ordered and relatively happy. In 1900, his only child, Kateryna, was born, and although the next year the loss of his father hurt him deeply, his friendship with Franko was strengthened and the two men arranged to build new homes next door to each other on an empty lot near the outskirts of the city.[50]

The new Hrushevsky home was really a small mansion, but Mariia, the professor's wife, kept it in good order. The rooms were decorated with Hutsul Kilims or thin woven carpets, which were scattered over the walls and floors. The professor's spacious study was ringed with shelves of books. (He had inherited a considerable library from his father, and he felt it to be his duty to enrich it.) A visitor might observe that the tables were all covered with books, journals, papers, and proofs. His writing desk too was thus covered because he almost never used it for writing; rather he would work for hours at a large standup desk placed in the middle of the study. Hrushevsky did this because, even while he was a young man, he was already quite short-sighted and had to look closely at the paper. 'What peace and modesty reigned in this room,' a guest remarked.[51]

Franko's somewhat smaller home was located next door. Franko's wife was not much of a housekeeper, and this house never had the orderly appearance of the

48 Levytsky, *Istoriia politychnoi dumky*, I, 354–60. Ivan Rakovsky, 'Prof. Mykhailo Hrushevsky u Lvovi,' pp. 82–3, also described these events and noted that, in general, the hardworking professor 'always gave our parliamentarians detailed information concerning Ukrainian scholarship whenever they had need of it.'

49 Polish, Galician Ukrainian, and Viennese papers all carried full reports of these events. *Slovenský přehled*, no. 5 (1902), translated Hnatiuk's article on the university question into Czech. In the Russian Empire, *Russkiia vedomosti*, no. 334, and *Pridneprovskii krai*, no. 1400, carried reports favourable to the Ukrainians, and *Novoe vremia* began to agitate for the foundation of a 'Russian' university in Lviv. This was rejected by the conservative *Iuzhnii krai*, no. 7210. See Serhii Iefremov 's note in *LNV* XVII (1902), p. 36.

50 *Avtobiohrafiia–1906*, p. 11; Doroshenko, 'Franko i Hrushevsky,' pp. 27–31.

51 Iu. Siry Iuryi Tyshchenko, 'Veleten ukrainskoi nauky: uryvok zi spohadiv pro M.S. Hrushevskoho,' *Ukraina* no. 2 (Paris, 1949), 79–80.

neighbouring mansion. Moreover, Mrs Franko did not get along with either Hrushevsky or his wife. In spite of these frictions, the working relationship between the two men endured. 'Once we had settled in next to each other,' Hrushevsky writes, 'my working morning would usually end with a conference between the two of us on the questions of the day.'

Before going into town, Franko would come to meet me with the results of his evening work, or with the results of his all-night work. (He mostly worked evenings and nights; I got up early, worked through the mornings and managed to finish off most of the day's work before noon.) We discussed the material , made the necessary corrections and changes, laid out the plans for the order of work, and also divided the correspondence.[52]

Franko would then go to the printers or the newspaper offices while Hrushevsky attended to university or social affairs. Often the two men would end their day with another meeting at which they would discuss the latest news and form a clear opinion about them. With interruptions, this daily regimen lasted almost seven years.[53]

Hrushevsky found Franko's cooperation and encouragement to be invaluable. For example, in 1901, possibly as a result of the uproar surrounding the Kievan Archaeological Congress and the formation of the National Democratic Party, the Russian censors banned distribution of *Literaturno-naukovyi vistnyk*. 'When they would no longer allow it in Ukraine and it became a local Galician publication,' Hrushevsky writes, 'I was rather overwhelmed with work and I wanted to get rid of it, and I withdrew my name from the journal. Franko insisted that I not do it, saying that I should at least look over the proofs. Franko said that he would thus feel stronger and more certain of himself – and I had to agree, although it was very difficult for me at that time.'[54]

The ban on *Literaturno-naukovyi vistnyk,* like the ban on the first volumes of

---

52 Hrushevsky, 'Apostolovi pratsi,' p. 16. Hrushevsky's memories of Franko should be checked against the account of Franko's daughter, Anna Franko-Kliuchko, who was, like her mother, very hostile to the historian. In *Ivan Franko i ioho rodyna* (Toronto, 1956), p. 51, she writes that her mother 'recognized that under the cover of affability, modesty, and concern, an egoistic nature was hiding, and some kind of instinctive hatred aroused her spirit against this person. Mother warned father against him, but father, being himself modest and noble, did not believe mother's warnings and often became angry at her for this.' Kliuchko's memoirs, as well, should be checked against the more accurate and less impassioned observations of Doroshenko, 'Franko i Hrushevsky,' *passim.* For Franko's friendship with the Hrushevsky family and his troublesome marriage, see Mochulsky, 'Z ostannikh desiatylit zhyttia Franka,' 252.

53 Hrushevsky, 'Apostolovi pratsi,' p. 16; Doroshenko, 'Franko i Hrushevsky.'

54 Ibid. Compare the reaction of Ukrainian writers in Russia, who were suddenly cut off from developments in Galicia. See, for example, Kotsiubynsky, *Tvory v shesty tomakh,* v, 311–12.

the *History of Ukraine-Rus'*, was a severe setback for Hrushevsky's pan-Ukrainian mission. Both in Russia and in the Western world, the achievements of Ukrainian scholarship remained little known. To break through the Russian ban, Hrushevsky turned to publishing in the Western European languages and began negotiations for a possible German translation of his monumental history. At first, the idea was poorly received; it was not until the beginning of 1903 that things really started to move. At this time, the Russian Higher School of Social Studies, which had been recently established in Paris, invited the professor to give a course in Ukrainian history. Hrushevsky accepted the proposal with enthusiasm and spent April and the beginning of May in Paris delivering his lectures and getting to know the famous sociologist and constitutional historian Maxim Kovalevsky, who was the principal founder of this 'Free Russian University.' Afterwards, Hrushevsky visited London, Leipzig, and Berlin and made some useful academic contacts. At this time he arranged for a French edition of his general lecture course and a German edition of the first volume of his great history.[55]

The summer of 1903 was a happy one for Hrushevsky. He spent much of it at his new summer cottage in the Carpathians reworking the Paris lectures into a Russian-language survey of Ukrainian history. This *Ocherk* or outline, his 'beloved' as he called it, ran into immediate problems: 'Both because of the censorship and for other reasons,' he informs us, 'the publishers did not want to take up such an uncertain book. One of the most liberal [Russian] publishing houses rejected it out of fear that the scheme of Ukrainian history, differing sharply from the accepted scheme of Russian history, would bring down the unfavourable judgment of Russian scholarly circles upon the book. Finally, after many vicissitudes, I decided to have the *Ocherk* printed at my own expense.'[56] It was a gamble, but it was a gamble that was eventually to pay off handsomely.

Problems with Russian publishing houses were only the tip of the iceberg. The Russian consulate in Lviv was watching Hrushevsky closely and those Ruthenians whom the Ukrainian sources call 'Muscophiles' fed information to their Russian friends. This resulted in hostile press reports appearing repeatedly in the conservative Russian press. Citizenship and passport complications ensued, and

55 *Avtobiohrafiia–1906*, pp. 11–12. Hrushevsky himself had to cover the costs of the German edition of his *Istoriia Ukrainy-Rusy*. The *Ecole russe des hautes études sociales* had been founded in 1902 by Kovalevsky (who was of Ukrainian origin), and the Armenian scholar Iury Gambarov. In 1903, it had some 250 students enrolled. (See the note in *LNV*, XXII [1903], 224.) In the next few years, Vinogradov, Miliukov, and Franko were all invited to give courses, and though Franko did not make it to Paris, enrolment grew. See *LNV*, XXXI (1905), 193–4, and Iu. S. Vorobreva, 'Russkaia vysshaia shkola obshchestvennykh nauk v Parizhe,' *Istoricheskie zapiski*, vol. CVII (Moscow, 1982), 333–4.

56 Ibid., p. 12.

for some time the historian did not dare to visit Dnieper Ukraine, although he always retained his Russian citizenship.[57] Moreover, the confrontation with the Poles continued, and his old foes within the NTSh continued their sniping.

The problems with his fellow Ukrainians were especially trying. Over the years, Hrushevsky's strong opinions, authoritative manner, and nervous energy grew to be more and more of a problem. Even his closest collaborators noticed the growth of an authoritarian demeanour. 'Hrushevsky was by nature an autocrat,' a younger contemporary later wrote, 'but in Galicia this side of his personality came out more and more thanks to his leading position in the NTSh and in Ukrainian society.'

This society was accustomed to bowing down before a wealthy, independent, and influential person. In addition, in the NTSh Hrushevsky felt like a 'master' to whom all had to listen. He could often be insensitive and sharp about making his will known to his co-workers . . . But this trait of his did not have a negative effect upon the society's affairs. Hrushevsky ran the NTSh with an iron hand, firmly preserving its pan-Ukrainian character and not allowing it to become a tool in the hands of the politicos.[58]

Broad-minded scholarship at the NTSh could thus survive intact; Hrushevsky's youthful affability could not. Over the years his nervous problems increased. Old adversaries, Shukhevych, Pavlyk, and others, used these weaknesses and repeatedly tried to cut away at his position in the NTSh. In 1901, Hrushevsky again resigned his posts at the society, and again, in complete confusion, the membership decided to ask him back. At the same time, the discontent slowly grew, and by 1904, there was significant opposition to his reelection to the presidency.[59]

The troubles at the NTSh combined with overwork to cause serious health problems for the historian. His nervous disability grew worse and he was plagued by blood rushing to his head and severe headaches; he was forced to moderate his hyperactive life-style. Indeed, the physicians assured him that all would be well if he would only rest. At first he could not, but in 1904, in the hope of relief, he made two brief trips to Italy, one of them in the company of Franko. These voyages did

---

57 *Avtobiohrafiia–1906*, p. 6; *Avtobiohrafiia–1926*, pp. 73–4; Rakovsky, 'Prof. Hrushevsky u Lvovi,' p. 82. In 1898, the Austrian government asked Hrushevsky to take out Austrian citizenship; this order was renewed by the university in 1899, to which Hrushevsky replied that he had requested 'of the Russian tsar to be released from Russian citizenship.' In 1912, the university and the Austrian government renewed their order, but to the outbreak of war in 1914 Hrushevsky retained Russian citizenship. See Wynar's note in *Avtobiohrafiia–1926*, pp. 73–4.

58 Doroshenko, 'Franko i Hrushevsky,' p. 33.

59 The internal politics of the Shevchenko Society have been analyzed in detail by Wynar, *Hrushevsky i NTSh*, pp. 46–54, *et passim*.

not completely cure his illness, but by the end of 1904 his malady had begun to abate.[60] This same year, surrounded by a small circle of friends and students, he quietly celebrated the tenth anniversary of his arrival in Galicia.[61]

Hrushevsky's voyages to Western Europe and, in particular, the example of the Paris-based Russian School of Higher Social Studies may have helped inspire the project of holding Lviv university courses in Ukrainian studies for the youth of Russian Ukraine. At any rate, in the summer of 1904, the recently founded 'Society of Friends of Ukrainian Scholarship, Literature, and Art' – an organization initiated by Hrushevsky – sponsored a summer school for young Ukrainians from the Russian Empire with courses in Ukrainian history (Hrushevsky), literature (Franko), anthropology (F. Vovk), language, and other subjects. It was hoped that the summer school would grow to become the kernel of an independent Ukrainian university.[62]

The school did attract a number of dedicated and intelligent students, some of whom eventually were to play an important role in the national rebirth. However, the time was inconvenient and the enrolment of students from Russian Ukraine was smaller than expected. Administrative pressure from the Polish authorities and disorders and political changes in the Russian Empire prevented the course from being repeated the following year.[63]

Positive developments in Russia compensated for the loss of the Lviv summer school. In particular, preparations were already under way for a great Congress of Slavists in Saint Petersburg. As at the time of the Archaeological Congress in

---

60 *Avtobiohrafiia–1906*, p. 13. For Franko's account of the journey with, as he put it, 'my dear friend, Professor Hrushevsky,' see his 'Römische Eindrücke,' in *Beiträge zur Geschichte und Kultur der Ukraine* (Berlin, 1963), p. 64.

61 M. Lozynsky, 'Mykhailo Hrushevsky ...', *Dilo*, 28 June 1910, refers to a 'modest anniversary ceremony.' Both the *Avtobiohrafiia–1906*, and a large and beautifully printed *Festschrift, Naukovyi Zbirnyk prysviachenyi prof. M. Hrushevskomu uchenykamy i prykhylnykamy ...* (Lviv, 1906), were prepared in connection with this anniversary. Franko, Krymsky, Lozynsky, and others contributed to the volume. As he wrote in a letter to Hnatiuk (4 November 1904; Old Style), M. Kotsiubynsky would also have liked to contribute, but was prevented from doing so by illness. See his *Tvory v shesty tomakh*, v, 387.

62 V. Doroshenko, 'Pershyi prezydent vidnovlenoi ukrainskoi derzhavy,' *Ovyd*, nos. 2–3 (Chicago, 1957), 27; Chykalenko, *Spohady*, pp. 226–7. Also see Wynar, 'Halytska doba,' pp. 14–15.

63 V. Doroshenko, who was one of the students from Dnieper Ukraine, writes in his introduction to Hrushevsky's *Vybrani pratsi*, p. 15: 'Without any doubt, these courses helped the youth from across the Zbruch in their national self-awareness. This was all the more true in so far as outside of their lectures, in a practical way, the students got to know the fashion of a constitutional state and the national achievements of their Western Ukrainian brothers gained through these free ways.' The most detailed description of the summer school is that of Dmytro Doroshenko, *Moi spomyny pro davne mynule (1901–1914)* (Winnipeg, 1949), pp. 50–8, who notes that Hrushevsky's lectures were dull compared with those of Franko and Vovk. The two Dorochenkos were not related.

Kiev, the Galicians were expected to attend. On this occasion, however, the organization of the congress was more firmly in the hands of scholars like Alexander Shakhmatov of the Russian Academy of Sciences and Professor Jagić of Vienna, who were sympathetic to the smaller Slavic nations. Moreover, the question of language – in particular, the status of Galician Ukrainian – was discussed at length beforehand.[64]

Even before his recovery from the nervous ailment, Hrushevsky had begun work on a major presentation for this congress. His paper, *The Traditional Scheme of 'Russian' History and the Problem of a Rational Organization of the History of the East Slavs*, was completed on 22 October 1903. When it was published the next year, this brief essay was to revolutionize thought about Ukrainian history.

The essay set out to define the limits and content of Ukrainian history. In what became known as his general 'scheme,' Hrushevsky pointed out the prevailing confusion between the old princely genealogical claims to the ancient Rus' heritage on the one hand, and the political and institutional history of the Muscovite state on the other. He also pointed out the intellectual confusion between the history of the 'Russian state,' and the different political and cultural histories of what he called 'the eastern Slavs'; that is, the Russians, the Belorussians, and the Ukrainians. Hrushevsky thought it unwise to mix princely genealogy, administrative history, and ethnohistory when he believed that each ran its separate course. On the ethnic and linguistic level, he saw Halych and Volhynia, and therefore Lithuania, as the true successor state to the Kievan. Muscovite history, and therefore Russian history, were something else. Thus the Ukrainian historical process, which included the history of Kievan Rus', had a dynamic all its own; the traditional scheme of Russian history originating in old genealogical claims to the Kievan heritage was inadaquate, misleading, and simply irrational.[65]

---

64 For an outline of the debate over the language question, see V., 'Kongress slavistiv u Peterburzi,' *LNV*, XXI (1903), 219–23, and L.P. Lapteva, 'S"ezd russkykh slavistov 1903g.' in *Issledovaniia po istoriografii slavianovedeniia i balkanistiki* (Moscow, 1981), pp. 261–78.

65 Hrushevsky's essay is available in numerous editions. I have used the English translation by Andrew Gregorovich, Ukrainian Free Academy of Sciences (Winnipeg, 1955), which contains a valuable bibliography and corrects certain mistakes of earlier translations. I have checked Gregorovich's translation against the first edition, which appeared in Saint Petersburg in 1904 (see note 68 below). Hrushevsky's position is stoutly defended in the more recent historiographical study by N. Polonska-Vasylenko, *Two Conceptions of the History of Ukraine and Russia* (London, 1968), which also outlines the traditional Russian 'Statist' view.

The Russian statists, beginning with N.M. Karamzin (1766–1829), claimed ancient Kiev for Russia and for Moscow. The conservative Moscow 'Slavophiles' agreed, but rejected European Saint Petersburg. S.M. Solovev (1820–79) managed to integrate into his history much of the Slavophile national flavour without rejecting the reforms of Peter I and Petersburg. V.O. Kliuchevsky (1841–

Hrushevsky wrote two other significant articles for the Slavic Congress. One of them dealt purely with the ethnic history of the eastern Slavs and argued against the Pogodin thesis concerning the supposed migration of the tribes of southern Rus' to the northern forest regions around Moscow. In this essay Hrushevsky identified the tribes that he believed to be the ancestors of the modern Ukrainians and extended and amended work that Academician Shakhmatov had already done on the formation of the various Russian dialects. Hrushevsky's final contribution to the congress dealt with the growth of archeology in the north Pontic area and was, in fact, a plea for more archeological work free from preconceptions dictated by traditional but rather slender literary evidence.[66]

The Congress of Slavists never took place. Conservative 'Slavophile' organizations representing extreme Russian nationalist opinion attacked and succeeded in sabotaging Academician Shakhmatov's efforts at organizing a meeting that would include presentations in all the Slavic languages. Simultaneously, Polish nationalist students in Austria led a fierce campaign against another congress organizer, the prominent Polish linguist J.O. Baudouin de Courtenay, accusing him of being a 'compromiser.' Nevertheless, the organizers started work on publication of the undelivered congress *Proceedings*; these included Hrushevsky's Ukrainian-language contributions.[67]

More generally, circumstances were beginning to favor an easing of the censorship. The imperial bureaucracy came under ever greater pressure from society as disorders in the countryside and unrest in the cities grew. Setbacks in the war against Japan brought about significant governmental changes. In August 1904, Prince P.D. Sviatopolk-Mirsky was appointed to the Ministry of the Interior. He immediately tried to calm the public temper by moderate reforms that sought to limit the tsar's power by the rule of law.

Hrushevsky decided to write personally to the new minister and sent him a letter

---

1911) added a socio-economic side, leaving the Kiev-Moscow-Petersburg scheme intact. See K. Grothusen, *Die historische Rechtsschule Russlands* (Giessen, 1962), and 'Die russische Geschichtswissenschaft des 19 Jahrhunderts als Forschungsaufgabe,' *Jahrbücher für Geschichte Osteuropas*, VIII (Munich, 1960), 32–61.

66 See 'Spirni pytannia staroruskoi etnografii,' and 'Etnografichni katagorii i kulturno-arkheologichni typy v suchasnykh studyiakh skhidnoi Evropy,' printed in the Russian Academy volume cited in note 68 below and also as separate booklets (Saint Petersburg, 1904). These articles are available in English as 'Some Debatable Questions in Old Russian Ethnography,' and 'Ethnographic Categories and Cultural-Archeological Groups in Contemporary Studies of Eastern Europe,' in Nicholas Chirovsky, ed. and trans., *On the Historical Beginnings of Eastern Slavic Europe* (New York: Shevchenko Scientific Society, 1976), pp. 13–38, and pp. 39–52.

67 See the general remarks of Lototsky, II, 467, who gives an excellent portrait of Shakhmatov. Lapteva, 'S"ezd,' argues that the outbreak of the war with Japan was the true reason why the congress never took place.

that he later thought 'hot and sharp.' As it turned out, Hrushevsky was not disappointed. By the end of 1904, the proceedings of the abortive Slavic Congress, including the contributions in the Ukrainian language, were published under the auspices of the Imperial Academy of Sciences in Saint Petersburg. This was an important event and did much to raise the prestige of the Ukrainian language, which was still widely seen as nothing more than just another peasant dialect. Thereafter, permission was also granted for the publication of Hrushevsky's multi-volume *History of Ukraine-Rus'*. In addition to this, a collection of his Ukrainian short stories appeared in Kiev, and the smaller *Ocherk*, which the historian had ventured to finance himself, appeared in Saint Petersburg amidst general acclaim. There is no doubt that Hrushevsky intended to use the 'spring' of Sviatopolk-Mirsky to greatest advantage.[68]

About this same time, in response to the repeated petitions of various Ukrainian representatives, the Council of Ministers took up the business of the abolition of censorship restrictions on what was still generally termed 'the Little Russian language.' The council asked for the opinions of the Imperial Academy of Sciences, of Kiev and Kharkiv universities, and of the governor-general of Kiev. The response of the academy was drawn up by a special commission headed by Academicians Shakhmatov and F. Ie. Korsh and showed the influence of Hrushevsky's essay on the traditional scheme of Russian history. The memorandum rejected the notion that a single pan-Russian (*obshcherusskii*) language existed and declared that Little Russian was an independent language that should be censored no more than the Great Russian language.[69] The memorandum of the

---

68 *Avtobiohrafiia–1906*, pp. 12–13. Hrushevsky's letter to Sviatopolk-Mirsky has never been published. The *Ocherk istorii ukrainskogo naroda* proved an enormous success and went through three editions: Saint Petersburg, 1904, 1911, and 1912. His 'Zvychaina skhema "russkoi" istorii i sprava ratsionalnoho ukladu istorii skhidnoho slovianstva,' was published along with his other contributions to the Congress of Slavists in *Stati po slavianovedeniiu*, part 1, ed. V.I. Lamansky (Saint Petersburg, 1904). This article has been photo-reprinted in Toronto by Andrew Gregorovich, no date. The nominal editor, Lamansky, was considered to be the 'patriarch' of Russian Slavists.

69 At this same time, Shakhmatov and Korsh were involved in the reform and simplification of Russian orthography. The point of such a reform was to bring the written language closer to the living language of the common people and thus facilitate the spread of mass education. A by-product of this reform, however, would be the further distancing of the Russian literary language from the Ukrainian vernacular, a process that had taken firm hold in the time of Pushkin. Thus it was natural for Shakhmatov, Korsh, and other figures concerned with mass education to be sympathetic to the Ukrainians, who, of course, thought along the same lines within their own sphere. The most extensive account of these events is in Lototsky, II, 348–81, who, along with other figures in the Saint Petersburg Ukrainian community, was coopted into the Academy's 'Commission on the Abolition of the Restrictions on the Little Russian Printed Word.' The enormous importance that the Ukrainians attached to the Academy's report (which was first printed as Imperatorskaia Akademiia Nauk, *Ob otmene stesnenii malorusskago pechatnago slova*, Saint

University of Kiev, which was drawn up by Hrushevsky's mentor Professor Antonovych, came to a similar conclusion, as did the responses of the governor-general of Kiev and the University of Kharkiv. Even the Holy Synod of the Russian Orthodox Church authorized printing the Gospel in the Ukrainian language and gave money for its publication.[70] The prospects for the free development of a dynamic Ukrainian culture, or *Ukrainstvo* as Hrushevsky then called it, were beginning to improve.

The weakening of restrictions upon the Ukrainian language and upon Ukrainian cultural institutions in Russia had enormous implications for the concept of the Galician Piedmont. During the period 1894–1904, Hrushevsky had concentrated upon building up local Galician institutions so that they could provide a cultural outlet for the creative energies of all Ukraine. His activity at the NTSh, his foundation of various publishing and cultural organizations, even his brief venture into political life were tied to a general pan-Ukrainian goal. In addition to this, a great deal of Hrushevsky's time was spent trying to break through the general ban on *Ukrainstvo* in Russia. The *Literaturno-naukovyi vistnyk*, attempts at participation in various scholarly congresses, publishing ventures in West European languages, and the growing prestige of the Shevchenko Scientific Society were all used to this end. The attempts were only partly successful, and the principal focus of Hrushevsky's activity remained in Galicia.

Throughout this period, Hrushevsky did his best to avoid the most petty issues of Galician public life. He tried to remain non-partisan. But his inward sympathies toward social and political radicalism came to the surface in his friendship and collaboration with Franko. Only the retreat of the two men into pure scholarship prevented an open break with more moderate Ukrainian politicians whose loyalty to the Habsburgs had never completely died. Most of the old populists or

---

Petersburg, 1905, iii + 96) is shown by its immediate translation and publication in *LNV*. It was also printed separately as *Peterburska Akademiia Nauk v spravi znesenia zaborony ukrainskoho slova* (Lviv, 1905; reprinted Munich, 1976). Hrushevsky wrote an introduction in which he pointed out the stress that the Academy placed upon 'the unnatural growth of Little Russian literature in Galicia – literature largely hostile to Russia,' which had been caused by the ban. He also noted that the report contained no talk of 'provincialism' or of the inequality of languages, but rather, as he said, showed real concern for the problem of illiteracy in Ukraine.

70 Hrushevsky published the Antonovych report in Kiev in 1909; that is, shortly after the latter's death and at a time when suppression of the Ukrainian language was again gathering force. See 'Zapyska Vol. Antonovycha v spravi obmezhen ukrainskoi movy' (text in Russian), *Zapysky Ukrainskoho Naukovoho Tovarystva*, III (Kiev, 1909), 33–9. On the question of the Ukrainian Bible, see Lototsky, II, 382–99. Hrushevsky kept the Ukrainian intelligentsia abreast of these developments in 'Sviate Pysmo,' *LNV*, XXXI (1905), 96 and 'Sviate Pysmo na ukrainskii movi,' *LNV*, XXXI (1905), 201.

narodovtsi had, of course, transformed themselves into modern-style National Democrats and declared themselves for a united and independent Ukraine to be achieved some time in the future; but for the present, the heart of their struggle was in Vienna and in Lviv. It was Hrushevsky who repeatedly reminded them to turn their eyes eastward.

Political thaw in Russia marked the beginning of a new period in the history of the Ukrainian movement. Dnieper Ukraine and Saint Petersburg became a new focus of Hrushevsky's activity. The ban on *Ukrainstvo* was beginning to crumble, and, with it, so too was Hrushevsky's provincial isolation in distant Galicia.

4

The Shift Back to Kiev 1905–1914

During the autumn of 1904 and the first months of 1905, the imperial Russian bureaucracy began to crumble under the weight of the unsuccessful war against Japan and growing civil disobedience. There were strikes in the cities and peasant uprisings in the countryside. The liberal opposition movement, organized into a 'Union of Liberation,' became more and more vociferous in its demands for civil liberties, for a constitution that would ensure the rule of law, and for a government responsible to the population as a whole. As the government hesitated between concessions and repressions, a period of uncertain but relatively open debate was beginning.

From his study in Lviv, Hrushevsky watched these momentous events with growing anticipation. He knew that a decisive moment was approaching: 'The earth is trembling and its foundation is being moved!' exclaimed the historian, echoing scripture. 'Bureaucratic-political autocracy in Russia, which even a few months ago was pretending to be hopelessly strong, has crumbled before our eyes. The idea of rebuilding Russia on a freer and more rational base has passed from the realm of theory and distant possibilities into a prime concern drawing the attention not only of the citizens of Russia, but also of the entire civilized world.'[1] In what were, in fact, Hrushevsky's first forays into the world of political journalism in the broad ideological sense, the historian urged his readers to support the general movement toward civil liberty and the elimination of arbitrary bureaucracy, but also urged them to take care of specifically Ukrainian needs. Hrushevsky wanted the Ukrainian intelligentsia to take advantage of the expected freedoms, especially the lifting of the ban on Ukrainian publications. He also urged the Ukrainian

---

1 See his 'Ukrainstvo i pytannia dnia v Rosii,' *LNV*, xxx (1905), 1–10, and reprinted in *Z. bizhuchoi khvyli: stati i zamitky na temu dnia 1905–1906* (Kiev, 1906), pp. 5–15. This article is signed March 1905.

intelligentsia to form organizations to print and distribute the new books, and – as they had done during the populist decades of the 1850s and 1860s – go into the countryside. Schoolteachers and reading clubs had to become a part of village life. 'Otherwise,' Hrushevsky maintained, 'the peasantry will be isolated from the Ukrainian literary movement just as not long ago the Russian village remained far removed from Great Russian literature.' He concluded: '*Ukrainstvo* in Russia must go beyond the idea of an ethnographic nationality; it must become political and economic and take up the organization of Ukrainian society as a nation.'[2]

As social disorders continued, so too did the constitutional debate. The liberals of the Union of Liberation demanded a constitution and the universal, equal, direct, and secret ballot. This liberal opposition, led by Peter Struve and Paul Miliukov, declared that it wanted a single 'All-Russian' parliament that would represent and legislate for the whole empire. Such a centralist position seems to have reflected a general symbiosis of liberalism and nationalism not unlike that already existing in Western Europe.[3]

Of course, there was no way that Hrushevsky could agree to such plans. They would leave the empire intact and the Russian element supreme. Rather, in May 1905, in the wake of government assurances on the language question, he elaborated a constitutional project of his own that reflected traditional Ukrainian yearnings for national autonomy. This daring and detailed project, which Hrushevsky first published in *Literaturno-naukovyi vistnyk,* would decentralize 'the state' to the point where it would be difficult to distinguish it from 'society.' For Hrushevsky, it seems, just and representative government did not grow primarily out of law and an orderly administration as it did with many of the liberals; rather, a 'progressive' and 'rational' rule meant participation in government by the people itself. The closer the government was to the people, the better it would be. In Hrushevsky's project, power was to be decentralized to the greatest possible extent and the local community and the region were to become the basic building blocks of political life. Hrushevsky believed that, in a land the size of Russia, a just and representative state structure could only be achieved through wide regional autonomy, which, if fully implemented, ultimately meant a kind of federalization of the empire. The very smallest minorities should be protected by proportional representation and the autonomy of the local community, and the national principle had to be taken into account in the definition of local self-government. Hrushevsky advised the various non-state nationalities that they 'should ensure that all Russia be organized on the basis of self-government,

2 Ibid., p. 10.
3 See, in particular, Richard Pipes, *Struve: Liberal on the Left* (Cambridge, Mass., 1970), and Thomas Riha, *A Russian European: Paul Miliukov in Russian Politics* (Notre Dame–London, 1969).

because only decentralization can ensure successful economic and cultural development of the provinces, and only the organization of self-government on a national basis into national territories can neutralize or minimize national conflict. This would make nationality what it should be – the underpinning of economic, cultural, and political development and not a subject of conflict.'[4]

Though Hrushevsky addressed his constitutional project to all 'progressive' elements of Russian society, and called it a 'corrective' to the plans of the Russian liberals, his notions about decentralization and autonomy were typical Ukrainian demands. They were akin to the ideas of the Cyril-Methodians, had parallels in the earlier constitutional project of Drahomanov, and bore traces of the influence of the French federalist theoretician Proudhon and his long-time disciple Antonovych. It is remarkable, however, that Hrushevsky, the historian, argued for Ukrainian autonomy not upon historical, but rather upon socio-economic, cultural, and 'rational' – that is, ethnic – principles.

Though Hrushevsky's program of 1905 clearly stood in the mainstream of Ukrainian political thought, not all of the historian's compatriots could entirely agree with him. Since the turn of the century, the Kharkiv lawyer Mykola Mikhnovsky had argued for Ukraine's national rights on the basis of the 1654 Treaty of Pereiaslav. Less concerned than was Hrushevsky with general humanitarian principles, Mikhnovsky had predicted that the near future would bring a general war of oppressor and oppressed nations, and he had urged his followers to face this struggle by aiming at nothing less than complete independence. His pamphlet *An Independent Ukraine* had for a time served as the program of the fledgling Revolutionary Ukrainian Party (RUP), and though the party's young members soon exchanged Mikhnovsky's purely nationalist program – 'Ukraine for the Ukrainians! Expulsion of our enemies!' – for one of socialism and national-territorial autonomy, their general impatience with the apolitical

---

4 The importance that Hrushevsky accorded his constitutional project is clear from the number of times that he had it printed. It first appeared as 'Konstytutsiine pytannie i Ukrainstvo v Rosii,' *LNV*, xxx (1905), 245–58, and as an offprint; it was reprinted in his *z bizhuchoi khvyli*, pp. 16–32, and was slightly abridged in a Russian edition as 'Na konstytutsionyia temy,' in his *Osvobozhdenie Rossii i ukrainskii vopros* (Saint Petersburg, 1907), pp. 121–31. (There is a photocopy of this very rare volume in the Widener Library, Harvard.) It must be stressed that Hrushevsky argued the importance of nationality on the grounds of 'rationality,' 'progress,' and 'representation.' There is no mention of 'national spirit' or any other such thing. Similarly, although probably for 'tactical' reasons, at this early date Hrushevsky avoids direct use of the words 'federalism' and 'democracy.' The chief censor of Ukrainian books in Kiev, S.N. Shchegolev, wrote in his *Ukrainskoe dvizhenie*, p. 157: 'From April to August, 1905, Prof. M. Hrushevsky placed a series of Russian articles in the Petersburg *Syn otechestva*. Skilfully dancing around the censor's pen, he pronounced "the unavoidable necessity for a basic restructuring of Russia."'

culturalism and legalist moderation of their elders remained undiminished.[5] Thus when Hrushevsky formulated his specific program of 1905, one RUP sympathizer thought the appeal to Russian liberals and the hope that Russified Ukrainians would return to the cause of their own people was useless. Hrushevsky's critic suggested that this energy would be better spent emulating the other non-Russian peoples who, he claimed, were busy with revolutionary activity and the production of an illegal national literature. The criticism must have struck the historian as being particularly apt, for he allowed it to be published in *Literaturno-naukovyi vistnyk.*[6]

As events unfolded, Hrushevsky observed that the tsarist government was making some linguistic and cultural concessions in the westerly Polish provinces where strong quasi-legal national pressures together with revolutionary turbulence had combined to force a change in official policy. Hrushevsky thought it ironic that, in areas of mixed Ukrainian-Polish population like Pidliashshia [Podlasie], the new policies would subject local people, who had largely refrained from revolutionary violence, to strong Polonizing influences. He noted that the government had seen the benefit of divide-and-rule tactics in Lithuania and had made some slight concessions to the anti-Polish Lithuanians. But the relatively loyal Ukrainians had still got absolutely nothing. In fact, the position of Polish landowners in Ukraine was even being strengthened. Hrushevsky could only marvel at what he thought was the absurd national policy of Russia, and, with the intensity of the Russian-Polish conflict in mind, he asked: 'Is a Polonized Ukraine less dangerous to Russia than a Ukraine loyal to her own nationality?'[7]

In the autumn of 1905, apparently for the first time in quite a while, Hrushevsky

---

5 For an early account of the history of the RUP, see V. Doroshenko, *Ukrainstvo v Rosii* (Vienna, 1916), pp. 34–40. Mikhnovsky's *Samostiina Ukraina* was first published in Lviv in 1900 and is quoted at length in Petro Mirchuk, *Ukrainska derzhavnist 1917–1920* (Philadelphia, 1967), pp. 19–27. The great burst of national enthusiasm that occurred at the turn of the century produced many declarations envisioning future independence: Iuliian Bachynsky's *Ukraina irredenta* first appeared in Galicia in 1895; both Hrushevsky and Franko set immediate decentralization and distant independence as goals of the National Democratic Party in 1899, and finally, Mikhnovsky's pamphlet appeared in 1900. What set Mikhnovsky apart, however, was his tough nationalist tone, his pessimistic attitude toward the Russian state, his premonition of war between nation and nation rather than just between states, and the consistency of his demand for full independence. While by 1905 Hrushevsky was again stressing federalism, and the RUP was transforming itself into the Ukrainian Social Democratic Labor Party (USDLP), which satisfied itself with national-territorial autonomy, the Mikhnovsky circle reorganized itself into a *Ukrainska Narodnia Partiia* and retained a program of unadulterated national independence. The new party remained small and had only a limited influence.
6 Prykhylnyk 'Erupivtsiv,' 'Ne kydaite biseru,' *LNV,* XXXII (1905).
7 M. Hrushevsky, 'Bezhluzda natsionalna polityka Rosii,' *Dilo,* no. 100, 18 May 1905.

ventured a trip to Dnieper Ukraine. He wanted, as he put it, 'to sound out the Ukrainian movement and agitate for the establishment of a new publication.'[8] Both Franko and Hrushevsky expected the war with Japan to have severe repercussions in Russia, and the historian was hopeful that his plans could be realized. In Kiev and Odessa there were already student demonstrations demanding the introduction of courses in Ukrainian literature, language, and history. Hrushevsky visited Kharkiv, Kiev, and Odessa, where his brother Oleksander was teaching at the university. He prepared to go to Saint Petersburg, but the continuing strikes, growing violence, and uncertain government policies caused him to change his plans and return to Galicia.[9]

Late on the evening of 18 October 1905 Franko returned from his habitual afternoon at the newspaper office and, standing at Hrushevsky's gate – adjacent to his own home – shouted out the glad tidings that he had just received: 'A constitution in Russia!' Hrushevsky and his family ran out to meet him and everyone shook hands through the gate.[10]

The rejoicing was somewhat premature. The tsar' s October Manifesto, which promised an elected Duma and basic civil liberties, was followed by a continuation of the struggle between the government and society. Though freedom of the press was discussed, and editors suddenly became more bold, administrative repressions continued. One response to the proclaimed liberties was the birth of a Ukrainian-language press in Dnieper Ukraine. But no special concessions were granted to the Ukrainians, there was no repeal of the legal ban on Ukrainian publications, no word about autonomy, and no improvement in the local administrative system. In December, Hrushevsky expressed his profound disappointment at the turn of events. It was not only the bureaucracy that he criticized. The various oppositional forces – Polish nationalists, Russian liberals, and assorted revolutionaries – seem to have completely ignored his proffered 'correctives,' and the historian urged the Ukrainian democratic intelligentsia to put no faith in the good will of these elements. He observed: 'The time of amorphous liberalism, when the most varied trends and causes could be covered under a few general phrases, is passing away.'[11] Going right to the heart of the matter, Hrushevsky criticized those 'progressive' Russians or Poles who seemed to think

8 *Avtobiohrafiia–1906*, p. 14; *Avtobiohrafiia–1926*, p. 73.

9 Ibid. Hrushevsky's autobiography gives the impression that he was in Dnieper Ukraine at the time of the proclamation of the tsar's October Manifesto. In September, he met with Kotsiubynsky in Kiev (*Tvory v shesty tomakh*, v, 422), but it is clear from other evidence (cited in note 10 below) that he returned to Galicia prior to the proclamation of the Manifesto. Chykalenko, *Spohady*, p. 365, mentions Ukrainian expectations with regard to the war with Japan.

10 'Apostolovi pratsi,' p. 16.

11 'Na ruinakh,' in *Z bizhuchoi khvyli*, pp. 33–43, esp. p. 41.

that all nationalism other than their own was a negative and backward phenomenon; he plainly declared the Ukrainian goal to be the open recognition of the Ukrainian nationality as a separate and independent entity of equal worth to its Slavic relatives.[12] In the following months, Hrushevsky continued to urge the Ukrainian intelligentsia not to be satisfied with anything less. Small deeds and ethnographic dilettantism would no longer do. Now was the time for political action.[13]

The boycott of the elections of 1906 by the radical left, Ukrainian as well as Russian, opened the field for the liberal parties. Most of the older generation of Ukrainian cultural activists, Hrushevsky's Kievan friends, had entered a small but influential Ukrainian Democratic-Radical Party, which was liberal in ideology and traced its lineage, through factional Democratic and Radical Parties, to a 'Ukrainian Non-party Organization' and the Kievan *Stara hromada*. The program of the UDRP differed from Miliukov's Kadets in that it included explicit demands for Ukrainian linguistic rights and autonomy.[14] Nevertheless, the two liberal parties cooperated during the elections, and, considering the extent of the continuing government harassment, both enjoyed considerable success.[15]

As soon as the elected deputies arrived in Saint Petersburg, the UDRP members, I.L. Shrah and P.I. Chyzhevsky, who had run under the Kadet banner in accordance with the agreement worked out with the Russian liberals, led the way in the formation of the Ukrainian 'club.' They were joined by many nationally

12 Ibid. He continues: 'The idea of Ukraine's renaissance on wide democratic and free principles has too old and important a history to agree to an examination before a Russian or Polish examination committee in order to get a diploma of progressiveness and liberality. The idea of the defence of the popular masses has been an inseparable part of it; the protest against slavery and autocracy, the lack of any national exclusiveness, the idea of the equal rights of brotherly peoples are the logical demands of its development.'

13 See, in particular, his 'Pershi kroky,' in *Z bizhuchoi khvyli*, pp. 46–53.

14 During his student years in Kiev, of course, Hrushevsky had been active in the *Stara hromada*. According to Chykalenko, *Spohady*, p. 312, when the General Non-party Organization was formed, Hrushevsky – upon his occasional visits to Kiev – was sometimes elected its head. The Democratic Party was formed in the fall of 1904, went through a split (a few members led by the headstrong Borys Hrinchenko walking out to form the Radical Party), and reunited on the eve of the elections. Hrushevsky wrote a brief introduction and published the program of the UDRP in *LNV*, xxxiv (1906), 194ff. More generally, see Chykalenko, *Spohady*, pp. 359–67, and Doroshenko, *Ukrainstvo v Rosii*, pp. 41–2.

15 According to Polonska-Vasylenko, *Istoriia Ukrainy*, ii, 422–4, out of some 524 Duma members (only 499 actually arrived) there were 102 deputies from Ukraine which elected 6 'moderates' (probably Octobrists), 36 Kadets, 2 Democratic Reformists (a liberal party sympathetic to Ukrainian autonomy), 4 autonomists, 28 *Trudoviki*, 5 Social Democrats, and 21 others. Hrushevsky was pleased with the election results and pointed out that they had been achieved in spite of the fact that the Ukrainians had done almost no campaigning. See his 'U ukrainskykh posliv rosyiskoi dumy,' *LNV*, xxxiv (1906), 540–5, and reprinted in *Z bizhuchoi khvyli*, pp. 79–84.

conscious peasant members who were either unaffiliated or associated with the socialist-leaning *Trudoviki*. Other Ukrainian peasant deputies naturally associated together and boarded 'with their own,' feeling like foreigners in the imperial capital. As the sittings began, some Russian members, especially Russian Kadets and conservative delegates, began to make fun of the '*Khokhly*' with their unusual language and rustic attire. This led to a very rapid growth in the size of the Ukrainian Club.[16]

The Club was soon strengthened by the presence of the famous historian who travelled to Saint Petersburg from Lviv. 'At that time,' the young activist Dmytro Doroshenko later recalled, 'all of us considered Hrushevsky to be the leader of the Ukrainian national movement in Russia.'

His great scholarly and public services, his extraordinary organizational talent, created for him great authority and deep respect. In our eyes, he was a symbol of pan-Ukrainian unification; in those days his word was law for us. He was at the height of his powers, full of energy and wide plans. With Hrushevsky's arrival in Petersburg everyone submitted to him without hesitation.[17]

From a hastily constructed study in Oleksander Lototsky's house, complete with telephone and stand-up desk, Hrushevsky fired off messages to previously inactive or uninterested people of Ukrainian background and to potential supporters among the other non-state nationalities and the Russians. Rising before the sun, the historian amazed his compatriots by his inexhaustable energy. His host observed: 'He did not simply exist, but seemed to be constantly afire.'[18]

Hrushevsky immediately became the ideological inspiration for the parliament-ary club's *Ukrainskii vestnik* and wrote a leading article for each number. In the Russian-language press, he repeated his arguments concerning the reorganization of the empire on the basis of national-territorial autonomy; he elucidated the relationship between agriculture and the national question, defended the idea of proportional representation, and wanted to abolish the educational quota, the 'pale

16 Lototsky, III, 11–14. Of the hundred or so members from the six Ukrainian provinces, close to half joined the Ukrainian Club, which was still growing when the Duma was dissolved (Polonska-Vasylenko, *Istoriia Ukrainy*, II, 422–4). In his general analysis of the Duma ('Z derzhavnoi dumy,' *LNV*, XXXV (1906), 95–102; *Z. bizhuchoi khvyli*, pp. 85–92) Hrushevsky says that 62 members declared themselves of Ukrainian nationality; that is, 14 per cent of total Duma membership. This number does not include those who thought of themselves as being primarily of Russian nationality and stated 'we too are Little Russians' (*tozhe Malorossy*). The Ukrainians, says Hrushevsky, comprised about 19 per cent of the population of the empire.

17 Doroshenko, *Spomyny pro davne mynule*, p. 83.

18 Lototsky, II, 155, and 'Diialnist Mykhaila Hrushevskoho'' *Dilo*, nos. 322–4, 28 November – 1 December 1934.

of settlement,' and, in fact, all civil restrictions on Jews.[19] Hrushevsky believed that the Ukrainian parliamentary club should define its goals clearly, so that gradually, as the national consciousness of its members and supporters deepened, the grouping could be turned into a true political party with an elementary political program.[20] At the meetings of the club, which were held jointly with the Saint Petersburg Ukrainian Society, Hrushevsky worked toward this goal. After several weeks of organizational work, the historian succeeded in composing a declaration concerning Ukrainian autonomy which was supposed to become the platform of the club. I. Shrah, the club's leader, was to read out this declaration together with a draft bill on nationality rights in the State Duma. However, on that very day, Tsar Nicholas II unexpectedly dissolved the assembly.[21]

During his brief stay in Saint Petersburg, Hrushevsky exercised an influence beyond the confines of the Ukrainian Club. He established contact with the influential constitutionalist Maxim Kovalevsky – newly arrived from Paris – the economist M.I. Tuhan-Baranovsky, and others who were increasingly drawn to the Ukrainian movement. He also worked with Academician Shakhmatov, who was by now something of a hero among the Saint Petersburg Ukrainians.[22] Moreover, the First Duma also saw the organization of a 'Union of Federalist-Autonomists' that included a number of Poles, Moslems, Balts, and others. This group, which Hrushevsky again seems to have helped to organize, was committed to the ideas of decentralization, proportional representation, and the full national development of all the peoples of the empire.[23] The chairman of the club's founding congress, the

19 See 'Vopros dnia (Agrarna perspektivy),' *Ukrainskii vestnik* (Saint Petersburg), no. 2, 28 May 1906; 'Natsionalnye momenty v agrarnom voprose,' *Strana* (Saint Petersburg), no. 154, 1906; 'Konets getto!' *Ukrainskii vestnik*, no. 7, 2 July 1906. Hrushevsky published similar articles in *Syn otechestva* (Saint Petersburg), and elsewhere. Most of these are reprinted in his collection of Russian-language polemics, *Ozvobozhdenie Rossii i ukrainskii vopros*.
20 M. Hrushevsky, 'Duma i natsionalne pytannie,' in *Z bizhuchoi khvyli*, pp. 93–9, especially p. 95.
21 Doroshenko, *Spomyny pro davne mynule*, p. 86.
22 'We Petersburg Ukrainians,' writes Lototsky (II, 348), 'called Shakhmatov according to his personal name "Holy Alexei the man of God," at which M.S. Hrushevsky on one occasion remarked – and not without ill-natured irony – that Ukrainians always pray to Muscovite saints.' Kovalevsky, a founder of the Party of Democratic Reform and a member of the First Duma, joined the Ukrainian Club and began to publicize the Ukrainian cause in the prestigious *Vestnik Evropy* and the newspaper *Strana*, both of which he edited. Tuhan-Baranovsky – Tugan-Baranovsky in Russian – contributed to *Ukrainskii vestnik* and later became a leader of the cooperative movement.
23 Lototsky, III, 28–37. Chykalenko, *Spohady*, p. 378, states that Hrushevsky was responsible for establishing relations between the Ukrainians and the other non-Russian nations gathered together in the Union of Autonomists. In his *Schodennyk* (1907–1917) (Lviv, 1931), p. 183, he is even more specific: 'In the First State Duma, by the efforts of the Ukrainians, most of all of M.S. Hrushevsky, a rather large block of autonomist-federalists (150 delegates) was organized and O.P. Obninsky, a Great Russian, but a sincere federalist, stood at their head.' On the other hand, Hrushevsky does not

Polish Slavist J.I. Baudouin de Courtenay, took a position similar to Hrushevsky when he declared that Russian nationalism was destroying the state and that only decentralization could save it.[24] Both the Ukrainian Club and the Union of Federalist-Autonomists were renewed in the Second Duma. But the arbitrary changes in the electoral laws that inaugurated the Third Duma drastically reduced the representation of the non-state peoples and the peasantry, and, as a consequence, both clubs were wiped out. Nevertheless, as Lototsky remarks, their brief existence had shown the new premier, Peter Stolypin, and indeed the whole empire, that the Ukrainians preferred to be considered true non-Russians – that is *inorodtsi* – and not just a quaint provincial variation of the Great Russian people.[25]

The initial failure of Russian democracy and the inauguration of reformed autocracy and gentry rule in the Third Duma was a severe blow to the Ukrainians. Looking back on the period, especially the first months of liberty, Hrushevsky believed that Russian Ukraine did not make full use of the brief opportunity that it had been given. The Kadets, he thought, had made serious tactical errors and society was tiring of anarchy. Russia was reaching a divide: 'either to go the road of anarchy and disintegration, or, after an interlude of exhaustion and apathy, to take up with new energy the renewal of the state and social order.'[26] Hrushevsky directed his readers to give themselves over to practical work and the establishment of a popular press and mass literature.[27]

It was not the first time that the historian had tried to spur his compatriots to

---

figure prominently in the account of either Lototsky, or A.M.B. Topchybashy, 'Soiuz avtonomystiv: z spomyniv pro pershu derzhavnu dumu v b. Rosii,' in L. Wasilewski and others, *Spohady, Pratsi Ukrainskoho Naukovoho Instytutu*, vol. VII (Warsaw, 1932), pp. 133–41.

24 Lototsky, III, 28–31. More generally, see Robert A. Rothstein, 'The Linguist as Dissenter: Jan Baudouin de Courtenay,' in *For Wiktor Weintraub: Essays in Polish Literature Language and History Presented on the Occasion of His Sixty-fifth Birthday*, ed. V. Erlich and others (The Hague–Paris, 1975), pp. 391–405. Lototsky, III, 28–31, juxtaposes Baudouin de Courtenay's position to that of Hrushevsky, who, in 'Natsionalnyi vopros i avtonomiia,' *Ukrainskii vestnik*, 21 May 1906, no. 1, and reprinted in *Osvobozhedenie Rossii i ukrainskii vopros*, pp. 68–80, argued that valuable energy was being wasted on national conflicts which necessarily degenerate into national chauvinism and that autonomy would prevent this by channelling these energies into creative cultural and economic development and the general renewal of society. Unlike Hrushevsky, Kovalevsky, the Professor of Law, argued for Ukrainian autonomy on historical grounds. At the same time, the Union of Autonomists contained Jews who rejected 'territorial' in favour of 'personal' autonomy, and Poles whose national claims conflicted with Ukrainians, Belorussians, and Lithuanians, as well as with the privileged Russians.

25 Lototsky, III, 35.

26 M. Hrushevsky, 'Persha richnytsia rosyiskoi konstytutsii,' *LNV*, XXXVI (1906), 327–31, and reprinted in *Z. bizhuchoi khvyli*, pp. 106–11.

27 Ibid., and also his 'Pislia dumy,' *LNV*, XXXV (1906), 330–4, and reprinted in *Z bizhuchoi khvyli*, pp. 106–11.

such action. Even before the First Duma had met, Hrushevsky had written to the wealthy patron of the Ukrainian national movement, Ievhen Chykalenko, asking for his cooperation in the transfer of *Literaturno-naukovyi vistnyk* from Lviv to Kiev. With the proclamation of the October Manifesto, the historian thought that it was time for the national 'energy' that had been built up in constitutional Austrian Galicia to be transferred back to Kiev, which he thought the natural centre of Ukrainian culture. Furthermore, with the emergence of a new Ukrainian press in Dnieper Ukraine, and one that from the start differed slightly from its Galician counterpart, Hrushevsky feared that each regional press might develop in its own direction and thus the national literature would be divided into two parts, as with Serbian and Croatian. Chykalenko was inclined to agree with Hrushevsky, but his collaborators in the new Kievan press, in particular Serhii Iefremov and the strong-willed Borys Hrinchenko, the editor of the first great dictionary of modern Ukrainian, did not jump to welcome the new competition. Hrushevsky was told that the political situation was still too unstable and that such a transfer would be too risky.[28]

Throughout 1906, Hrushevsky had busied himself with politics and public life in Saint Petersburg and Galicia. But by the autumn he noted that the situation in Kiev had not seriously changed and that the Kievan publications continued to diverge from the Galician ones. In December, he visited Kiev and carried on negotiations with Chykalenko about the transfer of *Literaturno-naukovyi vistnyk* and the possiblity of its merger with the latter's *Nova hromada*. This new Kievan paper was edited by Borys Hrinchenko, who did not take kindly to the idea of a merger, fearing, as was commonly said, that the 'bulava' or sceptre would pass to Hrushevsky. Eventually, Hrinchenko's friend and collaborator Iefremov began to write unflattering articles in the Russian-language press about the 'Galicianized' historian.[29]

Hrushevsky, on the other hand, was determined to go ahead with the transfer, and in December 1906, set out for all the world to see the arguments that he had previously made to Chykalenko.[30] In spite of martial law and continuing political uncertainty, the journal was moved to Kiev.

28 Chykalenko, *Spohady*, pp. 440–1. For a detailed analysis of these events, see M. Antonovych, 'Do vzaiemyn M.S. Hrushevskoho z S.O. Iefremovom,' *Ukrainskyi istoryk*, nos. 1–2 (1975), 91–9.

29 Ibid. Also see note 35 below. In his diary under an entry for 1910, Chykalenko describes Hrinchenko thus: 'in social life ... he was an extraordinarily difficult man ... Much of his extraordinary energy and health went into a struggle for the *bulava*, first with V.P. Naumenko, then with Hrushevsky and other "rivals"' (*Shchodennyk*, p. 127).

30 Hrushevsky's 'Halychyna i Ukraina' appeared simultaneously in the last number of the old edition of *LNV*, XXXVI (1906), 489–96, and in the Lviv daily *Dilo*, nos. 269–70 (1906). (It is reprinted in *Z bizhuchoi khvyli*, pp. 117–26.) In this article Hrushevsky writes plainly: 'In short, up to the present, Galicia has gone forward and Dnieper Ukraine has either stood still or gone beyond Galicia. Now

In the first number of the new Kiev edition, Hrushevsky explained the move in even greater detail. The *Literaturno-naukovyi vistnyk* would be printed and published simultaneously in both Kiev and Lviv; the new Russian government ban on Galician publications would thus be circumvented and both parts of Ukraine well served. A flexible editorial policy would allow Galicians to use their own orthography and style while Dnieper Ukrainian purists who preferred local idiom to what they considered to be Galician neologisms and who, in particular, insisted upon joining the reflexive 'sia' to the verb would be free to so.[31] In addition, Galician literary talents, like the political commentator Mykhailo Lozynsky and the young historian, Hrushevsky's pupil Ivan Dzhyzhora, would move to Kiev, as would the recent political refugee from the east, Iury Siry, who was to look after printing and distribution and set up a new Ukrainian bookstore.[32]

In the first numbers of the new Kiev edition, Hrushevsky repeated his general call to public action. He warned his readers that the Ukrainian movement should be progressive and unsullied by national 'exclusiveness' – he would tolerate no cries of 'Ukraine for the Ukrainians! Ukraine without Pole, Jew, or Russian!' But he demanded, as he carefully put it (no doubt with the censor's pencil in mind), the possibility of 'unceasing, wide, and all-sided development' for the Ukrainian masses, and for all society the 'free and successful development of *Ukrainstvo* as a people and as a nation in all the fullness of the conception of national life.'[33]

The personality conflicts and particularism of the Kievan *literati* did not cease

---

Ukraine will go along its own separate road and its distance from Galicia will grow with each step if care is not taken to shorten the distance between these roads. Should each go along its own road and rapprochement not be secured, in twenty or thirty years we will have before us two nationalities on one ethnographic base. This would be similar to the position of the Serbs and Croatians, two parts of one Serbian ethnic group divided in its political, cultural, and religious circumstances, resulting in complete alienation [*vidchuzhennia*].'

31 'Do nashykh chytachiv v Rosii' *LNV*, XXXVII (1907), 1–6. About this same time, Hrushevsky placed a series of articles in Chykalenko's new daily *Rada*. The theme was language. His basic point was that language should be first of all 'a tool for everyday cultural life, and not some kind of artistic creation appropriate only for hanging on the wall in church for adoration as before some hallowed "thing of beauty."' See his 'Pro ukrainsku movu i ukrainsku spravu,' *Rada*, January–April 1907, nos. 6 through 89, and reprinted under the same title in Kiev, 1917, especially p. 12. The above passage is also quoted in the discussion by Panteleimon Kovaliv, 'Mykhailo Hrushevsky u borotbi za ukrainsku movu,' in *Mykhailo Hrushevsky u 110 rokovyny narodzhennia*, pp. 42–55.

32 For details on these moves see Siry's memoir: 'Kyiv (uryvok z spomyniv),' *Literaturno-naukovyi zbirnyk*, vol. I (Hanover, 1946), pp. 45–77.

33 See Hrushevsky's major theoretical statement: 'Na ukrainski temy: "O liubvi k otechestvu i narodnoi gordosti,"' *LNV*, XXXVII (1907), 497–505; XXXVIII (1907), 111–24. While Polish critics thought the move reflected a new Ukrainian 'Muscophilism,' the conservative Russian nationalists and their Galician admirers saw it as an Austrian intrigue. For Hrushevsky's response to these contradictory accusations see 'Na ukrainski temy: kriachut vorony ...' *LNV*, XXXVII, 318–29.

with the transfer of *Literaturno-naukovyi vistnyk* and the disappearance of Borys Hrinchenko's unprofitable and ailing *Nova hromada*. Both Hrinchenko and Serhii Iefremov continued to begrudge Hrushevsky his power and central position in the Ukrainian movement; V.P. Naumenko, the proprietor of the older *Kievskaia starina* bookstore, did not welcome the new competition, and the historian's old mentor, I. Nechui-Levytsky, without knowing to whom he was speaking, railed at Siry about 'that Hrushevsky and that satanic Siry [who] want to make us into Galicians!'[34] Franko came to Hrushevsky's defence, but, burdened by a progressive disease of the nervous system – probably syphilis – and unwilling to move to Kiev, was unable to continue his work on *Literaturno-naukovyi vistnyk*. Early in 1908, Franko was struck down by a severe paralysis and mental disorder from which he would never completely recover. For all practical purposes, Hrushevsky lost his closest collaborator of the past decade.[35] Meanwhile, the elderly Nechui-Levytsky authored a brochure against his former protégé in which he accused the Lviv professor of replacing the pure Ukrainian language as it was spoken in central Ukraine with an artificial Galician language filled with Polonisms and archaisms.'The very worst of it,' recalled Siry many years later, 'was that [Nechui-Levytsky's] actions gave a great deal of material for attacks on the Ukrainian movement to none other than the Muscovite Black Hundreds. At every step they began to use his book in their attacks on our language, and, unfortunately, the old grandpa did not even notice it.'[36] At this same time, the Stolypin government was steadily regaining control of the country and as it did, the pressure on Ukrainian activists became more constant.

34 Y. Siry, 'Z moikh zustrichiv,' *Literaturno-naukovyi zbirnyk*, vol. III (Hanover–Kiel, 1948), pp. 55–69, especially p. 65. Also see his earlier memoir, 'Kyiv,' *passim*, and Chykalenko, *Shchodennyk*, p. 304.

35 Hrushevsky described Franko's illness and withdrawal from literary activity in 'Neduha d-ra Ivana Franka,' *LNV*, XLII (1908), 405–6. Franko's defence of Hrushevsky's position, which took the form of a critical review of Hrinchenko's *Nova hromada* – he said it deserved to die because it was poorly run – appeared in *Rada* but was blocked first by Hrushevsky and then by Chykalenko, who was appalled at this 'fraternal war.' In the end, Iefremov published his rejoinder in *Kievskie vesti*, but he never completely forgave Hrushevsky and ceased collaborating with the *LNV*. See Chykalenko, *Shchodennyk*, pp. 22–3; Antonovych, 'Do vzaimnyn,' pp. 95–6.

36 Siry, 'Z moikh zustrichiv,' p. 67. Siry's point is confirmed by an examination of Shchegolev, *Ukrainskoe dvizhenie*, pp. 267–70. Nechui-Levytsky's *Sohochasna chasopysna mova na Ukraini* (Kiev, 1907) and *Kryve dzerkalo ukrainskoi movy* (Kiev, 1912) both took a 'romantic-conservative' position on language, rejecting all loan words and neologisms, and, of course, the separate 'sia.' Hrushevsky's position, which reflected his concern for national unity, was summed up in his popular aphorism: 'Shchob nam z halychanamy ne dilytysia, treba viddilyty sia!' That is, 'In order to prevent a division with the Galicians, we must ourselves divide the sia!' According to Dr Vasyl Lev of the NTSh, New York, this reflected Hrushevsky's flexibility on the language question rather than any Galician predisposition. Lev points out that, in this same way, the historian

While the government continued to close the doors to any kind of open Ukrainian political life, Hrushevsky and his colleagues steadily shifted their activities to the cultural sphere. In 1907, Hrushevsky reprinted many of the polemical articles he had written over the course of the previous two years. He wrote several pamphlets on historical and public issues and made a contribution to the new Ukrainian daily press as well. In these articles, Hrushevsky argued in favour of an expansion of the primary school system with education in the native language.[37] From January to March 1907, in the wake of mass meetings at the University of Kiev, the Lviv professor, in the words of his critic Shchegolev, 'authored an apology for the pretensions of the students, placing in his *Literaturno-naukovyi vistnyk* a series of articles in which he hotly and passionately developed a program for the systematic Ukrainianization of the three South Russian universities.'[38] Hrushevsky wanted the introduction of courses in Ukrainian literature, history, and language; he wanted them taught in Ukrainian, and he thought that the creation of special chairs would be necessary to achieve this objective. The process had already begun spontaneously at various universities – for example, at Kharkiv and Odessa – but a ministerial veto put a stop to it.[39] During this same time, Hrushevsky summarized the populist position worked out in his great *History of Ukraine-Rus'* in his first major Ukrainian-language popularization of Ukrainian history. This popularization, titled *The Olden Days in Ukraine,* was directed toward the literate countryfolk and the 'quasi-

---

never acceded to the demands of linguistic purity and continued to write his name in the better-known and more convenient Russified form 'Hrushevsky,' never changing it to the more Ukrainian 'Hrushivsky' (interview of March 1981). In general, Chykalenko was sympathetic to Hrushevsky on the language question, but almost no one else among the Kievans would agree to a separate 'sia'; they stood firmly against its use in *Rada*. In the end, the Kievans won out and the unified 'sia' became the standard literary form – still used to the present day. See Chykalenko, *Shchodennyk*, pp. 181–2, and the discussions in Kovaliv, pp. 53–4, George Y. Shevelov [Yury Sherekh], *Die Ukrainische Schriftsprache 1798–1965: Ihre Entwicklung unter dem Einfluss der Dialekte* (Wiesbaden: Otto Harrassowitz, 1966), pp. 78–93, and Vasyl Chaplenko, *Istoriia novoi ukrainskoi literaturnoi movy* (New York, 1970), pp. 192–200, 220–1, 345–6.

37 His major collection of Russian articles, *Osvobozhdenie Rossii i ukrainskii vopros*, and his major collection of Ukrainian articles, *Z bizhuchoi khvyli*, were both reprinted in 1907, as were several smaller pamphlets containing the same ideas and some of the same essays. For a bibliography of these and of Hrushevsky's contributions to the daily press, that is, to *Rada* and *Dilo*, see D. Balyka and others, 'Materiialy do bibliohrafii drukovanykh prats Akademika Hrushevskoho za 1905–1928 rr.,' *Iuvileinyi zbirnyk na poshanu ... Hrushevskoho*, 3 vols. (Kiev, 1927–9), III, 9–13.

38 Shchegolev, *Ukrainskoe dvizhenie*, pp. 163–6, claims that both Polish students and the Jewish student who was shortly to assassinate Stolypin (September 1911) sympathized with the Ukrainian demands and participated in the Kiev disturbances. Thus, he argues, the Ukrainian movement, in spite of Hrushevsky's assurance, had to be considered dangerous to the Russian state.

39 Hrushevsky's major statement on the university question was *Vopros ob ukrainskikh kafedrakh i nuzhdy ukrainskoi nauki* (Saint Petersburg, 1907). His university projects are also detailed in Wynar, 'Halytska doba' pp. 19–22.

intelligentsia.'[40] Similarly, in the first mass periodicals for the peasantry of Russian Ukraine – which Hrushevsky had again been instrumental in establishing – the professor summarized his views on the language, educational, and national questions. Using short sentences, a simple vocabulary, and in his historical works anecdote and personal examples, Hrushevsky guided his rustic public to an appreciation of the practical importance and long-term significance of what he now regularly called the national-cultural movement. The whole purpose, in the terminology of Hrushevsky and his colleagues, was the enlightenment of the masses and the creation of a nationally conscious population.[41]

Pure scholarship as well as popular enlightenment continued to attract the historian's attention. One of Hrushevsky's favourite projects in this realm was the establishment of a Ukrainian Scientific Society in Kiev. By the end of 1906, a group of Kievan scholars, Hrushevsky among them, took advantage of the unofficial suspension of the ban on Ukrainian publications and managed to get formal approval for such a society. The stated goal of the new Ukrainian Scientific Society (UNT) was scientific research in the Ukrainian language and popularization of the various scientific disciplines. This was to be done through professional publications, scientific expeditions, and public lectures. On 29 April 1907, at the first general meeting of the society and in his capacity as president of the Lviv NTSh, Hrushevsky, to use his own words, 'greeted the new beacon of Ukrainian scientific thought; and those present, considering it necessary to document the close link of their scholarly work with that of the Lviv society (which up to now in all *soborna Ukraina* had carried on entirely on its own) elected the head of the Lviv society to be president of its first executive.'[42] In the following years, Hrushevsky remained at the centre of UNT activity; he initiated a vigorous publication program

40 *Pro stari chasy na Ukraini* (Saint Petersburg, 1907) was quickly expanded into a magnificent *Iliustrovana istoriia Ukrainy* (Kiev–Lviv, 1911), which was to see new editions in 1912, 1913, 1915, and 1917, four more in 1918, and another two in 1919. It has often been reprinted since. The volume is especially valuable for its illustrations, all of which are contemporary and are themselves historical documents. A second Ukrainian-language popularization, *Pro batka kozatskoho Bohdana Khmelnytskoho*, appeared in Kiev in 1909.

41 Hrushevsky initiated the highly popular *Selo* (1909–11), and, when the censor closed it down, *Zasiv* (1911–12), which turned out to be equally popular. These peasant weeklies largely replaced the older *Ridnyi krai*, which had been edited by the mother of Lesia Ukrainka, Olena Pchilka, who had been unable to ensure proper editing and distribution on her own. See Siry, 'Z moikh zustrichiv,' pp. 54–9, and also his *Pershi naddniprianski ukrainski masovi politychni hazeti* (New York, 1952). Some of Hrushevsky's contributions to *Selo* are collected in *Pro ukrainsku movu i ukrainsku shkolu* (Kiev, 1912). For his reflections on the closure of *Selo*, see 'Na ukrainski temy: nedotsiniuvannie,' *LNV*, LV (1911), 81–8. Shchegolev, who was the censor, thought *Selo* to be 'pan-Ukrainian, but with a sharp social-democratic tone sometimes approaching praise of anarchy' (*Ukrainskoe dvizhenie*, p. 175).

42 See Hrushevsky's official report: 'Ukrainske Naukove Tovarystvo v Kyivi i ioho naukove vydavnytstvo,' *ZUNT*, I (Kiev, 1908), 4–5.

modelled on the *Zapysky* of the NTSh, and managed to attract a number of eminent Russian as well as Ukrainian scholars to the ranks of the new institution.[43]

Calm 'scientific' disquisition and the prestige of the academic ivory tower saved the UNT from the harshest fines, arrests, and repressions to which most of the other Ukrainian organizations and publications were subject. The government was gradually gaining the upper hand in its continuing struggle with 'society' and, beginning in 1910, Stolypin began a general offensive against all non-Russian civic organizations. On 20 January, he sent out a bureaucratic circular forbidding the registration of all new non-Russian societies and publication ventures. But with regard to the Ukrainians, the minister had made a blunder: 'Unfortunately,' the Kiev censor S.N. Shchegolev noted, 'the circular united the concept of "non-Russian" [*inorodcheski*] with all of Ukrainian society, that is, with the organizations of the Ukrainian party.' Shchegolev continued:

Without a doubt, these societies are anti-state; they strive to develop centrifugal elements in the very body of the Russian people. They go on preaching their non-Russian tendencies in one of its branches and are therefore much more dangerous than the non-Russian associations working only on the accretions to the Russian national body or even on droplets within this body. The activity of the Ukrainian societies must be limited as much as possible. It is necessary to fight against them, but it is necessary to remember that these societies are made up of Russian people propagandized by 'estrangement-making' [*inorodchestvuiushchimi*] Russian agitators.[44]

Like the startled Kiev censor, some of the older Ukrainophiles viewed the circular as a costly but real recognition of their individuality and their status as a separate people. Hrushevsky, however, saw matters differently and responded with a clearly hyperbolic 'Hymn of Thanks' which sarcastically proclaimed that 'the circular should be emblazoned in golden letters in the history of the Ukrainian movement.'[45]

As it turned out, the professor was not far off the mark. Shortly afterward, his

43 A.A. Shakhmatov and F. Ie. Korsh were among the most prominent Russian scholars to join. By the end of its first year, the UNT counted 21 full members (ibid., p. 5) and by the end of its second, 60 members. Of these, there were 45 Kievan members, and 15 corresponding members. See 'Khronika UNT v Kyivi za 1908r'. *ZUNT*, II (Kiev, 1909), 153. The society expanded steadily and reached a high point of 181 members in 1914, by which time it had hundreds of lectures and many volumes of scholarly publications to its credit. See A.M. Katrenko and T.O. Suslo, 'Ukrainske Naukove Tovarystvo v Kyievi,' *Ukrainskyi istorychnyi zhurnal*, no. 5 (Kiev, 1967), 130–3, which is a cautious attempt by two Soviet scholars to 'rehabilitate' the society.

44 Shchegolev, *Ukrainskoe dvizhenie*, pp. 276–7.

45 M. Hrushevsky, 'Na ukrainski temy: hymn vdiachnosty,' *LNV*, V (1910), 46–51. Also see Lototsky's remarks cited in note 22 above.

compatriots were under renewed government pressure and even non-political educational societies and reading rooms for the countryfolk – the local *Prosvita* societies – one after another were closed down. In his commentary on these events, Hrushevsky recoiled in horror and declared that the persecution of such 'ultra-legal' Ukrainian institutions meant the death of Kostomarov-style moderation and loyalism, which, in order to win the trust of the government, had limited itself to popular education, ethnography, and *belles lettres*. Such persecutions with their accompanying charges of 'separatism' and 'Mazepism' were, in the historian's opinion, 'truly a marvellous tactic for rooting out all opportunism and Ukrainophile loyalism. There is no longer any place for them.'[46]

Stolypin did not leave his mistake in nomenclature uncorrected. A few months later, the government reverted to its earlier position and declared that the Ukrainians were no longer *inorodtsi* but one part of the great Russian people whose unity should not be tampered with. Once again, of course, this resulted in an offensive against the national movement. The authorities proceeded to attack Ukrainian publications and, in particular, the 'modernist' journal *Ukrainska khata*, which was trying to establish itself as an organ of radical, non-Marxist, and non-conformist youth. In response, Hrushevsky, who had earlier encouraged the literary activities of Mykyta Shapoval, the editor of the new journal, simply repeated and amplified his previous argument, saying that the 'nationalistic' course of the Russian government was, in fact, manufacturing 'separatism' and giving new opportunities to all those who wished to see a split in 'Eastern Slavdom.'[47] In general, Hrushevsky's polemics of this period consisted of a challenge to Russian society and to the tsar's government to live up to the ideals and promises set by the October Manifesto of 1905. Their tone is one of indignation and disappointment with the failings and hypocrisy of the imperial

46 M. Hrushevsky, 'Na ukrainski temy: v Velykyi Chetver,' *LNV*, L (1910), 337–41. Also see note 48 below. Quoting the Ukrainian journalist M. Zalizniak, Shchegolev stated that the main purpose of the *Prosvita* societies was 'education of the population in the Ukrainian national spirit and habituating society to work in the field of *Ukrainstvo*.' For his detailed account of the *Prosvita* societies see *Ukrainskoe dvizhenie*, pp. 272–8.

47 Hrushevsky, 'Na ukrainski temy: fabrykatsiia separatyzma,' *LNV*, LIV (1911), 128–34. Shapoval later became a leader of the Ukrainian Party of Socialist Revolutionaries (UPSR). In artistic questions, *Ukrainska khata* was to reject the genteel populism of the older generation of Ukrainophiles centred around the Kiev *Hromada* and associated organizations. Instead, it adopted a lively, rebellious, 'modernist' tone that the older generation (and later the Soviets) considered 'decadent.' In political questions, Shapoval and his sympathizers inclined to an agrarian socialism somewhat parallel to the Russian SRs. Thus the older Ukrainophiles such as Chykalenko and Iefremov were unfriendly to them and only the *LNV* and Hrushevsky himself revealed 'a certain tolerance' toward the new journal. In fact, Hrushevsky's personal secretary, Mykola Ievshan, soon gained a reputation as a leading modernist critic through his work on the journal. See Pavlo Bohatsky, *Ukrainska khata ... spohady*, ed. Sava Zerkal (New York, 1955), 15–16, 23.

administration and the leaders of Russian public opinion, both 'reactionary'and 'progressive.'[48]

The other side of Hrushevsky's approach consisted of a challenge to the Ukrainians themselves. The historian demanded that his compatriots shed their inferiority complex, give up their servility toward their Russian neighbours and the state, and cease their worship of everything foreign.[49] If the two sides could follow these prescriptions, a truly progressive and rational society, united by moral and not forced bureaucratic bonds, would be the result.

These general attitudes are reflected in Hrushevsky's position on various specific questions. For example, when Antonovych retired, and Hrushevsky, trying to fulfil a long-sought goal, expressed an interest in the vacant position, he was blocked by administrative pressures and by a thunderous defamation campaign carried on by the Black Hundreds, the local Russian nationalists, and their newspaper *Kievlianin*. The historian responded to these attacks with a characteristic determination and faith in eventual victory. 'We have no pretensions to those laurels which grow in the greenhouses of *Kievlianin*,' the historian informed his public, 'and we reject all offers that might link the title of university professor with the functions of an agent of the secret police.'

Ukraina fara da se! Ukraine will make itself . . . The course of human development, the sources of the human spirit, although they have their moments of weakness, go irresistibly forward, and in the very end the victors will be those who in their struggles and activity do not rely upon the lower instincts of violence, hatred, and obscurantism, but rather on the noble struggles of the human spirit toward freedom and development. A little sooner, or a little later, that is the only question.[50]

Such arguments, of course, had no effect upon the reactionary Russian nationalists gathered in the Black Hundreds, the Union of the Russian People, and the

---

48 See, in particular, Hrushevsky's bitter mockery of Russian stereotyping of the 'cunning Little Russian' who plans to separate the Hadiach district from the Poltava region, and also see his ironic exposé of Miliukov and the 'Kadet freedom'; which does not allow the Ukrainian countryfolk to read about aeroplanes in their own language, which closes reading halls and shuts down local cooperatives: 'Na ukrainski temy: slovo na malodushnykh,' *LNV*, XLIX (1910), 330–4.

49 M. Hrushevsky, 'Na ukrainski temy: hrikhy nashi,' *LNV*, XXXVIII (1907), 324–30.

50 M. Hrushevsky, 'Na ukrainski temy: hrim – ta ne z tuchi ... ' *LNV*, XXXIX (1907), 385–91. This article is a reply to a 'thunderous' attack that appeared in *Kievlianin*. Hrushevsky's critic maintained that all *Ukrainstvo* was false and that it was dangerous to Russia because it wanted to 'tear away Little Russia' from the Empire and set up a republic or renewed Hetmanate. The article was signed 'T.F.', though Hrushevsky, with his usual taste for irony – because of its crude tone, so he assures us – hesitated to assign it to his 'old professor,' T. Florinsky. Shchegolev, *Ukrainskoe dvizhenie*, p. 177, links the transfer of *LNV* with Hrushevsky's hopes of getting the Kievan chair and spending more time in Russia.

Kiev-based Russian Nationalist Party. These extremists were especially strong in the borderland regions where the Russian national identity was most seriously threatened. Thus Hrushevsky became a prime target for the attacks of reactionary figures like V.M. Purishkevich of Bessarabia and A.I. Savenko of Kiev. After the closure of the *Prosvita* reading halls, Savenko in particular attacked the Ukrainian Scientific Society on the pages of *Kievlianin* and *Moskovskie vedomosti*. The reading halls, he cried, were 'only agents, while the real manufacturer of the Ukrainomaniac idea of an independent Ukraine is the Kiev Literary Scientific Society named after Shevchenko. It has been transferred from Lvov by the main Mazepist, M. Grushevsky, and publishes the harmful journal *Literaturno-naukovyi vistnyk*.'[51] Elsewhere he continued:

Such figures as V.A. Bobrinsky are completely forbidden to enter the Austrian state under penalty of immediate imprisonment. While with us, the Mr Grushevskys and other Austro-Polish-Mazepist emissaries quietly travel through the country and carry on all the Mazepist propaganda and no one raises a finger! Austria has created a Mazepist Piedmont out of Galicia which is used by the united enemies of the 'Russian' people as a ram to ruin the unity and wholeness of Russia. And we, folding our hands, stand unmoved and sing out: 'Eat me up, dog!'[52]

Given the tone of these polemics, it is no wonder that Hrushevsky believed that the government and society had only temporarily exhausted themselves in their battle, and that, after a brief breathing space, the conflict would be renewed. The determined professor urged his countrymen to make good use of the narrow margin of liberty that they had acquired. The older Ukrainophiles should not sit back in satisfaction now that their long-sought goal – the lifting of the 1876 ban – had been unofficially achieved; local enthusiasts should not squabble over such petty concerns as how to dot the letter 'i' in the new orthography. The time for folksy 'dumpling style' local patriotism (*varenykofylstvo*) as he put it, was at an end; the time of national duty was at hand.[53]

51 In Chykalenko, *Shchodennyk*, p. 123. The diarist noted Savenko's errors: the UNT was not a literary society, did not publish the *LNV*, was not named after Shevchenko, and was not 'transferred' from Lviv. Rather it was an independent Kievan institution. On Savenko, who was a leader of the Russian Nationalist Club, see R. Edelman, *Gentry Politics on the Eve of the Russian Revolution: The Nationalist Party* (New Brunswick, NJ, 1980), p. 70 *et passim*.

52 Chykalenko quotes an entire Savenko article in *Shchodennyk*, pp. 248–52, and notes (pp. 254–5) that most Ukrainians demanding autonomy, Hrushevsky included, would prefer to be called 'Bohdanists' (after Bohdan Khmelnytsky, who fought for an autonomous Ukraine under either king, sultan, or tsar) rather than 'Mazepist' separatists. Also see Hrushevsky's 'Na ukrainski temy: Mazepynstvo i bohdanivstvo,' *LNV*, LVII (1912), 904–102.

53 M. Hrushevsky, 'Antrakt,' *LNV*, XLI (1908), 116–21.

In the face of continued persecution, Hrushevsky sought to stiffen the backbone of Ukrainian resistance by pointing out how far the nation had already come. It was not necessary to bow before demeaning Russian demands at the upcoming Chernyhiv Archaeological Congress – the Ukrainians were now strong enough to organize their own congress if it were necessary.[54] The historian remarked upon the evolution that had taken place since Gogol's time. After all, writes Hrushevsky, the author of *Taras Bulba* was no 'all-Russian on Ukrainian soil,' as the Black Hundreds, who were actually claiming him as their own patron, maintained. Rather, Hrushevsky continued, Gogol's static 'ethnographic' feeling for Ukraine was typical of his time and, if he were alive today, he would certainly be a nationally conscious Ukrainian in the modern sense.[55] Moreover, the historian advised his compatriots that if the administration and the police were to close down mass-distribution Ukrainian publications, Ukrainians should concentrate on science and scholarship; popularization would now come of its own.[56] All the same, being at present counted among the small nations and facing all the problems that smallness brings – problems of literary production, marketing, and distribution – Ukrainians could not afford, the historian piously stated, to quarrel incessantly among themselves. They must unite and bind their cultural achievements firmly to progress so that every small contribution would serve the cause of general human development.[57]

The great intensification of the polemical debate and the transfer of so much of

---

54 The Russian organizers had invited the Lviv NTSh, which would only attend if its Kievan counterpart, the UNT, could also come. The organizers agreed, but then tried to restrict the use of Ukrainian to a separate session. For Hrushevsky, who was already being branded a 'fanatic,' this was not enough: 'Things have changed since 1899,' he declared. See his 'Na ukrainski temy: ne pora,' *LNV*, XLIII (1908), 130–40. Kotsiubynsky, whom Hrushevsky at one point had asked to attend as a Ukrainian representative, described the meeting as having a 'state-police character.' See his letter of 30 July 1909 (Old Style) to Hrushevsky in *Tvory v shesty tomakh*, VI, 72–3.

55 M. Hrushevsky, 'Iuvylei Mykoly Hoholia,' *LNV*, XLV (1909), 606–10.

56 In his 'Na ukrainski temy: zamist novorichnoi,' *LNV*, LIII (1911), 57–65, Hrushevsky maintained that true culture was somewhat like a tree whose trunk was science or scholarship and whose branches, leaves, and flowers were popular culture.

57 In his 'Na ukrainski temy: ishche pro nashe kulturne zhytie,' *LNV*, LIII (1911), 392–403, Hrushevsky raised his pen in defence of the young Volodymyr Vynnychenko, who had been attacked for his 'pornography' by the Galician National Democrats. Hrushevsky said that Vynnychenko published his *Chesnist z soboiu* in Russian because *LNV* readers had threatened to boycott the journal if such 'porn' were published in it. This was, in the historian's opinion, a good example of the small-mindedness of a little nation that was driving its own writers into alien pastures. Hrushevsky's explanation must be taken with a certain amount of caution. Vynnychenko's private correspondence with Chykalenko (*Shchodennyk*, pp. 314–18) reveals that the writer had both financial and editorial disputes with Hrushevsky and already harboured a grievance against the journal.

Hrushevsky's activity to Dnieper Ukraine meant that the historian had to spend more and more time in Kiev. Though he still had academic responsibilities in Lviv, Hrushevsky escaped to the east as often as he could. At first, the Hrushevsky family would stay at the house of his sister, Hanna Serhiiovna; but it was not long before the entire family had got together to purchase a new building on Pankivsky Street. This multi-storeyed structure soon became a focal point in the cultural flowering that was then taking place in Dnieper Ukraine. Not only did Hrushevsky's immediate family move into the new quarters, but so did the family of his sister Hanna, and that of his brother Oleksander. They were soon joined by the printer Siry, and Vasyl Krychevsky, the greatest Ukrainian artist of the time and the designer of the famous Poltava Zemstvo building, which was constructed in the Ukrainian national style. In the spacious rooms of the new quarters, Hrushevsky gathered together a great new library and launched his wide-ranging plans for the expansion of Ukrainian scholarly and cultural life. Later, it was even said that Hrushevsky was a Mason and that the Kiev Masonic lodge, to which many prominent Ukrainian figures belonged, regularly met in the house. Meanwhile, brother Oleksander conferred with Siry about the workings of their new publishing house, 'Lan,' and Krychevsky turned the top floor of the building into a veritable museum. The artist's rooms held some 200 kilims and 250 ceramic pieces – all in Ukrainian styles. It was in these rooms that Krychevsky worked out the designs and illustrations for many of Hrushevsky's books, and when someone criticized the historian for living in a house that was not built in a Ukrainian style, it was Krychevsky who was assigned the difficult task of redesigning the building in an appropriate manner.[58]

By this time, Hrushevsky was undoubtedly the most famous and most vilified Ukrainian in the Russian Empire. On the one hand, he was widely praised in learned society and enjoyed the respect of some of the most eminent members of the Russian Academy of Sciences; he had been granted an honorary doctorate from Kharkiv University and had even won the prestigious Uvarov Prize (1910) for the second edition of his Russian-language outline of Ukrainian history.[59] With the

---

58 Iu. Siry, *Iz spohadiv pro ukrainski vydavnytsva* (Augsburg, 1949), pp. 4–8; Vadym Shcherbakivsky, *Pamiati Vasylia Hryhorovycha Krychevskoho* (London, 1954), pp. 16–17. Stakhiv, *Mykhailo Hrushevsky u 110 rokovyny narodzhennia*, p. 146, testifies that Arnold Margolin, a Jewish lawyer sympathetic to the Ukrainian cause, told him of Masonic meetings presided over by Hrushevsky in his house. L. Hass, 'Wolnomularstwo ukraińskie,' *Studia z dziejów ZSRR i Europy Sredkowej*, XVII (Wrocław, 1981), p. 35, lists Hrushevsky as a Mason.

59 Commenting, in *Rada*, no 156 (1910), on the award of the Uvarov Prize, the Kazan professor D.I. Korsakov drew a parallel between Kotliarevsky, Shevchenko, and Hrushevsky on the one hand, and Lomonosov, Pushkin, and Karamzin on the other. See Shchegolev, *Ukrainskoe dvizhenie*, pp. 113–14. About this same time, Hrushevsky was collaborating with M.M. Kovalevsky and M.I. Tuhan-Baranovsky in the composition of the first Ukrainian encyclopaedia, which was to appear in

help of academicians Shakhmatov and Korsh he was elected a corresponding member of the Imperial Academy of Sciences, while at the same time his old opponent, the slavist T.D. Florinsky (whose candidacy had been promoted by a reactionary 'Slavophile' group led by A.I. Sobolevsky), was rejected.[60] On the literary level, the best Ukrainian writers from the Russian Empire were solicitous in maintaining good relations with Hrushevsky. Lesia Ukrainka explained to Franko that she wished to be on good terms with Hrushevsky, in spite of his conflict with her old friend Mykhailo Pavlyk, and she continued to correspond with the historian and send in material to *Literaturno-naukovyi vistnyk* over the course of many years. Mykhailo Kotsiubynsky derived physical relaxation, spiritual sustenance and artistic inspiration from visiting Hrushevsky's summer home at Kryvorivnia in the Austrian Carpathians.[61]

On the other hand, Hrushevsky had already become the principal target of Russian nationalist attacks on the Ukrainians. For Shchegolev, in particular, the Lviv scholar was the head Mazepist, the 'mastermind behind Ukrainian causes,' the 'heresiarch [*eresiarkh*]'who had himself invented the Ukrainian language. Using the logic of the extreme right, Shchegolev criticized Hrushevsky's support for the abolition of the Pale of Settlement and maintained that the historian simply wanted to disperse the Jews throughout the rest of the empire and then give Little Russia to the Austrians, the Germans, and the Poles.[62] 'There was no kind of calumny or insinuation against the Ukrainian cause,' a contemporary observer later recalled, 'which did not cast an aspersion on the name of Mykhailo

four volumes under the title *Ukrainskii narod v ego proshlom i nastoiashchem*. Only the first two volumes were completed when war and revolution interrupted the work. Shchegolev (p. 433) sarcastically called Hrushevsky 'an unavoidable cementing element' in this work. More generally, see Lototsky, III, 155–66, who discusses the project in great detail.

60 Lototsky, II, 355–6, notes that Sobolevsky's group managed to block Ivan Franko's election, which was also favoured by Shakhmatov.

61 Kotsiubynsky's fascination with the Hutsul mountaineers, to which his most celebrated literary work, *Shadows of Forgotten Ancestors*, would be devoted, seems to stem from a visit to Kryvorivnia in the summer of 1910. In a letter of 27 August (9 Sept.) 1910 to Maxim Gorky, Kotsiubynsky writes: 'I promised to write you from Stockholm ... but ... I decided to spend my holiday resting in the Carpathians near the Hungarian border. I spent almost two weeks at the cottage of Prof. Hrushevsky and in truth I do not regret exchanging Sweden for the land of the Hutsuls' (*Tvory v shesty tomakh*, V, 207–10). Also see his letter of 16 (29) October to Hrushevsky (pp. 218–19). Kotsiubynsky returned the following year (pp. 278–9). For relations between Hrushevsky and Lesia Ukrainka, see Olha Kosach-Kryvynniuk, *Lesia Ukrainka: Khronolohiia zhyttia i tvorchosty* (New York, 1970), pp. 563, 646, 689, 692–3, 696–8, 704, 708, 795, 808–9, 838–40, 854.

62 Shchegolev, *Ukrainskoe dvizhenie, passim*. Referring to Hrushevsky's activities in Western Europe, Shchegolev, p. 112, writes: 'Out of love for the Germans and, perhaps, in gratitude to Bismarck for his project of a Kievan Kingdom, the professor published part of his work in German translation.'

Hrushevsky, so hated by the Russian reactionaries.'[63] On the very eve of the great war that was shortly to engulf all of Europe, the same monarchists who had accused the innocent Jewish worker Mendel Beilis of the ritual murder of a Christian boy were also accusing Hrushevsky of wanting to detach Little Russia from the empire and hand it over to Austria 'on an autonomous-federal basis.'[64]

Hrushevsky did not let these distortions of his political ideas go unanswered. In fact, when the Beilis trial finally ended, the historian directly addressed the twin problems of reactionary Russian nationalism and hostility to the Jews among the Ukrainian populace. In Hrushevsky's view, the normal process of enlightenment and progress in Dnieper Ukraine had been obstructed by Russian centralism, which had delayed the rebirth of native Ukrainian culture. Thus the ignorant lower strata easily fell victim to the lies of the Black Hundreds and other bearers of so-called 'general human' Great Russian culture. (These elements merely wished to distract the attention of the masses away from their true oppressors and exploiters.) Hrushevsky plainly stated that Ukraine was no stranger to bloody massacres in which large numbers of Jews had perished, but, at the same time, he claimed that the ritual murder accusation was a recent import from the Catholic West and was without precedent in Ukrainian lands, especially in those areas where traditions of liberty were strongest. Hrushevsky thought that it would take some time before the confused population recovered from the terrible lie that it had been fed for the previous two years, and he believed that the reputation of his country would be damaged for many years to come, but he took solace in the fact that, in spite of all the propaganda and pressure, twelve simple Ukrainian peasants had had the good sense to pronounce Beilis innocent and thus awaken the country from its nightmare.[65]

The hysterical campaign against Beilis, like the vicious personal attacks on

63 Lototsky, vol. II, 156–7, gives the example of the Hrushevsky Public School in Kiev. This school had been built with funds bequeathed by the historian's father (a long-time employee of the Ministry of Education) with the stipulation that it be named after him. The son contracted Krychevsky to build the structure and the whole venture had a strong Ukrainian flavour. The school was opened in 1911 and immediately became the target of a reactionary monarchist backlash (see, for example, Shechegolev, *Ukrainskoe dvizhenie*, pp. 420–1). By 1913, certain officials had managed to have the name of the school removed, saying that it was linked to that of the well-known 'Ukrainophile' Hrushevsky. The historian then ceased to provide funds for the maintenance of the institution on the ground that the change violated his father's will. An investigation by the ministry showed that the Kievan officials had knowingly confused the names of the long-time civil servant and his famous son. Also see M. Shumytsky, 'Ukrainskyi arkhitekturnyi styl ... ' *Iliustrovana Ukraina*, no. 8 (Lviv, 1913), 8–9.

64 See the discussions in Chykalenko, *Shchodennyk*, p. 437, and Lototsky, II, 157.

65 See M. Hrushevsky, 'Na ukrainski temy: po koshmari,' *LNV*, LXIV (1913), 268–71. Hrushevsky's 'Ukrainophile' acquaintance (and possibly a fellow Mason, note 58 above) Arnold Margolin acted in Beilis's defence.

Hrushevsky, could not set the clock back to the pre-1905 period of Russian and Ukrainian history. Before 1905, Hrushevsky could never have exposed the provocative tactics of his Russian monarchist enemies in a Ukrainian-language article published in Kiev. In spite of the dissolution of the First Duma and the Second Duma, in spite of renewed censorship, in spite of the Stolypin circulars and the negative atmosphere arising from the Beilis case, the Ukrainian movement survived and Hrushevsky continued to oversee the shift back to Kiev.

This did not mean that the monarchist offensive did not take a very high toll. After 1907, legal activity by Ukrainian political parties became difficult, numerous Ukrainian publications were closed down, and the *Prosvita* reading halls came under increased pressure. In the face of these difficulties, Hrushevsky's tactic was to retreat from political to cultural life, and, when necessary, from the popularization of high culture to pure scholarship. But he protested every step of the way, and he argued that each new example of national persecution increased the separatist danger to the Russian state. Moreover, whenever it was possible, Hrushevsky would reenter public life and again broach the essential questions of national politics.

In general, during the constitutional period which followed the revolution of 1905, Hrushevsky seemed to play the role of a moderate and a liberal who was anxious to make necessary reforms in the structure of the state and thus salvage it from revolutionary destruction. On the other hand, it was also true that, for all of his tactical flexibility, Hrushevsky had as yet made no concessions in principle that would change the basic direction of the Ukrainian national movement. The movement led by Hrushevsky would be popular, it would be progressive, and above all, it would not be stopped.

5
The Shift Continues 1905–1917

In spite of the repeated attacks of the Russian monarchist press, Hrushevsky continued to cross the border into Austrian Galicia and divide his time as equally as possible between Kiev and Lviv. In Galicia itself, the problems of Polish political predominance continued. For example, the struggle for a Ukrainian university remained one focal point of the professor's attention, and in 1907, in the wake of renewed and increasingly violent clashes between Polish and Ukrainian students, he composed his second memorandum to the minister of education, renewing the demand for a Ukrainian university and offering the help of the NTSh in staffing it with qualified teachers. Delegations to Vienna and the vociferous demands of the Ukrainian members of the *Reichsrat* brought only vague promises from the government about founding a new university within ten years. Student clashes continued and eventually one student, Adam Kotsko, was killed. Trials and the conviction of more Ukrainian students followed and Hrushevsky could do little more than mourn the death of the one that he dubbed 'the young hero' and urge the leaders of Ukrainian society to support the students more firmly.[1]

Other issues were also springing up. As early as 1905, Hrushevsky and Franko had become embroiled with the National Democratic politicians in a debate over the relative importance of a national theatre and the expansion of secondary education. When the Polish-controlled provincial legislature rejected a demand for funding to support a Ukrainian theatre, the Ukrainian politicians, taking a page from Czech cultural history, appealed to Ukrainian society to raise the money on its own through public subscription. Hrushevsky criticized the scheme, expressing

1 M. Hrushevsky, 'Nad svizhoiu mohyloiu,' *LNV*, LI (1910), 157–9. For a general outline of these events, see M. Lozynsky, *Notes sur les relations Ukraino-polonaises en Galicie pendant les 25 dernières années* (Paris, 1919). Kulczycki, *Ugoda polsko-ruska*, p. 56ff., provides a well-informed Polish view; Wynar, 'Halytska doba,' pp. 18–19, quotes from the text of Hrushevsky's memorandum.

the opinion that it was much more important to use the meagre Ukrainian resources at hand to extend the school system by building some new private gymnasia – the conservative Poles had limited the funding for public ones – than to waste them on building a prestigious but unnecessary theatre. These ideas were not favourably received by the politicians, and, though Franko rallied to his defence, the affair multiplied the number of the historian's enemies and marked the beginning of a new period of conflict with his Galician compatriots.[2]

These conflicts had both a public and a personal side. From the very beginning, Hrushevsky, the strong-willed visionary from Russian Ukraine, had run into problems with some of his Galician colleagues. Old adversaries like Shukhevych, whose daughter he had overlooked, and Pavlyk, whose attempts to politicize the NTSh he had resisted, both resented his power. Pavlyk, in particular, who should have been Hrushevsky's political ally, chafed under his authority and soon developed what Franko called 'a blind fanatical hatred' for the historian.[3] In the end, even Franko, his body and nervous system racked by illness and on the verge of a complete breakdown, began to have serious disagreements with his strong-willed friend and complained about him in his private correspondence.[4]

2 See Hrushevsky's 'Shcho zh dali,' *LNV*, XXIX (1905), 1–5, and 'V spravi ruskykh shkil i ruskoho teatru,' *LNV*, XXIX (1905), 11–19. Also see H. Luzhnytsky, 'Ivan Franko pro zavdannia i tsili teatru,' *Kyiv*, IV (Philadelphia, 1956), 156–63; Wynar, *Hrushevsky i NTSh*, pp. 54–55.

3 In his 'Mykhailo Pavlyk: zamist iuvileinoi sylvetky,' *LNV* (1905), and reprinted in *Ivan Franko pro sotsiializm i marksysm* (New York, 1966), pp. 191–233, Franko says (p. 231) that Pavlyk even hated and criticized Hrushevsky's *Istoriia Ukrainy-Rusy*, though he did not seem to understand Hrushevsky's method, or his basic ideas, or what was new and important in the work. 'This shows,' Franko concludes, 'that at its best, each of Pavlyk's attacks on it was dictated by a blind fanatic hatred, and not the slightest concrete reasons ... It is obvious that neither I nor Professor Hrushevsky can have anything against a concrete – and even severe – criticism of his history and all of his public activity. But to criticize it in the way that Pavlyk has is entirely unbefitting an active member of the Shevchenko Scientific Society.'

4 The closest thing to a real quarrel between Hrushevsky and Franko came toward the end of 1907, when Franko wished to publish his *Outline History of Ukrainian Literature* in book form, but the historian – short of contributors after the growth of a Ukrainian press in Dnieper Ukraine, and in the middle of his dispute with Hrinchenko and Iefremov – urged him to publish it serially in the *LNV*. If we can believe the ailing writer, Hrushevsky, who had encouraged his work at first, now tried to block its publication by the Publishing Society and the Philological Section of the NTSh. Somewhat hastily, Franko concluded that 'from a great follower and protector of my work, Hrushevsky has become its determined enemy.' Franko began to look elsewhere for a publisher, and when Hrushevsky went to Kiev, rumours spread about a break between the two men. Thereafter, the historian rushed back to Lviv to reassure the Galician public that their cultural leaders were in accord. In the end, as Franko informed F.K. Vovk: 'Prof. Hrushevsky has taken it as a point of honour to publish this literature, when it is ready, at the press of the Publishing Society and has already got a one-thousand-ruble honorarium for me so that I am no longer angry with him.' See Franko's two letters to Vovk (16–17 December 1907 and 20 February 1908), in *Literaturna spadshchyna Ivana Franka*, vol. 1 (Kiev, 1956), pp. 489–90, and his letter to Ie. K. Tryhubov (30

For his part, Hrushevsky's busy schedule, his abrupt and insensitive manner, and his high opinion of his own work was bound to alienate many. Commenting on the professor's conflict with the equally abrasive Hrinchenko, and on his scathing and ill-natured criticism of a recently published history of Ukraine which rivalled his own *Iliustrovana istoriia Ukrainy*, Chykalenko remarked that Hrushevsky was even envious of Drahomanov, whom he had never personally met. 'It was not enough for him,' writes the Kievan publisher, 'that all society recognized him as third in greatness among the greatest sons of Ukraine: Shevchenko, Drahomanov, and Hrushevsky; he wanted to stand second after Shevchenko, or even first.'[5]

The confidence and ebullience of Hrushevsky's character were of course, reflected in his approach to politics. Both in Galicia and in Dnieper Ukraine, the historian adhered to principles that he would not compromise and voiced demands that required radical change. His appeal to Russian liberals, his program for the unhindered development of the Ukrainian nationality, and his project for the general restructuring of the Russian Empire raised the ire of many a conservative tsarist bureaucrat. But Hrushevsky's attitude toward Austria-Hungary and the ruling Galician Poles appeared to be even more uncompromising, since there are no appeals to 'progressive' Polish society and no concerns for the welfare of the Habsburg monarchy to be found in his writings.

Hrushevsky's attitude toward the Habsburg monarchy was, in fact, quite clear. Shortly after his arrival in Galicia in the 1890s, he had quickly become convinced that the 'compromise' with the Poles had been a fraud; the Poles, he thought, had never intended to make any basic changes in the political system. With the exception of the first few months of 1900, when he had helped to found the National Democratic Party – whose leaders and policies he soon came to distrust – the historian had avoided direct involvement in political life. In 1907, however, at

November 1907), in *Tvory*, xx, 615–18. Of course, Soviet writers have tried to see ideological overtones in the incident and blame Franko's nervous breakdown upon Hrushevsky's 'autocratic' and miserly character. See, for example, Mykytas, *Ideolohichna borotba navkolo spadshchyny Ivana Franka*, pp. 154–6, and Bass, *Ivan Franko*, pp. 225–7.

5 The rival history was by Mykola Arkas. Chykalenko, *Shchodennyk*, pp. 152–3, also remarks upon Hrushevsky's anger at learning that to boost circulation *Rada* was to distribute a free copy of Arka's book to its subscribers. He continues: 'It is certain that great people also have great ambition, but in Hrushevsky one must forgive this fault more than in anyone else, because for his great talent, for his colossal work, he received neither financial compensation, nor titles, but only fame. Unfortunately, he did not realize that his fame would have been even greater if he had not belittled his predecessors and contemporaries but rather valued each according to his service.' In turn, Lototsky, II, 154, tells us that when Hrushevsky visited Saint Petersburg, he (Lototsky) took up the matter of the Arkas affair with the historian, who argued with him for a long time, but in the end, 'with his customary smile and with mischievous sparks in his eyes said: "And so, do not I also have the right to make a mistake?"'

the time when universal manhood suffrage was being introduced into the Austrian half of the monarchy and the number of Ukrainian seats in the *Reichsrat* was significantly increased, Hrushevsky again began to take an interest in Galician public life. Though he did not formally join any political party, he once again frequented the meetings of the National Democrats. At these meetings Hrushevsky urged the party to take a bold stand on basic national and political questions and to avoid any compromises with the Ruthenian traditionalists who were generally known as 'Muscophiles.' He thought himself proved right when the Ukrainian parties, independently of their Ruthenian rivals, and only in alliance with the Jewish Zionists, won a clear victory at the polls.[6]

In Hrushevsky's eyes, however, the victory was not complete. The Ukrainian parliamentarians were soon ignoring his advice and negotiating with their traditionalist Ruthenian rivals toward a 'consolidation' of forces into a single parliamentary club to represent the entire Ruthenian/Ukrainian nationality. There were debates as to the program and name of the club. Would it be Ruthenian (*Rus'kyi*/*Ruthenisch*) or Ukrainian? How would it stand in relation to the national question in Russia? At conferences and in the press, Hrushevsky spoke out against any compromises on the national question. He thought that popular antipathy toward the Poles was the only force uniting 'all Ruthenians' and that the Ukrainian election victory, which had been guaranteed by a firm commitment to social action at the village level, was so great (twenty-five deputies) that 'consolidation' with the five remaining Ruthenian deputies (who, at any rate, were thought of as 'hardline Muscophiles' – *tverdi moskvofily*) was not worth the loss of a clear and modern national identity. It would be a backward step and only lead to national demoralization. In Hrushevsky's view, it was not simply a question of nomenclature; it was a matter of progress versus reaction. If the consolidation took place, the historian predicted a negative result:

As in the old days, we would have a Ruthenenklub – just as if we had not changed at all during the last ten years! This would be a *Rus'kyi kliub* in our language. Some will write it *s'* '*Rus'kyi*,' and otners with a double *s*, '*Russkii*,' and it will again be possible to say that there are no Ukrainians in Galicia, but only *Russkie*. And a German will once again ask: *Ruthenen und Rumänen ist's einerlei*? ['Are Ruthenians and Romanians the same thing?'] . . . At the present time, the formation of a Ukrainian [*ukrainisch*] club in the Vienna parliament would be an enormous demonstration [to Europe of the existence of] the modern Ukrainian movement, the unity of the Ukrainian people, the solidarity of Austrian and

---

6 For a general discussion of the elections, in which there was still considerable administrative pressure against the Ukrainians, see Levytsky, *Istoriia politychnoi dumky*, II, 442–4. For Hrushevsky's reaction, see the articles cited in notes 7 and 10 below.

Russian *Ukrainstvo,* and this would strengthen the moral powers of both the Ukrainian movement in Russia and national progress in Austria . . . Away with Ruthenianism![7]

Hrushevsky's view eventually prevailed, and a Ukrainian club with a clear national program was formed. However, the debate over the relationship between Austrian Ruthenians, Dnieper Ukrainians, and Great Russians produced an unexpected result. Two of the former Ruthenian deputies (that is, the group generally known as Muscophiles), declaring 'an end to Ruthenianism,' proclaimed themselves to be of Russian nationality and tried to address the Austrian parliament in Russian. There now seemed to be a clear distinction between those who remained true to the traditionalist Old Ruthenian position which was basically that of local patriots, and those who viewed themselves as Russians.[8]

Hrushevsky saw no future in Galicia for either of the these national orientations. 'Panrussianism,' as he called it, was linguistically and geographically divorced from Galician life, while the Old Ruthenians, who had been the conservers of local historical tradition, had already seen their publications slowly Russified and their former constituency express a preference for the Ukrainian position. Moreover, in Hrushevsky's opinion, when the Ruthenian parliamentary delegates declared that they were Russians, they had only unmasked a reactionary Galician Muscophilism which had always been closely allied with the Russian Black Hundreds. Hrushevsky believed that a few of the wiser politicians among the 'Muscophiles' would see that Panrussianism could have no popular base in Galicia and he thought that these men would continue to hide their Muscophilism under the coat of Ruthenianism; there would always be some Ukrainian representatives who would be willing to compromise with them. 'I am certain of this,' concluded Hrushevsky, who continued to be adamantly opposed to such a consolidation, 'and therefore it is with great pleasure that I welcome the ''New Era'' initiated by the Galician Black Hundreds and I reiterate their cry: ''An end to Ruthenianism!'' Away with national duplicity. Away with renegades!'[9]

---

7 M. Hrushevsky, 'Het z rutenstvom!' *Dilo,* no. 129, 27 June 1907. The principal 'Muscophile' newspaper, *Galichanin,* also opposed the 'consolidation,' viewing it as a betrayal of the *russkoi narodnoi idei.* See the brief discussion in Levytsky, *Istoriia politychnoi dumky,* II, 445ff.

8 Ibid., and pp. 452–3. Also see Mykola Andrusiak, *Narysy z istorii halytskoho moskvofilstva* (Lviv, 1935), pp. 51–2, who dates the actual split somewhat later, during debates in the provincial assembly. Paul Magocsi, 'Old Ruthenianism and Russophilism: A new Conceptual Framework for Analyzing National Ideologies in Late Nineteenth Century Eastern Galicia,' *American Contributions to the Ninth International Congress of Slavists Kiev 1983,* vol. II, ed. P. Debreczny (Columbus, Ohio: Slavica, 1983), pp. 305–24, refrains from use of the 'opprobrious' term Muscophile, carries the split back to the 1890s, and thinks that the two non-Ukrainian national orientations existed in a less definite way even prior to this.

9 M. Hrushevsky, 'Na ukrainski temy: "Konets rutenstva!"' *LNV,* XL (1907), 135–47.

Hrushevsky was confident that the Ukrainian national movement was closely tied to the social and economic aspirations of the common folk and for this reason he did not fear an open competition with those elements espousing conservative political, economic, and linguistic views. He noted that the lack of a popular base was already causing these elements to look to the ruling Poles for political support, and he was not surprised at the alliance between Polish conservatives and 'Muscophiles' (that is, both Old Ruthenians and newly declared Russians) in the provincial elections of 1908. But the Polish authorities carried out the elections in a violent and obviously fraudulent manner which returned a disproportionately large delegation of 'Muscophiles' to the provincial assembly. The Ukrainian public was outraged and a young student, Myroslav Sichynsky, who claimed to be avenging a certain peasant, Marko Kahanets, who had been killed for protesting against election fraud, assassinated the viceroy, Count Andrzej Potocki. Social tensions mounted in Galicia as enraged Polish nationalists attacked Ukrainian institutions and shops, while the Ukrainians voiced support for the assassin. Hrushevsky's reaction was well argued, theoretical, and especially firm: holy scripture and ancient law, he began, forbid murder. Modern states, however, carry out organized murder with impunity; they even compel reluctant citizens to participate in it. A case in point is the present situation, one of relentless oppression and violence. The two possible protests of those caught within such an inextricable situation are suicide and assassination. Hrushevsky continues: there have been a great many suicides among our young people recently, all of them for social and not personal reasons, all of them without effect. Therefore, 'Polish cries for repressions against *Ukrainstvo* on account of the recent assassination, the desire of blood for blood in the given situation, can only be uttered by madmen – or provocateurs . . . because the cup has already run over.'[10]

The years which followed were ones of sharp Polish-Ukrainian conflict in Galicia, but these conflicts were soon elevated to a higher international level by the development of a new cultural and political phenomenon: Neoslavism. In 1908,

10 M. Hrushevsky, 'Krov,' *LNV*, XLII (1908), 380–5. Sichynsky was sentenced to death, but, in response to the appeals of Ukrainian parliamentarians, and probably in view of the explosive political situation, Emperor Franz Josef reduced the penalty to twenty-five years' imprisonment. Sichynsky was eventually smuggled out of prison and out of the country to America, where he became prominent in the Ukrainian-American community. During the war, together with the Czech leader, Professor Masaryk, he participated in the foundation of the 'Mid-European Democratic Union,' and after the revolution he corresponded with Hrushevsky. See chapter 8, notes 37 and 42. More generally, see M. Shapoval, *Zi spomyniv Myroslava Sichynskoho* (Podebrady, 1928); Mariia Omelchenkova, *T.G. Masaryk (1850–1930)* (Prague, 1931), pp. 270–4; Makukh, *Na narodnii sluzhbi*, pp. 162–4; Lozynsky, *Notes sur les relations Ukraino-polonaises*; and Wasilewski, *Ukraina i sprawa ukraińska*, pp. 180–2, who writes that it was the Polish National Democrats who 'organized something in the nature of pogroms against the Ukrainians' and thereafter made common cause with the 'Muscophiles' against them.

Roman Dmowski, the leader of the extreme Polish nationalists of the Polish National Democratic Party, expanded the cooperation with the Galician 'Muscophiles' by announcing a new Russophile course. In the hope of further concessions from post-1905 Russia, he declared his loyalty to the tsarist state and initiated a policy of cooperation with Russian liberals and Czech Panslavs who were in the process of renewing the old Slavophile movement in what was hoped would be a somewhat more liberal form. The whole movement assumed that German expansion was the principal danger to the Slavic peoples and that cooperation among the Slavs would somehow bring liberal reform to Russia. The year was marked by celebrations and congresses which stressed the theme of Slavic cultural unity and held out the possibility of political cooperation between the Austrian and Russian empires.[11]

Hrushevsky was not impressed. He was long familiar with Dmowski's militant anti-Ukrainian position and extremist 'all-Polish' views; he knew that it was the Polish National Democrats who had attacked Ukrainian shops after the Potocki assassination. Moreover, Hrushevsky was beginning to lose faith in Russian liberals, and was soon to come into conflict with the Czech Neoslav Karel Kramář. In general, the Ukrainian historian believed that Neoslavism was little more than dangerous talk. There were already Czech-Polish confrontations in Silesia; Polish chauvinism in Galicia continued unabated, and the Russian state did not cease to persecute its non-Russian subjects. Romantic Panslavism, Hrushevsky declared, in which Ukraine had played an honourable role, was, regrettably, a thing of the past; its modern equivalent was based on racial hatred, imperialistic power politics, and simple hypocrisy. Talk of liberating the Macedonians from the Turks and the Pomeranian Kashubians and the Lusatian Sorbs from the Germans was all very fine, but the historian warned:

We will not go down this path. We have our own Macedonia at home to think about . . . We can sympathize with the closest rapprochement of progressive Slavic groups inspired by the ideas of liberation and progress, of the struggle against all violence, backwardness and

11 The older Slavophile organizations such as the *Slavianskoe Blagotvoritelnoe Obshchestvo* remained staunchly monarchist and consistently reflected an expansionist Russian nationalism. They were hostile to the Ukrainian movement and financially supported the conservative Old Ruthenian and pro-Russian (Muscophile) elements in Galicia. In 1908, however, an *Obshchestvo Slavianskoi Kultury* was founded in Moscow by F.A. Chudnovsky; it stressed the value of 'the individual characteristics of every nationality.' F.Ie. Korsh was elected its president, and the society was the only one of its kind to tolerate Ukrainian cultural aspirations. See Lototsky, II, 469, who says that, in general, Slavic congresses and societies provided fertile ground for reactionary, anti-Ukrainian propaganda. On Dmowski and the Neoslavs, see the brief remarks of P. Wandycz, *The Lands of Partitioned Poland* (Seattle and London, 1974), pp. 324–5, and Wasilewski, *Ukraina i sprawa ukraińska*, pp. 180–2, who discusses Dmowski's alliance with the Galician 'Muscophiles.'

obscurantism – but not such a fraternity as would not distinguish between right and left, between progressives and reactionaries, in the name of the Slavic race and racial hatred for the Germanic world.[12]

Hrushevsky declared that he was as much opposed to German as to every other kind of imperialism; but he advised his readers that the Ukrainians should not give up European culture, of which Germany was a part, for the sake of imperialist instincts and racial fantasies.[13]

It was not long before Hrushevsky was predicting the demise of Neoslavism, which he considered to be simply an alliance of convenience. As events unfolded, he came to see the purpose of this alliance as the strengthening of the Czech predominance over the German minority in autonomous Bohemia and of the Polish predominance over the weaker Ukrainians in Galicia, and also the promotion of Polish-Russian cooperation at the expense of the Ukrainians, Belorussians, and Lithuanians. Taking a page from Drahomanov, Hrushevsky reiterated his earlier stance and advised the Slavs to forget Balkan adventures and deal with 'the Turks back home.' Furthermore, he criticized the Ukrainian representatives in the *Reichsrat* (whom he thought too enamoured of the Austro-Slav idea) for voting in favour of the Austrian annexation of Slavic Bosnia without consulting the local population.[14]

Hrushevsky proposed what he thought was a practical alternative to both Neoslavism and the political-cultural isolation that its rejection might bring Ukrainians. He suggested that the real friends of the Ukrainian people were those with whom they had most in common, those with whom they shared a common history, and those who faced the same problems. Hrushevsky suggested cooperation with the neighbouring Belorussians and Lithuanians. All three

12 See Hrushevsky's 'Na ukrainski temy: ukrainstvo i vseslovianstvo,' *LNV*, XLII (1908), 540–7, and the brief discussion in Hans Kohn, *Panslavism: Its History and Ideology* (New York, 1960), pp. 246–51. Also see Hrushevsky's 'Kinets polskoi yntryhi,' *Dilo*, no. 131 (1908), in which he mocks the Russian monarchist legend which claimed that the 'Mazepist' movement was simply a product of Polish anti-Russian intrigues. This article first appeared in *Kievskaia mysl* (Kiev), no. 136 (1908).

13 Hrushevsky, 'Ukrainstvo i vseslovianstvo.' At the height of the Neoslav movement, O. Trehubov, the Ukrainian priest and member of the State Duma, unsuccessfully tried to arrange a meeting between the monarchist Slavophile leader, Count V. Bobrinsky, and a reluctant Hrushevsky. See Lototsky, II, 468–9.

14 See 'Na ukrainski temy: na novyi rik,' *LNV*, XLV (1909), 115–26. The Ukrainian members, it seems, supported the annexation partly, like the Czechs and South Slavs, in the hope of attaining a Slavic majority in the empire, and partly in return for some concrete political concessions in Eastern Galicia. It was characteristic of Hrushevsky to disapprove of such compromises, and this criticism was certainly one element in his growing conflict with the Ukrainian National Democrats. Compare Chubaty, 'Dodatkovi spomyny ... ' pp. 78–9, and accompanying editorial note.

nations, he pointed out, shared a common heritage and faced the twin evils of Great Russian nationalism and Polish chauvinism; all three were the battleground between Catholicism and Orthodoxy; and all three had common economic and social conditions. Hrushevsky suggested a program of quiet, consistent cultural cooperation. Ukrainian publications should take an interest in Belorussian and Lithuanian developments and give space to contributors from these countries; perhaps the latter would respond in kind. Ever mindful of the Russian censor, he concluded with the aesopian benediction: 'From sea to sea and from mountain to mountain, let the germ of freedom spread across the wide Ukrainian, Belorussian, and Lithuanian lands. Let the fruitful and life-giving grain of culture and self-recognition grow. Let it persevere through frost and fire and all the blows of hostile elements.'[15]

Hrushevsky's strong stand against Neoslavism was not appreciated in certain Polish and Russian circles. It was not long before rumours began to circulate that the Ukrainians, and Hrushevsky in particular, had been bought off by German marks. In the summer of 1910, Polish newspapers in both Russian Poland and Galicia were alive with articles about a certain Rakowski, who claimed to be a retired Prussian secret agent. Rakowski produced documents purporting to show that the Shevchenko Scientific Society and other Ukrainian organizations and publications were in the pay of the German Kaiser. It was not long before the monarchist Russian newspapers and conservative Russian nationalists began to repeat the story.[16] Hrushevsky, who had denied the rumours even before the

15 Hrushevsky, 'Na novyi rik,' pp. 124–6. Also see his 'Ukraina, Bilorus', Lytva,' *Dilo*, no. 29 (1909), and 'Ukraine, Weisrussland, Litauen,' *Ukrainische Rundschau*, no. 2 (Vienna, 1909), 49–52, in which the historian expresses the hope that the Lithuanians will draw their fellow Balts into such an alliance. There is a hostile description of this project in Shchegolev, *Ukrainskoe dvizhenie*, pp. 335–7, who observes that this alliance remained Hrushevsky's declared program for at least three years and that 'in his struggle against general Slavic ideals, he is ready to enter an anti-Russian union.' Elsewhere (p. 280) Shchegolev writes that Hrushevsky maintained contacts in Riga with his 'university friend,' a certain Marshinsky, that the newspaper *Pribaltiiskii krai* was favourable to the 'Ukrainophiles,' and that a Latvian paper had even sponsored literary evening parties promoting cooperation between the two peoples. O. Ohloblyn, 'Mykhailo Serhiievych Hrushevsky,' *Ukrainskyi istoryk*, nos. 1–2 (1966), p. 13, writes (with a certain degree of exaggeration) that 'Hrushevsky was always in favour of a hermetically sealed unification of three peoples: Ukrainian, Belorussian, and Lithuanian, which, in his opinion, had all the preconditions for the creation of a Black Sea–Baltic federation with Ukraine at its head.'

16 The story began in *Kurier Warszawski*, whence it spread to the three Lviv papers (*Słowo Polskie*, *Kurier Lwowski*, and *Dziennik Polski*) and two Cracow ones (*Czas* and *Głos Narodu*). Thereafter, it was repeated with embellishments by *Utro Rossii*, no. 76 (1912), and by Shchegolev, *Ukrainskoe dvizhenie*, pp. 489–92, who, however, admits that the Rakowski documents were untrustworthy. For Chykalenko's exasperated reaction to *Utro Rossii*'s allegation that *Rada* (which ran a large deficit every year) received German money, see his *Shchodennyk*, pp. 303–4.

Rakowski story broke, reacted strongly to the new accusations, and pointed out that the only German marks coming into Galicia were the hard-earned wages of Ukrainian seasonal workers in Silesia. He informed the Poles (who were then celebrating the anniversary of the historic 1410 battle of Grunwald/Tannenberg in which they had defeated the Teutonic Order) that in light of the bloody battles between Ukrainian and Polish students at the university, and fierce conflicts elsewhere, the planned celebrations of this common Slavic victory had, in fact, turned into a funeral for the aged union of Poland and Rus'.[17]

The debate over the Ukrainian relationship to the Neoslav movement took still another twist in 1911 when the Czech leader, Karel Kramář, visited Russia on a Panslavic cultural mission. In an interview with a conservative Saint Petersburg paper, Kramář made some serious allegations about the Ukrainian movement, describing it as 'essentially unnatural, anti-Russian, and therefore anti-Slavic.' Moreover, he was quoted as saying that it 'has always found the strongest support on the part of the Austrian government and some of the most influential circles in Vienna.' He ended by pointing to the danger that 'war can break out between Russia and Austria on account of Galicia, because a dangerous anti-Russian fireplace is being heated up there, the flame of which must jump across to southern Russia and kindle unrest and rebellion among the Russian people itself.'[18] Of course, this was anything but news for the Russian monarchist press, which had been convinced from the start that the Ukrainian movement was little more than an Austrian invention. It was not long before there were fantastic reports circulating about an Austrian map that showed southern Russia marked off as a Ukrainian kingdom and none other than Professor Hrushevsky as king.[19]

---

17 In 'Na ukrainski temy: pokhorony unii,' *LNV*, LI (1910) 289–98, Hrushevsky rejected the idea of a resurrected Polish-Lithuanian Commonwealth, repeated his Belorussian-Lithuanian proposal, and invited those Poles who truly wished to cooperate with Ukrainians to unite heart and soul with the 'local population' as a group of Right-Bank 'Ukrainians of Polish Culture' led by Wacław Lipiński had recently done. Also see his earlier statement: 'Na ukrainski temy: na novyi rik,' *LNV*, XLV (1909), 115–26, and the reaction of Shchegolev, *Ukrainskoe dvizhenie*.

18 These passages are quoted in Shchegolev, *Ukrainskoe dvizhenie*, pp. 478–80, who cites *Novoe vremia* (Saint Petersburg), no. 12804 (1911).

19 Ibid., pp. 485–500, citing *Rada*, no. 91 (1912), which in turn refers its readers to the monarchist *Novoe vremia* for the beginning of April 1912. Shchegolev (pp. 483–4) also discusses Franz Josef's first use of the term 'Ukrainian' (instead of the traditional 'Ruthenian') with regard to his Eastern Galician subjects and points to an analysis in the London *Times* which guessed that the emperor did this in order to weaken Russia and attain internal peace on the eve of new Balkan adventures. The journalist in question, Henry Wickham Steed, expanded upon this theory in his *The Habsburg Monarchy* (London, 1913), pp. 127–9, 289ff., stating that Austria would probably make concessions to the Galician Ukrainians (such as the long-awaited university) if Austro-Russian relations took a turn for the worse, while the Galician Ukrainians would have to wait a long time for their university if these relations improved, 'unless Russia turns the tables on Austria by establishing a Little Russian university at Kieff.'

All these reports drew a storm of protest from Ukrainian leaders. In Kiev, the newspaper *Rada* protested its loyalty to a renewed Russia, while in Saint Petersburg, Academician Shakhmatov and the local Ukrainians tried to convince the visiting Czech leader, Professor Masaryk, of the deeply native and democratic nature of the Ukrainian movement. Meanwhile, Hrushevsky had already reiterated his interpretation of the Neoslav phenomenon and repeated his condemnation of all imperialism. He pointed out that Austria had handed Galicia over to the Polish gentry a long time ago, and that the Ukrainian population had got whatever it had by plain struggle and not by any imperial favours.[20]

In general, the reactionary Russian press could make no greater mistake than to label Hrushevsky an Austrophile. Since what he considered to be the failure of the compromise of 1890, the historian had steadily become more critical of Austrian rule in Galicia and had begun to urge the Ukrainian politicians to stand in opposition to this rule and not to betray basic national principles for the sake of minor or illusory concessions. When, after the electoral victory of 1907, in spite of his admonitions the Ukrainian parliamentary club agreed to cooperate with the Austrian premier, Baron Beck, and then continued this cooperation after the central government failed to curb the abuses of the Potocki administration – even tolerating the reprisals against Ukrainian institutions which followed the Potocki assassination – Hrushevsky began to view the situation as a repeat performance of 1890. The Ukrainian Club's flirtations with those whom he considered to be reactionary Muscophiles, its support for the annexation of Bosnia, and its vote in favour of raising new recruits for the Austrian military completed Hrushevsky's alienation from the politicians. On the one hand, these were basic violations of the historian's high-minded 'progressive' and anti-imperialist ideas about national development; on the other hand, in his opinion nothing significant was received in exchange and the Ukrainians were once again left to the mercy of the governing Poles. 'In the very end,' Hrushevsky concluded in an article that marked his final break with the Ukrainian National Democrats, 'all the promises of the Austrian rulers end by advising us to negotiate the Ukrainian demands with the Polish Club.'

Such was the advice of Kazimierz Badeni, who in the role of Austrian Viceroy had initiated a compromise; such was the finale of the last negotiations with Baron Beck, who also initiated an agreement with the Ukrainian Club . . . The Austrian government will in no way make any concessions to the Ukrainians without the Polish *placet*. But the Polish *placet* is a hopeless dream . . . As long as the Austrian government treats the Ukrainians not as an Austrian nationality, but as Polish subjects, as long as it does not dare to fulfil Ukrainian

20 See Hrushevsky's 'Na ukrainski temy: v slavianskykh obiimakh,' *LNV*, LVI (1909), 394–409, Chykalenko's *Shchodennyk*, pp. 303–4, and Lototsky, II, 357, for events in Petersburg.

requirements without a view to the will of the Poles – then there cannot be talk about any kind of understanding with the Austrian government.[21]

The historian's disillusionment with what he called the secretive, inconsistent, and unprincipled conduct of the Galician politicians eventually passed over into a general condemnation of Galician public life. He thought the Galician leaders to be too weak, too passive, and too unresponsive to the demands of the general population. By contrast, he praised the bravery and the energy of the Dnieper Ukrainians, who had the spark of revolution about them. He compared them to Sichynsky, who was the exception that proved the Galician rule. What was needed in Galicia, he concluded, was a consistent and relentless policy of opposition to both the local Polish 'lords of the situation' and to the Austrian government that collaborated with them at the expense of the Ukrainians. When Hrushevsky collected all his criticisms of Galician public life and had them reprinted in book form under the title *Nasha polityka,* retribution was not long in coming.[22]

By 1913, Hrushevsky's old enemies in the NTSh had joined ranks with the National Democrat politicians in a common front against their antagonist. They were strengthened by the support of some of the professor's older and more talented students who had outgrown their master's heavy authority. These combined forces, the veterans led by Shukhevych, the politicians led by Kost Levytsky, and the young rebels led by Stepan Tomashivsky, began a campaign to remove Hrushevsky from his powerful position at the head of the NTSh. On the eve of the society's annual general elections, an anonymous brochure appeared and, without the historian's knowledge, was distributed to a good portion of the Galician membership. *Nasha polityka i Prof. Hrushevsky* accused the historian of being unrealistic in his approach to Galician public life, of running the society despotically, and of attaining personal enrichment at the expense of the NTSh.[23] At the general meeting that followed, a surprised Hrushevsky faced his personal and his political enemies who were out in full force.

They were successful in their main purpose. The scholar failed in his bid to have a special committee immediately investigate the charges against him and he left the

21 M. Hrushevsky, 'Realna polityka na halytskim grunti,' *LNV,* XLVII (1909), 555–65, and reprinted in his *Nasha polityka* (Lviv, 1911), pp. 40–57, especially pp. 45–6. Also see the brief remarks of M. Lozynsky, 'Mykhailo Hrushevsky: 25-lit ioho literaturnoi diialnosty,' *Dilo,* 28 June 1910.

22 See, in particular, the essays 'Dva roky halytskoi polityky' and 'Mali dila,' in *Nasha polityka,* pp. 17–39, 58–70. In the latter essay, Hrushevsky put it very carefully, saying that 'long-suffering endurance' and passive resistance were the principal strengths of the Galicians.

23 *Nasha polityka i Prof. Hrushevsky* may have been written by Tomashivsky, who was joined in his opposition by the geographer Stepan Rudnytsky, the painter Ivan Trush, and others. Its content is summarized in Wynar, *Hrushevsky i NTSh,* pp. 59–62, who pieced together some fragments from the Lypynsky Archives in Philadelphia.

proceedings in protest; thereafter, a new executive composed of former 'opposit-ionists' was elected. The supporters of the historian only managed to get him reelected to the presidency on the third ballot, and with a very slim majority at that. Moreover, the new executive immediately developed a plan for a new constitution for the society that would extend voting rights to the non-academic members (like the politicians, Levytsky, Romanchuk, and Volodymyr Bachynsky), while simultaneously depriving the members from Dnieper Ukraine of the right to send in proxies to any member of the administration. This was clearly directed against Hrushevsky, who had long been the main representative of the Dnieper Ukrainians.[24]

Hrushevsky was throughly shaken. In spite of many conflicts in the past, the manner, the extent, and the ferocity of the personal attack against him had caught him off guard. He now resolved to submit his resignation, wash his hands of the whole affair, and concentrate most of his energies on his work in Dnieper Ukraine. 'Without regard to the outcome of this battle,' he informed Chykalenko in Kiev, 'I feel myself morally free from any further suffering for the sake of Galicia, and in general, I think that this is the "day of absolution". For twenty-five years I have "organized"; I have endured all kinds of injuries. My nerves have been shattered on this rocky road. It is enough. No one can expect any more from me – and I have no nerves left for it. These twenty-five years would count for fifty in different and in better circumstances.'[25] Memoranda were published in his defence; Chykalenko, V.M. Leontovych, and V.M. Shemet arrived from Kiev to defend his honour before the next general meeting; his Galician supporters urged him to carry on, but Hrushevsky had made up his mind. On 1 April 1914, the new executive registered a letter from their long-time president in which he declared that he could continue in his post no longer. With this 'revolt of the midgets against a giant of scholarship,' as a younger contemporary put it, an era came to an end.[26]

The Dnieper Ukrainians were quite aware of the difficulties between Hrushevsky and the Galicians. Many years later, one of them, a man who himself was soon to come into conflict with the famous scholar, summarized the matter thus:

They accused Hrushevsky of being an authoritarian, of running the society autocratically

24 *Khronika NTSh*, no. 56 (1913), 2; Chykalenko, *Shchodennyk*, pp. 387–9; Wynar, *Hrushevsky i NTSh*, pp. 62–4.

25 Chykalenko gives the letter (dated 23/25 August 1913) in full in his *Shchodennyk*, pp. 387–90.

26 Makukh, *Na narodnii sluzhbi*, p. 80. Dzhydzhora for the Galicians and Doroshenko for the Easterners both composed memoranda in defence of Hrushevsky. As well, a fierce polemic raged between Rudnytsky (writing in *Dilo*) and Hrushevsky's former critic, Iefremov (writing in *Rada*), who now rallied to the historian's defence. See the detailed account by Chykalenko, *Shchodennyk*, pp. 396–407, and the analysis in Wynar, *Hrushevsky i NTSh*, pp. 66–8.

and disposing of its funds arbitrarily. That Hrushevsky was a difficult man, had unlimited ambition, could not bear to have significant people beside him, and surrounded himself with little people who could flatter him, that he could not tolerate, for example, even the most carefully worded review of his book if it was not filled with praise – all of this we knew, but in our eyes it was a petty detail when compared to his great service to *Ukrainstvo,* and we greeted him enthusiastically, or to put it better, we overlooked his 'sins' all the more because in the eyes of our enemies he embodied in his person the entire Ukrainian movement and they concentrated all of their hatred upon him. He was the consistent target of [all of] their malicious attacks, inventions, denunciations, and slanders. No one would be able to preserve healthy nerves and equanimity under such conditions![27]

Though Hrushevsky's humour suffered considerably from these assaults, his energy and daring did not. He took every opportunity to break through the remaining physical and administrative restrictions that prevented open discussion of the rising 'Ukrainian question.' So in 1912, when the difficult problem of the Kholm province – claimed as their own by the conservative Polish gentry, reactionary Russian bureaucrats, and populist Ukrainian schoolteachers alike – was debated in the Russian State Duma, a Kadet member named Nikolsky read out a bold letter from Hrushevsky which, as the indignant censor Shchegolev put it, 'in part revealed to the Duma the monstrous pretensions of the [Ukrainian] party.'[28]

Hrushevsky did not really expect to get a sympathetic hearing from the Third Duma. After all, it was dominated by the conservative 'Octobrist' Party and the newly formed Russian Nationalist Party, which generally favoured aggressive Russifying policies, and by members of the extreme right who eagerly cheered the pogroms against Jewish ghetto and Ukrainian cultural society alike.[29] However, he did think the institution an important forum for the education of the general

---

27 D. Doroshenko, *Moi spomyny pro davne mynule*, p. 158. Doroshenko visited Lviv at this time, and gives a good summary of the Galician 'revolt.'

28 Shchegolev, *Ukrainskoe dvizhenie*, p. 149, citing 'Stenogrammy' in the paper *Rossiia*, and *Rada*, nos. 18 and 111 (1912). Hrushevsky agreed with government plans to separate Kholm from 'Congress' Poland and put it under the governor-general of Kiev because, as he said, this would be a 'lesser evil' than its continued domination by the Poles. Of course, he would have preferred its annexation to an autonomous Ukraine. See his 'Na ukrainski temy: vidluchenie Kholmshchyny,' *LNV* LIX (1912), 3–12, and the discussion in A.Ia. Avrekh, *Stolypin i tretia duma* (Moscow, 1968), 114–15, 139–40.

29 Under new election laws that favoured the landowning gentry, the Ukrainian parties lost all of their representatives in the Duma. They were almost entirely replaced by reactionary Russian nationalists such as the *Kievlianin* editor, V.V. Shulgin. There were a few nationally conscious Ukrainian priests and countryfolk elected, but as Chykalenko remarked (*Shchodennyk*, pp. 290, 342), the priest feared the authorities and the peasants did not want to see the Duma dissolved again 'and lose money that they would never have been able to make without the Duma.' Only Professor I.V. Luchytsky of Kiev, now a Kadet member, represented the Ukrainian intelligentsia. But he was very old, had many commitments outside the Duma, and was ineffective on the school question

public. Thus in late 1912, when a somewhat more liberal Duma was elected, Hrushevsky was anxious not to lose the new opportunity.

Hrushevsky was most happy to cooperate with the *Trudoviki* or Labour Party. Many members of this party were of non-Russian background and the whole party had displayed concern for Ukrainian interests in the Kholm debate. But the Ukrainian historian was also willing to work with the Kadets, who were badly divided on the Ukrainian question, and even with the Social Democrats, who wanted to use national problems as a tactical tool. In a theoretical tract composed about this time, Hrushevsky called on all 'progressives' and all nationalities to unite in the cause of decentralization and national territorial autonomy.[30]

On his frequent visits to Kiev, Hrushevsky always met with the old circle of Ukrainian liberals, the moderates of the Ukrainian Democratic Radical Party, who were now reorganized into a non-party Society of Ukrainian Progressives (*Tovarystvo Ukrainskykh Postupovtsiv* or TUP). The TUP tried to unite all democrats who supported Ukrainian autonomy.[31] As in 1905 and 1907, so too in the elections of 1912 this group joined together with the local Kadets and advised them on the national question. They also worked together with the *Trudoviki*. On 8 June 1913, Chykalenko noted in his diary:

Our agreements with the *Trudoviki* and the Kadets were not in vain. In the autumn the

when it counted. See Lototsky, III, 58–63, who writes: 'At the start, there was even some talk that the members from Ukraine were gathering to put together a "right" Ukrainian club. Even this created a commotion and M.S. Hrushevsky wrote angry letters to me on the subject and thundered away in the press. But this rumour was a simple fairy-tale: the Ukrainian Duma members were not so brave.' Hrushevsky's 'Nova Duma i Ukraintsi,' *Rada* (Kiev), no. 38 (1907), was not available to me.

30 In 'Na natsionalnyia temy: k vopros o natsionalno-territorialnoi avtonomii,' *Russkoe bogatstvo*, no. 1 (Saint Petersburg, 1913), 225–43, Hrushevsky defended the notion of national-territorial autonomy against a Jewish critic, V. Medem, who had, in connection with recent Polish-Jewish clashes over city government in Congress Poland, wanted to replace it with 'personal' autonomy. Hrushevsky thought local autonomies within regional ones, and proportional representation, to be the best correctives.

Though Miliukov and other Kadets had supported Luchytsky's modest proposal for a partial Ukrainianization of the primary schools, their party program rejected the federal idea, and one of their leading members, Peter Struve, even thought Ukrainian cultural 'separatism' to be more dangerous than political 'separatism.' This position was, of course, in direct conflict with that of Hrushevsky. See Richard Pipes, 'Peter Struve and Ukrainian Nationalism,' *Harvard Ukrainian Studies*, III–IV (Cambridge, Mass. 1979–80), 675–83. For his part, in his terse notes on the Ukrainian question, Lenin called Iefremov a 'Spracharbeiter!!' and noted 'reaktsiia!!' in his marginalia on Hrushevsky. (The exclamation points are Lenin's.) See *Leninskii sbornik*, XXX (Moscow–Leningrad, 1937), 18, 25–6.

31 Władysław Serczyk, *Historia Ukrainy* (Wrocław, 1979), p. 305, remarks that the TUP was founded in 1908 by Hrushevsky and Iefremov, but from Chykalenko's diary (pp. 179, 183–4) it is clear that Hrushevsky had no part in the foundation of this organization and even wanted to remake it to his own taste.

Trudoviki promised to submit a bill on [Ukrainian-language] public schools, and the Kadets one on chairs [of Ukrainian studies] in the universities. Now, during the budget debate, a whole series of speakers (Shingarev, Miliukov, Kerensky, Dziubinsky, Petrovsky) have spoken about the situation of the Ukrainians in Russia, at which the [Russian] nationalists Savenko and Skoropadsky answered with insinuations of 'Mazepism,' and in the end, the President of the State Duma, Rodzianko, declared that the Ukrainian people does not want and does not need the Ukrainian language in school.[32]

The debate created a great uproar in the press. While the monarchist papers lauded Savenko and his friends, the Ukrainians went into a furor of activity. Making good use of parliamentary privilege – which guaranteed exemption from the censor's pen – Hrushevsky and his colleagues had the debates reprinted and also sent a note of solidarity to each of their parliamentary defenders. The note cited the necessity for 'the immediate nationalization of education' and included the traditional demand for autonomy. The *Trudoviki* and Kadets had this declaration printed in their papers.[33]

Rodzianko's speech, in particular, caused a strong reaction. This conservative landowner, himself of Ukrainian Cossack lineage, had maintained that when he worked in the Katerynoslav *Zemstvo* in 1905, the villagers rejected offers of having the October Manifesto translated into the Ukrainian language, because, as he said, they did not understand this artificial invention; he claimed that they preferred to have it in Russian. In response to these words, the villagers of the Katerynoslav area (who, with the help and influence of the famous Cossack enthusiast D.I. Iavornytsky, had preserved the sole surviving *Prosvita* Society in all Russian Ukraine) collected some sixteen hundred names for a note of protest. They sent this note to their deputy, the head of the Bolshevik group in the Duma, H.I. Petrovsky, who had it printed in *Pravda*, whence it was reprinted in *Rada* (no. 211, 1913), and elsewhere. In Kiev, Chykalenko heard that 'this protest, signed by such a great number of villagers, has made a great impression on the Duma deputies.'[34]

In his public discussion of these events, Hrushevsky reaffirmed the usefulness of the cooperation with the *Trudoviki* and the Kadets. Pointing to the enthusiasm of the Katerynoslav countryfolk, he warned both the conservative Rodziankos – the

32 Chykalenko, *Shchodennyk*, pp. 379–80.
33 Ibid., pp. 380–1, states that the document was distributed for signature in all the Ukrainian towns, and a note was attached warning that only those persons who were independent of the administration and the zemstvos should sign, since there was a possibility of repressions against the signatories. About two hundred signatures were collected.
34 Ibid., p. 381. *Pravda* was closed down shortly afterwards. Petrovsky was actually elected from the workers' curia of Katerynoslav gubernia.

doubting 'we too are Little Russians,' as he scornfully called them – and also the unsympathetic or hostile elements among the Kadets that the Ukrainian movement was no fiction, but a very real phenomenon and a logical development of historical, economic, and social conditions. He concluded that for the Ukrainians, who lacked both freedom of open debate and economic power, the floor of the Duma had taken on great significance.[35]

The cooperation of Hrushevsky's TUP colleagues with the Russian liberals and the general ideals of autonomy and federalism with a reformed Russia did not go unchallenged. After the revolution of 1905, Dmytro Dontsov, a young Social Democratic émigré from Dnieper Ukraine, used a number of public forums in Galicia to criticize the general orientation of the Ukrainian national movement. Like Hrushevsky, Dontsov was critical of the older Ukrainophiles who had fearfully eschewed politics, but unlike Hrushevsky, he saw no prospects for the reform of Russian society. Dontsov thought that the Russian influence on Ukraine was politically deadening and socially negative and that it should be replaced by civilizing Western European influences. He urged the liberal Ukrainian intelligentsia to give up its admiration for Russian culture and cease being 'national hermaphrodites.' He thought that the TUP leaders and other cultural activists who preached autonomism and federalism had simply translated into modern terms the 'Muscophilism' of the old Cossack officer class which had sold out its country for guarantees of noble status. The liberal-democratic intelligentsia led by Hrushevsky, Dontsov claimed, were the partisans of an unnecessary and harmful 'Modern Muscophilism.'[36]

Dontsov proposed a fundamental change in orientation and wrote that the moment to implement such a change had arrived. A major conflict seemed to be looming between Russia and Austria, and Dontsov proposed a complete separation of Ukraine from Russia and the formation of a Ukrainian Crown Land within the Austrian Empire. Every piece of Ukrainian territory taken by relatively progressive Austria, Dontsov believed, would strengthen the whole Ukrainian nation and would be a step forward. Discarding both independence and federation with Russia, Dontsov advocated a *Realpolitik* of political separatism. In 1913, this

35 M. Hrushevsky, 'Na ukrainski temy: ukrainska debata,' *LNV* LVII (1913), 153–61. Hrushevsky's reference to economic power was occasioned by a Polish commercial boycott of non-Polish institutions. In general, Hrushevsky's relations with the Poles were filled with tension. It seems that Hrushevsky feared Polish pretensions in Right Bank Ukraine and was very annoyed by, as he put it, 'that disagreeable science, appearing of late, of sincerely zoological, unconcealed national egoism which the privileged representatives of national struggles – the Polish nationalists – have given to the Russian progressives' (p. 156).

36 See D. Dontsov, 'Natsionalni hermafrodyty,' *Nash holos* (Lviv), nos. 9–10 (1911), 417–26, and also his brochure *Moderne moskvofilstvo* (Lviv, 1913), which is analysed and quoted at length in M. Sosnovsky, *Dmytro Dontsov: politychnyi portret* (New York and Toronto, 1974), pp. 93–7.

daring thesis was accepted at the Second All-Ukrainian Congress of Students held in Lviv.[37]

Dontsov's challenge did not go unanswered. The day after the student congress had ended, Mykhailo Mohyliansky, a Ukrainian cultural activist and member of the Kadet Party, penned a defence of traditional Dnieper Ukrainian autonomist ideals and the evolving alliance with the Russian liberals. In the Saint Petersburg paper *Rech,* he called Dontsov's proposals 'political adventurism' and quoted from Hrushevsky's criticisms of the Austrophile course of the Galician Ukrainian politicians. Their concessions had yielded nothing; their policy was bankrupt. It is unfortunate, Mohyliansky concluded, that in Galicia Hrushevsky is merely 'a voice crying out in the wilderness,' but it must be noted that the student body of Russian Ukraine was not properly represented at this congress and its decisions do not reflect the opinion of the mainstream of the Ukrainian national movement in Russia.[38]

Mohyliansky's traditional autonomism and rejection of the separatist position adopted at the Second All-Ukrainian Congress of Students was quickly seconded by most of Dontsov's comrades in the Ukrainian Social Democratic Party (USDLP).[39] Of course, even this moderate position could not satisfy either reactionary Russian monarchists like *Kievlianin* editor V.V. Shulgin or professional Russian revolutionaries like the Bolshevik leader, V.I. Lenin. Neither the extreme Right nor the extreme Left on the Russian political spectrum would have anything to do with the Russian liberals and their moderate Ukrainian allies.[40]

The TUP moderates were undeterred. They continued to declare their loyalty to automonist and federalist ideals and to keep in contact with various democratic

---

37 Dontsov's presentation to the congress was published as *Suchasne polithyche polozhennia natsii i nashi zavdannia* (Lviv, 1913), and is discussed in Sosnovsky, *Dontsov,* pp. 98–107.

38 M. Mohyliansky, "Vseukrainskii" s"ezd studenchestva,' *Rech,* no. 174, 29 June 1913.

39 See Lev Iurkevych, 'Z nahody vseukrainskoho studentskoho z'izdu,' *Dzvin* (Kiev), no. 9 (1913), 236–41, and the discussion in Myroslav Yurkevych, 'A Forerunner of National Communism: Lev Iurkevych (1885–1918),' *Journal of Ukrainian Studies* no. 12 (1982), 50–6. Iurkevych labelled Dontsov a 'bourgeois nationalist' and was instrumental in having him expelled from the USDLP. For the criticism of another USDLP member, see Mykola Porsh, 'Pro "moderne moskvofilstvo" (z nahody broshry D. Dontsova *Moderne moskvofilstvo*),' *LNV,* LXIV (1913), 360–71, who is somewhat less severe. Porsh wrote that the liberal intelligentsia were not Muscophiles, but rather Ukrainianizers, that Dontsov would do better to criticize his fellow Marxists, among whom there was more than enough Muscophilism, and that he glossed too lightly over German and Austrian imperialism.

40 V.I. Lenin, 'Cadets on the Question of the Ukraine,' in *Collected Works,* vol. XIX (Moscow, 1963), pp. 266–7. In this brief article, Lenin, who had just finished reading both Shchegolev and a pamphlet by Hrushevsky (see note 30 above), lashed out at Mohyliansky for his 'real chauvinist badgering of the Ukrainians for "separatism."' At the same time, Lenin rejected the separatism of what he called 'social-nationalists of the Dontsov type.'

elements among the Russians. When government officials banned the centennial celebrations of Shevchenko's birth – planned for March 1914 – some TUP members approached the *Trudoviki* and Kadets to raise the matter in the Duma. The latter two responded quickly with an 'interpellation' on the ban, but shortly afterward were outdone by the Social Democrats, who registered questions on the repression against the Ukrainian movement in general. After consulting with his Kievan colleagues, the Kadet leader, Paul Miliukov, decided to go to Kiev to discuss the matter directly with the Ukrainian leaders.[41]

The Kiev Kadets, led by Baron F.P. Shteinhel, were very sympathetic to the Ukrainian movement. They argued before their reluctant northern colleagues that, should their party take a negative position on the matter, the growing strength of the movement would be translated into electoral support for the more sympathetic *Trudoviki*. On the appointed day, in Shteinhel's house, ten Ukrainian representatives led by Hrushevsky met with Miliukov and ten local Kadets.[42]

Hrushevsky told Miliukov that the Ukrainians would deal with both Kadets and *Trudoviki*, that they supported parliamentary government, autonomy, and a federal reorganization of the state. Thus, he concluded, it was evident that the Ukrainians were not separatists working for German marks and Austrian crowns, but just the opposite, and, in fact, for many years the Kievan Ukrainians had actually supported the Lviv Shevchenko Society with Russian rubles. While Miliukov copied down notes in shorthand, other speakers discussed the general level of national consciousness, the school question, the role of the *Prosvita* societies, books, the press, and other matters; Hrushevsky spoke a second time on the university question. Miliukov then said that he and the Kadets agreed with most of the Ukrainian demands but could not go along with what Hrushevsky had said about autonomy or federalism. He said that in Poland and Finland autonomy was possible because it had a historical base, but not in Ukraine. Moreover, he considered federalism to be a means of drawing different states together (as in America), but in Russia this would mean breaking up the country.[43]

In a forceful extemporaneous speech, Hrushevsky replied that autonomy and

41 Chykalenko, *Shchodennyk*, pp. 415–17. Lototsky, II, 419–20, says that Miliukov with his practical and logical approach to politics was an exception among the Saint Petersburg Russian intelligentsia who, he claims, were generally indifferent to and ignorant of national questions. For a Ukrainian translation of the texts of the three interpellations, see Orest Starchuk, 'Shevchenko i chetverta derzhavna duma,' *Zbirnyk materiialiv naukovykh konferentsii kanadskoho NTSh* (Toronto, 1962), 82–99.

42 Chykalenko, *Shchodennyk*, p. 417. Of the ten local Kadets, seven counted themselves Ukrainian, two counted themselves *obshcherusskie*, and there was one Jew who quietly left when he heard that the Jewish question was not going to be discussed. The only Great Russian present was Miliukov himself.

43 Ibid., pp. 422–3.

federal reorganization had been a Ukrainian demand from the time of the Society of United Slavs, through the Cyril-Methodians, to Drahomanov and the present. He repeated his familiar argument that federalism would in the end strengthen the whole state. Miliukov, caught somewhat off guard, replied by saying that he had never opposed Ukrainian self-determination, but that the Ukrainian ideals were so distant that at present there was no point arguing about them.[44]

In a general article published at about the same time as the meeting with Miliukov, Hrushevsky discussed both political developments in Russia and the Ukrainian question as a topic of international debate. The historian noted that Ukrainian affairs were for the first time becoming a matter of lively discussion throughout Europe. With the growth of international tensions, he observed, the peoples living in the borderlands between the Russian Empire and its European neighbours were beginning to weigh the odds in a war which would most certainly be fought on their soil. Meanwhile, within Russia itself, the forces of decentralization were growing. The Siberians, Hrushevsky noted, were voicing demands for autonomy, and among the Russian progressives there was a weak but significant 'left-wing' which desired the support of Ukrainian and other national groups. However, Hrushevsky would not commit himself to any of these possible allies. 'I do not put any hope in this "left-wing" of the Russian progressives,' he confessed, '[and] I always was and I remain today a true opponent of any reckoning on "Europe," on some sort of international political combination.' In a way that was characteristic of him, Hrushevsky the theoretician concluded: '[only] that strict position of principle in which the ideologues of the Ukrainian movement in Russia have placed *Ukrainstvo* gives it special significance among the varied national and political trends that lie beyond Ukrainian affairs. *Ukrainstvo* has a great future in the centre of these trends and combinations.'[45]

International political trends and the general orientation of the Ukrainian national movement played an important role in the Duma debate on the ban of the Shevchenko celebrations. In his keynote speech, Miliukov registered his support

44 Ibid., pp. 424–5, where Chykalenko remarks: 'But it is hard to believe Miliukov. For example, he assures us that he recognizes the right of the Ukrainians to self-determination, but this is not true, because at the Congress of Journalists in 1905 he – admittedly in an unofficial and private conversation with us "non-Russians" – firmly declared himself as a centralist-leveller.' Many years later, Miliukov recalled this meeting with the TUP leaders, a meeting which Chykalenko's diary says was very hurried because Miliukov was only in Kiev for a single day. In his *Political Memoirs 1905–1917* (Ann Arbor, 1967), p. 287, the Kadet leader wrote: 'I made a special trip to Kiev where I had long conferences with a group of honoured Ukrainian "progressivists." My tactic was to focus on their comparatively moderate demands ... the TUP leaders were satisfied with this and agreed to set aside in the future their demand for a "federation" and to exclude separatism completely. Only Professor Hrushevsky tried to deceive and hide his real intentions.'

45 M. Hrushevsky, 'Na ukrainski temy: nova khvylia,' *LNV*, LXV (1914), 22–30.

for Ukrainian schools and cultural institutions because, as he said, the movement was deeply democratic and not an Austrian invention. He maintained that Hrushevsky and his colleagues were no 'Mazepist'-separatists, but rather 'Bohdanist'-autonomists who were trapped between Savenko and the Russian nationalists on the one hand and Ukrainian extremists like the émigré Dmytro Dontsov on the other. The Kadet leader outlined Dontsov's argument, pointing out that this Ukrainian socialist and advocate of separatism had even accused autonomists and federalists like Hrushevsky of spreading Russian cultural influences – Modern Muscophilism – in Galicia. Miliukov ended by saying that he was against autonomy or federalism, which would be harmful and dangerous for Russia, but that as the English journalist Henry Wickham Steed recently had pointed out, persecution of the Ukrainians in Russia could be used to advantage by Austria, while timely cultural concessions would turn the movement in the opposite direction.[46]

The government did not lift the ban on the Shevchenko celebrations and about a week after Miliukov's speech in the Duma, that is, during the first days of March 1914, there were mass demonstrations in Kiev. These were the first mass demonstrations ever staged by the Ukrainian movement in Russia. Thousands of people gathered in Saint Sophia square and for two consecutive days the streets of Kiev rang with patriotic songs. At times, the national colours, the blue and yellow banner, could be seen. Even certain 'Little Russian' elements among the police and city administration temporarily joined in. Afterwards, the monarchist press claimed that the crowds had shouted 'Long live Austria! Down with Russia!' and Savenko's Russian Nationalist Club demanded that the Ukrainian Scientific Society and the Ukrainian press be closed down and that Hrushevsky be barred from reentering Russia.[47]

46 *Gosudarstvennaia Duma: Stenograficheskii otchet*, 19 February 1914, pp. 901–16, and quoted in full in Chykalenko, *Shchodennyk*, pp. 425–33. Also see A. Bilousenko [O. Lototsky], 'Ukrainskie dni v Gosudarstvennoi Dume,' *Ukrainskaia zhizn*, no. 3 (Moscow, 1914), 7–18, and Riha, *A Russian European*, pp. 210–11, who points out that Miliukov accused Savenko and friends of being the real manufacturers of separatism and that this fitted in with Miliukov's general theory that the government was unnecessarily 'creating enemies at home.' During the war, part of Miliukov's speech was translated into English in *Ukraine's Claim to Freedom*, ed. E. Bjorkman and others (New York, 1915), pp. 106–8. The most recent discussion is in Sosnovsky, *Dontsov*, pp. 107–9.

47 Chykalenko, *Shchodennyk*, pp. 436–7. The demonstrations took place without the cooperation of the TUP, which feared provocations and charges of treason. The Ukrainian youth, especially students, made most of the preparations and sought the cooperation of the Russian SRs and Social Democrats. The Russians were not interested and, in marked contrast to the local Georgians, Armenians, and Poles, refused to participate. For a first-hand account by one of the organizers, see Mykola Kovalevsky, *Pry dzherelakh borotby* (Innsbruck, 1960), pp. 155–62. For the account of another young participant see Vasyl Dibert, 'Studentska demonstratsiia 1914 r. v Kyievi,' *Vilna Ukraina*, no. 45 (1965), 47–52.

Hrushevsky himself was aware of the significance of all these events. No longer could the Ukrainian movement be ignored, no longer could it be explained away as just so much foreign intrigue. Kadets like Miliukov, who thought that a formula could be devised in Saint Petersburg to solve the riddles of the various national regions, were very much mistaken. The Kadets, Hrushevsky explained, say that decentralization will lead to competition among the various nationalities and result in a general loss of freedom; we say this opinion is based on ignorance of the national question. Ukraine and all other national regions, every ethonographic entity, should be granted national-territorial autonomy; historic claims should be set aside. This might prevent, but certainly would not cause, such a *bellum omnium contra omnes*.[48]

Hrushevsky then turned to the foreign press, which in the wake of Miliukov's famous speech had become even more interested in the newly emerging 'Ukrainian question.' On the one hand, the influential German publicist and scholar Theodor Schiemann urged his government towards an aggressive anti-Russian policy and wanted to see Ukraine annexed to Austria in return for Austrian territorial concessions to Germany. On the other hand, the bellicose Austrian journalist Heinrich Friedjung, undaunted by recent scandals that had destroyed much of his credibility, cited Miliukov's speech and theorized that Russia supported Slavophile and Russophile agitation in Galcia to weaken Austria, while the latter supported the Ukrainians there and should carry this policy into Russian Ukraine as well, since any future war over Balkan questions would most certainly be carried on in the Ukrainian lands.[49]

Hrushevsky flatly rejected the theories of Schiemann and Friedjung, whom he thought to be the inspirers of Great Power diplomacy. He argued that real gamblers do not show their cards beforehand and that therefore this Ukrainian card must be a bluff. Moreover, he claimed that the Austrian influences on *Ukrainstvo* were

48 M. Hrushevsky, 'Na ukrainski temy: siianie vitra,' *LNV* LXV (1914), 24–31. A few months earlier, Hrushevsky had happily noted that at a large Congress of Public School Teachers in Saint Petersburg the various non-Russian delegates had spontaneously united with common resolutions on national and educational problems and opposed both the official nationalism of the bureaucracy and also the new liberal centralism, and had turned 'an animated nationalistic atmosphere' into an occasion 'for cultural and social liberation.' See his 'Novye lozungi,' *Ukrainskaia zhizn*, no. 1 (Moscow, 1914), 5–10.

49 Hrushevsky, 'Siianie vitra,' does not cite any specific articles by Schiemann or Friedjung. On Schiemann, who preached a preventive war against Russia, see Peter Borowsky, *Deutsche Ukrainepolitik 1918* (Lubeck and Hamburg, 1968), pp. 29–30. On Friedjung, see Steed's *Habsburg Monarchy*, 100–5, 259–60. According to H. Grebing, 'Osterreich-Ungarn und die Ukrainische Aktion,' *Jahrbücher für Geschichte Osteuropas*, VII (Munich, 1959), 270–96, and Oleh Fedyshyn, *Germany's Drive to the East and the Ukrainian Revolution 1917–1918* (New Brunswick, NJ, 1971), pp. 18–41, Austria feared Ukrainian revolutionaries more than Russian nationalists and refrained from exploiting Ukrainian anti-Russian sentiment before the war.

steadily weakening and could only be revived by the hostility to everything Ukrainian of the Russian bureaucracy and Russian nationalists.[50]

In general, Hrushevsky was extremely critical of both Austrian and Russian imperialism and could in no way be called an Austrophile. But he was equally critical of the territorial pretensions of the various Balkan states that were in continual conflict with one another. Rational solutions to these problems and the genuine attempts of Turkish decentralizers and constitutionalists, he thought, were ruined by racial hatreds and imperialist intervention. The rivalries of the Balkan Slav states had exposed the sham of Panslavism and added to the 'war-psychology' of Europe. In fact, all Europe, he wrote, is caught up in 'hurrah-patriotism' and is beginning to grind away at militarist tunes; and for the sake of Russian prestige, for the Slav idea, and the interests of Russian imperialism, even ardent pacifists like Miliukov join in. The liberators and progressives, the sincere defenders of culture, justice, and humanity have become militarists who discard moderation and say that war cannot be humane. 'This is a terrible warning,' the historian concluded, 'the *memento mori* of our contemporary civilization and life.'[51]

The assassination of the supposedly Slavophile Archduke Franz Ferdinand on 28 June 1914 was another step toward Armageddon. Each of the Austrian nationalities had expected something from this heir to the throne. In the case of the Galicians, many Poles and some of the Ukrainian National Democrats associated Franz Ferdinand with an aggressive anti-Russian Balkan policy and rumours of a Ukrainian Habsburg kingdom. Of course, Hrushevsky, who even in 1914 was still a Russian subject, did not share this view. Rather, he argued that the late crown prince was just another conservative Catholic aristocrat, in whom it had been wrong to put any special hopes. Like Franz Josef, he would never have broken with the Poles, and in foreign policy had even hoped to renew the conservative Three Emperors' League. Thus, the historian warned, it was incorrect to see the prince as an irreconcilable enemy of Russia who wished to use the 'Mazepist' elements as the Austrian guards of the East. Hrushevsky concluded firmly: 'The legend upon which some Galician circles wanted to base their policies, and by which the enemies of *Ukrainstvo* wished to explain its general evolution, has dissipated. Like a fantasy, like a dream, like smoke, it is gone.'[52]

50 Hrushevsky, 'Siianie Vitra.' On the other hand, Hrushevsky was willing to work with Schiemann's political opponent, the conservative constitutionalist and well-known Russophile Otto Hoetzsch, whom he had first met in 1905. See the latter's 'Michael Hruševskyj,' *Zeitschrift für osteuropäische Geschichte*, IX (Berlin, 1935), 161–4.
51 M. Hrushevsky, 'Pislia balkanskoi viiny,' *LNV*, LXIV (1913), 321–2.
52 M. Hrushevsky, 'Saraievska tragediia,' *LNV*, LXV (1914), 424–31. This article was published shortly before the proclamation of war and was soon confiscated by the Austrian authorities. Thereafter, disciplinary action began against the author. See Dmytro Doroshenko, *Moi Spomyny*

The outbreak of the war caught Hrushevsky vacationing with his family at his summer home in the Carpathian mountains. He was no longer involved in the NTSh, had finished his work at the university, and after twenty years of teaching was preparing for retirement; but all transportation was taken over by the military and there was no possiblity of returning to Lviv. Moreover, the Polish authorities urged on by Roman Dmowski's National Democrats (Endeks), were using the war as an excuse to strike out at the Ukrainian intelligentsia and it was even growing dangerous to stay in the mountains. Hrushevsky's younger contemporary Volodymyr Doroshenko, who was in contact with him at the time, explains:

The Polish Endeks (the *wszechpolacy*) hated Hrushevsky, considering him to be the main driving force behind the Ukrainian national movement in Galicia. And because the Galician administration was in the hands of the Poles, any local official or police commander could use the state of war to kill the 'father of the Hajdamaki' under some pretext of his being a Muscophile and enemy of Austria. The situation of Hrushevsky and his family was all the more dangerous in that the Poles and their Hungarian friends were at that time furiously attacking our nationally conscious people and without trial hanging a lot of innocents for some supposed Muscophilism and spying for Russia . . . Again, if the Poles did not get them, there was no good to be expected from the Muscovites should they reach [the summer home at] Kryvorivnia, because the Russian Black Hundreds hounded Hrushevsky as the leader of Ukrainian separatism and called the government to punish the 'cursed Mazepist.' Thus some military officer or Russian chauvinist could use the state of war and on his own destroy 'the father of the Mazepists,' even expecting a government award for this.[53]

Doroshenko and his friends, idealistic socialist émigrés from the Dnieper region, had recently formed a Union for the Liberation of Ukraine (SVU), which aimed to attain Ukrainian independence under Austrian auspices. Through its contacts with the Austrian general staff, this group arranged safe passage to Vienna for the Hrushevsky family. On 24 September the professor and his companions arrived in the Austrian capital, where the Galician political leaders had just formed a Supreme Ukrainian Council . Even more than the union, this

pro nedavne mynule (1914–1920) (Munich, 1969), p. 35. Also see the brief remarks of Panas Fedenko, 'Mykhailo Hrushevsky v nautsi i politytsi,' *Vilna Ukraina*, no. 52 (1966), 6. About two weeks earlier, Hrushevsky had what must have been a pleasant conversation with the wandering English scholar R.W. Seton-Watson, who was already proving himself a friend to the smaller peoples of Austria-Hungary. Seton-Watson was sympathetic to the Ukrainians and clashed with the Neoslav Kramář on their fate. He did not, however, share Hrushevsky's pessimism with regard to Franz Ferdinand. See Hugh and Christopher Seton-Watson, *The Making of a New Europe: R.W. Seton-Watson and the Last Years of Austria-Hungary* (London, 1981), pp. 100–2.

53 V. Doroshenko, 'Pershyi prezydent vidnovlenoi ukrainskoi derzhavy,' *Ovyd*, no. 2–3 (Chicago, 1957), 28; idem, 'Zhyttia i diialnist Mykhaila Hrushevskoho,' in *Vybrani pratsi*, pp. 17–18.

council was strongly Austrophile in character and, moreover, was composed of many of those figures of whom Hrushevsky had been so critical over the past years. Feeling politically isolated, and being closely watched, the historian decided to go to neutral Italy, where he might be able to acquaint himself with the situation on the other side of the front. He promised the SVU members that he would try to keep in contact with them through neutral states.[54]

Once in Italy, Hrushevsky telegraphed his Kievan friends and in reply received a summons to return home immediately. 'My stay abroad,' he writes, 'had given the enemies of *Ukrainstvo* an excuse for various insinuations and it was very difficult for the Ukrainians just then . . . Though I did no political work abroad, I had to listen to my countrymen and in the middle of November chose to go to Kiev.'[55] Before his departure, Hrushevsky happened upon a correspondent for a liberal-leaning Russian newspaper and discussed the 'inevitable' federalization of Russia with him.[56] From Italy, he made his way to Romania and back into the Russian Empire.[57]

Once in Kiev, Hrushevsky immediately met with the TUP leaders and the members of the Ukrainian Scientific Society. They were eager for news from the outside world and hopeful that the historian's connections with influential Russian

---

54 Ibid.; Andrii Zhuk, 'Prof. M. Hrushevsky i Soiuz Vyzvolennia Ukrainy v rokakh pershoi svitovoi viiny,' in the Public Archives of Canada, National Ethnic Archives, Andrii Zhuk Collection, vol. xv, file 24. The *Soiuz Vyzvolennia Ukrainy* was organized by the Ukrainian Social Democrats (USDLP) Volodymyr Doroshenko and Andrii Zhuk, by the Ukrainian Socialist Revolutionary Mykola Zalizniak, and the former Ukrainian Social Democrat and declared separatist Dmytro Dontsov, who had already begun his shift toward a more militantly nationalist position. The SVU's main role was in propaganda and diplomatic work and it was influential in getting the Ottoman minister Talaat Bey to declare an independent Ukraine as a war aim (November 1914). The *Holovna Ukrainska Rada* coordinated the policy of the main Galician political parties and was headed by Hrushevsky's political foe Kost Levytsky. It was important in the formation of the Galician military units called the Sich Riflemen (*Ukrainski Sichovi Striltsi*).

55 'Avtobiohrafiia Mykhaila Hrushevskoho, 1914–1919,' *Ukrainskyi istoryk*, nos. 1–2 (1966), 99. This brief memoir was originally published in the Canadian newspaper *Ukrainskyi holos* (Winnipeg), nos. 16–21, April 1920. Also see L. Wynar, 'Chomu Mykhailo Hrushevsky povernuvsia na Ukrainu v 1914 rotsi?' *Ukrainskyi istoryk*, nos. 3–4 (1967), 103–8.

56 M. Mukhyn, 'Prof. M. Hrushevsky (1866–1934),' *Vistnyk*, IV (Lviv, 1936), 194–202, especially 195, citing Mikhail Osorgin, 'Vstrechi,' *Poslednie novosti*, 10 April 1933, who worked for *Russkie vedomosti*.

57 V. Doroshenko, 'Pershyi prezydent,' p. 28 and 'Zhyttia i diialnist,' pp. 17–18; *Avtobiohrafiia– 1926*, p. 85. It seems that even before Hrushevsky had left Austria, the Poles who controlled Lviv University had begun 'disciplinary action' against him for (presumably 'Muscophile') statements made in 'Saraievska tragediia.' Afterwards, an order for his arrest went out from the Austrian authorities and his NTSh critic, S. Tomashivsky, was called to give evidence. See Iu. Gerych, 'Do biohrafii M. Hrushevskoho,' *Ukrainskyi istoryk*, nos. 1–2 (1972), 66–84, and the accompanying remarks of L. Wynar, pp. 85–90.

scholars would help protect them from the heavy hand of the wartime censor. At a special meeting of the Scientific Society, Hrushevsky told a hushed circle of Ukrainian activists about the persecution of the Ukrainian intelligentsia in Galicia. He said that the principal centre of émigré activity was now Vienna, that the SVU had been formed, and that the Galician representatives in the *Reichsrat* and provincial assembly had formed a Supreme Ukrainian Council, but that it had little influence since Austria did not count upon recovering the province. Hrushevsky also told the TUP leaders about a plan to form Ukrainian national legions in Austria and of the SVU plan to do political and cultural work among the many thousands of Ukrainians in the Russian ranks who were expected to be captured and taken as prisoners-of-war. It was late at night by the time the anxious circle decided to send a warning to the SVU: be cautious in pronouncements 'in the name of all Ukraine.' Such caution was necessary, Hrushevsky said, because there were irresponsible Ukrainian Socialist Revolutionaries in Vienna who were simply in the pay of the Austrian General Staff.[58]

By early the next morning, the Kiev police officials had received word that Hrushevsky was in the city, and they immediately searched his house in an attempt to arrest him. But, rising early, as was his habit, the historian had already gone away to a meeting. Upon learning that the police were at his home, Hrushevsky and his friends approached General Khodorovych of the Kiev General Staff and asked for an explanation. While Khodorovych made inquiries, Hrushevsky stayed at Baron Shteinhel's house. That evening Hrushevsky returned to the military headquarters and, in compliance with an order 'from up above,' was arrested. He was accused of 'Austrophilism' and locked up in Lukianivsky Prison.[59]

The veteran Ukrainian leader was not the only one to suffer. The outbreak of war had given the government and excuse for new repressions against the entire Ukrainian cultural movement. All Ukrainian-language publications were closed down and cultural activities ground to a halt. Florinsky and Shchegolev were active in Kiev, and what little Ukrainian activity there was now took place in Moscow and Odessa, where the censors were somewhat less strict. The TUP went completely underground.[60]

58 D. Doroshenko, *Spomyny pro nedavne mynule*, pp. 38–9. According to Wynar, 'Avtobiohrafiia M. Hrushevskoho z 1906 i 1926 rokiv iak dzherelo,' p. 130, this meeting took place on either 20 or 21 November. In the fall of 1914, Mykola Zalizniak (note 54 above) left the SVU to form a separate Committee which carried on anti-Russian activities in Bukovina. See D. Doroshenko, *Istoriia Ukrainy 1917–1923*, 2 vols. (Uzhhorod, 1932), I, 31. Andrii Zhuk, 'Prof. M. Hrushevsky i SVU,' p. 14, argues that the SVU was no less representative of the Ukrainian people than was the TUP, and minimizes the political differences between Hrushevsky and the SVU.

59 D. Doroshenko, *Spomyny pro nedavne-mynule*, pp. 39–41.

60 Ibid. Also see the contemporary note in *Ukrainiskaia zhizn*, no. 2 (Moscow, 1915), p. 81, and Chykalenko, *Shchodennyk*, pp. 448ff.

It did not, however, abandon its most famous member to his fate. While Hrushevsky sat in Lukianivsky Prison, and Russian police searched his home in occupied Lviv, efforts to obtain his release began. Dmytro Doroshenko was dispatched to Petrograd to lobby the members of the Duma on the professor's behalf. Some members seemed sympathetic, and Kerensky himself promised to go to Kiev and investigate, but in general the response was not enthusiastic. *Kievlianin* claimed that the professor had organized his Lviv students into Galician legions to fight against Russia. There were rumours that Hrushevsky was to be put on trial.[61]

The situation began to change when the Commander of the Kiev Military District, a certain General Trotsky, proposed to send Hrushevsky to Siberia for the duration of the war. With the help of Shakhmatov, Korsh, and Maxim Kovalevsky, a press campaign was waged for the release of the well-known historian. A committee of professors, with the rector of Petrograd University, D.D. Grimm, at its head, submitted a memorandum to the minister of education Count Ignatev, to the effect that Russia did not have so many professors that it could treat them in such a manner and that every university in Russia would be honoured to have Hrushevsky on its staff. Soon other universities and the Academy of Sciences seconded Grimm's appeal. They asked that, instead of Siberia, he should at least be allowed to settle in a city with a university.[62] Even the outspoken Ukrainophobe Peter Struve,[63] who was in the process of quitting the Kadet Party because of his hard line on the Ukrainian question, acknowledged that there had been no basis for Hrushevsky's arrest, that it was only a kind of

61 D. Doroshenko, *Spomyny pro nedavne-mynule*, pp. 39–41. Lototsky, II, 157, quotes *Kievlianin* (19 September 1914). In his *Avtobiohrafiia–1914–1919*, p. 99, Hrushevsky writes: 'From the very beginning of the war an order had gone out for me in Kiev: as soon as I should arrive, I must be searched, arrested, and sent to Siberia as the dangerous leader of the Ukrainian movement. And, in fact, four days after my arrival, they searched my home, took all my books and papers, and threw me into prison. The searches did not produce any evidence that I had anything to do with the formation of the Rifle Regiments and because I was so far removed from any Austrophile course, they could not find anything against me. They finished going through my papers and they wanted to send me to Siberia for Christmas, but since the Russian occupation authorities were then searching my house in Lviv and sending the collected material to the Kiev police, the fumbling about began anew and I was held in prison under very close guard and kept in solitary confinement. I was not even allowed to receive books from outside.' According to Kovalevsky, *Pry dzherelakh borotby*, pp. 171–2, who was also a Lukianivsky prisoner at the time, Hrushevsky's natural dignity and optimism soon won him the respect of his jailers. He also managed to communicate secretly with the other prisoners.

62 S. Iefremov and H. Semeshko, 'Prof. M. Hrushevsky,' *Kalendar kanadyiskoho Rusyna na rik 1917* (Winnipeg), pp. 177–82.

63 Struve's remarks are quoted in *Ukrainskaia zhizn*, nos. 3–4 (Moscow, 1915), 179, and also in Lototsky, II, 158.

preventive measure, and that the government had no business arresting 'people of learning' in the first place. Meanwhile, outside of the Russian Empire, as far away as New York City, Ukrainian emigrant workers held a public demonstration protesting the persecution of their National Leader.[64]

All these efforts were not in vain. 'Hrushevsky was supposed to be exiled to Siberia,' the historian writes of himself, 'but at the last minute a Petersburg friend, so *Novoe vremia* joked, succeeded in "inserting the letter M," and instead of Siberia, Simbirsk was made the place of exile.'[65] Hrushevsky remained in Simbirsk with his wife and daughter, was occasionally visited by oppositional politicians like Alexander Kerensky, and worked on a popular *Universal History* until the autumn of 1915, when, at the behest of the Academy of Sciences, the authorities transferred him to Kazan, which had a university. One year later, in September 1916, he was allowed to live in Moscow, but was still kept 'under close surveillance' and not allowed to visit Ukraine or to lecture or speak publicly.[66]

All this time the press campaign continued. There were caricatures of the professor in the liberal newspapers. They showed Hrushevsky decked out in a fur coat, his *History* under his arm, pursued by barking dogs bearing the names of the monarchist newspapers: *Novoe vremia, Moskovskie vedomosti, Kievlianin, Russkoe znamia,* and *Dvuglavii orel.*[67] Exile and the prohibition against public activity weighed heavily upon him, as did the destruction of Ukrainian life in Galicia and the suppression of the Ukrainian press in Russia. 'For the first time,' writes Lototsky, his old friend from university days in Kiev, 'the spirit of this strong character was broken. His letters to me were so sad that I was even ashamed of him; he answered that I did not understand him.'[68]

Despite Lototsky's impressions, however, even in Kazan and Moscow Hrushevsky does not appear to have given way to despair. Under the very eyes of the police, he initiated the reactivization of the Moscow TUP; he also helped edit Symon Petliura's *Ukrainskaia zhizn* and the sole Ukrainian-language weekly left in the empire, *Promin*; he was instrumental in the establishment of a publishing cooperative and the transfer of the work of the Ukrainian Scientific Society (UNT) to Moscow. And all the while he continued to work on his great *History.*[69] On the

---

64 C. Manning, 'Ukrainians and the United States in the First World War,' *Ukrainian Quarterly*, XIII (New York, 1957), 346–54, especially 349–50.
65 *Avtobiohrafiia–1926*, p. 85. According to *Ukrainiskaia zhizn*, no. 2 (1915), 81, Hrushevsky left Kiev on 20 February (Old Style).
66 Ibid., pp. 85–6.
67 M. Mukhyn, 'Prof. M. Hrushevsky (1866–1934),' *Vistnyk*, no. 3 (Lviv, 1936), 197.
68 Lototsky, II, 159.
69 *Avtobiohrafiia–1926*, p. 86. Also see O. Salikovsky, 'Pro odnu nenapysanu knyhu,' *Kalendar-almanakh 'Dnipro' za 1925 rik* (Lviv). In 1916, both the Moscow *Ukrainskaia zhizn*, no. 12, and

political level, police supervision did not prevent Hrushevsky and his colleagues from holding secret discussions with various oppositional figures among the Russians. The historian later wrote: 'Maksim Gorky came to us for consultations concerning a radical daily to be published by him. It was to have united all revolutionary and progressive forces. The future Russian dictator, Kerensky, came and called a conference on common action by representatives of various radical and revolutionary groupings. Thus I was well oriented in the stream of contemporary feelings, hopes, and plans.'[70]

As soon as was possible, Hrushevsky replied to *Kievlianin's* charges about the Galician legions, the Ukrainian Sich Riflemen. He said that he had always opposed the 'Austrian orientation,' had taken no part in the organization of the units, and was not responsible for the actions of his students, just as Professor Kulakovsky, the *Kievlianin* writer, was not responsible for his own, that is Hrushevsky's, Ukrainian position, even though he had once been a student of this very same Kulakovsky.[71] The scholar also mocked the latest monarchist accusations to the effect that Miliukov had invented the Ukrainian movement while he himself had only invented 'the idiotic Ukrainian grammar.'[72] In fact, by the beginning of 1916, he was exploring the limits of censorship by publicly deploring the official nationalism that, in its eagerness for war, had crushed the cultural development of the non-state peoples. He boldly refered to the war itself as that 'orgy of barbarism seizing the more cultured lands of the world.'[73] These were statements fully in keeping with his own attitudes and goals, but very much out of step with the patriotic enthusiasm of both the Russian government and its liberal critics. The difference was not without significance for the year of revolution that was so swiftly approaching.

When in February 1917 crowds of soldiers and citizens surged through the streets of Petrograd and overthrew the inept and unpopular government of Nicholas II, the 'Ukrainian question' had already emerged as a real issue of the day and Hrushevsky stood in the centre of the controversy surrounding it. From 1905,

the Vienna *Vistnyk Soiuz Vyzvolennia Ukrainy*, no. 127, celebrated Hrushevsky's fiftieth birthday with special issues in his honour.

70 M. Hrushevsky, 'Z nedavnoho mynuloho (selianstvo v revoliutsii),' *Pysmo z Prosvity*, nos. 7–8 (Lviv, 1922).

71 M. Hrushevsky, 'Vetkhii prakh,' *Ukrainskaia zhizn*, no. 10 (1915), 85–92, and also printed in the Kadet paper *Rech* (Petrograd), no. 281 (1915).

72 M. Hrushevsky, 'Neskolko slov ob Ukrainstve,' *Rech* (Petrograd), no. 156 (1916).

73 M. Hrushevsky, 'V godovshchinu voiny,' *Ukrainskaia zhizn*, no. 7 (Moscow, 1915), 5–8; 'Novyi god,' *Ukrainskaia zhizn*, no. 1 (1916), 5–9. From Chykalenko's diary (pp. 449–50), it is clear that Hrushevsky's inclination toward pacifism was secretly shared by a great many Ukrainian activists.

when he had first proposed decentralizing federalist 'correctives' to the constitutional plans of the Russian liberals, until 1914, when it came down to hard bargaining with Miliukov on the price of Ukrainian electoral support, Hrushevsky had set the tone to the Ukrainian cultural and political movement. In 1905, the historian had announced the entry of *Ukrainstvo* into Russian political life. The entry was a stormy one, plagued by the resistance of the bureaucracy and the vitriolic attacks of Russian nationalists. But by 1914, Ukrainian parties occupied a number of different points on the political spectrum and there were even mass demonstrations in the streets of Kiev. Thus Russian nationalist claims that the Ukrainians were merely a party and not a nationality could no longer be taken seriously; there could no longer be any doubt that the Ukrainian movement was a genuinely popular phenomenon and not the invention of a few dreamy intellectuals.

Hrushevsky stood at the head of the 'national-cultural movement,' and was convinced that it was liberating, enlightening, and progressive in nature. He thought this process to be natural and 'rational,' while he saw its enemies, the Russian autocracy and its 'nationalist' supporters, as being backward reactionaries standing in the way of popular education and civil liberty. Hrushevsky was the populist who had become the greatest living symbol of the Ukrainian national revival, even though he never once called himself a 'nationalist.' In fact, for this bearded and bespectacled professor, the terms 'nationalist' and 'nationalistic' even seemed to connote something negative, something exclusive, and something chauvinistic. It must be remembered that in general, in the pre-1917 Russian Empire, and especially in the western borderlands of this state, the term 'nationalist' was most frequently applied to conservative or reactionary monarchists, especially the members of Savenko's Russian Nationalist Club. These were the protagonists of 'all-Russian' (*obshcherusskii*) culture who were the enemies of the Ukrainian national movement. The mainstream of the Ukrainian movement, on the other hand, was considered to be 'autonomist-federalist' by its participants and 'separatist-Mazepist' by its foes.

The situation was somewhat different in Austrian Galicia, where the national movement was already more intense. Here Hrushevsky was not so much the outstanding symbol of the national revival as he was the symbol of pan-Ukrainian unity. In Galicia, he was still the conscience of the national cause, but after 1905, as he continually shifted the focus of his activity to Russian Ukraine, the pugnacious historian became more and more impatient with the realities of Western Ukrainian political life. This led one perspicacious Polish critic to think that Hrushevsky was just an old-style radical from the east, who, like his Russian models, did not understand constitutionalism and underestimated the value of real cultural achievements for the sake of abstract and inexorable principles.[74] Among his fellow Ukrainians too it was no surprise that, upon the outbreak of hostilities in 1914, the patriarch of *Ukrainstvo* returned to his beloved Kiev.[75]

In the years that preceded the war and revolution, Hrushevsky's position on the national question seems to have had two sides. On the one hand, he stood for the entry of the non-state peoples into public life and the transformation of the Russian Empire into a federal state. Timely concessions by this state would benefit its population and ensure it a prolonged life; inflexibility would only bring its destruction. Such was Hrushevsky's prognosis for the immediate future.

The distant future was another matter. It seems that, like Antonovych, Hrushevsky saw deep historical forces at work behind the national question. These forces – geographic, social, and economic – were unrelenting and were part of a historical process that would shake the Russian state to its very foundations. Thus, while he thought decentralization to be inevitable, he also looked ahead toward some sort of national independence. In fact, for Hrushevsky, full independence was a consistent and logical culmination of national development. Along with Franko he had stressed this point in 1899 in Lviv at the foundation of the Ukrainian National Democratic Party, and he ventured to mention it again in 1905 in the midst of his polemics on the national question in Russia.[76] This vision of future statehood and independence was the other side of his approach to the national question.

After 1905, however, Hrushevsky was either unwilling or unable to state his distant goals as clearly as he did his immediate objectives. His philosophic vision of future possibilities fell into the background as he became more involved in practical politics in the Russian Empire. His discussion of the question of independence, which had never been very extensive, receded as the rhetoric of

---

74 See Kulczcki, *Ugoda polsko-ruska*, pp. 40–1, who considers Drahomanov to have been a multifaceted European, in contrast to Hrushevsky, whose thought, he says, 'from certain vantage points carries traits of barbarism.' In what seems to be a reply to the Austrophile and Polonophile Dontsov, who had accused Hrushevsky and the autonomists of 'Modern Muscophilism,' Kulczycki writes: 'Prof. Hrushevsky is not a Muscophile, only a Ukrainian nationalist, but all his sympathies lie with the Russian state. Being a sort of (philosophical) radical, he is still able to come to an agreement with people in Russia who have nothing in common with radicalism and he directs all his hatred against the Pole whom he considers more dangerous to the Ukrainians [*Rusinów*] than are the Russians.'

75 See, for example, Volodomyr Levynsky, *Tsarska Rosiia i ukrainska sprava* (Montreal, 1917), pp. 105–7. Levynsky, who was a Ukrainian Social Democrat, thought Hrushevsky merciless in his criticism of Austria and the Poles, but an 'opportunist' in the Russian sphere.

76 See the quote from Hrushevsky's 'Edinstvo ili raspadenie?' *Ukrainskii vestnik*, no. 3 (Saint Petersburg, 1906), in Levynsky, *Tsarska Rosiia*, pp. 105–7.

federalism came to the fore. During the war, in spite of numerous difficulties, he continued to publish extensively on the evils of centralization and the travail of the Ukrainian and other non-state peoples.[77] By 1917, his stand in favour of the full national development of all peoples, his concern for weak and scattered minorities, his condemnation of extreme nationalisms of all sorts, his objection to imperialism, and his consistent promotion of Ukrainian autonomy had probably made him the most celebrated federalist thinker in the Russian Empire.

77 See the discussion in Levynsky, *Tsarska Rosiia*, who refers primarily to Hrushevsky's articles in the wartime Russian press. Simultaneously, however, the SVU was translating and reprinting selections from his works in other lands. (Hrushevsky had checked this material and given his permission for their publication during his brief stay in Vienna in 1914. See Zhuk, 'Hrushevsky i SVU.') The most widely circulated essay, which appeared in French and German as well as English, was his *Historical Evolution of the Ukrainian Problem* (English edition, London, 1915; reprinted in Cleveland, 1981). It aroused an immediate response. See, for example, the defence of the Polish historical role in Ukraine by Dr Czef. [Czesław Frankiewicz?], *Poglądy historyczne Prof. M. Hruszewskiego w kwestji ukraińskiej w świetle krytyki naukowej* (Lublin, 1916). Even Franko, shortly before his death, in a letter (4 November 1915) to SVU member V. Doroshenko, expressed impatience with the wide circulation given Hrushevsky's writings and made an angry reference to his 'false historical conceptions.' For obvious reasons, Soviet interpreters – in books, political pamphlets, and even radio broadcasts – have read too much into this remark. Doroshenko explains it as the anxiety of a dying man at not having his own most recent work published by the SVU. See Doroshenko, 'Ivan Franko i Mykhailo Hrushevsky,' pp. 17–18.

6

The Struggle for a Ukrainian State 1917–1918

During the last days of February 1917, troops of the Petrograd garrison, and, in particular, members of the Volhynia training regiment, which consisted largely of raw Ukrainian recruits, refused to shoot at the crowds of workers and women who had for some days filled the streets of the Russian capital demanding 'bread and freedom.' The rebels were soon joined by other regiments. and it was not long before police officials and the tsar's ministers were hiding in fear of the revolutionary mobs. Power devolved to the streets, to a spontaneously formed worker and soldier council or 'soviet' in which labour leaders and socialist politicians played a leading role, and to a more conservative committee of the Duma. The latter, in consultation with the new Petrograd Soviet, hastily formed a provisional government. The power of Nicholas II had dissolved and the once powerful Romanov monarchy came to an abrupt end.[1]

When word of the revolution in Petrograd reached Kiev, the Commander of the Kiev Military District, that same General Khodorovych who had reluctantly arrested Hrushevsky some three years before, called together a committee of the various local civic organizations to help preserve order. At first, the Ukrainians seemed to be well represented in this committee and Baron Shteinhel was elected chairman; later on, however, as the initial euphoria and confusion passed, the Civic Committee (IKSOO) was seen to be a more purely Russian institution associated with the new Provisional Government. On another level, the Kiev

---

1 The Ukrainian role in the Petrograd events is described by Lototsky, III, 314–21, and is mentioned in most general histories of the revolution. Pavlo Khrystiuk, *Zamitky i materiialy do istorii ukrainskoi revoliutsii,* 4 vols. (Vienna, n.d.; reprinted New York, 1969), I, 9, claims that the Petrograd Ukrainian organizations 'had prepared' the Volhynians for their revolutionary actions. Some contemporaries later saw it as rough justice which compensated for the rape of occupied Lviv during the war. See, in particular, the idiosyncratic but often perceptive reflections of Dr K.U., *Pershyi napad Rosii na Lviv (1914) v 40-littia kontr-napadu Ukraintsiv na Peterburh (25. II. 1917–1925. II, 1957)* (New York, 1957).

proletariat, which was still largely made up of Russian or Russified workers, emulated their Petrograd counterparts and formed a council, that is soviet, which similarly looked to the north for inspiration. Simultaneously, however, the Ukrainian leaders, Hrushevsky's TUP associates, formed their own council – Rada in Ukrainian – which quickly attracted the support of the various Ukrainian organizations and transformed itself into a 'Central Rada' to represent all Ukrainian national interests. Though he was still in Moscow, Hrushevsky was elected head of the new institution. It was expected that his arrival would help settle disputes as to the relative representation of the various Ukrainian organizations and parties. Hrushevsky's wife, Mariia Sylvestrivna, was in close contact with the influential TUP leaders and by telegraph informed the exiled professor of the rapid succession of events.[2]

In Moscow, Hrushevsky immediately began to lobby the new authorities concerning traditional Ukrainian grievances – censorship, police restrictions on Ukrainian publications, the closure of Ukrainian societies and institutions, etc. – to which was now added the liberation of those surviving Galicians who had been arrested and exiled during the war. 'At the beginning of March,' writes Hrushevsky, 'when Kerensky, who was already a member of the revolutionary government, arrived in Moscow, I tried to see him since I had known him well for a very long time.'

I wished to bring to his attention those Ukrainian grievances which we had so recently discussed when he had visited me at Simbirsk. But I found out that old ties had lost their power now that my old acquaintances and friends were sitting in the places of the old tsarist ministers! The people to whom I turned simply refused to let me see Kerensky; they claimed that the man on whom the fate of all Russia now depended did not have time for such petty concerns. This was the attitude of our friends of yesterday toward our grievances. Only by letter could I remind Kerensky of the most pressing concerns to which the new lords of Russia had to attend.[3]

Despairing of achieving anything concrete in Moscow, the professor answered the call of his TUP friends and boarded a train for Kiev.

Hrushevsky's trip to Kiev did not pass without incident. During the night a fire suddenly broke out in the sleeping-car in which the professor was travelling. He

2 On the role of the Civic Committee, compare the hostile account of Khrystiuk, I, 13–16, and the more favourable one of Dmytro Doroshenko, *Istoriia Ukrainy 1917-1923,* 2 vols. (Uzhhorod, 1930–2; reprinted, New York, 1954), I, 40–3. More generally, see Oleh Pidhainy, *The Formation of the Ukrainian Republic* (Toronto, 1966), pp. 33–44. For the role of Mariia Sylvestrivna, see Ie. Chykalenko, *Uryvok z moikh spomyniv za 1917* (Prague, 1932). p. 10.

3 Hrushevsky, 'Z nedavnoho mynuloho.'

barely managed to escape with his life, and all of his things, including his clothes and some rare sixteenth-century Ukrainian books that he had been carrying, were destroyed in the fire. At five in the morning of 14 March, that is, about two weeks after the outbreak of the revolution, and two days after a great Ukrainian demonstration in Petrograd – the first such demonstration since 1914 – it was a very tired scholar who walked home in his underclothes, coat, and slippers, through the quiet streets of the City of Saint Volodymyr.[4]

The next day, Hrushevsky immediately went to the Pedagogical Museum building, a graceful monument of local architecture decorated with Ukrainian motifs which the Central Rada had begun to use for its sittings. 'I remember his arrival,' a young cooperative worker recalled many years later. 'I was standing in the "lobby" of our parliament with a few military officers. The entrance doors opened, and in walked Hrushevsky. Everyone immediately recognized him: his grey beard, glasses ... But [we were stunned by the sudden appearance of this legendary figure and] no one could utter a word when he said: "My name is Hrushevsky. Is the Central Rada somewhere in here?"'[5]

It usually was, but on that particular day, a Kiev district cooperative workers' congress was taking place in the Museum building. The congress welcomed the bearded historian and immediately elected him its honorary president. It was not long before the cooperators passed a resolution demanding reorganization of the empire into a federal republic with territorial autonomy for Ukraine.[6]

The following day, the Central Rada, with Hrushevsky now at its head, called for the assembly of a 'Ukrainian National Congress' to express the wishes of the nation. Local Russian leaders reacted negatively, and at a joint meeting of representatives from the Civic Committee, the Kiev Soviet, and the Central Rada, Hrushevsky and the other Ukrainian activists, Vynnychenko and Doroshenko, faced angry questions from the champions of 'Russian Democracy.' The latter feared that the National Congress would turn out to be a Ukrainian Constituent Assembly which would locally supplant the role of the All-Russian Constituent Assembly that was being planned in Petrograd. Hrushevsky tried to calm Russian fears and explained that although the Ukrainians did, in fact, want autonomy, this

---

4 *Avtobiohrafiia–1914–1919*, p. 99. In this autobiography, Hrushevsky notes that travel was very difficult in the days immediately following the revolution. D. Doroshenko and F.P. Matushevsky waited for him until 4:00 a.m. See the former's *Spomyny pro nedavne-mynule*, p. 87. For the exact date see Doroshenko, *Istoriia*, I, 44.

5 M.I. Mandryka, 'Deshcho za roky 1917 ta 1918 (Prodovzhennia),' *Ukrainskyi istoryk*, nos. 3–4 (1977), 75–82, especially 78–9.

6 The congress also demanded immediate use of the Ukrainian language in the schools, courts, and all civil and government institutions. One delegate was applauded when he called out 'for a free Ukraine, for independence, and for our native language and its use in school!' See Doroshenko, *Istoriia*, I, 46; Khrystiuk, I, 17–18.

was in no way contrary to the revolutionary slogans of decentralization and the self-determination of peoples. The Congress would only sanction the Central Rada. Propounding the centralist postion, Nezlobin, the Russian SR and chairman of the Workers' Soviet, angrily replied that 'the demand for autonomy is a stab in the back for the Russian revolution,' and that 'Russian Democracy would answer all attempts at carrying it out with bayonets.' Hrushevsky ended by asking ironically: 'With whom have we met here? With friends or with enemies?'[7]

Revolutionary celebrations and meetings filled the next few days, and in view of Nezlobin's threats, the Ukrainians tried to appear as strong as possible and began calling their compatriots to Kiev from various outlying towns. On 16 March, the streets were filled with yellow and blue standards, as well as red flags, as crowds celebrated 'the holiday of liberty.' The following day Hrushevsky participated in a conference which discussed ways of putting an immediate end to administrative repressions in occupied Galicia and Bukovina.[8] On the 18th, the first Ukrainian secondary school opened and the City Council decided to switch to Ukrainian-language instruction at the school founded by Hrushevsky in honour of his father.[9] Finally, on Sunday, 19 March, the Ukrainian organizations staged the greatest national demonstration that the city had yet seen.

At the prescribed time thousands of workers, schoolteachers, schoolchildren, soldiers, marching bands, civilians of all kinds, and even government officials filled the streets and paraded under the Ukrainian flag and portraits of Shevchenko. They marched to the central square before the City Council building. Hrushevsky joined the members of the Kiev Prosvita Society and marched along. Bystanders could easily spot him by his long beard and glasses. At the City Hall, General Khodorovych saluted the parade, and on behalf of the city government, Baron Shteinhel welcomed the marchers and pointing to Hrushevsky said: 'Before you stands the finest son of Ukraine, her spiritual leader, the martyr for the sake of her rebirth who has just now returned from exile.' The crowd burst into enthusiastic cheers: '*Slava batkovi Hrushevskomu!*' The historian then addressed the throng. He spoke of Shevchenko and the Cyril-Methodian ideals and the need to build a free autonomous Ukraine 'within a free league [*spilka*] of peoples of the Russian Federative Republic'; he asked the crowds to swear before the symbols of the

---

7 See Iakiv Zozulia, *Velyka ukrainska revoliutsiia ... kalendar istorychnykh podii za liutyi 1917 roku – berezen 1918 roku* (New York, 1967), p. 9. Doroshenko *Istoriia*, I, 57, explains that even at this early date Hrushevsky conceived autonomy to be organized locally and only later to be sanctioned by the All-Russian Constituent Assembly. Khrystiuk, I, 31–2, makes an important point of Hrushevsky's final remark. Also see Doroshenko *Spomyny pro nedavne-mynule*, pp. 91–2, and R. Mlynovetsky, *Narysy z istorii ukrainskykh vyzvolnykh zmahan 1917–1918rr.* (Toronto[?], 1970), pp. 155–8, who gives a detailed description of this meeting.

8 Zozulia, *Kalendar*, p. 10.

9 Doroshenko, *Istoriia*, I, 41–2.

nation never to abandon these ideals. With outstretched arms the assembly cried: 'We swear! We swear!' Amidst further cheers and patriotic songs Hrushevsky was lifted over the shoulders of the crowd to the balcony above. More speeches, more song, and further acclaim followed. Afterwards, the assembly moved on to Saint Sophia square, where official resolutions on autonomy were drafted and, amidst church bells and general acclamation, a priest spoke out for 'one's own power, truth, and freedom in one's own home.'[10]

This first great demonstration of Ukrainian strength was of considerable significance. The crowds had numbered over one hundred thousand people and for the first time, as contemporaries noted, thousands upon thousands of ordinary workers and city people had joined in. One of the TUP stalwarts later recalled: 'By its grandiose character, by its life-giving spirit, and by its enthusiasm, it surpassed all of our expectations. For the first time, we all felt the solid ground below our feet; we felt ourselves masters in our own house. After the demonstration, the congresses began.'[11]

The first meeting that was held during the period of organizing and conventions that followed was the TUP Congress of 25 March. Hrushevsky, of course, was elected chairman. The gathering opened with the TUP executive proposing a resolution concerning the gradual enactment of Ukrainian autonomy by 'legal' means. Then quite unexpectedly, in a fiery speech, Hrushevsky proposed a resolution of his own urging the immediate introduction of autonomy so that other problems – social questions and the expected peace with the Central Powers – could be quickly dealt with. A young delegate from Petrograd, Oleksander Shulhyn, spoke against the historian's resolution and pointed to the difficulties – with large, hostile minorities, and Russian forces quartered in Kiev and all across Western Ukraine – that too fast a pace would provoke. In the end, though both speeches were heartily applauded, the executive's resolution, which stressed legality, passed easily, and the historian was left somewhat dissatisfied.[12]

---

10 The text of Hrushevsky's speech along with the resolutions and a general description of the Ukrainian demonstration is given in *Visti z Ukrainskoi Tsentralnoi Rady u Kyivi*, no. 2, 19 March 1917; reprinted in *Ukrainskyi istoryk*, nos. 1–3 (1978), 152–9, especially 153. There is also a very detailed description in N. Hryhoriiv, *Spohady 'Ruinnyka': iak my ruinuvaly tiurmu narodiv a iak my buduvaly svoiu khatu* (Lviv, 1938), pp. 166–73.

11 Doroshenko, *Spomyny pro nedavne-mynule*, pp. 88–90.

12 Shulhyn [Alexandre Choulguine] writes in his *L'Ukraine contre Moscou (1917)* (Paris, 1935), pp. 108–9, that Hrushevsky 'parlait avec une conviction profonde, appuyée sur une ample et très logique argumentation. Il témoigna d'un grand esprit de prévoyance en émettant des doutes sur les capacités du gouvernement provisoire pour accomplir sa tâche. Au moment où tout le monde voulait encore être optimiste (on n'était que le 25 mars, 1917), Hrouchevsky fut le prophète du mal et de l'anarchie qui devaient venir.' Also see Hrushevsky's brief comments on 'the minimalism of the moment' in 'Z nedavnoho mynuloho,' and Oleksander Shulhyn, 'Mykhailo Serhiiovych

At the same congress, it was decided that the TUP would transform itself into a regular political party called 'the Union of Ukrainian Autonomist-Federalists.' The various component units were to be given considerable room for 'self-determination.' Hrushevsky's sometime critic Serhii Iefremov was elected leader.[13] At a separate meeting of one of the organizations affiliated with the TUP, Chykalenko proposed to renew the publication of *Rada* under the name *Nova Rada*. However Hrushevsky objected, saying that *Rada* had never been very popular. Chykalenko replied that his son, who had just returned from Petrograd, had said that *Rada* had already had an enormous influence among the guard regiments there and that it was imperative to renew it immediately. Chykalenko got his way and *Nova Rada* appeared shortly afterward. But the historian's relations with the TUP veterans were turning decidedly cool.[14]

In spite of these disagreements, Hrushevsky still contributed to *Nova Rada*. His articles immediately changed the tone of the Ukrainian pronouncements. Gone were the pious greetings to the Provisional Government; gone was the self-imposed concentration on purely cultural goals. 'A great moment has come!' the historian exclaimed. 'The chains that were the cunning policy of the Muscovite Tsardom have fallen from Ukraine.'

Nothing could be more erroneous than to dig out the old Ukrainian petitions and again hand them over to the government as a statement of our present demands ... If our demands of five, four, three, and even one year ago had been granted then, they would have been accepted by Ukrainian society with deep gratitude ... but they can in no way be considered a satisfaction of Ukrainian needs, 'a solution to the Ukrainian question' at the present moment! The Ukrainian question no longer exists. What does exist is a free and great Ukrainian people which weaves its fortune in the new conditions of freedom.

Hrushevsky then appended his own program, a program that reflected the enthusiasm aroused by the great national demonstration of the previous week. The timid counsels of the TUP liberals were left far behind as he wrote: 'We must feel the pulse of national [*narodnoho*] life and enter into the rhythm of its being. It will be the only law by which we will abide. We will announce it to all whether they

---

Hrushevsky: iak polityk i liudyna,' in *Zbirnyk na poshanu Oleksandra Shulhyna (1889–1960)*, *ZNTSh*, vol. CLXXXVI (Paris–Munich, 1969). 143–55. This disagreement is not mentioned in standard histories of the revolution like that of Doroshenko, *Istoriia*, I, 50.

13 Ibid.; Zozulia, *Kalendar*, p. 11.

14 See Chykalenko, *Uryvok z moikh spomyniv za 1917*, pp. 12–13. who complains that Hrushevsky sometimes revealed an ambivalent attitude toward the 'bourgeois' daily *Rada*.

like it or not.' This was to be done gently and tactfully, but decisively and without let-up. He concluded: 'The will of our people must be done.'[15]

Hrushevsky's turn to the left did not go unnoticed among his older colleagues. 'We, the collaborators of Mykhailo Serhiiovych, his true old guard,' Doroshenko writes, 'began to observe, with no little astonishment, that he was no longer with us. He frequented the clubs of the young SRs, began to take counsel with them, and to surround himself with them, while he spoke with and advised us very little.'[16] When old friends broached the subject in private conversations, the historian explained that real power now lay with the youth and that the masses would quickly follow their lead. Therefore, it would be better to stand at their head from the beginning and thus prevent too much extremism. Of course, some of the veterans accepted Hrushevsky's explanations, but this did not prevent a certain amount of resentment at his desertion to the left, especially when he avoided the company of his former friends and did not advise them to follow him into the ranks of the new organizations.[17] Later on, both the TUP veterans and the more purely nationalist elements, that is, those people who stood for complete independence, would accuse the historian of betraying his non-partisan position at the head of the entire Ukrainian national movement for the sake of populist theory and the adulation of the youth. But in the beginning, Hrushevsky's enormous prestige and undeniable ability swept all before it and the various parties rallied around this living symbol of the nation.

During these first months, Hrushevsky set out to explain the Ukrainian ideals in the simplest way so that as many people as possible could become acquainted with them. To a population which had recently been forbidden the very use of the term 'Ukrainian,' he explained who the Ukrainians were and what they wanted. Shevchenko, he thought, had decided the nomenclature; an autonomous Ukrainian

15 M. Hrushevsky, 'Velyka khvylia,' *Nova Rada* (Kiev), no. 1, 25 March 1917; reprinted in *Vilna Ukraina* (New York, 1918), and in *Vybrani pratsi*, pp. 113–16. Also see the brief discussion in Richard Pipes, *The Formation of the Soviet Union* (New York, 1974) [originally published 1954], p. 54. M. Ieremiiv, 'Za lashtunkamy Tsentralnoi Rady (Storinky zi spohadiv),' *Ukrainskyi istoryk*, nos. 1–4 (1968), 103, writes that, at first, the Central Rada had 'a purely patriarchal character, but with Hrushevsky's return to Kiev, and his eager appearance among the Ukrainian political parties, everything changed and vital political action began.'

16 Doroshenko, *Spomyny pro nedavne mynule*, pp. 87–8.

17 Ibid. Chykalenko, *Uryvok*, says that Hrushevsky felt that he alone could see that power had passed to the street and that a new era had opened. Lototsky, III, 356, explains that Hrushevsky avoided him so much that, in order to discuss the reasons and consequences of his desertion, he had to go call on him uninvited and during the very early hours of the morning. It might be added that when Lototsky had first arrived in Kiev on 25 March, Hrushevsky managed to pacify a number of Central Rada members who were incensed at Lototsky for the moderate stance of the Petrograd Ukrainian National Council (ibid., p. 348). Also see Shulhyn, *L'Ukraine contre Moscou*. p. 110.

legislative assembly (*soim*) would decide the political and economic questions.[18] To those who were unfamiliar with federalist theories and the idea of autonomy, he explained just what autonomy was, and why 'a full political autonomy approaching complete independence' was the most desirable political arrangement for Ukraine.[19] He also published some new historical studies, the most important of which concluded that Ukraine had retained the right of statehood (*derzhavne pravo*) after the Treaty of Pereiaslav (1654) in which the Ukrainian population swore fealty to the Muscovite tsar. These events seemed to take on great significance in 1917 when the bonds of loyalty to the Romanov monarchy were dissolved and the question of Ukraine's constitutional status seemed reopened.[20] He also republished a number of other works as well.[21]

On 6 April, following the various party congresses, the Ukrainian National Congress finally met. On this clear spring day, about nine hundred delegates from all parts of Ukraine approved of the general course taken by the Central Rada; they recognized it as the legislative organ of the Ukrainian people, and urged the immediate organization of autonomy to be later confirmed by the All-Russian Constituent Assembly. Then came the reelection of the president (*holova*) of the Rada. One of the younger delegates later recalled:

The entire congress with a single voice and great enthusiasm elected Mykhailo Hrushevsky in an open vote. But he insisted upon a secret ballot, foreseeing that our enemies would cast a shadow upon the propriety of the election and criticize its openness. For this reason the congress went through the long procedure of secret balloting which resulted in the unanimous election of Mykhailo Serhiiovych.[22]

18 M. Hrushevsky, *Khto taki Ukraintsi i choho vony khochut* (Kiev, 1917). On pp. 3–4, he recalls the importance of Shevchenko and writes: 'It was not long before the difference between the name of the Little Russians and of the Ukrainians was felt. All people of Ukrainian background who were indifferent to both Ukraine and Ukrainian life called themselves Little Russians. While those people who cared about and set as the goal of their life the welfare of the Ukrainian people called themselves Ukrainians. This was not publicly discussed, but it was felt, and the government took note of it and the authorities and the censor began to suspect the name Ukraine and remove it from books and newspapers.'

19 M. Hrushevsky, *Iakoi my khochemo avtonomii i federatsii* (Kiev, 1917), and reprinted in *Vybrani pratsi*, pp. 142–9. In this essay Hrushevsky distinguished six different forms of social organization: (1) full Centralism; (2) administrative or bureaucratic decentralization; (3) narrow or wider self-administration (*samouprava*); (4) narrow or wider autonomy; (5) incomplete or non-sovereign statehood; (6) completely independent statehood. Ukraine, he thought, was best suited to fit into the second last category.

20 M. Hrushevsky, *Pereiaslavska umova Ukrainy z Moskvoiu 1654 roku* (Kiev, 1917).

21 See, in particular, the collection of historical essays *Z polytychnoho zhytia staroi Ukrainy: rozvidky stati promovy* (Kiev, 1917), and the collection of short stories *Sub divo* (Kiev, 1918).

22 Kovalevsky, *Pry dzherelakh borotby*, p. 281. Actually, there were a few votes against Hrushevsky as opposed to 588 in favour. See Doroshenko, *Istoriia*, I, 59.

There were elections to the Rada as well, and these were carried out according to a formula worked out by the historian. The formula integrated both the party and the territorial principles and was meant to be the first step in the country's autonomous reorganization. The territorial subdivisions were meant to be both electoral units and governmental districts, which would themselves retain a degree of autonomy and eventually include the representatives of the national minorities – Russians, Jews, and Poles – as well.[23] Since the Peasant Union (*Selianska spilka*) was the strongest national organization in all parts of the country, the Ukrainian SRs (UPSR) who predominated in it soon obtained an absolute majority of delegates to the Central Rada. In view of their wider experience and higher education, the more moderate elements led by the Ukrainian Social Democrat (USDLP) Vynnychenko and the Autonomist-Federalist Iefremov did retain a dominant role in the Rada's presidium. The whole congress, as contemporaries unanimously relate, was carried out in a pleasant atmosphere in which venerable cultural activist and passionate young military conscript freely mixed. By this time, the ever-present Hrushevsky clearly symbolized the unity of the nation, and in particular, the continuity of the national movement from elderly Ukrainophile to youthful patriot.[24]

In the weeks following the Ukrainian National Congress, Hrushevsky retained his position at the centre of the national movement. In articles published in *Nova Rada* he argued that all Ukrainians now agreed upon a program of national-territorial autonomy and federalism. This was, he argued, the moderate, middle, position, between simple apolitical cultural aspirations and a program of complete independence. The persecutions and repressions of 1914–17 had already destroyed the base for the first position and there could be no return to it; further displays of Russian centralism would only push the Ukrainians toward full independence.[25] Hrushevsky argued that all over the Russian Empire the various nationalities – Lithuanians, Belorussians, Estonians, Latvians, and Moldavians – were busy organizing their own lives. Ukrainians must do so too, and on the life-or-death question of national autonomy, they could not afford to delay and put

23 Doroshenko, *Istoriia*, 1, 60.
24 Kovalevsky, *Pry dzherelakh borotby*, p. 281; Doroshenko, *Istoriia*, 1, 60, and *Spomyny pro nedavne-mynule*, pp. 93–5; Khrystiuk, 1, 38–9; Hryhoriiv, *Spohady 'Ruinnyka,'* pp. 240–6. Also see B. Martos, 'Pershi kroky Tsentralnoi Rady,' *Ukrainskyi istoryk*, nos. 3–4 (1973), 99–112, who, admitting to the presence of some workers and villagers, considers the congress to have been primarily a gathering of the Ukrainian intelligentsia. Outsiders like the Zionist A.A. Goldenveizer. 'Iz Kievskikh vospominanii,' in S.A. Alekseev, ed., *Revoliutsiia na Ukraine po memuaram Belykh* (Moscow–Leningrad, 1930), p. 6, remark upon Hrushevsky's 'magical authority' over this multitude.
25 M. Hrushevsky, 'Povorotu-nema,' in his collection of articles *Vilna Ukraina* (Kiev, 1917), and *Vybrani pratsi*, pp. 117–20.

all their trust in some projected All-Russian Constituent Assembly in which centralist tendencies might prevail. The Ukrainian ideals must be immediately put into action.[26] Of course, the historian advised, all extremism must be avoided. The minorities must be guaranteed their rights, and contacts must be established with 'our closest brothers, the Belorussians.' The Hungarian and Polish models, which proclaim national liberty while at the same time oppressing other peoples, must be avoided. He concluded: 'We will firmly oppose all chauvinist tendencies ... The defenders of the Ukrainian nationality will not be nationalists.'[27]

While Hrushevsky discoursed upon the advantages of a free Ukraine, his ideas were already being put into action. It was not a simple matter. For example, the Ukrainian soldiers quartered in Kiev were particularly anxious to form their own military units. There were disputes between the soldiers and the local military authorities. The Central Rada supported the soldiers while the Civic Committee opposed them. Cabinet changes in Petrograd ensued and the war minister, Alexander Guchkov, and the foreign minister, Paul Miliukov, resigned.[28] Meanwhile, on 23 April, after prompting from Petrograd, the Kiev Soviet leaders attempted to form a united council/soviet/rada of worker, peasant, and soldier deputies. From the start, conflicts broke out between the Russian-dominated worker delegation and the Ukrainian-dominated peasant delegation. Nezlobin was elected chairman and there were no Ukrainians on the presidium. The peasants managed to get Hrushevsky elected honorary chairman, but when the Russians tried to reduce village representation, the peasants walked out in protest. That was the end of the united council.[29]

The end of May and the beginning of June saw Vynnychenko and a delegation from the Rada travel to Petrograd to present the Ukrainian demands to the Provisional Government. Both the government of Prince Lvov and the

26 M. Hrushevsky, 'Vid slova do dilia,' *Vilna Ukraina* and *Vybrani pratsi*, pp. 121–5.
27 M. Hrushevsky, 'Narodnostiam Ukrainy.' Also see 'Chy Ukraina tilky dlia Ukraintsiv?' Both are in *Vybrani pratsi*, pp. 126–32. As early as March, a Jewish lawyer from Chernyhiv, Arnold Margolin, had met with Hrushevsky to discuss the widening of the national movement beyond its traditionally narrow ethnic and party base. Margolin, *Ukraina i politika Antanty: zapiski evreia i grazhdanina* (Berlin, n.d.), p. 54, writes that 'Hrushevsky understood me from the very first words that I spoke, and he agreed with me. But at that time he was simply inundated with work at the Central Rada, and apparently was unable to carry through to completion the respective reform in the structure of the Ukrainian parties.' Margolin was of liberal disposition, a friend of Illia Shrah, and defence counsel in the Beilis case.
28 Guchkov had visited Kiev at the time of the Ukrainian National Congress but would not agree to the formation of Ukrainian regiments. He and Miliukov resigned on 5 May. M. Mikhnovsky, a true nationalist who stood for complete independence, and other members of the nationalist Polubotok Club began organization of the Ukrainianized Bohdan Khmelnytsky Regiment immediately after Guchkov's departure from Kiev.
29 Doroshenko, *Istoriia*, 1, 72–3; Zozulia, *Kalendar*, pp. 12–14.

Menshevik-led Petrograd Soviet were unsympathetic; only the Bolsheviks recognized the theoretical right of the Ukrainians to self-determination.[30] Meanwhile, Hrushevsky remained in Kiev, where he continued to chair the sessions of the Central Rada and various other meetings. He was given an especially warm reception at the First All-Ukrainian Congress of Peasants, which, in fact, was practically a convention of the strongly SR Peasant Union. It was a very large gathering and many country schoolteachers attended. The congress was still in session when a telegram from the Petrograd government arrived: the demands for immediate autonomy were rejected. The Ukrainians were advised to wait for the proposed All-Russian Constituent Assembly. With an acute sense of drama, Hrushevsky, just as he was closing the congress, read out the telegram to the crowds, and concluded: 'The holiday of the revolution has ended. The time of danger has come! Ukraine must be organized! Only the Ukrainian people should decide its own future!' The audience answered with loud cheers of 'Long live a free Ukraine. We will build our own life!' The congress sent 133 new members to the Central Rada.[31]

A few days later, delegates began arriving in Kiev for the Second All-Ukrainian Military Congress, which had been forbidden by the new war minister, Alexander Kerensky. The city administration even threatened to disperse the congress by force of arms. Nevertheless, under the protection of the Ukrainianized Bohdan Khmelnytsky Regiment, the soldiers met in the Kiev Opera House. Meanwhile, Hrushevsky and the Rada leaders, now thoroughly convinced of the need for unilateral action, prepared a 'Universal' or special manifesto to the nation. The basic text of the Universal, which was essentially a declaration of Ukrainian autonomy, is said to have been composed by Vynnychenko, but there is no doubt that Hrushevsky completely agreed with the contents. When the deputy chairman of the Rada, the moderate Serhii Iefremov, hesitated to sign the document, both Hrushevsky and Vynnychenko, as a witness relates, 'set about convincing Serhii

---

30 Vynnychenko, I, 156–84, gives a moving account of the hostile reception in Petrograd. He says that 'peace and land' lay at the heart of the Ukrainian demand for autonomy. Kovalevsky, *Pry dzherelakh borotby*, pp. 334–42, gives an even more detailed picture of the reception. The Ukrainians from the guard regiments, he says, were exuberant; Prince Lvov was polite but made no concessions; Victor Chernov, the SR minister in charge of land reform, was optimistic about Russian democracy but had suddenly turned into a convinced centralist; the Menshivik, Chkheidze, who headed the Soviet, was rude and completely hostile, and Maksim Gorky, who was close to the Bolsheviks, could give Vynnychenko no firm commitments.

31 Khrystiuk, I, 65-8; Doroshenko, *Istoriia,* I, 82–3. Also see Borys Martos, 'Pershyi vseukrainskyi selianskyi z'izd,' *Kalendar 'Dnipro' na rik 1940* (Lviv), and reprinted in the *Journal of Ukrainian Studies,* no. 6 (Toronto, 1979), 20–8, who describes the warm welcome accorded Hrushevsky. The telegram and related documents are collected in R.P. Browder and A. Kerensky, *The Russian Provisional Government 1917 Documents,* vol. I (Stanford, 1961), pp. 376–9.

Iefremov of the necessity for the promulgation of this first historic act of the Ukrainian people.'

Mykhailo Hrushevsky nervously stroked his grey beard and finally, unable to bear it any longer, put the text of the First Universal in front of Iefremov, and pointed with his finger to the most important part which proclaimed Ukrainian autonomy. Serhii Iefremov took thought for a moment, reread the text, and finally stood up and said to us: 'We are taking a great responsibility upon ourselves.' Later he added: 'I agree to this text of our First Universal.'[32]

Thus the declaration of Ukrainian autonomy was unanimously approved by the various Rada leaders, that is, by the Presidium. Immediately afterwards, it was also carried in a full session of the Central Rada, whose members rose to greet the declaration with stormy applause. That evening the soldiers at the Military Congress heard the news. They shook the walls of the Opera House with their enthusiasm.[33]

The next day, at a solemn ceremony in Saint Sophia Square, in the presence of Hrushevsky and the members of the Central Rada, of the Ukrainian hierarchs and clergy, and of an enormous throng of civilians and soldiers, the Universal was read out to the nation. When the words 'From today the Ukrainian people will create its own life' were pronounced, thousands broke into cheers. The ringing of church bells, patriotic songs, and parades followed. Hrushevsky took the salute of the new Ukrainian regiments. Non-Ukrainians greeted him as well. The colonel of a Don Cossack regiment saluted the professor and said in Russian: 'Mister President! The Don Cossacks salute a Free Ukraine and its government!'[34]

The Ukrainian reaction to the First Universal exceeded the expectations of the Rada leaders. National organizations suddenly sprang up throughout the country and voluntary financial contributions flowed into Kiev from the villages. Even the

---

32 Kovalevsky, *Pry dzherelakh borotby,* pp. 351–3. According to Kovalevsky, the commission for drafting the Universal was formed from all parties, but unlike the plenary sessions of the Rada it did not have an SR majority, and an SR draft proposal was turned down as too revolutionary and lacking an explanatory apparatus; Vynnychenko's more moderate phraseology, which included an appendix about hopes for good future relations with the Russians, was accepted instead. Both Vynnychenko and Hrushevsky, says Kovalevsky, believed that the document should lay out the basic state structure. The text of the Universal is given in Zozulia *Kalendar,* pp. 65–8, and is translated in Taras Hunczak, ed., *The Ukraine 1917–1921: A Study in Revolution* (Cambridge, Mass., 1977), pp. 382–5.

33 Volodymyr Kedrovsky, *1917 Rik Spohady* (Winnipeg, 1967), pp. 133–40, and Kovalevsky, *Pry dzherelakh borotby,* pp. 353–4, give vivid descriptions of Vynnychenko's sudden appearance at the congress and his reading of the Universal.

34 Kovalesky, *Pry dzherelakh borotby,* pp. 355–6; Zozulia, *Kalendar,* p. 17.

heavily Russified and generally hostile City of Kiev was temporarily overawed by the strength of the Ukrainian response.[35] On the other hand, Russian reactions were uniformly negative. Prince Lvov went over the heads of the Central Rada leaders with an appeal to the Ukrainian people that advocated revolutionary unity. *Rech,* which in the past had consistently objected to monarchist insinuations against both Hrushevsky and the Ukrainian movement, now angrily called the act 'yet another link in the German plan to dismember Russia.'[36]

When the Universal was proclaimed, the Provisional Government was in the process of launching its major offensive against the Germans and could give the matter little attention. Nor could it react to the subsequent formation of a General Secretariat or Ukrainian administration. It was the end of June before the new foreign minister, M. Tereshchenko, and the minister of posts, I. Tsereteli, arrived in Kiev, where they were joined by Kerensky, who was on his way home from the front. Only then did real negotiations with the Rada leaders begin.[37]

35 Kovalevsky, *Pry dzherelakh borotby,* pp. 357–60; Doroshenko, *Istoriia,* I, 93; Borys Martos, *The First Universal of the Ukrainian Central Rada* (New York, 1968); reprinted from *The Ukrainian Quarterly,* XXIV, no. 1 (New York, 1968). The essay by Martos is directed primarily against the next generation of Ukrainian nationalists who criticized the moderation of the 'autonomists,' Vynnychenko and Hrushevsky, and maintained that the national mood and political situation justified a declaration of independence. See, for example, Petro Mirchuk, *Ukrainska derzhavnist 1917–1920* (Philadelphia, 1967), p. 85, who claims that even Hrushevsky in his writings of the time 'asserted that it would not have been difficult to separate Ukraine from Russia at that moment.' Mirchuk, however, neither quotes Hrushevsky to this effect, nor cites a reference.

36 See the 'Appeal of the Provisional Government to the Ukrainian People,' and '*Rech* on the First Universal' in Browder and Kerensky, I, 385–7. After the revolution, it was a very bitter Miliukov who complained that the Provisional Government had from the beginning tried to accommodate the Ukrainians. 'But from Kiev came ever greater demands emanating from a ready plan for the national-territorial detachment of Ukraine in its widest bounds. "Father" M.S. Hrushevsky was the inspiration for these strivings,' claimed Miliukov, 'for he had acquired experience in the national struggle in the Austrian Slav arena in Galicia, and now applied to the struggle with Petrograd "centralism" those indirect and subtle strategies that had already been tried in the struggle with Vienna ... The content of the "Universal" was very characteristic of Hrushevsky's policy. On the one hand, he in no way broke the formal tie with the central government; on the other hand, in actual fact, he entered into open combat with the government, using its tolerance and passivity to widen and deepen the base of the Ukrainian movement, the limited and intellectual character of which was involuntarily contained in the Universal itself." See P. Miliukov, *Istoria Vtoroi Russkoi Revoliutsii, Tom Pervyi,* in 3 parts (Sophia, 1924), I, 154–5, 159–60.

37 Doroshenko, *Istoriia,* I, 110–11. Tereshchenko was born in 1888 into a Ukrainian peasant family that had grown rich in the wheat trade during the Crimean War. The family invested in sugar refining and soon possessed large estates in the Kiev area. Tereshchenko had been an Octobrist to 1917, and moved leftward thereafter. He had no contacts with the national movement, but, according to Doroshenko (p. 112), 'displayed a certain local patriotism,' almost exclusively hiring local people, that is, Ukrainians, to run his estates. Tsereteli was a Menshevik leader and the son of a famous Georgian poet.

On 29 June, Hrushevsky, Vynnychenko, and Petliura met with the Petrograd ministers in the Central Rada Building. The Ukrainians assured the ministers that they were not separatists, as the Russian press was claiming. Hrushevsky explained that federalism and autonomy were the traditional aspirations of the Ukrainian people. Petliura said that there were nationalists, especially in the army, who were much more radical than the majority in the Rada. These, he said, exercised the same pressure in Ukraine as did the extremists and Bolsheviks in Petrograd. Vynnychenko, it seems, laid out a plan for Ukrainian autonomy in which the newly created General Secretariat would have full administrative powers and be responsible to the Central Rada. This was rejected by the ministers. Negotiations continued and at 5:00 p.m., Hrushevsky went outside to take the salute of the Ukrainian army – the Bohdan Khmelnytsky and Polubotok Regiments – that paraded past the building in which the negotiations were taking place. The timorous ministers remained inside during the parade, but Kerensky ventured out afterward and the soldiers greeted him. By the next day, a compromise was reached. A General Secretariat 'responsible to the Rada and subject to confirmation by the Provisional Government' would become 'the highest regional authority of the Provisional Government in Ukraine.' The national minorities would enter the Rada and Ukrainian military units were to be permitted 'in so far as they be deemed technically feasible by the minister of war.' The Rada acknowledged that it would not arbitrarily establish autonomy before the convocation of the All-Russian Constituent Assembly. These points were to be announced in a Second Universal of the Central Rada and a special 'Declaration' by the Provisional Government.[38]

Hrushevsky seemed to be pleased by the agreement. When the Second Universal and Declaration were read to a plenum of the Rada, he declared: 'We are passing to a higher stage and are getting *de facto* autonomy for Ukraine with a legislative and an administrative organ – the Rada and the Secretariat. We have to be aware of the fact that having got these organs, everyone and everything must submit to them in order [for the Central Rada] to pass from a moral form of

38 The fullest descriptions of the negotiations, in which Hrushevsky and Tsereteli seem to have been the major players, is in I.G. Tsereteli, *Vospominaniia o fevralskoi revoliutsii,* 2 vols. (Paris–The Hague, 1963), II, 138–49. According to Doroshenko, *Istoriia,* I, 112–13, who cites a contemporary pamphlet by Hrushevsky: *Ukraina i Rosiia* (Kiev, 1917), Kerensky was generally silent, but in a separate meeting with the Ukrainian Military Committee objected to national-territorial reorganization of the army. Tereshchenko proved a moderate, and Tsereteli thought all 'misunderstanding' could be ironed out if only the correct wording could be found. According to Tsereteli (p. 142), Hrushevsky 'spoke Russian with difficulty and continually mixed in Ukrainian expressions.' Tsereteli thought that Petliura was 'even more inclined to extremism' than were Hrushevsky and Vynnychenko, but all realized that 'the vast majority of Russian Democracy' would go only so far.

authority to a legal one.'[39] The assembly responded heartily and the Universal was accepted with a comfortable majority.

The satisfaction, however, was short-lived. Even before the Second Universal had been issued, the Ukrainian Democratic-Agrarian Party, which was made up of small landholders, and a strongly nationalist Union of Ukrainian Statehood, inspired by Mykola Mikhnovsky, began to call for complete independence.[40] Such sentiments were also strong in the Polubotok Regiment, and in response to the compromise with Petrograd, and when news came of the failure of the military offensive against the Germans – that is, on the night of 5 July – the regiment surrounded the Rada building and took control of the main points in Kiev. When all power was in their hands, the soldiers hoped that the Rada would feel confident enough to declare immediate independence, call the army back from the front, and conclude a separate peace with the Central Powers. The Bohdan Khmelnytsky Regiment, however, after some hesitation, remained loyal to the Rada and disarmed its nationalist comrades. The Rada was saved and the Polubotok men were eventually compelled to depart for the front. At the insistance of the Russian authorities, the Bohdan Khmelnytsky Regiment soon followed them.[41]

The Rada had only survived at the price of its revolutionary momentum. After the failure of the Polubotok coup, the radicals in the army, especially those nationalists who sympathized with Mikhnovsky and his group, would no longer look to the Central Rada for leadership. Hrushevsky and his followers were blamed for losing a golden opportunity, for giving up real independence for the sake of a precarious legal autonomy, and for disbanding the national army at the very moment when it was most needed. Among the socially conservative Ukrainian nationalists who had given real direction to the soldiers' demands for demobilization and land, Hrushevsky was hereafter labelled a spineless autonomist and an ineffectual pacifist who had betrayed the national cause. It was a charge that would grow with the years and would eventually come to dominate one school of thought in the history of the Ukrainian revolution.[42]

39 In Doroshenko, *Istoriia*, I, 16, who writes: 'This was the moment of triumph for Hrushevsky's policy, and the Central Rada gave its leader a fitting ovation.' For the Ukrainian text of the Second Universal see Zozulia, *Kalendar*, pp. 68–70, and for an English translation see *The Ukraine 1917–1921: A Study in Revolution*, pp. 385–7. The Declaration of the Provisional Government is in Browder and Kerensky, I, 389–90.

40 See the discussion in Pidhainy, pp. 119–20.

41 Ibid., pp. 121–5; Doroshenko, *Istoriia*, I, 364–9; Zozulia, *Kalendar*, pp. 19–21.

42 See, for example, the memoir of P. Mlynovetsky, 'Do tak zvanoho' 'Polubotkivskoho perevorotu,''' in *Almanakh Kalendar Homonu Ukrainy 1962* (Toronto), pp. 159–66, and his later history *Narysy z istorii ukrainskykh vyzvolnykh zmahan 1917–1918* (Toronto, 1970), which considerably exaggerates the strength of the movement for independence and bitterly attacks Hrushevsky's autonomism.

The Second Universal and the compromise it represented had equally significant repercussions in Petrograd. Though Prince Lvov and a majority of his ministers accepted the arrangement and the liberal paper *Den* saw the compromise as a personal victory for Tsereteli and Tereshchenko and 'a severe blow for the Ukrainian nationalists,'[43] four Kadet ministers, including A.I. Shingarev, resigned in protest. Some observers even thought that the ministers had been outwitted by Hrushevsky. In *Rech* (7 July 1917) the influential Kadet jurist, Baron Nolde, called the agreement 'an undoubtedly one-sided act of legalistic state trickery which on one side reflects the experienced hand of an old European warrior raised in the school of subtle political formulas and complex political in-fighting, and on the other side, the inexperienced and completely unwarranted revolutionary enthusiasm [of the Petrograd ministers].'[44] Given the objections, the criticism, and the reluctant approval that the Kiev agreement elicited from both the Russian and the Ukrainian sides, there is no doubt that it was a true compromise in which both parties had made significant concessions.[45]

Once the agreement with the Provisional Government was reached, and the Russian, Jewish, Polish, and other minorities entered the Central Rada, the operation of this 'revolutionary parliament' began to take on a regular form. The minorities entered both the full Rada, which sat from time to time, and also the executive General Secretariat and the smaller legislature, the 'Mala Rada,' which was in continual session.[46] In fact, the assembly functioned much like a parliament in the Western sense. Hrushevsky and the presidium sat in the centre of the main assembly hall of the Pedagogical Museum facing a semicircle of legislators. The Autonomist-Federalists, who in keeping with the spirit of the times were now

43 See '*Den*' on the Second Universal,' in Browder and Kerensky, I, 393–4.
44 In Doroshenko, *Istoriia*, I, 117. Nolde's fierce criticism of the agreement seems to have been more directed against judicial vagueness and legal contradiction than against the actual principle of autonomy. The article is also quoted at length by Miliukov, *Istoriia Vtoroi Russkoi Revoliutsii*, I, 232–5. who says that Prince Lvov's cabinet had not given the 'Triumvirate' the power to conclude an agreement in Kiev. Hrushevsky (*Ukraina i Rosiia*, p. 7, cited by Doroshenko, *Istoriia*, I, 113) says that the ministers told him that 'they had been given full powers to come to an agreement with the Central Rada.' After the resignation of the Kadet ministers, which, Miliukov informs us, was not due to the Ukrainian question alone, 'the ministers of the Kadet Party of National Liberty, in order to show that they had nothing at all against the regional autonomy of Ukraine ... put regional autonomy into their party program and created a commission to work out a bill on the subject' (p. 236).
45 This is the thesis of Iakiv Zozulia, 'Druhyi universal ukrainskoi tsentralnoi rady ta ioho pravno-istorychna vartist, '*Vilna Ukraina*, nos. 55–6 (1967), 10–16.
46 On 12 July the eighteen representatives of the minorities first participated in the Mala Rada. (The full Rada ended its first sitting 1 July, the day after the departure of the Petrograd ministers.) The Kiev Civic Committee accorded the various non-Ukrainian parties and organizations their seats. For a breakdown of the representation, see Zozulia, *Kalendar*, p. 20.

renamed the Socialist-Federalists, and the other moderates were in the first rows in the middle. They were surrounded by row upon row of members sporting the grey military clothing that marked one as a 'comrade' and was then the fashion even in civilian circles. These were the SRs, the representatives of the Peasant Union, the non-party socialists, the Social Democrats, and the members from the minorities. A conservative Ukrainian observer writes:

In the middle was the President, Prof. M. Hrushevsky. Of course, it would have been difficult for him to hide his bourgeois affiliation because everyone could see his beautiful six-storey stone house in Kiev, and his highly cultured manner was visible to all. But the long grey beard and universally respected authority of 'father Hrushevsky' covered everything. His youthful deputy, the twenty-two-year-old student Mykola Shrah (son of the famed activist, Illia Shrah), and two young secretaries, Mykhailo Ieremiiv and Mykola Chechel, both in military attire – entirely typical 'comrades' – stood in strange contrast to him.[47]

All accounts agree, however, that Hrushevsky chaired the assembly with great skill. 'He ran the sessions of the Rada quietly but authoritatively,' writes the Ukrainian Social Democrat Borys Martos, 'so that complete order reigned even in the plenary sessions of the Great Rada in which over seven hundred people participated. Moreover, many in this multitude were unaccustomed to such gatherings.'[48] With prompting and a little leeway from the president, even the most awkward and rustic of speakers managed to make his point and sit down. With some difficulty, Hrushevsky was even able to control the galleries, which were often filled with young students or soldiers who were quick to let their preferences be known. At the same time as he was doing this, he corrected the proofs of his latest essays and delighted in joking on the side with Ieremiiv that this speaker was a common 'prattler' while that one was a lofty 'nightingale.'[49]

47 Doroshenko, *Spomyny pro nedavne-mynule,* p. 157.
48 Borys Martos, 'M.S. Hrushevsky iakym ia ioho znav,' *Ukrainskyi istoryk,* nos. 1–2 (1966), 74–5. Martos continues: 'As a participant, I can testify that at the sessions of the Central Rada there was such order as is not always apparent in Western parliaments. I do not recall any Rada member using rough or abrasive language in the heat of a polemic; nor do I recall any group shouting down a speaker as sometimes happens in parliament, nor do I recall a case of parliamentary obstruction.'
49 Ieremiiv, 'Za lashtunkamy Tsentralnoi Rady,' p. 102–3; Martos, 'Hrushevsky,' pp. 74–5, adds by way of criticism that he was often irritated when Hrushevsky allowed a boring or repetitive speaker to carry on too long. 'But now,' Martos reflects, 'I understand Hrushevsky's condescension in this matter. He was acting like a father to them, allowing for their inexperience in public speaking because under the regime of the tsars almost none of the common people had an opportunity to take part in such assemblies.' The historian's phenomenal ability to work, and even do two things at the same time aroused the ire as well as the admiration of his contemporaries. A few months later,

As President of the Rada, Hrushevsky fulfilled other functions as well. It was his task to mediate disputes between the various Ukrainian political parties. Although he was unsuccessful in achieving a concensus that would include all the national minorities, he did have a powerful influence upon the Ukrainians.[50] For a long time he held the passionate and impatient SRs in check, while they gained badly needed experience in public life. The old professor seemed to be instructing almost everyone. Martos recalls accidentally stumbling into a session of the Commission on the Constitution in which Hrushevsky was lecturing to a panel of novice jurists upon the principles of Western constitutionalism.[51] Only the very young seemed to be able to keep up with the ubiquitous scholar. 'He was a veritable powerhouse of energy,' his admiring secretary, Ieremiiv, later wrote, 'and with rapid movements, and clear and concrete expressions, he passed on this energy to the young. He walked very quickly, and always ran through the vestibule of the Central Rada building, and our older people were greatly irritated by this.'[52]

While Hrushevsky chaired the Central Rada in Kiev, events in Petrograd moved quickly. The failure of the Bolshevik insurrection and the resignation of the Kadet ministers, and then of Prince Lvov, left Alexander Kerensky as the strongman of the Provisional Government. And with the defeat of the Bolsheviks, the new premier felt strong enough to reject the Rada's detailed bill putting into effect the principles of the Second Universal. Instead, Kerensky sent a 'Temporary Instruction' to the Rada's General Secretariat. This Instruction narrowed the geographical base of the Central Rada's authority and also limited the competence and Ukrainian character of the General Secretariat which was now cast in the role of an 'organ of the Provisional Government.'[53]

Vynnychenko noted in his diary (*Shchodennyk*, vol. I [Edmonton–New York, 1980], p. 288) that 'I have given all of my attention throughout all of this year to the creation of the Ukrainian state, but I just do not have the ability of Hrushevsky to use everything for my own good and proof read brochures while at the same time announcing the law of the Ukrainian Republic.'

50 Margolin, p. 52, writes: 'There was no struggle of parties, but rather a struggle of nations in the Central Rada, and this made for an abnormal situation ... It is true, the Zionists and the Folkspartai always took a neutral position, and the Poles had no really defined policy, but this did not change the general impression.'

51 Martos, 'Hrushevsky,' pp. 76–7; Kovalevsky, *Pry dzherelakh borotby,* p. 392, remarks that Hrushevsky carried out all these functions from a small office, hidden almost in the basement of the Pedagogical Museum, which was crowded with committees and departments of various sorts.

52 Ieremiiv, 'Za lashtunkamy,' p. 102.

53 On 16 July, the Mala Rada passed a 'Statute for the General Administration of Ukraine,' which clearly stated that a General Secretariat of fourteen portfolios was to control the entire administration of Ukraine and be responsible to the Central Rada. (Text in Zozulia, pp. 79–80, and in Browder and Kerensky, I, 394–6.) A delegation carried this statute to Petrograd and was urged to be firm in its discussions with the government. Kerensky avoided the Ukrainian delegation and sent his 'Instruction' to Kiev instead. It limited the authority of the Rada to Kiev, Poltava, Volhynia, Podillia, and part of Chernyhiv gubernia, reduced the Secretariat to nine portfolios and insisted that

This breach of the earlier compromise caused a great commotion in Kiev. For three days the issue was hotly debated in the Rada. The SRs insisted that the Instruction be rejected. In view of the growing power of the Provisional Government, and the absence of the Ukrainian military units, Vynnychenko and the moderates devised a resolution that strongly criticized the Instruction but took it 'into consideration.' This formula was accepted by a slim majority, but, nevertheless, it caused great indignation among the SRs, who fiercely criticized Vynnychenko and even turned against Hrushevsky, who, though he may have urged firmness in negotiations with Petrograd, seems to have stood close to Vynnychenko on how to react to the Instruction. Hrushevsky offered to resign, but the SRs declared that they still had confidence in the presidium and would not accept his resignation.[54] Questioning of Vynnychenko continued, however, and upon his resignation, the more moderate Doroshenko, who was believed to have useful connections in Petrograd, was asked to form a new General Secretariat. In the eyes of Hrushevsky and the SRs, however, Doroshenko's program proved too conciliatory and he too was induced to resign.[55] Once again, it fell to Vynnychenko to form a cabinet.

While Vynnychenko gathered together his third and most moderate cabinet, the general mood in Russia shifted steadily to the right. In view of Petrograd's continued resistance to Ukrainian demands, the Ukrainian SRs (UPSR) turned more and more toward the work of arousing the masses and establishing connections with the other 'non-state' peoples of the former Russian Empire who aspired toward autonomy or independence. In the compromise worked out by Tsereteli and Hrushevsky, the Rada leaders had been asked not to encourage the national movements of the other non-state peoples of the empire; but when Kerensky discarded this agreement, the Ukrainians felt free to strengthen their connections with these movements.[56]

---

four of these be held by non-Ukrainian representatives. The first article reads: '... The General Secretariat, appointed by the Provisional Government from recommendations submitted by the Central Rada, shall be the highest organ of the Provisional Government with jurisdiction over matters of local government in Ukraine.' See the text in Browder and Kerensky, I, 396–7, and the discussions in Khrystiuk, I, 113–4, and John S. Reshetar, *The Ukrainian Revolution* (Princeton, 1952), pp. 68–71.

54 Doroshenko, *Istoriia*, I, 131–2.

55 Ibid., pp. 134–5, and *Spomyny pro nedavne mynule*, pp. 160–3. Doroshenko states that although Hrushevsky was the most severe critic of his program of cooperation with the Provisional Government, he also wanted him to remain at his post 'at any price.' The SRs, however, had already come to an agreement with Vynnychenko. Also see Kovalevsky, *Pry dzherelakh borotby*, p. 415.

56 Kovalevsky, *Pry dzherelakh borotby*, p. 404, explains that at the time of the compromise, Tsereteli, in particular, insisted that the Rada not support the other non-Russians. He writes: 'Russian circles stood in fear of a Ukraine that would stand at the head of a block of the old empire's non-Russian peoples who were trying to renew their own statehood.'

Hrushevsky, in particular, had always advocated cooperation among the non-state peoples. As early as April, the Ukrainian National Congress had called for a 'Congress of Peoples' to initiate such cooperation. As soon as the General Secretariat had been formed, it had declared the convocation of a Congress of Peoples to be one of its principal tasks.[57] Invitations now went out to the Belorussians, the Baltic and Caucasian peoples, the Cossacks, Moslems, Jews, and Poles. On 8 September, some hundred delegates from these nationalities gathered in Kiev for a congress that lasted a full week. The Provisional Government reluctantly acknowledged the existence of the congress and sent its representative. Hrushevsky, it seems, had put much effort into the gathering and in consequence was elected its honorary chairman. In his keynote address, he welcomed the delegates, outlined the Ukrainians' historical commitment to federalism, and, in response to Russian criticism, said that Ukrainian federalists did not see their program as a step toward independence, but rather 'in those other terms which have been expounded by the progressive thinkers of humanity; that is, the road toward a European federation, and then a federation of the whole world.'[58] In its final resolutions, the congress called for a restructuring of the state along national and federal lines; it called for the guarantee of proportional

---

57 Volodymyr Soiko, 'Z'izd narodiv u Kyievi 1917 roku,' *Ukrainskyi istoryk,* nos. 3–4 (1977), 14–25. This declaration was made on 27 June (Old Style), that is before the Petrograd ministers had come to Kiev. For the text, see Zozulia, *Kalendar,* p. 81ff. Presumably Tsereteli had tried to have the congress postponed or cancelled, but when the Instruction finally arrived, Hrushevsky and the Rada leaders went ahead with the project.

58 Hrushevsky's remarks deserve quotation at length: '... I have to declare that for the Ukrainian federalists (who form the principal tendency in Ukraine) and for all the great mass of the people of Ukraine, federalism is not a transitory step toward state independence! On the contrary, for us Ukrainians, state independence does not lie in the future but in the past. We have already experienced life as an independent state. On the basis of the Treaty of Pereiaslav which guaranteed our state rights we joined Russia, but the old dynasty illegally took away these rights of ours. The Ukrainian people has never given up these rights, just as other peoples, who have also possessed state independence, have not given them up either. And, when we now announce the principle of federalism, we declare our will in the sense of confirming the maintenance of our state rights. But at the same time, we do not see federalism as a step toward independence, but rather in those other terms which have been expounded by the progressive thinkers of humanity; that is, the road toward European federation, and then federation of the whole world.' Printed in *Svobodnii soiuz* (Kiev), no. 1, October 1917, 30–1, and reprinted in Stoiko, 'Z'izd narodiv,' p. 24. Also see 'Promova Prof. Hrushevskoho (na z'izdi narodiv v Kyievi),' *Ukrainske slovo* (Lviv), no. 248 (1917), 1. In his description of the Congress of Peoples, Miliukov, *Istoriia Vtoroi Russkoi Revoliutsii,* III, 100–3, who was in Petrograd at the time, once again dismissed Hrushevsky's rhetoric and claimed that, while independence was officially rejected, 'in private declarations, the Ukrainians often acknowledged that federation was only a step for them toward full independence.' On the other hand, according to Stoiko,'Z'izd norodiv,' the Finns did not attend and the Poles only sent observers because both of these peoples were already determined upon independence.

representation and personal autonomy for scattered peoples and minorities like the Jews. The resolutions specifically mentioned autonomy for Belorussia and Latvia, the right of the Cossacks to an independent existence, and Provisional Government recognition of the right of the Lithuanians to a sovereign statehood, which would include Prussian Lithuania and certain lands that had already been promised to the Poles. The congress also resolved to found a permanent Council of Peoples (*Rada narodiv*) to be based in Kiev. Hrushevsky was elected its first president.[59]

The general drift to the right, which had preceded the Congress of Peoples, climaxed on 27 August, when General Kornilov pronounced himself dictator and declared his intention of saving the country from complete anarchy. In fact, the action had exactly the opposite effect. Democrats everywhere rallied to the banner of liberty, and in Kiev, Ukrainians, supporters of the Provisional Government, and Bolsheviks joined together in a Committee to Defend the Revolution. While Kornilov was arrested and incarcerated near Mohyliv on the upper Dnieper, in Kiev more conservative military personnel were dismissed and the monarchist newspaper *Kievlianin* was temporarily closed down.[60] Chykalenko heard that, had the plot succeeded, Kornilov's followers intended to charge with high treason and hang Hrushevsky, Chykalenko himself, and even Professor Antonovych, who had died several years before.[61]

The revolution, it seemed, was saved, but what little order had existed now disappeared. The military was in complete disarray. The Bolsheviks now openly organized armed detachments of Red Guards, and small Ukrainian landholders organized vigilante units of 'Free Cossacks.' While the Congress of Peoples was still in session, the Mala Rada with its SR majority, over the objections of the members from the minorities, passed a resolution calling for a Ukrainian Constituent Assembly.[62] It appeared that Hrushevsky, who at the very beginning

59 The council was given the task of publishing a bi-monthly journal to propagate the federal cause. The first issue of *Svobodnii soiuz* contained the congress deliberations; the second contained a brief article by Hrushevsky, 'Chas probil' (listed in Oleh and Oleksandra Pidhainy, *The Ukrainian Republic in the Great East European Revolution: A Bibliography*, vol. VI, part 2 [Toronto–New York, 1975], p. 152.) The congress resolutions are also given in Khrystiuk, II, 20-3, and Stoiko, 'Z'izd narodiv,' pp. 18–20. The Ukrainian historian later attempted to draw European attention to these events in his article: 'The Congress of the Allogenian [sic!] Peoples of Russia,' *Eastern Europe*, I, no. 5 (Paris, 1919). Insinuating disloyalty to Russia, Miliukov, *Istoriia*, III, 100–3, later maintained that only 'a specific political trend' was represented at the Congress of Peoples. In fact, among many nationalities the decision to attend was a sign of preference for a pro-Russian solution to the national question. For the example of the Estonians and Latvians see the brief discussion in G. von Rauch, *The Baltic States* (London, 1974), p. 31.

60 Doroshenko, *Istoriia*, I, 145–6; Zozulia, *Kalendar*, p. 24.

61 Chykalenko, *Uryvok z moikh spomyniv za 1917*, p. 24.

62 Doroshenko, *Istoriia*, I, 155–6; Zozulia, *Kalendar*, p. 24.

of the revolution had broken with his older colleagues on this issue, was about to see his plans put into action.

In private UPSR conferences, Hrushevsky warned his followers that the revolution was reaching its climax and that the collapse of Russia was now inevitable. He outlined the three forces opposing the Ukrainians – reactionary monarchist generals, Kerensky's inflexible Russian Democracy, and revolutionary Bolshevik centralists – and said that it was necessary to mobilize all the SR forces and strengthen the kernel of the Ukrainian state. The SRs had been left out of Vynnychenko's last cabinet, and Hrushevsky explained to them that they were 'that revolutionary reserve which must take power at the critical moment.'[63] About this same time, the historian paid a visit to his old friend, the moderate Chykalenko. 'He was in a very bold mood, and exuded confidence,' the publisher later wrote of his historian friend.

In the summertime, he had written to me [while I was in the countryside] ... saying that my absence from Kiev had affected him personally very deeply. Now, however, he lacked for nothing, because he enjoyed a great popularity among the majority of the Central Rada members, who were almost all either real or false SRs. I tried to caution Hrushevsky against the SR approach to the agrarian question in Ukraine, because it would make everyone who owned more land than the working norm into an enemy of the Ukrainian state, and one could not build a state on the basis of the proletarian class alone. He answered by saying that he would adhere to the majority: whatever it decided, so it would be. I expressed the fear that the anarchy that was breaking out everywhere might once again produce a monarchy and we would only be left – God willing! – with Ukrainian schools. He only smiled, like an old experienced man at a naive boy.[64]

By 17 October, it seemed that a fresh conflict with the Provisional Government could not be avoided. Word spread that a judicial investigation concerning the declaration about a Ukrainian Constituent Assembly had been ordered, that funds for the General Secretariat had been held up, and that Vynnychenko and other secretaries were ordered to Petrograd.[65] The Third All-Ukrainian Military

---

63 Kovalevsky, *Pry dzherelakh borotby*, pp. 417–8. It is possible that Kovalevsky grants Hrushevsky rather too much foresight.

64 Chykalenko, *Uryvok*, p. 24.

65 Vynnychenko, *Vidrodzhennia natsii*, II, 58–9; Doroshenko, *Istoriia*, I, 157. This version is accepted by Reshetar, p. 80, and Pidhainy, p. 164. There is no doubt that Vynnychenko and other secretaries were ordered to Petrograd to explain 'reports on agitation in Ukraine in favour of convoking a sovereign Constituent Assembly' (Browder and Kerensky, I, 401), but many years later Kerensky denied all knowledge of judicial proceedings against the Central Rada as a whole, and, according to Borshchak, Hrushevsky was also unaware of any. See O. Kerensky [A. Kerensky],

Congress, one of the largest of all the Ukrainian congresses, was then convening, and it supported the secretaries and suggested that they should not go to the Russian capital. The assembly received Vynnychenko and Hrushevsky warmly and, as usual, elected Hrushevsky as its honorary president. In his major speech, Hrushevsky discussed the question of a Ukrainian Constituent Assembly and for the first time mentioned the possible establishment of a 'Ukrainian People's Republic' (*Ukrainska Narodnia Respublyka*). He urged the Ukrainian soldiers to join together with the Central Rada and said that he was confident that the national-political struggle would conclude successfully. 'Hrushevsky's words about the creation of a Ukrainian People's Republic,' writes a close observer, 'elicited an enthusiastic response from the congress. They got a long and thunderous reception.'[66]

On 24 October, three secretaries, Vynnychenko, Steshenko, and Zarubin, decided to test the intentions of the Provisional Government and they left for Petrograd. When they arrived in the Russian capital, however, the Provisional Government no longer existed. The Bolsheviks under Lenin and Trotsky had taken control of the city, toppled Kerensky's government, and formed a 'Council of People's Commissars' to govern the country. These were the basic events that came to be sanctified in Communist historiography as the Great October Revolution. By evening, the news had reached Kiev, and Hrushevsky immediately called an emergency session of the Mala Rada. That same night a 'Committee of the Land in Defence of the Revolution in Ukraine' was formed. The next few days saw Kiev turn into an armed camp with three rival centres of power: the Central Rada continued to sit in the Pedagogical Museum, the Bolshevik-dominated Soviet of Workers' and Soldiers' Deputies occupied the former Imperial residence, and the supporters of Kerensky gathered around the military staff headquarters. At an emergency meeting of the City Council, the old Russian nationalist leaders, Hrushevsky's monarchist enemies, Shulgin and Savenko, joined together with the Russian SRs, Kadets, and Mensheviks in support of

---

'Chy rosiiskyi tymchasovyi uriad buv rozpochav sudove slidstvo proty tsentralnoi rady?' *Ukraina*, no. 9 (Paris, 1953), 795–6.

66 Khrystiuk, II, 39–40. Of course, this did not imply support for total Ukrainian independence. For example, *Nova Rada*, no. 169, reported that when the representative of the Socialist-Independentist Party – Mikhnovsky's nationalist followers – a certain Makarenko, made his opening remarks and tried to explain his party's position, 'he was not able to finish, since the President of the Congress [presumably Hrushevsky] cut him off, saying that he must only greet the congress and not explain his party's program . . . A certain part of the congress supported this intolerant position of the President and did not even allow him to finish his greeting, cutting off his every word.' In Doroshenko, *Istoriia*, I, 159–60.

Kerensky, and at the same time fiercely attacked the Central Rada. Fighting broke out between the Bolsheviks and the Staff, that is, Provisional Government supporters, and at one point, the latter had batteries of artillery trained on the Rada Building.[67]

A Cossack Congress called pro-Kerensky Don Cossacks back from the front and the Staff recalled the Czech legion and other units favourable to the Provisional Government. The approach of the disciplined Czechs threatened to upset the balance of power and on the night of 27 October, in hurried discussions of the Mala Rada, Hrushevsky urged direct negotiations with them; others suggested bombarding the legions as they approached the city. Hrushevsky's position was narrowly carried and the next day Czech emissaries met with Hrushevsky and Vynnychenko and happily declared their neutrality in the struggle for Kiev.[68] This same day, fighting between the Bolsheviks, who were trying to take over the city, and forces loyal to the Provisional Government was reaching a climax. At the critical moment, the Rada threw its support behind the rebels and occupied strategic points in the city. Ukrainian units now more or less controlled Kiev. The General Secretariat was immediately enlarged by several portfolios and now claimed jurisdiction over all nine gubernias with a clear Ukrainian majority. Galician prisoners were finally freed from their camps and the Ukrainian Sich Riflemen stood at the disposition of the Central Rada. In the Mala Rada, Hrushevsky presided over discussions on the proclamation of the Ukrainian People's Republic. Over the course of a full week a Third Universal was prepared, and, partly at the insistence of the Jews and other minorities, a stress was placed on the continued desire for a federal tie with Russia.[69] On 7 November, Hrushevsky presented the final text of this document to the Mala Rada. In his introductory remarks, he emphasized the chaos and strife that was spreading across Russia and the need 'to save Ukraine from anarchy and civil war.' He said that the revolutionary gains of Ukraine would benefit all Russia and the Third All-Ukrainian Military Congress had demanded the proclamation of the Ukrainian People's Republic, and in response the Rada had prepared such a proclamation. Hrushevsky then read out the Third Universal, which declared the Republic,

---

67 Zozulia, *Kalendar*, p. 27. On the City Council meeting see Khrystiuk, II, 43–4. More generally, see Pipes, pp. 71–2, and Pidhainy, pp. 189–92.

68 Zozulia, *Kalendar*, pp. 28–9. The Czech leader, Professor T. Masaryk, who had met Franko in Prague and had got to know Hrushevsky and other Ukrainian figures during the war, was personally inclined to sympathize with the Ukrainian national movement. See E. Borschak [I. Borschak], 'Masaryk et l'Ukraine,' *Le monde slave*, no. 2 (Paris, 1930), 467–80.

69 Zozulia, *Kalendar*, pp. 33–4; M. Rafes, *Dva goda revoliutsii na Ukraine* (Moscow, 1920). p. 56, as cited in J. Borys, *The Sovietization of Ukraine 1917–1923* (Edmonton, 1980), p. 114.

defined the territory of the state, and set a date for the election and convocation of the Constituent Assembly. The members of the Rada responded enthusiastically.[70]

On 9 November, in what was now becoming a tradition, after a few words by Hrushevsky, the Universal was solemnly proclaimed in Saint Sophia Square to the accompaniment of church bells, speeches, and military parades. French, Italian, and Belgian military officers, obviously disconcerted by the Bolshevik style of revolutionism and Lenin's Decree on Peace, showed their support for the new republic by their presence.[71]

The proclamation of the Ukrainian People's Republic was the culmination of Hrushevsky's work of the preceding months. From the very first days after the outbreak of the February revolution, the veteran Ukrainian leader had unequivocally reiterated what he believed to be the traditional goals of the national movement. These went beyond the simple cultural concessions and political liberties that might be possible in a unitary state, but they did not reach the point of complete state independence. As he had first suggested in 1905, as he had insisted before Miliukov in 1914, so too in 1917 Hrushevsky clearly set forth the case for a Ukrainian state having wide autonomy within a federation of peoples of the former empire. With the proclamation of the People's Republic, the first part of this formula, autonomous Ukrainian statehood, had been achieved. Only the second part, the establishment of federal relations with related peoples, remained.

In setting out the traditional demands for Ukrainian autonomy, Hrushevsky affirmed his commitment to the cause of the common people and vowed that the demands of the masses would always be his own. During these first months of revolution and state-building, Hrushevsky was fortunate in so far as both the land-hungry Ukrainian peasantry, who were unwilling to share their rich soil with their counterparts to the north, and the restless peasant-soldiers of the former Imperial Army, who were anxious to return home to get their share, both strongly supported the demands for autonomy. Thus the returned martyr, the 'father' of the nationally conscious intelligentsia, did in actual fact very quickly become the hero for the whole nation. So great was Hrushevsky's popularity that a jealous Vynnychenko warned the SR Kovalevsky that 'our old man ... wants to be a

70 Doroshenko, *Istoriia*, I, 178–82, quotes from Hrushevsky's speech, gives the Ukrainian text of the Universal, and states that it was accepted by the Mala Rada in a vote of 42 in favour and 4 abstentions. Zozulia, *Kalendar*, pp. 71–3, establishes a somewhat more authentic text, which is translated in *The Ukraine 1917–1921: A Study in Revolution*, pp. 387–91. For the text, of Hrushevsky's speech see: 'Promova Hrushevskoho (20.XI.1917) pered oholoshenniam universalu tsentralnoi rady,' *Ukrainske slovo* (Lviv), no. 291, 1918.
71 Doroshenko, *Istoriia*. I, 183; Zozulia, *Kalendar*, pp. 35–6.

dictator.' The latter, however, thought the admonition absurd, for in his view, Hrushevsky's commitment to popular rule was unbreakable and his attachment to democratic forms and parliamentarism almost 'pedantic.'[72] It was an interpretation shared by others.[73]

On the other hand, the historian's association with the SRs irritated and alienated his oldest friends and colleagues. The TUP veterans had expected him to stand above class interests and be non-partisan in his relations with the various Ukrainian political parties, and they resented and could not understand his movement to the left. They explained it in different ways: Doroshenko hypothesized that the historian was using social slogans to attract the masses to the national cause; on the other hand, Lototsky thought that Hrushevsky had become unbalanced by the disasters, slanders, and persecutions of the war and the sudden liberties and adulation that succeeded it. But in spite of these doubts, during the revolution itself even these moderates were more or less swept along by the revolutionary current and did not question the authority of the Ukrainian parliament and its universally respected leader. It was only later that the TUP veterans claimed that their former champion had sunk to the level of short-sighted sloganeering at the time when the unlettered masses had the greatest need for wise leadership.[74]

Mikhnovsky and the nationalists of the Polubotok Club had a somewhat different attitude toward the historian. Even before the revolution, Mikhnovsky had set a fully independent Ukrainian national state as his goal and had criticized Hrushevsky's influence in Galicia.[75] During the revolution, the nationalists concentrated their energy on the military, and, like the Bolsheviks, tried to use the peasant-soldiers' desire for demobilization to overthrow the authority of the Provisional Government. But when the day of reckoning came, the nationalist-led Polubotok Regiment did not have the moral authority to overthrow the Central Rada, which stood at the head of the national movement. The nationalists only hoped to stiffen its resolve. Hrushevsky and the Central Rada, however, did not avail themselves of the opportunity that the nationalists had given them and

72 Kovalevsky, *Pry dzherelakh borotby,* pp. 366–7. Vynnychenko also complained to Chykalenko about Hrushevsky's flirtations with the SRs, whom Chykalenko considered simple demagogues. See Chykalenko, *Uryvok z moikh spomyniv,* p. 21.

73 See, in particular, Ievhen Onatsky's essay 'M. Hrushevsky: chestnist z narodom,' in his *Portrety v profile* (Chicago, 1965). pp. 285–97.

74 See Doroshenko, *Istoriia,* I, 75–6 and Lototsky, III, 357. Iefremov's *Nova Rada* did publicly criticize the Central Rada's radical course, but as Chykalenko later acknowledged (*Uryvok z moikh spomyniv,* p. 23), under revolutionary conditions it would have been impossible for the Rada to follow any other policy.

75 For Mikhnovsky's earlier criticism of Hrushevsky see chapter 3, note 14 above.

remained true to their agreement with Petrograd. The Polubotok coup failed and, in consequence, the bulk of the Ukrainian army was sent to the front. Civil war and its attendant anarchy were temporarily prevented, but the Ukrainian government was left practically defenceless.

In the crucial weeks that followed, no one in the Ukrainian government emulated the nationalists (or the Bolsheviks for that matter) by forming volunteer units of Ukrainian revolutionary guards. Vynnychenko was unconcerned, Petliura only tried to Ukrainianize disintegrating regular units, and Hrushevsky was busy chairing the revolutionary parliament. Thus, when the Provisional Government finally fell, only the Central Rada's renewed reputation as an opposition force, the chance presence of the soldiers of the Third All-Ukrainian Military Congress, the brief alliance with the Bolsheviks, and good timing permitted the survival of the Ukrainian government and the proclamation of the Ukrainian People's Republic. At this time, it seems, both Petliura and Hrushevsky became aware of the pressing need for a new Ukrainian army. Vynnychenko alone maintained his anti-militarist posture and continued to rely solely on the effects of propaganda.[76] It remained to be seen whether this would be enough to save the Ukrainian régime in the trials to come. Failure would most certainly cause the single-minded nationalists to denounce Hrushevsky and the other Rada leaders in the harshest of terms.

76 On Hrushevsky, Onatsky, pp. 288–9, writes: 'Hrushevsky was not a militarist, but those err who think that some supposed 'professorial approach' prevented him from understanding the need for decisive military action. To the contrary, I know very well that the necessity for the creation of a Ukrainian army was one of his most worrisome [hryzotlyva] thoughts. I recall that the only time that I saw 'father Hrushevsky' in a state of deep depression – the only time that this depression appeared during the entire period of our common labour in the Central Rada, was for a very short moment ... when the government of Kerensky fell ... the Bolsheviks were rising in Kiev ... even all the anti-Ukrainian minorities and those who had previously cried that the Ukrainian movement was "a knife in the back of the revolution" were turning to the Central Rada to take all power into its hands ... and we were militarily unprepared.' Shortly after these events, Vynnychenko, who was inclined to compromise with the Bolsheviks, dismissed Petliura from his post as war minister. It seems that it was only after his dismissal that Petliura threw himself into the organization of a volunteer army. See V. Ivanys, *Symon Petliura: Prezydent Ukrainy* (Toronto, 1952), pp. 51–3.

7
The Ukrainian People's Republic 1918

In the last days of the Provisional Government, at a time when official Petrograd hummed with rumours of Ukrainian Germanophilism, Hrushevsky spared no effort to reassure the representatives of the Western Allies that the Ukrainian émigré organizations in central Europe did not represent the Ukrainian people as a whole and that the Central Rada was committed to the same goals as the Western democratic states.[1] With the Bolshevik coup and the proclamation of the Ukrainian People's Republic, Western military and diplomatic representatives – the French in particular – hoped that the Ukrainians would continue the war against Germany. The French General Tabouis was encouraged in these hopes by both the Ukrainian foreign secretary, O. Shulhyn, and by the war secretary, Symon Petliura; in turn, Tabouis and the newly arrived British representative, Picton Bagge, moved toward official recognition of the Ukrainian People's Republic. Masaryk and the Czech National Council also recognized the new Ukrainian régime, and the French offered financial assistance and elaborated a plan for close cooperation between Romania, Ukraine, the Don Cossack government, and other non-

---

1 The French journalist and partisan of the stateless peoples, Jean Péllissier, had met with the Rada leaders in the autumn of 1917, and made an enthusiastic report to a doubting French ambassador. On 19 October 1917, Péllissier printed a letter from Hrushevsky in the Petrograd *Journal de Russie*. 'I authorize you,' Hrushevsky began, 'to affirm categorically in my name and in the name of the Central Rada that [the émigré] Stepankivsky has no right to speak in the name of the Ukrainian people, of which the Rada is the only official representative, that we formally disavow these declarations according to which Ukraine should remain neutral, that until the war is over we do not want to have any connection with the Ukrainians in emigration and will always remain on the same ground as Democratic Russia and the allies.' Quoted in I. Borshchak [E. Borschak], 'La paix ukrainienne de Brest-Litovsk,' *Le monde slave*, nos. 4–8 (Paris, 1929), 42–3. Borshchak thinks that this letter characterized the general attitude of the Central Rada leadership from February to October 1917. There is a detailed description of Péllissier's mission in Pidhainy, p. 291ff. For Hrushevsky's previous relations with the émigré SVU, see chapter 5, pp. 116–18.

Bolshevik elements that might be willing to continue the war against the Central Powers.[2] At closed meetings of the Rada leaders, which were held in the middle of the night in Hrushevsky's office, the historian supported Shulhyn's position on accepting the French aid, at least as a bargaining tool for use against the Central Powers in the expected peace talks. He stood firmly against Mykola Porsh's position, which, on the basis of Marxist theory, argued against the acceptance of French aid.[3]

It was not only the representatives of foreign governments that flocked to Kiev after the Bolshevik revolution in the north. Thousands of conservative Russian officers and their families arrived in the city hoping to find refuge from the chaos reigning in the Russian heartland. In general, these newcomers were thoroughly hostile to their Ukrainian hosts and took the side of the local Russian nationalists against them. Though they may not have been familiar with the other Ukrainian leaders, the famous 'Mazepist,' Hrushevsky, was well known to them, and, when they recognized him on the street, they could not refrain from casting hostile glances and muttering threatening words against him under their breath. The historian's personal bodyguard would immediately stand alerted, and Hrushevsky and his companions would quicken their pace.[4]

With the disappearance of the Provisional Government, relations between the Bolsheviks and the Central Rada grew steadily worse. At first, Lenin's followers hoped to take over the Rada by means of a large All-Ukrainian Congress of Soviets, which they thought they could control. Local Red Guards would oversee the event and do the rest. But on 29 November, on the very eve of the congress, Ukrainian units, strengthened by the arrival of the heroes of the February revolution, the Petrograd guard regiments, set about disarming the Bolshevized elements in Kiev. When the congress finally met on 4 December, in spite of the Bolshevik agitators who stood at the door telling the simple countryfolk that Hrushevsky was a millionaire who owned thousands of acres of land all over Ukraine and that the General Secretariat was just a group of generals who wanted to run the country, almost all of the two thousand delegates supported the Rada. Moreover, the congress delegates were stunned by an unexpected 'ultimatum'

2 See Shulhyn, *L'Ukraine contre Moscou*, p. 165ff., and the detailed discussion in Pidhainy, pp. 297–304, who makes good use of French and other Western documents.

3 Shulhyn, *L'Ukraine contre Moscou*, pp. 168–9. Porsh had earlier promised the returned émigré Stepankivsky that he would try to influence Hrushevsky toward full independence and peace with Germany. See Pidhainy, p. 309, who cites a German intelligence report.

4 A. Berehulka, 'Liutyi 1918 roku v Kyievi,' *Biuleten soiuzu buvshykh ukrainskykh voiakiv u Kanadi*, no. 10 (Toronto, 1962). 13–16. Berehulka was in charge of the small detachment of six or seven soldiers which formed Hrushevsky's personal guard. The historian was on good terms with these soldiers, including the sentries posted at his house. See L. Bachynsky, 'Malyi spomyn,' *Zhinocha dolia*, nos. 15–16 (Kolomyia, 1935), 12–13.

from Lenin's government. Even the Kiev Bolshevik leaders were divided on the meaning of the ultimatum, some considering it a 'misunderstanding.' The ultimatum threatened war unless the Rada re-armed the local Red Guards and stopped the movement of Don Cossacks toward their home, where the non-Bolshevik General Kaledin ruled. In his major address, Hrushevsky declared that the Central Rada was prepared to resign or be reorganized in accordance with the Bolshevik demands if that was really what the delegates wanted, but as to the ultimatum it was simply interference in Ukrainian affairs. Hostile action, he informed a supportive audience, would be repulsed by force of arms if necessary. Hrushevsky concluded by addressing his Russian critics directly: 'What happens in Ukraine is our business and not yours.'[5]

The outbreak of war between the Petrograd Council of People's Commissars and the Ukrainian People's Republic coincided with the opening of peace talks between Russia and the Central Powers at Brest-Litovsk. In its Third Universal, the Ukrainian government had insisted that 'peace negotiations begin at once'; it could not afford to be outbid by the Bolsheviks in the game of making peace. Thus on the very day that negotiations began at Brest (9/22 December), in a note to the Western and neutral states, the Central Rada expressed its desire for a democratic and general peace. The stress on a 'general' peace enabled Shulhyn to present the project to the Entente representatives in the most favourable light possible, and Tabouis, in the words of the Ukrainian foreign secretary, 'considering it inevitable, no longer protested against our sending a delegation to Brest-Litovsk.'[6] This same day, the Mala Rada, presided over by Hrushevsky, hurriedly chose a delegation of young socialists – the SRs M. Holubovych, O. Sevriuk, M. Poloz, and M. Liubynsky and the SD M. Levytsky – to go to Brest as observers. Neither Vynnychenko nor Shulhyn gave the delegation any firm instructions, and only one long conference with Hrushevsky prepared them for their task. At this meeting the professor treated the novice diplomats to a general lesson in geopolitics. He talked about the economics of the Black Sea basin and the ethnography of the western Ukrainian lands: Eastern Galicia, Bukovina, Kholm, Trans-Carpathian Rus', and

5 Khrystiuk, II, 72. For the full text of Hrushevsky's speech see 'Na Ukraini ide pokhodom vorozhe viisko. Promova Prof. Hrushevskoho do vseukrainskoho z'izdu rad robitnychykh, selianskykh i soldatskykh deputativ,' *Dilo,* no. 307 (1917). For the text of the ultimatum see Pipes, *Formation of the Soviet Union,* p. 119. At this point, Hrushevsky announced the issue of a new Ukrainian currency and asked for a display of confidence in it. The congress replied enthusiastically with applause and shouts of '*Slava batkovi Hrushevskomu!*' See Doroshenko, *Istoriia,* I, 223. On the Bolshevik agitators at the door see the brief remarks of Serhii Shelukhyn, 'Doba tsentralnoi rady,' *Vilna Ukraina,* no. 52 (1966), 29–49, especially 30. For a general study of the significance of the Congress of Soviets see my 'The First All-Ukrainian Congress of Soviets and Its Antecedents,' *Journal of Ukrainian Graduate Studies,* no. 6 (Toronto, 1979), 3–9.

6 Shulhyn, *L'Ukraine contre Moscou,* pp. 169–70.

Pidliashshia. Holubovych would come later with fuller instructions. As the hesitant young men departed, they were told: 'You will manage somehow and do the best for our interests.'[7]

Strangely enough, Hrushevsky's briefing proved to be sufficient preparation for the young negotiators. In fact, while simply observing the verbal duels of the aristocratic German diplomat Richard von Kühlmann and the fiery Russian revolutionist Leon Trotsky, they managed to get their delegation recognized by both parties, in spite of the official 'state of war' supposedly existing between Kiev and Petrograd. Since Trotsky did not really seem to be interested in signing a peace treaty, and as the Ukrainian-Russian war grew more serious, the Germans turned to the Ukrainians for the contraction of a separate peace. Further instructions came from Kiev, and Holubovych – seemingly at Hrushevsky's suggestion – opened the direct bargaining with a demand for the cession of the western Ukrainian lands. This proposal was rejected out of hand by the Austrian representative, Count Otto-kar von Czernin. Finally, on 4/17 January 1918, in hope of obtaining Ukrainian wheat for hungry Vienna, the Germans and Austrians agreed to the annexation of the Kholm district and parts of Pidliashshia by an independent Ukrainian state. The Ukrainian delegation returned to Kiev to inform Hrushevsky and the government of the offer.[8]

The diplomats returned to a Kiev very different from the one they had left a few weeks before. The swift march of the Bolshevik armies had destroyed the euphoria resulting from the Rada's victory at the All-Ukrainian Congress of Soviets. By the end of December, Kharkiv, Chernyhiv, Poltava, and Katerynoslav had already fallen to the Red Guards. Everyone recognized the pressing need for an immediate peace with the Central Powers. But Ukraine was still theoretically an autonomous part of a fictitious Russian federation, and its international status remained unclear.[9] Only a formal declaration of independence could unequivocally resolve

---

7 See O. Severiuk, 'Beresteiskyi myr: uryvky zi spomyniv,' in *Beresteiskyi myr*, ed. I. Kedryn (Lviv–Kiev, 1928), pp. 145–6.

8 Sevriuk, 'Beresteiskyi myr,' pp. 145–6. For the chronology, see Zozulia, *Kalendar*, p. 46. More generally, see Reshetar, pp. 104–7, and the relevant chapters of the classic works by J.W. Wheeler-Bennett, *Brest-Litovsk: The Forgotten Peace, March 1918* (London, 1939), and Fritz Fischer, *Germany's Aims in the First World War* (New York, 1967).

9 As late as 30 December/12 January Hrushevsky met with Tabouis, who had just been named 'Commissar of the French Republic in Ukraine,' and complained to him that the declaration of the American president – Wilson's Fourteen Points, which supposedly dealt with national self-determination, – completely ignored Russia and Ukraine. Hrushevsky said that Ukraine was, in fact, already independent, but a federation might be possible in the future. He then reminded Tabouis that he was the president of the Council of Peoples, and while Ukraine, the Crimea, Belorussia, and the Balts were represented in it, Poland and Russia were not. See General Tabouis, 'Comment je devins Commissaire de la Republique Française en Ukraine,' in *Spohady, Pratsi ukrainskoho naukovoho instytutu*, vol. vii (Warsaw, 1932), pp. 142–64, especially pp. 157–8, and

the issue. When the question was debated in the Rada, Iefremov's Socialist-Federalists and some of the Ukrainian Social Democrats declared that such an important step could only be taken by the forthcoming Ukrainian Constituent Assemly. Hrushevsky, however, who very seldom spoke in the ordinary discussions of the Rada, was visibly disturbed by these deliberations. The leader of the UPSR, Kovalevsky, noticed this. He later recalled:

Although Hrushevsky controlled himself, one could see the trembling in his visage, and at the same time feel his deep anxiety about the future of the Ukrainian state, which had been born in the revolutionary storm . . . When almost everyone had expressed his opinion about the declaration of independence, Mykhailo Hrushevsky passionately argued against the idea of putting off this act until the convocation of the Constituent Assembly. He pointed out that, since the recent territorial elections, the Central Rada represented the will of all levels of the Ukrainian nation [*narod*], and that 'any delay means death,' because, in the midst of the revolutionary tempest, decisive action was necessary to create a broader perspective for furthering the struggle for liberation.[10]

The authority of the bearded historian decided the matter and the leading figures in the Rada immediately set about composing a 'Fourth Universal.' On 9/22 January three separate texts were ready. 'Of the three,' writes Kovalevsky, 'the shortest was the project of Mykhailo Hrushevsky.'

In its preamble it affirmed that throughout the centuries which followed the loss of its statehood, the Ukrainian people had expressed its unquenchable desire for national liberation, and that finally the time had come for realizing the great ideal which was the complete independence [*nezalezhnist*] of Ukraine and the practical sovereignty [*samostiin-ist*] of her state. In response to this, the Central Rada, as the representative of all strata of the Ukrainian people, pronounces the independence of the Ukrainian People's Republic and

---

the summary in Pidhainy, p. 498. Also see Vynnychenko, *Vidrodzhennia natsii*, II, 243, who says that international relations demanded a resolution of this situation. Vynnychenko, however, stresses relations with the Entente, confining the Central Powers to a single paragraph.

10 Mykola Kovalevsky, 'Iak proholosheno IV universal: pamiat Mykhaila Hrushevskoho, '*Dilo*, no. 239, 15 December 1934, and reprinted in *Vilna Ukraina*, no. 52 (1966), 17–19. Hrushevsky's mention of elections is probably a reference to the 27 December/9 January election to the Ukrainian Constituent Assembly, which was carried out in all areas not yet under Bolshevik control. There were places for 301 members, but only 171 were elected (Zozulia, *Kalendar*, p. 45). In view of the dispersal of the All-Russian Constituent Assembly in Petrograd, the Rada also called all its Ukrainian members to gather in Kiev and join in the work of building the Republic. Many did. See, for example, the memoir of a member for the Kherson Gubernia, I. Havryliuk, 'Chertvertyi universal: spohady,' *LNV*, XCV (1928), 16–24, who was an eyewitness to the events that followed.

directs the government to implement the organization of the state which is to be a democratic republic.[11]

Vynnychenko proposed an alternative text, and a third one was worked out by the Ukrainian SRs, Mykyta Shapoval and Mykola Saltan. These texts were considerably longer and contained declarations about the redistribution of land, the reorganization of commerce, and general social and economic questions. All three drafts were then given to a constitutional commission. While a nervous Kiev – all too accustomed to idle soldiers and occasional gunfire – waited, this commission worked out a final text which incorporated the essential parts of Hrushevsky's original and added a few paragraphs on social and economic questions.[12]

On 10/23 January, the Mala Rada discussed the final text of the Fourth Universal. The national minorities, who were generally unsympathetic to the declaration of independence, insisted that a long-expected law on national-personal autonomy be adopted first. The next day, the bill on national-personal autonomy was passed and the Universal received its 'second reading.'[13] Toward midnight, a fifteen-minute recess was called, and the galleries quickly filled with men in Cossack dress, soldiers, and members of the general public, many of whom also sported proletarian military attire. Several Ukrainian members of the All-Russian Constituent Assembly were also present. All had heard that a declaration of independence was about to be made.[14]

At twenty minutes past midnight, Hrushevsky opened the meeting with a brief speech. He said that because of the new fratricidal 'holy war' declared by the so-called 'People's Commissars,' there was such disorder in the country that adequate elections to the Ukrainian Constituent Assembly could not take place. Thus in order to make peace and ensure order, on 9/22 January the Central Rada had decided to issue its Fourth Universal. Everyone then rose and listened closely as Hrushevsky began to read. 'People of Ukraine!' the document began, 'By your

---

11 Kolvalevsky, 'Iak proholosheno IV universal.'
12 Ibid. Kovalevsky and Zozulia, *Kalendar*. p. 46, both say that the third proposed text was worked out jointly by Shapoval and Saltan, but Sava Zerkal, 'Do statti "Iak proholosheno IV universal,"' *Vilna Ukraina*, no. 54 (1967). 64, claims the distinction for Shapoval alone and cites Doroshenko, *Istoriia*, I, 263, to strengthen his case.
13 For the text of the law on National-Personal Autonomy, which at first envisioned self-government for Russians, Jews, and Poles under their own National Unions, see Zozulia, *Kalendar*, pp. 85–6. Goldenveizer, p. 20, writes that 'in reality, the projects of the minorities on national autonomy did not meet with any particular resistance.'
14 Doroshenko, *Istoriia*, I, 263–4; Havryliuk, 'Chetvertyi universal'; Ostap Voinarenko, *Pro samostiinist UNR: de koly i iak vona proholoshuvalas ta iakyi buv ii zmist!* (Winnipeg, 1966). The latter two accounts stress that the Central Rada did not have complete control of the capital even at this time.

efforts, your will, and your word, a Free Ukrainian People's Republic has been created on Ukrainian soil. The ancient dream of your ancestors – fighters for the freedom and rights of the workers – has been fulfilled.' Hrushevsky read on. He described the Bolshevik invasion and the Ukrainian desire for peace. When he read out the heart of the declaration – 'From this day forth, the Ukrainian People's Republic becomes independent, subject to no one, a Free, Sovereign State of the Ukrainian People' – the packed galleries broke out in cheers and applause. Hrushevsky then continued. The General Secretariat was renamed the 'Council of People's Ministers' – more cheers; the Bolsheviks would be expelled –cheers; land, private property, and the banks were to be taken over by the state – cheers; the national-personal autonomy of minorities was confirmed – cheers again; and possible establishment of federal ties with other people's republics was to be deferred until the convocation of the Ukrainian Constituent Assembly, which would be the highest authority in the land. The document was dated 9/22 January 1918, the day when the Ukrainian Constituent Assembly was originally supposed to have met, and the day that work on the Universal had begun. The declaration was easily passed with almost all the Ukrainian members voting 'for,' only a few members (mostly Russian Mensheviks) voting 'against,' and a few other members – the representatives of the national minorities – abstaining. Hrushevsky declared the Universal accepted and the walls of the Pedagogical Museum shook to the strains of the patriotic hymn 'Ukraine has not yet passed away.'[15] Afterwards, Vynnychenko and others made speeches expressing the hope that the Fourth Universal would become a rallying point for a socialism which would begin in Ukraine and lead to 'a federation of socialist republics of the whole world.'[16] When the cheers gradually died away, the Rada turned to other business, and continued its work long after the galleries had emptied.

15 For the text of the Universal see Zozulia, pp. 73–7, and the translation in *The Ukraine 1917–1920: A Study in Revolution*, pp. 391–5. For the voting, see the accounts of Doroshenko, Havryliuk, and Voinarenko cited above. Doroshenko counts 39 for, 4 against, and 6 abstentions. He says all Ukrainians supported the measure. But Voinarenko, pp. 18–20, gives a vivid description of the voting that does not accord with this assertion. He writes: 'Prof. Hrushevsky voted first. In a self-assured, decisive tone, he clearly pronounced his "for!" One by one, the others followed. When it was the turn of Viktor Kovalsky, a member of the USDLP, he said: "In accordance with party discipline, I vote 'for'. But I was, I am, and I will be against Ukrainian independence!"' The galleries reacted angrily to this declaration. Later, when the Ukrainian SD Ievhen Neronovych also voted 'no,' 'a boisterous uproar broke out in the galleries. People cried: "Out with him, traitor, shame!" Stamping and hissing started and led to the ringing of the order bell, which Prof. Hrushevsky pointed in every direction, trying in vain to quieten the continuous hubbub.' When the noise diminished, voting continued, and none of the other negative votes, or abstentions by members from the non-Ukrainian nationalities, seems to have caused such an uproar. The sole Polish socialist representative voted in favour of the Universal; the sole Polish conservative abstained.

16 Doroshenko, *Istoriia*, 1, 261–9; Voinarenko, pp. 21–4.

In an article written shortly after the declaration of independence, Hrushevsky stressed the difficulties of the task ahead. He urged his countrymen to forget the illusions of the united revolutionary 'front' proclaimed by the Russians. Rather, he wanted them to unite in the great duty of building the Ukrainian Republic. 'Then,' he concluded, 'the proclaimed independence will become the firm foundation of the security of our statehood and of the social structure for which our working people are waiting.'[17]

Vague promises about the future re-establishment of federal relations did not satisfy the Rada's opponents. The proclamation of the Fourth Universal produced an immediate reaction among the Russian, Jewish, and Russified proletariat of Kiev. Bolshevik elements began openly testing Ukrainian military strength. Strikes and fighting spread throughout the city. More conservative Russian elements stood to the side or even joined in the protest. In the face of this determined opposition, the Ukrainians were very unsure of themselves. Soldiers of the Ukrainianized regiments were proving susceptible to Bolshevik propaganda, and the two major parties, the USDLP and the UPSR, which had originally intended to go only as far as autonomy, were suspicious of each other. Vynnychenko was resentful of Hrushevsky, and Hrushevsky did not seem to trust Vynnychenko.

The successful march of the Bolshevik armies from Russia and rising Bolshevik strength in Kiev itself brought matters to a head. Vynnychenko's government, which had been very apologetic about issuing the Fourth Universal in the first place, had proved itself unable to fight against its Social Democratic comrades from the north and was under strong SR pressure to resign. In accordance with Hrushevsky's plan, the SRs wanted to take over the government and issue the Fourth Universal themselves, but somehow Vynnychenko managed to hold on a little longer. Finally, on 14/27 January, in view of the general uncertainty and spreading chaos, Vynnychenko proclaimed a state of siege in Kiev and named an energetic young soldier, Mykhailo Kovenko, as City Commandant. That same evening, Kovenko, at the head of a Free Cossack Unit composed of nationally conscious proletarians, marched into an SR party conference in the Rada building and interrupted the speaker, Mykola Saltan, who was talking about the formation of a new SR government determined to resist the Muscovites. Kovenko arrested several left-wing SRs who were rumoured to favour an understanding with the Bolsheviks. The prominent SR and former editor of *Ukrainska khata* Mykyta Shapoval, who had just refused to join such a government because he thought it too

17 M. Hrushevsky, 'Velykyi oboviazok,' in *Vybrani pratsi,* pp. 36–7. In a second article, Hrushevsky explained that Ukrainian independence was unavoidable for two reasons: (1) to conclude peace; (2) to clarify the situation and make possible a firm response to the Bolshevik invasion of Ukraine. See 'Ukrainska samostiinist i ii istorychna neobkhidnist,' in ibid., pp. 37–9, which, however, does not rule out future federation with friendly neighbours.

conservative, exonerated his party comrades from most of the blame for this violation of parliamentary privilege:

Formally, the government of Vynnychenko was still in office; the SD Porsh was war minister, M. Tkachenko was minister of internal affairs. Kovenko was under Porsh. Thus the *arrest* of the members of the Central Rada and of our Central Committee was *the doing of the Social Democrats*. They might have had the personal cooperation of [just] a few right-wing SRs. One cannot assert otherwise because Hrushevsky, for example (who associated with the right SRs), knew nothing about it. After the arrest of the 'leftists,' Saltan's list [of ministers] was quickly accepted. This became the cabinet of Holubovych . . . Hrushevsky protested sharply against the arrests and as a result, if I am not mistaken, the arrested men were released.[18]

It was in this atmosphere of confusion and universal mistrust that the government of Holubovych was formed. Hrushevsky's expectations about the SR 'revolutionary reserve' had not exactly gone according to plan. Nevertheless, Kovenko's decisive action seems to have stiffened the backbone of the weak and uninspiring Holubovych government to the extent that it was able to react to the general crisis.[19]

In fact, the Ukrainian People's Republic was in the midst of the deepest crisis that it had yet faced. Bolshevik armies were marching on Kiev from the north and from the east. Under the influence of Bolshevik propaganda, the Ukrainianized regiments formed earlier in the year had almost completely melted away, and the majority of those who held their ranks – including one regiment named after

18 Mykyta Shapoval, 'Narodnytstvo v ukr. vyzvolnomu rukhovi,' *Vilna spilka,* no. 3 (Prague, 1927–9, 95–128, especially 106. Shapoval says that SR pressure forced Vynnychenko's resignation, but that, simulaneously, the UPSR began to split into three groupings. The formation of a government, he explains, forced the SRs to decide what kind of revolution they were promoting. 'In our Central Committee,' writes Shapoval, 'the majority was for social revolution ... the minority for "bourgeois revolution."' The three groupings in the party were: '(a) The extreme left: for social revolution in full union with the Bolsheviks. (b) The Centre: for an independent Ukraine, social revolution, and an understanding on interstate relations with the Bolsheviks. (c) The right: for war against the Bolsheviks and for a Bourgeois revolution. In the extreme left were Poloz, ... Shumsky, and others. In the centre were: Shrah, Lyzanivsky, Okhrimovych, Hryhoriiv, myself, and others. On the right were: Saltan, Chechel, Holubovych, Zhukovsky, Sevriuk, and others, who were in fact led by Hrushevsky, who was not a member of the party.' Shapoval may well exaggerate the distinction between the 'centre' and the 'right.'

19 See, for example, Doroshenko, *Spomyny pro nedavne mynule,* p. 216, who believes that by arresting the Bolshevik-leaning parliamentarians in the very parliament building, Kovenko brought the confused legislators to their senses and saved the situation. He adds: 'Old Hrushevsky pulled his beard at such a breach of parliamentary privilege, but the deed was done and there was no turning back.'

Hrushevsky – now declared themselves neutral in the struggle for Kiev. There only remained some Free Cossacks, the well-disciplined Sich Riflemen, and a small army of volunteers – the Ukrainian Haidamak Host of Slobidska Ukraine – organized by Petliura after the dogmatically anti-militarist Vynnychenko had dismissed him. When Petliura marched off to meet one of the invading armies, the Bolshevik uprising began in earnest. The Reds took the Arsenal, the Main Post Office and Telegraph. Meanwhile, at Kruty, on the road to Kiev, an important battle took place and a battalion of four hundred student volunteers was wiped out by the approaching Red Guards. In the historical literature, this engagement eventually gained the reputation of a Ukrainian Thermopylae, a classical allusion which followed the example of the funeral oration pronounced a few weeks later by Hrushevsky over the graves of the fallen heroes.[20]

But Kiev would not fall so easily. The remaining Ukrainian units held their ground. On 15/28 January, in the vain hope of rallying the population behind the Republic, the Ninth Plenary Session of the Rada was held. Hrushevsky, as usual, reported on the activity of the Mala Rada, and various laws were confirmed including the Fourth Universal.[21] Afterwards, the Mala Rada continued its work, but the situation grew more and more dangerous. Fierce battles raged in the streets. 'One morning,' writes one of the Ukrainian members of the All-Russian Constituent Assembly who had come to Kiev, 'the Bolsheviks succeeded in disconcerting our forces so that a battle began close to the Central Rada Building.'

Blood was already flowing in the University Park . . . Bullets were whistling by the Central Rada, which was in session. But the composure and desire of the members to finish their work was extraordinary. No one took it into his head to cast his work aside and look for a safe refuge. Even when the Bolsheviks were almost up to the Rada Building and when bullets were hitting the glass dome and broken glass was raining down on the assembly hall, the members did not budge from their places.[22]

Hrushevsky was the single dominant personality during the period of the Holubovych government, and he was determined to hold Kiev until a peace could be signed with the Central Powers. It was hoped that the main body of the Galician Sich Riflemen and the Ukrainian prisoners-of-war in Germany, which the émigré Union for the Liberation of Ukraine had organized into a number of nationally

20 M. Hrushevsky, 'Promova pid tsentralnoiu radoiu na pokhoroni Sichovykiv Studentskoho Kurenia 19 Bereznia 1918 roku,' in his *Na prozi novoi Ukrainy* (Kiev, 1918), p. 85, and reprinted in *Vilna Ukraina* nos. 55–6 (1967), 16–17. Hrushevsky's speech, written only after the bloody battle for Kiev had ended, began: 'Dulce et decorum est pro patria mori ...'
21 Doroshenko, *Istoriia*, I, 278; Zozulia, *Kalendar*, p. 48.
22 Havryliuk, 'Chetvertyi Universal,' p. 18. Also see Doroshenko, *Istoriia*, I, 185.

conscious and well-disciplined 'Bluecoat divisions,' would be permitted to come to help.[23] At any rate, in Kiev the fighting continued. Petliura returned victorious over one Bolshevik army and joined in the battle for Kiev. Then a mounted regiment of several hundred soldiers with armoured cars arrived unexpectedly from the Western Front, and after wandering through the city, came to the Rada Building. The soldiers touched their caps and asked to see some members of the Central Rada and 'Father Hrushevsky' in particular. The Ukrainian leader, complete with rimless glasses and beard, soon appeared. While horses, men, and armoured cars waited outside, a brief discussion took place in the vestibule of the Pedagogical Museum:

'Well, here I am. What do you want, children?' said [Hrushevsky] in a slow and reassuring voice. Pause. The commander [of the newcomers], who once again removed his hat, replied: . . . 'Without any orders we have come from far-off Belorussia to defend the Ukrainian working people. Without any orders, we have come here to Kiev, to you, father. On the front they told us that all of you here were pure bourgeois, and we have come to see. But we cannot make it out: we do not know who is fighting with whom and what they are fighting about in Kiev.' [A second man added] . . . 'We have everything we need to defend the Ukrainian working people from the foe, whatever it leads to!'

Hrushevsky answered that the visitors had been lied to at the front. He said that the Rada was not bourgeois, and to prove his point, he introduced an active peasant member of the Rada, and then an ordinary worker who was on several legislative commissions. Other ministers spoke afterwards, and when suddenly an urgent call came for military support, the soldiers immediately responded by joining in on the Ukrainian side. This was the last reinforcement that Ukrainian Kiev was to receive.[24]

On 22 January/4 February, Petliura's 'Haidamaks' retook the Arsenal; most of Kiev was again in Ukrainian hands and public services were returning to normal. But the next day a newly arrived army of Red Guards led by Muravev – a brutal former tsarist officer whom Antonov-Ovsienko, his superior, thought somewhat deranged – began to bombard the city with heavy artillery from the opposite side of the Dnieper River. Cannon mounted on armoured trains added to the destruction. Meanwhile, in the city itself, a rumour spread that the Bolsheviks wanted to destroy Hrushevsky's great house on Pankivska street. As the house was now well

23 M. Hrushevsky, *Iliustrovana istoriia Ukrainy z dodatkom ... za roky 1914 do 1919* (Winnipeg, n.d., but probably 1919), p. 550.

24 Vsevolod Petriv, *Spomyny z chasiv ukrainskoi revoliutsii (1917–1921)* part I (Lviv, 1927), p. 100. This unit was the Ukrainianized Hordienko Mounted Regiment organized and commanded by Colonel Petriv.

guarded, the Reds decided to bombard it from afar. On the morning of 24 January/6 February, Hrushevsky, who seems to have known that something was afoot, introduced some soldiers from the guard to his wife and daughter, and gave them a brief guided tour of the building. He showed them the museum with its Greek, Scythian, and Sarmatian artifacts, and the library with its ancient manuscripts; he then left for the Central Rada Building. Shortly after he had left, Muravev's Red Guards fire-bombed the house with cannon from their armoured trains. The historian's daughter and wife, Kateryna and Mariia Sylvestrivna, as well as Vasyl and Ievhenia Krychevsky and others fled for their lives. Hrushevsky's ailing mother had to be carried out from the blaze; she died from the effects a few days later. Hrushevsky's library and museum were completely destroyed. So too was Krychevsky's art studio and museum on the top floor and the library of Iury Siry. The most celebrated cultural centre of Ukrainian Kiev was burnt to ashes and its inhabitants scattered. 'I firebombed Hrushevsky's great house,' Muravev later boasted, 'and for three days and nights it burned like a bright bonfire.'[25]

The destruction of Hrushevsky's house was only the beginning. By noon, the bombardment was general; house-to-house fighting continued. But let us quote the professional historian who was an eyewitness to this terrible strife. Hrushevsky writes:

Almost every day, a few points changed hands several times: now the Bolsheviks held them, now the Ukrainian army. The heroic efforts of the few thousand men who were free could not suffice in a struggle in which they were fired upon from outside of the city and from within, from the gates and from the windows; they could not suffice when betrayal oozed up everywhere leaving nothing certain. People were exhausted from the constant nervous strain. On both sides the ferocity reached extremes. All of the passions of the civil war came out into the open. The population began to lose its sense of equilibrium and complain against the Central Rada for trying to hold out so long and for putting the city in danger of being destroyed. Ten days passed in this way.[26]

Once Hrushevsky's house had been destroyed, the Bolsheviks concentrated their fire on the Central Rada Building, which was in the same general area as the Church of Saint Sophia and the ruins of the historic 'Golden Gates.' That same

25 Muravev is quoted in *Kievskaia Mysl* (Kiev), no. 17 (1918), and by Hrushevsky, 'Na perelomi,' in *Vybrani pratsi*, p. 51, note 1. Berehulka, pp. 15–16, describes the scene and was one of the soldiers whom Hrushevsky guided through the structure before the bombardment. Ievenia Krychevska, 'Pozhezha budynku Mykhaila Hrushevskoho,' *Novi dni*, no. 105 (Toronto, 1958), 13–20, gives a very detailed personal recollection of the bombardment of Kiev and the destruction of Hrushevsky's house.
26 Hrushevsky, *Iliustrovana istoriia Ukrainy*, p. 551.

evening, the Holubovych cabinet avoided the Rada Building and met at the more closely guarded War Ministry offices in Galagan College, which in pre-revolutionary days had been an institution renowned for its 'Ukrainophile' sympathies. The meeting was brief. One of the ministers declared that resistance was no longer possible and that nothing was left but for every man to save his own life. Suddenly Hrushevsky's gavel hit the table: 'And the Ukrainian Republic? Is it left to die? No! If we cannot defend Kiev, we will retreat and recoup our forces, but we will not surrender.' The majoity supported their tough-minded patriarch.[27]

The evacuation began on the afternoon of the next day, that is, on 25 January/7 February. Hrushevsky and his wife and daughter, accompanied by a guard of two hundred Sich Riflemen, left the city in the direction of Zhytomyr to the west. That same night, other members of the government, the Central Rada, and the various units of the Ukrainian army followed. Although good order prevailed, the evacuation was carried out very quickly and many prominent figures (including Doroshenko and the ministers, Khrystiuk and Kovalevsky) were left behind. Muravev's army entered the city unopposed on the morning of the 26th; they searched everywhere for Hrushevsky, but he was gone.[28]

By 28 January/10 February, Hrushevsky and the government of the Ukrainian People's Republic were quartered in the Gubernia Commissar's Residence in Zhytomyr, where the Ukrainian forces were shortly afterwards reorganized. For a while, Hrushevsky was busy dealing with nervous local officials who feared a bombardment similar to the one that had caused so much destruction in Kiev. He also spoke with some Czech legionnaires who were turning against the Ukrainians because of the negotiations with their German enemies. Soon, however, the approach of Bolshevik forces threatened to encircle the Ukrainians and the government decided to withdraw further west to Sarny in northern Volhynia.[29]

27 Shulhyn, *L'Ukraine contre Moscou*, pp. 204–5. Shulhyn writes that 'the figure of Hrushevsky dominated' the meeting. Also see Hrushevsky, *Iliustrovana istoriia Ukrainy*, p. 551, Khrystiuk, II, 127, Doroshenko, *Spomyny pro nedavne mynule*, p. 220, and others who say that the Ukrainian government retreated 'to save the city from complete ruin.'

28 Zozulia, *Kalendar*, p. 52. Zozulia's account is supported by several eyewitnesses. However, M. Ieremiiv, in a letter to L. Wynar (*Ukrainskyi istoryk*, nos. 3–4 [1967], 124) claims that Hrushevsky's wife and daughter were almost left behind 'and Mrs Hrushevsky and her daughter ran to me when everyone had already left for Sviatoshyn on the road to Zhytomyr and in tears told me that their house was burning. I gave them the last automobile with the chauffeur Borys.' Also see Doroshenko, *Istoriia*, I, 328, and Khrystiuk II, 127–8.

29 Hrushevsky, *Iliustrovana istoriia Ukrainy*, p. 553, gives a brief description of this retreat. There is a more detailed description in Ia. Zozulia, 'Obloha Kyieva, vidstup ukrainskoi armii na Volyn,' *Za derzhavnist*, XI (Toronto, 1966), 42–64, and S. Kachura, 'Perebuvannia uriadu ukrainskoi respublyky v Sarnakh (Spohady),' *Ukrainski visti* (Munich), no. 28 (1968), 3–7.

The destruction in Kiev and the retreat to Volhynia amounted to a real catastrophe for Hrushevsky. On the national level, the Central Rada was dispersed and the authority of the Ukrainian government extended little further than the railway line along which it was fleeing, and the Ukrainian People's Republic seemed to be about as concrete as a wisp of smoke. On the personal level, his home was destroyed, his mother killed, his family in danger. Hrushevsky himself, though he appeared firm and impassive to the soldiers and cadres who bustled about him, must have been in a terrible psychological state. Something elemental was happening inside him, and he thought that something elemental was happening to Ukraine as well. On 4/17 February, when he finally sat down to write, his theme was 'Purification by Fire.' For the first time, he lashed out directly at Bolshevik hypocrisy. He contrasted Bolshevik propaganda, which recognised the self-determination of nations, as it claimed, 'up to complete separation,' and Bolshevik actions, which simply amounted to beating up the insolent 'Khokhol' who had actually dared to raise his head and throw off the Muscovite yoke. These Russian Bolsheviks, these Red converts to 'federalism,' put the word to a very original use. 'I do not know if the federalist idea can survive this heavy blow, which the self-proclaimed federalists, Lenin and Trotsky, have dealt to it,' the Ukrainian leader despaired. 'It will be very difficult for anyone to call himself a federalist while Lenin and Trotsky are doing so, and while this "federalism" is in actual fact the most evil kind of terroristic centralism.'[30] From Hrushevsky's point of view, both revolutionaries and counter-revolutionaries had risen up and given general battle to Ukrainian national life, and they did this – to use the old nationalist slogan – for the sake of 'a single indivisible Russia.' Nevertheless, the anarchy and flames had simplified matters. A purification had taken place. Hrushevsky drew the inevitable conclusion:

People have been blown to pieces, but so have ideas. Not only have cities been destroyed, but so have traditions. Much has been consumed in this great conflagration, and much will burn yet. People are coming out of it renewed and they look at the world with new eyes.

Among other things, the historic, cultural, economic, and other ties between the Ukrainian and Great Russian peoples are being burned up. The history of these two 'brotherly peoples' seems to be reaching that stage which the other Slavic brothers – the Ukrainian and Polish – reached earlier on.

Previously, the Ukrainian people had to deal with a bureaucracy and government which Great Russian society to some degree rejected. Now we have the self-evident fact of a struggle between the Great Russian and Ukrainian peoples themselves.

One attacks. The other defends itself.

30 M. Hrushevsky, 'Ochyshchennia ohnem,' in *Vybrani pratsi*, pp. 40–3.

The history of these two 'fraternal peoples' has reached the stage discussed in the Biblical tale of the first brothers: And God asked: Cain, where is your brother?[31]

Hrushevsky's policy was in ruins and the very existence of the Central Rada was in danger, but the last breath of life had not yet passed from Abel's charred and blistered body. Volhynia, at least, was cleared of Bolshevism, and further south, a vigorous young officer named Iurko Tiutiunyk was raising a highly effective army of Free Cossacks and going on the offensive against Red units on the Right Bank. Most important, however, Ukrainian eyes, and especially those of Hrushevsky, who was the only one to have personally seen the other side of the front, were turned toward Brest-Litovsk, where, though he did not yet know it, a peace treaty had already been signed. This treaty guaranteed the immediate exchange of all prisoners-of-war, including the well-disciplined and nationally conscious Ukrainian Bluecoat and Greycoat Divisions formed in the prisoner-of-war camps in Germany and Austria.[32]

Hrushevsky himself had played an indirect, but significant, role in the negotiations leading up to the conclusion of this treaty. He had been the only government figure to brief the Ukrainian diplomats when they had first set out as observers; again, he had been the only one to give them instructions when they returned with the Austro-German proposals on the eve of the Fourth Universal.

In general, with regard to international politics Hrushevsky was in a very difficult position. Years of monarchist insinuations and Russian nationalist propaganda had made him very sensitive to allegations of Austrophilism or of being influenced by 'German marks.' His guarded reserve in relation to the war effort had only changed after the Bolshevik seizure of power in Petrograd. In hopes of establishing formal relations with foreign states, he had fully supported Shulhyn's policy of cooperation with the democratic Western powers and France in particular. But Hrushevsky and Shulhyn soon discovered that the Entente demanded a continuation of the war, while the Ukrainian population wanted peace. Moreover, in the face of the growing Bolshevik danger, Britain and France could offer no substantial aid, while the Central Powers had control over the Ukrainian Sich Riflemen and the Grey and Blue Divisions. Thus when Vynnychenko's government fell and that of Holubovych took office, Hrushevsky recognized the necessity of reaching an immediate agreement at Brest, but at the same time forcefully seconded the new prime minister's unsuccessful request to

31 Ibid.
32 From the beginning of the war, the SVU had concentrated on gathering together and raising the national consciousness of Ukrainian prisoners captured by the German and Austrian forces. Separate camps housed some eighty thousand prisoners, who were taught reading, writing, history, literature, and choral music. See Doroshenko, *Istoriia,* I, 35ff.

the Francophile Shulhyn to stay on as foreign minister. 'Peace with the Central Powers,' he told a despairing Shulhyn, 'has certainly become inevitable, but if you stay, the Entente powers will recognize that we have been forced into this position and that, above all, our political orientation has not changed.'[33]

Thus when the Ukrainian negotiators returned to Kiev, Hrushevsky was still struggling with the paradoxes of his position in between the Entente and the Central Powers. How could he obtain an immediate peace and rally the Galicians and the Greycoats to the support of the Ukrainian Republic without risking future relations with the Western democracies? During those nervous last days in Kiev, Hrushevsky determined to strike a hard bargain with the Central Powers and at the same time push ahead for an immediate peace settlement. The paradox was not yet resolved, but that could not be helped.[34]

On the eve of the proclamation of the Fourth Universal, the recently returned Ukrainian diplomats informed Hrushevsky that the Austrians would not give up any of their Ukrainian territories, as he had demanded. The Central Powers would only concede Kholm [Chełm] and parts of Pidliashshia [Podlasie], which had been a part of Congress Poland and thus under the former Russian Empire. Hrushevsky complained to the young diplomats that not all of Ukrainian Pidliashshia had been included. Moreover, he would not ignore the fate of Austrian Galicia, where he had spent so many years building up Ukrainian national institutions. He decided to stand by the principle that he had first adopted in 1899, when he had helped to organize the Ukrainian National Democratic Party: a united and independent Ukraine might be put off to the future, but, in the meantime, the Austrian Ukrainians had to be liberated from Polish subjection; they had to be recognized as a separate Austrian nationality. 'Hrushevsky agreed,' writes Sevriuk, who was now named to lead the delegation back to Brest, 'that peace might be concluded on condition that Eastern Galicia and Northern Bukovina be united as a separate Austrian Crown Land.'[35]

33 Shulhyn, *L'Ukraine contre Moscou*, p. 179. Shulhyn could not accept this argument, saying that if he stayed on and signed a peace treaty with the Central Powers, he would be called a traitor to the Entente. Hrushevsky jumped at this remark. Shulhyn writes: 'The moment that I said this, Hrushevsky became extremely nervous. He ended by saying that a political person had to do whatever was necessary in a given situation and that this was the only rule that I was bound to go by. This did not budge me an inch, and I resigned anyway.'

34 Ibid.

35 Sevriuk, pp. 155–6. According to Doroshenko, *Istoriia*, I, 296, Hrushevsky had set the creation of a fully autonomous Ukrainian Crown Land as a *conditio sine qua non* for carrying on further negotiations. Reshetar, p. 107, says that the appointment of Sevriuk to head the delegation back to Brest 'probably was prompted by the fact that Hrushevsky envisioned the youth as the husband of his only daughter Catherine, who had a romantic interest in him.' Reshetar gives no source for this information.

The Treaty of Brest-Litovsk, which was signed a few days later, gave the Ukrainian delegation most of what it asked for. Ukraine was recognized as an independent state, Kholm and much of Pidliashshia were ceded to it, and, to foil the Poles, who would most certainly object to the scheme, a secret agreement was worked out on the unification of Eastern Galicia and Northern Bukovina. On the other hand, the Ukrainian People's Republic was compelled to sell the Central Powers the grain that Vienna needed so badly; the Austrians proved unwilling to transfer the Sich Riflemen from occupied western Volhynia, and it would take some time to mobilize the Greycoat and Bluecoat Divisions for action in Ukraine.[36]

Several hours after the Treaty of Brest-Litovsk had been signed, the Ukrainian diplomats received news of the fall of Kiev. The treaty did not provide for direct German military assistance to the Ukrainian Republic, but by now immediate help of some sort seemed to be absolutely necessary if the Ukrainian government was to be saved. In Brest, it was not even known where the government was. The Germans therefore approached Mykola Liubynsky of the Ukrainian delegation and advised him to make a formal appeal to the German people for military assistance. After consulting with Sevriuk, who was in Vienna, Liubynsky did so, and German troops began to prepare for their advance eastward across the Ukrainian front.[37]

Hrushevsky had been counting on the arrival of Ukrainian troops, not Germans, and news of the German advance seems to have taken him by surprise. The clearest evidence for this is a passage in Sevriuk's memoirs describing a meeting with the Ukrainian leader:

Before 9 February (New Style), so far as I can remember, no one in the delegation had ever spoken about the possibility of a 'friendly' German advance into Ukraine. I must stress that before the conclusion of peace, it had never been discussed with the Austro-German delegates: there was also no discussion of it during our stay in Kiev. In this regard, I must mention a meeting with Professor Hrushevsky in a railway carriage somewhere between Sarny and Zhytomyr. This happened after the peace when the Germans were moving into Ukraine. The two of us were alone and Professor Hrushevsky cried.

36 The text of the treaty and the secret protocol concerning Galicia are given in Zozulia, *Kalendar*, pp. 94–8. For a good general discussion see Fedyshyn, *Germany's Drive to the East*, pp. 60–86, who has translated the various documents into English (pp. 271–82). The importance that Hrushevsky attached to the prisoners-of-war is indicated by the fact that he also sent the recently arrived SVU member O. Skoropys-Ioltukhovsky to join the delegation at Brest and get the Grey and Blue Divisions back to Ukraine as quickly as possible. See Doroshenko, *Istoriia*, 1, 36–8.

37 Doroshenko, *Istoriia*, 1, 333–5, gives the text of the 'Appeal to the German People.' On the basis of German documents, Fedyshyn, *Germany's Drive to the East*, pp. 89–91, clearly establishes that this was done at Hoffman's suggestion, after the matter had already been discussed in Berlin. The Bluecoats, it was believed, would not be ready for action for a month or two, and Hoffman had some doubt as to whether they could pacify Ukraine without German help.

Sevriuk continues:

The German march into Ukraine was the drama of his personal life. Those who, in their hatred for everything Ukrainian and by lies and by slander, had linked his name with either Austrian or German intrigues, had got a new weapon into their hands. What an irony! What a bitter and unmerited fate![38]

What turmoil at that moment occurred within the depths of the historian's inner soul we shall probably never know, for to the casual observer, or to anyone who read his pronouncements of the time, he appeared as firm and resolute as ever. Indeed, he even seemed to be optimistic. In announcing the Treaty of Brest-Litovsk to his people, Hrushevsky pointed out that only the Ukrainian government had succeeded in bringing the unwanted imperialist war to an end. The Bolsheviks, on the other hand, promised peace but never delivered it. In fact, they did everything possible to destroy the Ukrainian People's Republic and prevent it from concluding peace. The Entente too had attempted to keep Ukraine in the war. But the government of the Ukrainian People's Republic kept its promise to the people and concluded an honourable and democratic peace which returned ancestral Ukrainian lands and secured the Republic's international status. He concluded optimistically: 'This is proof of the high authority of the Ukrainian government and its parliament, the Ukrainian Central Rada. This is the guarantee and the beginning of a quick and full victory over all of the country's enemies.'[39]

The Germans tried to be as unobtrusive as possible. They allowed the Ukrainian troops to do most of the fighting and enter recaptured towns in triumph. German soldiers were ordered to keep a low profile, treat the local population with the respect befitting an allied people, and cooperate with Ukrainian officials.[40]

Hrushevsky quietly followed the newly victorious Ukrainian troops and their German allies back to Kiev. In this city, which was now well acquainted with both civil war and Bolshevik rule, he met a passive proletariat, a relieved bourgeoisie, and a national intelligentsia that was happy to see the reestablishment of a Ukrainian government.[41] Shortly after his arrival, Hrushevsky issued an official

38 Sevriuk, pp. 159–60.
39 M. Hrushevsky, 'Myr zemli nashii!' in *Na prozi novoi Ukrainy* (Kiev, 1918), and reprinted in *Vybrani pratsi*, pp. 47–8. About this time Hrushevsky sent to Brest the railroad commissar, Serhii Kachura, to examine communications and arrange for the smooth annexation of Kholm and Pidliashshia. See Kachura, p. 7.
40 Khrystiuk, II, 146; Vynnychenko, *Vidrodzhennia natsii*, II, 303; Fedyshyn, *Germany's Drive to the East,* pp. 90–103.
41 Doroshenko, *Istoriia*, I, 337. In his *Spomyny pro nedavnemynule*, pp. 232–3, Doroshenko describes the elation of Ukrainian circles upon the arrival of Petliura and the first units of the Ukrainian army which marched through the capital in a victory parade. Ukrainians filled the streets, while Jews and 'Muscovites' generally stayed home. For non-Ukrainian reactions see Goldenveizer, pp. 26–7.

statement that explained what the Kievans already seemed to know: the Germans had come for their own reasons, but were favourably inclined toward the Ukrainian state. The government had not dealt with them until the Bolshevik invasion made it unavoidable. The Austrians would not allow the Galicians to help their Eastern brethren, and the prisoners-of-war were still being mobilized. Thus the Germans had come and would only stay until the country had been cleared of its enemies. German soldiers would not steal, but would pay for their daily needs, and the population should give them what they required.[42]

On the other hand, Hrushevsky warned various reactionaries against trying to take advantage of the German presence. In an article composed immediately after the return to Kiev, he wrote that the fall of Bolshevism and the restoration of order might tempt some to dream of the abolition of the real achievements of the revolution, that is, the liberties and social reforms of the Third and Fourth Universals. The government, however, would resist this and would retain its socialist character. He concluded: 'Our struggle with Bolshevism is at the same time a struggle with counter-revolution . . . We will not build a republic for the bourgeoisie, but for the working masses of Ukraine, and we will not retreat from this position.'[43]

In theoretical tracts written after the return to Kiev, Hrushevsky laid out the principles that he thought should be the basis of a new Ukraine. His old ideas, which were formulated in a 'political testament' written before the fall of Kiev, had been burned together with his papers in the destruction of his house; he would not return to them. The Bolshevik invasion, he was now convinced, had dissolved all moral ties to Russia. The Muscovite orientation no longer existed. It was being replaced by a renewed Western orientation which had its roots in Renaissance and medieval times and led through the old market cities of Breslau [Wrocław] and Danzig [Gdańsk]. This tie was cultural and economic. On the other hand, the traditional Ukrainian attraction southward, toward Byzantium and Istanbul, was also being renewed. This would eventually become a real 'Black Sea orientation' based upon geographic proximity. In other words, cultural ties drew the Ukrainian nation westward, while geography turned it south and east. Hrushevsky insisted that these economic and cultural connections had nothing to do with imperialist temptations. In spite of all his recent disappointments, Hrushevsky's ultimate ideal was still a federation of the world. This broader federation could only begin with the voluntary federation of countries that were closely related in economic and cultural terms. But to bring this about, more practical work was necessary.

42 M. Hrushevsky, 'Choho pryishly nimtsi na Ukrainu,' *Ofitsiialni povidomlennia Dumky* (Kiev, 1918), and reprinted in *Vilna Ukraina*, no. 52 (1966), 27–8, and in Doroshenko, *Istoriia*, I, 335–6.
43 M. Hrushevsky, 'Povorotu ne bude!' in *Na porozi novoi Ukrainy* and reprinted in *Vybrani pratsi*, pp. 49–50.

The fact that we sing beautifully, observed Hrushevsky, but cannot put together a disciplined army to defend our liberties shows how much more work has to be done. A proper balance between physical and spiritual needs must be struck and this will be the moral foundation of a truly 'Great Ukraine.' Hrushevsky concluded that a Great Ukraine, with clear moral principles at its base, would strengthen and enrich the cause of all humanity.[44]

Hrushevsky devoted an entire essay to describing his vision of a Great Ukraine. He began with the peasantry, which he considered to be the primary foundation of his ideal. The Ukrainian populists of the nineteenth century had pointed the way; their more cautious successors would be wrong to be frightened by the radical reforms to the revolutionary Ukrainian government. The Ukrainian revolution was very different from the ones that had taken place in the West. 'Our history,' Hrushevsky wrote, 'has gone along different paths.'

We have no creative healthy working bourgeoisie and that which is called a bourgeoisie is predominantly a parasitical element nurtured by the old régime and incapable of creative work . . . The Ukrainian proletariat is still extraordinarily weak . . . Therefore our revolution has happened differently from those of the West . . . [Our revolution] has at its foundation the interests of the working peasantry . . . This peasantry, although it will not expand in relative terms (because of industrialization, the growth of an industrial proletariat, and related intellectual – that is, intelligentsia and quasi-intelligentsia – occupations), will nevertheless continue to grow in absolute terms and will retain, perhaps forever, a primary social and political role . . . Future generations of villagers will have the great mission of representing the Ukrainian People's Republic, a Great Ukraine, before the world. [In this sense,] it will be the single state of the working people that will serve as a model and a school for the other democracies of the world.[45]

Turning to the cities, Hrushevsky referred to the Czech model, which saw the decline of German predominance throughout the nineteenth century. Polish and Jewish elements still predominated in Ukraine's cities, but this had to change with the foundation of the Ukrainian state. The Jews, in particular, had to be granted full autonomy and encouraged to give up their Russifying practices in favour of their own national life and greater appreciation for the Ukrainian culture, which – borrowing from their Russian masters – they had been accustomed to deprecate

44 See the essays 'Na perelomi,' 'Kinets moskovskoi oriientatsii, 'Nasha zakhidnia oriientatsiia,' 'Oriientatsiia chornomorska,' 'Novi perspektyvy,' 'Kultura krasy i kultura zhyttia,' and 'Velyka Ukraina,' all in *Vybrani pratsi*, pp. 51–89. There is a discussion of these writings in V. Modrych-Verhan, 'Mykhailo Hrushevsky iak publitsyst,' in *Mykhailo Hrushevsky u 110 rokovyny narodzhennia*, pp. 76–86.
45 M. Hrushevsky, 'Pidstavy velykoi Ukrainy,' in *Na porozi novoi Ukrainy* and reprinted in *Vybrani pratsi*, pp. 90–4. Also see Modrych-Verhan, pp. 87–8.

and oppose. In turn, Ukrainian leaders would do everything possible to rout out and neutralize anti-Semitism. Anti-Jewish feelings, the historian believed, had only recently arisen as a result of vulgar nationalism and the participation of some Jews in Bolshevik excesses. In fact, relations with the Jews would be easier to mend than would relations with the Poles who had lost their great estates with the socialization of the land. It is to be hoped, Hrushevsky concluded, that national autonomy would not keep Polish cultural institutions islands of clerical reaction and chauvinism in a great democratic and socialist sea.[46]

From minority rights, Hrushevsky turned to the state itself. It would be a democratic 'people's' state going beyond the bourgeois republics of the West to approach 'socialism' whenever possible. Old suspicions about the state, wrote this most famous of populist historians, must be discarded. Decentralization on the American model would protect civil liberties. There would be no bureaucratic-police rule. For example, schools would be partly controlled by local organs of self-government, and partly by national organs. The army, which in the past was always a threat to democracy, would eventually be replaced by a popular militia. Given such a reordering of affairs, the nation might continue along the path of spiritual and economic liberation in its own democratic state.[47]

Having reiterated his commitment to the cause of the people, to the democratic principle, and the revolution, Hrushevsky once again retired to the sacred precincts of the Pedagogical Museum where the Mala Rada had reassembled for legislative work. Indeed, even during the retreat to Zhytomyr and Sarny, the diminished but undissolved Rada had never ceased to issue progressive, if somewhat idealistic, legislation. In various obscure towns along the railway line, laws were passed about the socialization of the land, about the introduction of the New Style calendar, a new monetary system, a coat-of-arms for the Republic, Ukrainian citizenship, and the abolition of gubernias in favour of a new system of thirty self-governing 'lands,' somewhat similar to American states.[48]

Hrushevsky played a crucial role in all of this activity. The new autonomous administrative system was almost entirely his creation and conformed to his theories about decentralization of the state. The design of the national coat-of-arms had been researched beforehand by Dmytro Antonovych, supported and amended slightly by Hrushevsky, and then executed by his friend, the artist Krychevsky. Its essence was the trident which had appeared on the coins of Volodymyr the Great (d.1015) and which Hrushevsky saw as symbolic of the Ukrainian claim to the

46 Ibid., pp. 94–9.
47 Ibid., pp. 99–110. Also see Modrych-Verhan, pp. 89–98.
48 The texts of these laws are in Doroshenko, *Istoriia*, I, 286–94, and Zozulia, *Kalendar*, pp. 87–92. For a description of the daily sessions of the Mala Rada at this time see Kachura, p. 7.

heritage of the ancient Kievan state.[49] The historian played a lesser role in the elaboration of the land law which abolished private property, but once it was formulated, he loyally supported it. In general, during the chaotic period in Zhytomyr and Sarny, the person of Hrushevsky continued to stand in the centre of what remained of the Ukrainian government and act as a magnet for the national forces. It was he who kept the Mala Rada functioning. The young men of the Holubovych cabinet looked to him for reassurance and leadership. He gave them what he could: a clear statement of principles and a symbol around which they could rally.

When the full Mala Rada, which included the members from the national minorities, reassembled to consider the legislation that had been passed at Zhytomyr and Sarny, fierce debates arose over the radical course of the government. There were allegations of chauvinism and demands that the Holubovych government resign. Hrushevsky, who was by this time quite openly the strongest personality in the government, managed to defuse a ministerial crisis by coopting several Social Democrats and Socialist-Federalists into the cabinet. As a result, the Brest Treaty passed the first stages of ratification and the accusations of chauvinism ceased. On the other hand, the divisions within the UPSR were aggravated to the extent that a united party no longer existed. The anti-German 'left' led by Shumsky and Poloz was deserting to the Bolsheviks, while Hrushevsky's followers, the 'right' who formed the government, had become, in the words of one ambitious SR critic, 'simply given to intrigues [intryganskym].'[50] The government had been temporily saved, but the governing UPSR, which was the largest party in the land, was in a complete shambles.

The general condition of the country was not much better. The Ukrainian state had only a very small army of its own to enforce its will and the recent Bolshevik ascendancy had thoroughly disorganized the administration. Anarchy still reigned in the countryside, and hostile Russian elements gathered around the Kiev City Council. Russian landowners on the Left Bank joined together in a Union of Landlords (*Soiuz zemelnikh sobstvennikov*), while the Polish gentry on the Right Bank used their personal contacts with Poles in the Habsburg service to ensure Austrian intervention on their behalf. With German help, Russian and Polish landlords undertook punitive expeditions against the recalcitrant peasantry. A

49 For Hrushevsky's remarks on the new Ukrainian coat-of-arms, see his 'Tryzub – Ukrainskyi herb,' *Narodnia volia* (Kiev), January 1918, and reprinted in *Vilna Ukraina*, nos. 59–60 (1969), 91. On its execution see Roman Klymkevych, 'Diialnist Mykhaila Hrushevskoho v tsaryni ukrainskoi heraldyky i sfrahistyky,' *Ukrainskyi istoryk*, nos. 1–2 (1966), 82–90.
50 Shapoval, 'Narodnytstvo v ukr. vyzvolnomu rukhovi,' pp. 107–8. More generally, see Hrushevsky, *Iliustrovana istoriia Ukrainy*, pp. 554–8.

recently formed Farmers' or Democratic Agrarian Party (*Ukrainska Democratychna khliborobska Partiia*), which represented the wealthier villagers who had just gathered in a great congress in Poltava gubernia, sent a two-hundred-man delegation to present the Farmers' concerns about the reigning anarchy to the plenary session of the Central Rada. Hrushevsky, however, was unbending in his commitment to the revolution and refused to allow the delegation to address the assembly. The government leaders rejected all of their demands, including a modest amendment to the law on the socialization of all land.[51]

By the beginning of April, the Germans were starting to worry about peasant reluctance to sow their fields. On 6 April, the German commander, von Eichhorn, ordered his subordinates to ensure that the fields be sown; on 12 April, Hrushevsky, Holubovych, and the Ukrainian government protested to Eichhorn against the order, but were told that they could call themselves the government only because Germany stood behind them.[52] Angry debates in the Rada followed, and a few days later, in the UPSR newspaper *Narodnia volia*, Hrushevsky declared that an amendment to the land law under foreign and landlord pressure would be a betrayal of the peasantry.[53] In fact, Hrushevsky's resistance to outside interference went beyond the realm of principles. He was downright tactless in his treatment of the Germans and this had a disastrous effect upon their relations with the Ukrainian government. The moderate Doroshenko, who witnessed the course of events in growing alarm, later explained:

In general, official Ukrainian circles received the Germans very coldly, like occupiers rather than allies. No one made any effort toward rapproachment, friendly relations, or [exchange of] information. When the Germans arrived in Kiev, the capital of Ukraine, they thought that they would meet Ukrainians, but with the exception of government institutions, they were nowhere to be found. Meanwhile, Russian, Jewish, and Polish circles did

51 Doroshenko, *Istoriia*, II, 17; Khrystiuk, II, 159. In his *Spomyny pro nedavne-mynule*, p. 236, Doroshenko writes: 'The requests of the Farmers were really very modest. They wanted the Central Rada to consider its land law, to receive into its body the Farmer delegates, and arrange for new elections to the Ukrainian Constituent Assembly, because the one which had taken place during the Bolshevik invasion was carried out in total chaos and rendered very questionable results: many Bolsheviks and [other] enemies of the Ukrainian state had been elected.'

52 Doroshenko, *Istoriia*, II, 18–19; Reshetar, p. 124; Fedyshyn, *Germany's Drive to the East*, pp. 124–7.

53 M. Hrushevsky, 'Stara istoriia,' *Narodnia volia*, no. 59 (Kiev, 1918); reprinted in *Vilna Ukraina*, no. 57 (1968) 4–6, and quoted at length in Khrystiuk, II, 161–2. This number of *Narodnia volia* is dated 18 April by the editors of *Vilna Ukraina* and 21 April by Khrystiuk. Hrushevsky later wrote: 'When German representatives paid me official visits in my capacity as president of the Central Rada, I warned them in the firmest possible way against going along with various reactionary elements which were calling them to introduce an order that would be favourable to the landlords and capitalists.' See *Avtobiohrafiia–1914–1919*, p. 100.

everything possible to approach, befriend, and inform the Germans, and one can imagine how they informed them about Ukraine and her young state! Extraordinary dryness and brusqueness were characteristic of Professor Hrushevsky's personal relations – and I have known him since 1904 – and these characteristics of his set the tone of the Ukrainian government's relations with the Germans from the moment that they first arrived in Kiev. This was true of Ukrainian civilians, the military, government people, and official circles. No welcome and no meetings other than purely official business. Meanwhile, non-Ukrainian Kievan 'society' did just the opposite and 'worked on them' as much as they could.[54]

About the middle of April, rumours began to spread about some kind of German action against the Central Rada. 'General Groener, their real leader,' Hrushevsky tells us, 'came to an understanding . . . with the local rightist Ukrainian parties and asked to have a confidential conversation with me, but I refused, asking him to approach the responsible ministers directly.'[55] On the 24th, following the disappearance of a prominent Jewish banker who was alleged to have violated the Rada's commercial laws, the German military took over police functions and the criminal courts. On the 26th, the Germans disarmed those Bluecoats who had already arrived in Kiev. On the 27th, the Socialist-Federalists withdrew from the government.[56] About this same time, Ievhen Konovalets, the commander of the Sich Riflemen, told several prominent UPSR members that the Germans were plotting a coup. When he got no clear response, Konovalets went to Hrushevsky himself and informed him of the danger. To Konovalets's great surprise, Hrushevsky was unruffled and assured him that he had just spoken with a representative of the German command, Stolzenberg, and had received a firm assurance that there was no threat to the Central Rada.[57]

On 27 and 28 April, there were stormy debates and denunciations of the reactionary German military in the Mala Rada. Liubynsky was criticized for not sufficiently defining the German role before calling them in; Vynnychenko attacked German imperialism, and Holubovych made a distinction between the German military and the German government. About 4:00 on the afternoon of the 28th, the representative of the Jewish Bund and critic of the German alliance, M. Rafes, was speaking, when someone approached Hrushevsky, who was seated in the president's chair, and whispered something into his ear. Hrushevsky said nothing, but after a few minutes, told Rafes that his time was up. Rafes continued

54 Doroshenko, *Spomyny pro nedavne-mynule*, p. 237.
55 *Avtobiohrafiia–1914–1919*, p. 100.
56 Fedyshyn, *Germany's Drive to the East*, pp. 105–32, describes the growing conflict in great detail. There is a summary in Reshetar, pp. 127–8.
57 Ievhen Konovalets, *Prychynky do istorii ukrainskoi revoliutsii*, 2nd ed. (n.p., 1948), p. 6.

to speak. A few minutes later Hrushevsky again told Rafes that his time was up. Rafes still continued to speak. Suddenly, a German officer and a number of armed soldiers burst into the hall. The officer marched up to Hrushevsky, pointed a revolver at him, and shouted in broken Russian: 'In the name of the German command, hands up!' The intruding soldiers pointed their guns and all present except Hrushevsky raised their hands. Deathly white, and not moving from the Presidential Chair, Hrushevsky said in a trembling voice in Ukrainian: 'In the name of the Ukrainian Central Rada, I protest against this shameful attack of the German command against the legal Ukrainian government.' The officer read out a list of names: Tkachenko, Liubynsky, Kovalevsky, etc. Those who were present stepped forward and were marched out. The others were then ordered into adjoining rooms and sent home. Hrushevsky was still sitting in the Presidential Chair when the German officer standing next to him holstered his revolver, and without saying another word, walked out and left the Ukrainian leader completely alone.[58]

The next day the members of the Rada who were still free quietly met in the Pedagogical Museum to discuss the situation. Hrushevsky informed the newly cautious circle of parliamentarians that he had lodged a protest with the German authorities, and that the Germans had returned some of the papers that they had seized. There was silence. Later, the meeting was opened as a session of the Mala Rada. With what must have been grim feelings of unreality, defiance, and acquiescence, the shaken legislators ratified a constitution for the republic, amended the land law as the Democratic Agrarians had requested, and formally elected Hrushevsky president of the republic.[59]

About this same time, Konovalets arrived at the Rada building with an armed detachment of Sich Riflemen. He had just come from the German command, where he had been told that there was no coup under way and that the attack on the Rada had been a mistake. He was told that only a few Rada members who were plotting against the Germans were to have been arrested. Konovalets conveyed

58 Doroshenko, *Istoriia*, II, 34, gives an accurate picture of the scene. All of the first-hand accounts agree on essential points concerning Hrushevsky. Goldenveizer, pp. 84–5, writes: 'The soldiers raised their guns. Everyone except Hrushevsky stood up and raised his hands. With raised hands and a sarcastic smile on his face, Rafes was standing at the speaker's podium. Porsh (as a sign of his German loyalties, it seems) raised his hands with a copy of *Neue Freie Presse* in one and his passport in the other ... Later, I said to an SR standing next to me: "Now you see how thoughtless it was to be without power and carry out a policy opposed to those who have power. Why did you not go along with the Germans for a while?"' Also see A. Ilnytsky, 'Rozhyn nimtsiamy tsentralnoi rady: spohad,' *Vilna Ukraina*, no. 52 (1966), 24–7.

59 Doroshenko, *Istoriia*, II, 34–5. The new land law allowed private possession of land of up to 30 desiatyny. In his *Avtobiohrafiia–1914–1919*, p. 100, Hrushevsky says that the Germans arrested, searched, and confiscated some papers from him because of his refusal to talk to Groener.

this information to the Ukrainian leaders. 'I found Professor Hrushevsky and Premier Holubovych severely depressed and very disoriented,' the colonel later wrote. 'When I asked what we should do with the armed guard of the Central Rada and what we should do with the government, I did not receive any clear answer. They only told me: keep in contact with the War Ministry and ask again for an explanation from the Germans.'[60]

This same day the conservative forces made their move. The members of the Union of Landowners met under the protection of some five hundred armed Russian officers, and, with the German authorities looking on, proclaimed a well-known general of Ukrainian background as 'Hetman of All Ukraine.' In Saint Sophia square, where only a few months earlier the Ukrainian People's Republic had been proclaimed, Pavlo Skoropadsky was acclaimed ruler of 'the Ukrainian State' (*Ukrainska derzhava*) to the music of church bells and the singing of 'Many Years.' Within the next twenty-four hours all government ministries were in the hands of the new Hetman's largely 'Little Russian' supporters. Three of these men were killed when the Sich Riflemen put up a brief resistance around the Central Rada building.

The short life of the Ukrainian People's Republic marked a profound turning point in modern Ukrainian political history. Just when an autonomous Ukrainian state was in the process of being established, the Bolshevik revolution in Russia and the subsequent invasion of Ukraine dashed all hopes for a peaceful resolution of the national question. Almost against their will, Hrushevsky and the other Ukrainian leaders were forced to make a declaration of independence for which they knew the population as a whole was not prepared. Moreover, the very idea of state independence seemed culpable to them and they took pains to show that they had not completely forsaken the federal ideal.

It was no use. Their assurances were hollow, the Bolsheviks relentless, and the Central Powers insistent. As Hrushevsky himself could clearly see, traditional Ukrainian autonomism, the orientation toward Russia, was consumed in the conflagration that had destroyed his house. Henceforth, the Ukrainian national movement waged a true war of independence.

For the bulk of the Ukrainian intelligentsia, the realization of the necessity for war had come too late. Hrushevsky had ignored it, Vynnychenko had denied it,

60 Konovalets, p. 6, notes that had Hrushevsky not expressly denied the existence of a German threat, the Sich Riflemen would have immediately come to the defence of the Central Rada. He writes: '*This express and categorical declaration of the President of the Central Rada was the only reason that the German attack on the Central Rada Building (28 April) caught us unprepared.* Prof. Hrushevsky enjoyed such authority among us that after his declaration we discarded the idea of strengthening the guard of the Central Rada and, as was usual, put only honorary sentries in place.'

and Petliura only turned to a volunteer army when all other means of defence were blocked. In February or April, 1918, it was well and good to talk about the necessity for a small, well-disciplined army, but this was merely a belated admission that Mikhnovsky and the Polubotok nationalists had been proved right. The anti-militarist ideologue of the national movement, Hrushevsky, only made this admission when the Bolsheviks were threatening Kiev. Vynnychenko never brought himself to make it.[61]

It was Hrushevsky's commitment to principles and his propensity for theory that prevented him from becoming a practical revolutionary politician. This is clearly revealed in his dogmatic adherence to the democratic process, his concentration on purely parliamentary work, his lofty but inconsequential theoretical writings, and his stubborn refusal to change the law that had abolished private property. He would not compromise with the middle strata of peasantry, who could have been the backbone of a free Ukrainian state, and, outside of his official capacity, he would not even talk to his German protectors. Such 'principled' conduct was both noble and 'progressive,' but it quickly alienated the only possible allies in a very critical situation.

Hrushevsky's old colleagues from the TUP were aware of these faults. Although Doroshenko had sat in the Central Rada and voted with the others in favour of various socialist laws, and the moderate Chykalenko knew that the Central Rada could not do otherwise, both men later thought that, in the heat of the revolutionary struggle, Hrushevsky had succumbed to demogoguery, naivety, and personal ambition. Doroshenko assures us that many thought the Holubovych government was inept because Hrushevsky could not tolerate rivals and always surrounded himself with weak personalities.[62] Chykalenko, who had always abhorred SR extremism and thought the UPSR to be purely Russian in ideological content, sadly concluded: 'When M. Hrushevsky returned with a German army from Zhytomyr, and instead of building a petty-bourgeois peasant state, stood at the head of the Socialist Revolutionaries and proclaimed publicly and in print that the Central Rada would show the world a 'model socialist state,' I saw that the Muscovite proverb – "every wise man is silly enough" – applies very well to our respected professor.'[63]

---

61 This question took on great significance in the 1930s, when, under the general influence of militant nationalism, and in particular of the nationalist ideologue Dmytro Dontsov, Hrushevsky was plainly accused of ineffectual pacifism, corrupt Muscophilism, and being pro-Soviet. For the attack on Hrushevsky see the series of articles by M. Mukhin scattered through various numbers of the Lviv *Vistnyk* for 1936. For some remarks by Dontsov himself see his *Dukh nashoi davnyny* (Prague, 1944), pp. 38, 45. For an early defence of Hrushevsky, which admits that he only spoke in favour of an army in February–March 1918, see M. Andrusiak, 'Dumky Hrushevskoho pro potrebu ukrainskoi armii,' *Litopys Chervonoi Kalyny,* VII (Lviv, 1935), 7–8.

62 Doroshenko, *Spomyny pro nedavne-mynule,* pp. 216–17.

63 Chykalenko, *Spohady,* p. 385.

It was easy to identify Hrushevsky's personal shortcomings and tactical mistakes when the game was already up. But the degree to which the professor could actualy manipulate the situation remains an open question. Clearly, during the first months of the revolution, Hrushevsky's prestige was enormous and his influence considerable. At that time, his theories coincided with the aspirations of the masses. But as events rapidly unfolded, it seemed more and more as if Hrushevsky was merely riding the crest of a great wave that no man could possibly control. In legal terms, his position was largely symbolic.[64] Moreover, by the beginning of 1918, the historian's theoretical postulates were no longer in harmony with the immediate demands of the population. When the crisis finally came, very few cared for democratic forms and very few were willing to fight for the Central Rada. Although he found it necessary to rely upon German help, Hrushevsky could not bear to cooperate or fraternize with his unwanted (uninvited, he later claimed)[65] conservative allies. Thus he alienated both the general population to whom he was committed and the German guests who protected but embarrassed him. It was the failure to resolve this dilemma that sealed the fate of the Ukrainian Central Rada.

64 In his *Avtobiohrafiia–1914–1919*, p. 100, Hrushevsky writes: 'Although all responsibility fell upon me, in reality I had a very limited influence and only a moral one at that: in legal terms, my role was purely formal. As head of the Central Rada, I chaired its meetings and represented it before the outside world. The majority decided everything and all executive power was in the hands of the General Secretariat.' On 24 March 1918, during the period when Hrushevsky was supposed to be the most powerful figure in the Holubovych government, an Austrian observer reported: 'Der Vorsitzende der grossen Rada ist der gewesene Professor für ruthenische Geschichte an der Lemberger Universität Herr Hruschewski; ein idealistischer Theoretiker, der sich aber nur mit den grossen politischen Ideen befasst und das Ministerium besonders in der volkswirtschaftlichen Tätigkeit in keiner Weise beeinflusst.' See Theophil Hornykiewicz, *Ereignisse in der Ukraine 1914–1922*, vol. I (Philadelphia, 1966), p. 334.
65 *Avtobiohrafiia–1914–1919*, p. 100.

8

The Liberation Struggle at Home and Abroad
1918–1924

The coup of General Pavlo Skoropadsky met with very little resistance. Colonel Arkas of the Rada's cavalry guard and Colonel Slyvinsky of the General Staff deserted to the new Hetman. Some of the Sich Riflemen put up a brief resistance around the Central Rada building, but soon retreated to their barracks while negotiations with the Hetman's representatives began.[1]

While the Hetman consolidated his rule, the Hrushevsky family accompanied the Sich Riflemen to their barracks. Though there was very little fighting and the general population greeted the coup calmly, the retreat of the President of the Ukrainian People's Republic did not pass without incident. Hrushevsky writes: 'When the followers of the Hetman were besieging the Central Rada building, the Sich Riflemen took me together with my wife and daughter to their barracks. During the process, some Muscovite tried to stab me with his bayonet, and lunged at me, but, instead of me, wounded my wife.'[2]

Once the party was safely at the barracks, there were secret conferences about what should be done. Petliura, Porsh, Konovalets, Mykola Shrah, Mykola Chechel, Mykola Kovalevsky, and others were present. At one point, representatives of the Hetman, who was under German pressure to continue in the path of

---

1 Doroshenko, *Istoriia*, II, 38–9; Konovalets, pp. 5–9.

2 *Avtobiohrafiia–1914–1919*, p. 100. For a much fuller eyewitness account see M. Marenin, 'Dvi zustrichi z Prof. Hrushevskym,' *Lysty do pryiateliv*, no. 4 (New York, 1960), 7–10. The would-be assassin at first tried to shoot Hrushevsky, who was seated with his wife and daughter in a car, but the rifle would not fire. After three attempts, he ran at the historian with fixed bayonet but was pushed aside by Marenin, who was standing nearby. Mariia Sylvestrivna's wound could not have been serious, because Hrushevsky told Marenin that everyone was all right and no medical assistance was required. The would-be assassin was dressed in the uniform of a Sich Rifleman, came from the Lemko region of Galicia, and was generally described as a 'Muscophile' by his former comrades. He was taken away and shot shortly afterwards. Doroshenko, *Istoriia*, II, 39, says that the bayonet 'scratched' Hrushevsky's hand.

statehood and independence established by the Central Rada, were sent to ask Hrushevsky and Chechel to ratify the unpublished law confirming the peace with the Central Powers. Hrushevsky firmly refused, and the Hetman was compelled to sign and publish the measure on his own.[3]

While Konovalets negotiated with the Hetman's supporters, Hrushevsky and the Rada leaders agreed that, in the face of overwhelming German strength, open resistance in Kiev was impossible. It was decided to smuggle Hrushevsky out of the capital and carry on resistance in some different form. Late one evening, the Sich Riflemen dressed Hrushevsky in a long overcoat, tucked his beard inside, and smuggled him past the German sentries and into the countryside, where his family still owned a small cottage. The Hetman did not pursue the fallen Rada leaders, and Hrushevsky was left in peace during the next several months.[4]

The new regime assumed the form of a dictatorship with all executive and legislative power temporarily in the hands of the Hetman and ministers appointed by him. All property laws enacted by the Russian Provisional Government and the Central Rada were abolished. However, the Hetman promised basic civic liberties, a moderate program of land redistribution that would break up the large estates, and the future election of a Ukrainian parliament or *soim*. The Hetman tried unsuccessfully to attract the support of the moderate Ukrainian parties, especially the Socialist-Federalists. Among the Ukrainians, only the Democratic-Agrarians, that is, the *Khliborobska Partiia,* and a few of the more conservative veterans of the national movement like Dmytro Doroshenko and Viacheslav Lypynsky supported him. Some Ukrainian exiles like the famous Austrophile, Dontsov, returned to work in the Hetman's administration. But on the whole, the Skoropadsky regime rested largely on the more conservative classes, on those Russian landowners who wished to reconstruct the Russian Empire from a safe base in Ukraine, and on the bayonets of the German military.[5]

Nationally conscious Ukrainian circles, the more moderate political parties led by Iefremov's Socialist-Federalists, and the postal, telegraph, and railroad workers formed an independent organization to represent their interests. The Ukrainian National-State Union (*Ukrainskyi Natsionalnyi-Derzhavnyi Soiuz*) acted as a quasi-legal opposition and criticized the conservative economic and national policies of the Russian Kadets and Octobrists who held key positions in the Skoropadsky government. The National Union also helped to offset the influence of the Union of Industry, Commerce, and Finance (*Protofis*), which was pro-Russian in orientation and generally supported the government. At first the

3 Khrystiuk, iii, 69; Kovalevsky, *Pry dzherelakh borotby,* pp. 487–8.
4 Kovalevsky, *Pry dzherelakh borotby,* p. 487; Marenin, 'Dví zustrichi.'
5 Reshetar, pp. 147–207, *passim*; Taras Hunczak, 'The Ukraine under Hetman Pavlo Skoropadskyi,' in *Ukraine 1917–1921: A Study in Revolution*, pp. 61–81.

USDLP and the UPSR, which were basically revolutionary parties, did not join the National Union. Hrushevsky played no role in its formation.[6]

Though the elected president of the defunct Ukrainian People's Republic was cut off from political developments in the capital, he must have been aware of the crisis that was developing in the countryside where he now resided. The punitive expeditions against the peasantry, which had begun during the last days of the Central Rada, were becoming a regular feature of the new regime, and by the summer were producing a growing number of local peasant uprisings. In the countryside around Kiev, the uprisings (in which the UPSR and the Peasant Union seemed to have played some role) began to take on special significance. Khrystiuk informs us that the SR peasant leader, M. Shynkar, who headed the largest SR insurgent group in the Kiev area, 'held discussions with the President of the Central Rada.'

They discussed the need to transform the movement into a pan-Ukrainian peasant-worker uprising. [Shynkar] called on old Hrushevsky to go to the insurgents and stand at the head of the movement, assuring him that his name alone would be enough to ignite all the peasants and workers of Ukraine and consume in its fires the landlord bourgeois dictatorship. But circumstances did not favour it.[7]

It was probably in the chaos surrounding these events that Hrushevsky's country home was destroyed. Thereafter, he moved back to Kiev, where he lived in semi-secrecy in the shell of his burnt-out house.[8]

Throughout the summer, the Skoropadsky regime tried to balance between Russia and Ukraine, reaction and reform. The Hetman asked Doroshenko to Ukrainianize the cabinet, but in spite of considerable efforts, the latter could find no one who would cooperate. The Hetman made progress in the nationalization of the school system and founded two new Ukrainian universities, but still remained unpopular among the national intelligentsia, who were accustomed to seeing themselves as the champions of the peasantry. His minister of education, M.P. Vasylenko, created a commission of scholars including the mineralogist, Vladimir Vernadsky, to found a Ukrainian Academy of Sciences. Hrushevsky heard about the project and sent his brother Oleksander to ask Vernadsky to come and discuss the project with him, since he was still in hiding and could not come to Vernadsky. The latter secretly met with Hrushevsky and discussed the plans for an academy. Both men thought the project important, but disagreed on the model along which the academy should be organized.[9] Shortly afterward, the Hetman asked

6 Reshetar, pp. 151–2; Hunczak, 'The Ukraine under Skaropadskyi.'
7 Khrystiuk, III, 61.
8 *Avtobiohrafiia–1914–1919*, p. 100.
9 Hrushevsky preferred the Western European system used at the NTSh, which stressed the

Hrushevsky himself to take on the presidency of the new institution. Skoropadsky later recalled:

> I was of the opinion, and everyone else agreed with me, that this high and honourable place in Ukraine belonged to Hrushevsky alone. I had always esteemed Hrushevsky as our greatest historian; I respected him for his courage, about which I had often heard . . . It seemed to me that if he became President of the Academy, it would be of great benefit to Ukrainian scholarship . . . Therefore, I made inquiries as to his position on the matter. The answer was a categorical negative.[10]

Perhaps Hrushevsky could already see that the Skoropadsky regime would not last much longer. In fact, by the time the academicians were gathering for their first formal meeting, the war in Western Europe was coming to an end and the Germans were preparing to go home. The Social Democrats and the SRs had entered the National Union and Vynnychenko was already standing at its head. Thereafter, the failure of a last attempt at compromise and the imminent German departure led the Hetman to declare 'federation' with Russia. In response, the National Union established a Directory of five men – including Vynnychenko and Petliura – to head an insurrectionary government. They were soon joined by independent peasant insurgent armies, each under its own *Otaman* or Cossack-style leader. By 14 December 1918, the bulk of the Hetman's army had deserted to the rebels, Skoropadsky had abdicated, and the victorious Sich Riflemen once again patrolled the streets of Kiev. Hrushevsky was not asked to participate in or head the uprising; he played no part in it and only came out of hiding when the Ukrainian insurgents were already in control of Kiev.[11]

humanities; Vernadsky preferred the Russian system, which was more elaborate and placed an emphasis on laboratories and research institutes for the physical sciences. See Vernadsky's memoir: 'The First Year of the Ukrainian Academy of Sciences (1918–1919),' *Annals of the Ukrainian Academy of Arts and Science in the USA,* XI (New York, 1964–8), 3–31. Also see N. Polonska-Vasylenko, *Ukrainska Akademiia Nauk (Narys istorii),* 2 vols. (Munich, 1955–8), I, 15–16. According to D. Anastas'in and I. Voznesensky, 'Nachalo trekh nationalnykh akademii,' *Pamiat': istoricheskii sbornik,* vol. V (Moscow–Paris, 1981–2), 165–225, the new Ukrainian academy, with its special function as a centre for strengthening the self-awareness and assertiveness of the nation and for attaining international recognition of Ukrainian culture – aspects that Hrushevsky clearly wished to stress – was to serve as a model for the national academies of other Soviet Republics and exerted an especially strong influence on the Belorussians. Anastas'in and Voznesensky conclude (p. 166): 'There was nothing similar to it in the practice of academies of sciences throughout the entire world.'

10 Quoted in Polonska-Vasylenko, *Ukrainska Akademiia Nauk,* I, 15–16.

11 *Avtobiohrafiia–1914–1919,* p. 101. During this brief retirement from political life, 'seeking relief from difficult experiences in literary-scholarly work,' Hrushevsky completed his *Vsesvitna istoriia,* and devoted himself to ancient history, and the history of the Middle Ages. See *Avtobiohrafiia–1926,* p. 87.

The historian later explained this long period of political inactivity in terms of principles. He condemned both the Hetman and his opponents. 'I did not want to take part in social or political life,' writes Hrushevsky, 'because I did not want to give the impression that I had come to terms with the current state of affairs which had been set up through German violence and the bourgeoisie's betrayal of its own people.' He explains:

The Hetman tried to appease me with some kind of appointment; as, for example, President of the Academy. (The supporters of the Hetman hastened to organize it so that they could link his name with this cause for which the real heroes of Ukrainian scholarship had worked dozens of years and at a time when scholarship brought no financial rewards.) Of course, I refused this proposition; I would have nothing to do with the Hetman's Academy. On the other hand, I had no desire to seek any ties with the political action which was concentrated in the newly created 'National Union.' Right-wing groups which had conspired with the Germans against the Central Rada were leading it and now they were reviling the Rada and trying to organize a bourgeois Ukrainian government on the basis of an understanding with the Hetman and the Germans. But in the end the Hetman gave the Ukrainian bourgeoisie nothing and joined with the Russian bourgeoisie to reconstruct a united Russia.[12]

Judging by Hrushevsky's account, it was he who was refusing to cooperate with both the Hetman and also with his opposition. But if the Hetman felt that he could make use of Hrushevsky, the National Union and the Directory that emerged from it did not. Personal antagonisms seem to have played a definite role. Of the National Union leaders, Iefremov had a history of disagreements with the historian, and it was his party, the Socialist-Federalists, that had deserted the Holubovych government on the eve of the Hetman's coup; the SFs remained a voice for moderation and compromise within the National Union. Moreover, the new head of the National Union, Vynnychenko, was jealous of Hrushevsky's fame and authority – as can be seen in his diary, where he called the historian 'a spiteful, dishonest old man.'[13] Finally the SR leader, Mykyta Shapoval, who was a principal organizer of the uprising against the Hetman and should have informed Hrushevsky of the course of events, seems to have been angry with the former president for previously favouring the inept Holubovych as premier over himself.

12 *Avtobiohrafiia–1914–1919*, pp. 100–1.
13 Vynnychenko, *Shchodennyk*, I, 316. During the reign of Skoropadsky, Vynnychenko noted at one point that there were difficulties publishing Ukrainian books (p. 288): 'Perhaps it will even become impossible to publish them. My books are still unpublished. I have given all my attention throughout all this year to the creation of the Ukrainian state, but I just do not have the ability of Hrushevsky to use everything for his own good and proofread brochures while at the same time announcing the law of the Ukrainian Republic.'

In consequence, it appears, Shapoval excluded the historian from the deliberations of the conspirators.[14]

With the Directory's restoration of the Ukrainian People's Republic, Holubovych, Oleksander Zhukovsky, and other members of the former SR government were released from prison. Hrushevsky himself immediately reentered public life. At SR party conferences held during the first days after the fall of the Hetman, Hrushevsky and his followers argued that the sole legal government of the country was still the Central Rada and that it should be immediately reconvoked. Shapoval and a majority of the party faithful rejected this idea, because they thought that the Central Rada had been discredited when it called the Germans to Ukraine and when it was so docile in the face of the Hetman's coup.[15]

Even before the Directory had captured Kiev, Shapoval and Vynnychenko had agreed that it would be impractical to recall either the Central Rada or the Ukrainian Constituent Assembly which had been elected during the first Bolshevik invasion. Nevertheless, some kind of legitimization was necessary, and Vynnychenko proposed the idea of a Toilers' Congress (*Trudovyi Kongress*) composed of delegates from the peasantry, the workers, and the soldiers. This reflected Vynnychenko's expectations that some kind of understanding could eventually be worked out with Moscow. On the other hand, Petliura, who headed the military and enjoyed considerable personal popularity, was suspicious of Vynnychenko and doubted whether negotiations with Moscow could prove fruitful. In a USDLP congress held in Kiev (10–12 January 1919), both men agreed that Russian proletarian chauvinism and the absence of a native Ukrainian proletariat were serious problems and that the Toilers' Congress alone could decide how much power should be held by the Directory and how much should be held by local worker-peasant councils/radas/soviets, which might fall into the hands of the Russian Bolsheviks. Both Vynnychenko and Petliura rejected the position of the left wing of their party, which demanded immediate government by local councils. In general, the members of the Directory believed that, in the face of a new Bolshevik invasion and widespread chaos, a firm hand was necessary if independence was to be preserved.[16]

Once it was clear that there was no possibility that the Central Rada would be

14 See the discussion in M. Stakhiv, *Ukraina v dobi dyrektorii UNR*, 6 vols. (Scranton, Pa., 1962–5), I, 70–1.
15 Shapoval, 'Narodnytsvo v ukr. vyzvolnomu rukhovi,' p. 109. Shapoval admits, however, that Hrushevsky did call a secret meeting of the Central Rada to protest the Skoropadsky coup. The appeal met with a very feeble response.
16 There was even some talk of establishing a temporary dictatorship. See Reshetar, p. 217ff., and M. Bohachevsky-Chomiak, 'The Directory of Ukrainian National Republic,' in *The Ukraine 1917–1921: A Study in Revolution*, pp. 92–3.

recalled, Hrushevsky was left with the choice of supporting a Directory of men who were personally antagonistic to him and would not heed his political advice, or going over to the alternative suggested by the left or Independent SDs and the left wing of the UPSR, the pro-Soviet *Borotbisty*. This left-wing block supported the idea of rule by local peasant-worker councils. At this point, it seems, the historian once again turned sharply to the left. While Hrushevsky's SR rivals, Shapoval and Hryhoriiv, were busy with government work in the Directory, the historian endeavoured to build up his following in the UPSR and in the Peasant Union. The Kiev Gubernia Peasant Congress (21–4 December 1918) greeted him 'warmly' and declared itself in favor of local control over the representatives of the central power, but also declared its faith in the Directory.[17]

On another level Hrushevsky's dissatisfaction with the *status quo* resulted in a conflict at the Ukrainian Academy of Sciences. In early January 1919, at a meeting of the UNT, Hrushevsky proposed to reorganize the Academy that had been founded under the Hetman and replace it with a new institution that would have a more clearly Ukrainian character. It is probable that the historian wished to put into action the ideas that he had outlined to Vernadsky some months before. These would stress research in the humanities carried out in the Ukrainian language. The Academy's permanent secretary, A. Iu. Krymsky, the genealogist V.L. Modza-levsky, and others firmly opposed Hrushevsky's plans. Petliura seemed to stand somewhere in the middle and issued a special decree or law (*Zakon* no. 25, 3 January 1919) accepting the recommendations of the Ukrainian Scientific Society, in fact of Hrushevsky, reorganizing but not exactly abolishing the Academy. Although new restrictions were put on publishing in the Russian language, the Ukrainian Academy of Sciences which had been organized under the Hetman survived.[18]

During the following weeks, the Directory went ahead with its plans for the Toilers' Congress. The Galician Ukrainians also became involved. With the collapse of the Central Powers and the dissolution of the Habsburg Monarchy, the Ukrainians of Eastern Galicia had declared their independence; their leaders had already signed a preliminary agreement for the unification of the Western Ukrainian Republic and the Ukrainian People's Republic and now they were asked to send their delegates to the Toilers' Congress and take part in a formal Act of Union (*Akt sobornosty*). On 22 January 1919, in Saint Sophia Square, the

17 Khrystiuk, III, 45–6; Shapoval, 'Narodnytsvo v ukr. vyzvolnomu rukhovi,' p. 109
18 Polonska-Vasylenko, I, 17–18; Vernadsky, p. 25; Stakhiv, 'Deiaki materiialy pro svitohliad Hrushevskoho,' pp. 230–1, quotes an interview with the historian published in *Nash prapor* (Lviv), 11 January 1924, in which Hrushevsky refers to an attempt to 'reorganize' the academy. 'But due to the disapproval of S. Petliura, who was overseeing cultural affairs, this reorganization was not carried to its conclusion and I did not enter the Academy.'

representatives of Galician and Dnieper Ukraine enthusiastically declared their national unity within the Ukrainian People's Republic. The Galician representatives were promised that their region would enjoy a wide degree of autonomy. Among the Galician representatives present were several members of the Radical Party, including the writer Vasyl Stefanyk. Hrushevsky mixed easily with this group and was seen talking to the peasant leader, Ivan Sanduliak, 'as if with an old friend.'[19]

The next day the Toilers' Congress began in earnest. Three general trends emerged among the delegates: a 'right' trend which strongly supported the Directory and stood for democratic socialism, a 'centre' trend which opposed the Directory leadership and wanted a form of conciliar (soviet/rada) government as a temporary measure, and a 'left' trend represented by deserters from the UPSR, the *Borotbisty,* who were openly in favour of Soviet-style government.[20] Hrushevsky, who was elected to the congress by the peasants of his native Chyhyryn District, was a leader of the 'centre' trend, and his followers attempted to get him elected president of the congress. The Directory members M. Shapoval and Fedir Shvets objected and used their influence among the various party groupings to block his candidacy. The SRs and Peasant Union finally agreed to leave the post temporarily vacant and only a congress vice-president and general secretary were elected.[21]

For Hrushevsky, the principal issue at the congress was neither foreign, nor agricultural, nor even national policy; rather it was the question of power. This comes out very clearly in his own account of the organization of the congress. He describes the course of events in the following terms:

At first [before the Directory had entered Kiev], a Toilers' Congress composed of peasant, soldier, and worker delegates was proposed. At later party conferences in Kiev this plan was changed and the delegates of peasants, workers, 'intellectual workers,' and those professional organizations that had taken an active part in the revolt were invited . . . But this change, dictated by moderate Ukrainian groups, provoked the discontent of the Peasant Union, which approved a resolution supporting the immediate organization of local councils [*rady*] of peasant and worker deputies and the transfer of power to them . . . The SRs of the centre formed a majority at the congress. (Almost all the peasants joined them.) With the left, they expressed their dissatisfaction that the 'toiler' principle proclaimed by

19 Kovalevsky, *Pry dzherelakh borotby,* pp. 536–7; Stakhiv, *Dyrektoriia,* III, 13–16. Sanduliak had been a Radical member of the Galician Provincial Assembly (1908–13) and had written on village life for the peasant-oriented Lviv newspaper *Batkivshchyna.* See the note in the *Entsyklopediia Ukrainoznavstva,* vol. VII (New York, 1973), p. 2706.
20 Khrystiuk, IV, 57ff.; Ivanys, *Petliura,* pp. 86–7.
21 Stakhiv, *Dyrektoriia,* III, 18–19, citing an account by Olkesander Mytsiuk, who was at the time minister of internal affairs.

the directory had not been developed or put into action, and that, rather, government policy showed signs of doing away with this principle.

Hrushevsky then described how the Bolshevik invasion drove public opinion to the right and how a block coalesced around the socially conservative Galician delegation. The congress was disturbed by the swift approach of Bolshevik troops:

The right pressed the Congress to close as quickly as possible. It succeeded in obtaining a slight majority because of the secession of the left and the abstinence of the centre; it passed a resolution to elect commissions to function between sessions [that is, until the next congress or Constituent Assembly]. Full power remained in the hands of the Directory while local councils would serve as instruments of control.[22]

From other accounts, it is clear that the victory of the Directory (and especially of Petliura, who replaced Vynnychenko at its head as soon as the failure of negotiations with Moscow became clear) was made possible by a deep split within the UPSR. In fact, the conflict within this party turned out to be a central event at the Toilers' Congress. Some SRs supported Shapoval and the Directory; others supported Hrushevsky and 'Toilers' Councils.' As can be seen from the passages quoted above, Hrushevsky and his followers claimed that the approach of the Bolsheviks and the atmosphere of growing anxiety had stampeded the congress into supporting the Directory. But there can be no doubt that had the professor obtained the full support of the UPSR, he would have emerged victorious.[23]

When the Toilers' Congress had closed, the Directory began the immediate evacuation of Kiev. Shapoval and the other SR members of the government left the city. At this same time, that is, on the afternoon of 28 January, the SRs who had stayed behind – they were mostly of the 'Central' trend – held their last party conference. In the absence of Shapoval, Hrushevsky's group was successful in taking over the Central Committee of the party, ordering all SRs to withdraw from the government, and passing a resolution that called for the transfer of power to peasant and worker councils.[24] Hrushevsky later explained the difficulties and advantages of the conciliar/rada/soviet principle. He noted that councils had been resisted in Ukraine because they were seen 'as capitulation to Bolshevism and its political pretensions.'

It was forgotten that the soviet principle was not a Bolshevik invention. It had been

22 M. Hrushevsky, *La lutte sociale et politque en Ukraine 1917, 1918, 1919* (Prague, 1920), pp. 33–4.
23 See Khrystiuk, IV, 65ff., and the discussion in Stakhiv, *Dyrektoriia,* III, 37–8.
24 Khrystiuk, IV, 74; Shapoval, 'Narodnytsvo v ukr. vyzvolnomu rukhovi,' p. 110. Also see the discussion in Stakhiv, *Dyrektoriia,* III, 153–5.

popularized at the beginning of the revolution by the Social Democratic Mensheviks. The Bolsheviks had only used the soviet principle to their own advantage. Simultaneously, it was deformed and discredited. Peasant representation was reduced to nothing and the dictatorship of the proletariat was the marching order . . . The Bolsheviks bound this order to a Russian federation which really meant a restoration of the old principles of Russian domination . . . However, the left-leaning socialist groups of Ukraine put sentiment aside and, looking coldly at the situation, saw that the conciliar/soviet principle had to be accepted for a short time, [that is,] until circumstances permitted [the implementation of] full democratic principles.[25]

Having made his point within the UPSR, Hrushevsky joined the crowds of refugees that were packing the trains and fleeing westward to the snow-covered plains of Boishevik-free Podillia. The government ministers and administrators retreated to Vinnytsia, while a good part of the Ukrainian intelligentsia gathered in Kamianets-Podilsky, where the Hetman had recently allowed a Ukrainian university to be founded. Hrushevsky was bound for the latter city, but on the way, his train once again ran into trouble. A fierce snowstorm derailed it and several people were injured or killed. Most of the survivors were compelled to continue their journey on foot; Hrushevsky and a few other notables made their way to Kamianets on horseback.[26]

While Petliura and the government resisted the Bolsheviks and tried to come to terms with the Entente, which had aleady landed troops in Odessa, Kamianets quickly became a centre of opposition. In the opinion of the conservative Doroshenko, who was tied neither to the Directory nor to its leftist opponents, 'Professor Hrushevsky was the soul of this opposition.'[27]

Hrushevsky and his followers would have nothing to do with the government or any of the institutions that stood under its protection. Because the university had been founded by the Hetman, and Professor Ohiienko, a government figure, was its rector, Hrushevsky boycotted the institution and in a kind of competition founded a local branch of the UNT. Thereafter, his SR supporters took over the newspaper *Zhyttia Podillia,* which had been run by a group of university professors. From this tribune Hrushevsky spoke against an alliance with the Entente and in favour of an understanding with the Bolsheviks. The historian supported a government by worker-peasant councils.[28] Finally, toward the end of March, in view of the Bolshevik successes and the complete panic reigning in government circles, Hrushevsky's supporters used the Toilers' Congress law, which allowed local councils to oversee the agents of the central government, in

25 Hrushevsky, *La lutte sociale et politique,* p. 35.
26 Doroshenko, *Spomyny pro nedavne-mynule,* p. 430.
27 Ibid., p. 431.
28 Ibid.

order to organize a local worker-peasant congress and a Committee for the Defence of the Republic. As in the days of the Mala Rada, Hrushevsky was the honorary President of the Congress. He was not an actual member of the Committee, but there can be no doubt that he supported it. For four days this 'revkom,' as Doroshenko called it, ruled Kamianets and the surrounding area. It enjoyed the support of the local sugar workers and the peasantry; it organized a communal police, removed a few unpopular administrators, and kept order while the Directory was busy fighting the Bolsheviks. By the fifth day, the Directory's armies had secured the front and Petliura's emissary arrived. At one point, it seems, the Directory feared that Hrushevsky was organizing a Soviet government at Kamianets. In the confusion surrounding the dissolution of the Committee, several of Hrushevsky's followers were arrested and the historian himself was threatened. In the eyes of Petliura and the government, the Kamianets Committee had disrupted the front that they were trying to establish against the Bolsheviks. It had to be dissolved.[29]

Hrushevsky salvaged what he could from his experience as the unofficial head of the Kamianets worker-peasant congress. He later noted that the arrested men were quickly released and that, because of the Kamianets events, Petliura had been forced to change his cabinet and shift his orientation away from the Entente. Moreover, Hrushevsky later claimed that his trust in popular rule had not been misplaced. With an air of learned objectivity, he writes: 'Having had the opportunity of observing the working of a congress and a council . . . I have the general impression that for a while worker councils were a very appropriate institution which were able to serve as a powerful measure against anarchy as well as against counter-revolutionary reaction. They possessed the confidence of the working class and unified its forces with those of the intellectual socialists.'[30] On the other hand, the lessons of the Kamianets experiment were rather ephemeral: the Directory remained in power, Petliura and the army were quickly becoming the major force in what remained of the Ukrainian People's Republic, anarchy with its accompanying pogroms against the Jews was about to spread throughout large parts of the country, and Bolshevik hostility with its consequent geopolitical dilemma did not change. Immediately after the dissolution of the Kamianets Committee for the Defence of the Republic, Hrushevsky resolved to go abroad.[31]

29 See ibid., and I. Mazepa, *Ukraina v ohni i buri revoliutsii 1917–1921*, 3 vols. (2nd edition, n.p., 1950), I, 140–9, which is the most detailed account of the 'Kamianets revolution.' There is some confusion over the actual title of Hrushevsky's committee. Mazepa called it the Committee for the Defence of the Republic, Doroshenko called it the Committee for the Defence of the Revolution, and Hrushevsky himself called it the Committee for the Defence of Ukraine. Also see Stakhiv, *Dyrektoriia*, VI, 167–76.
30 Hrushevsky, *La lutte sociale et politique*, p. 41.
31 In his *Avtobiohrafiia–1914–1919*, p. 101, Hrushevsky hints, and in his 'V pershii delegatsii

The historian had considered going abroad even before the evacuation of Kiev. At that time, he had elaborated a project for sending representatives of the two major socialist parties to Western Europe to do propaganda work and to oversee the operation of the Republic's nascent diplomatic corps. This plan was eventually amended and Hrushevsky was allowed to go to the Paris Peace Conference as a representative of the UPSR. According to Hrushevsky, the foreign delegations of the two major revolutionary parties – the UPSR and the USDLP – had been promised a voice in all political negotiations.[32]

From Kamianets, the historian travelled to Stanyslaviv (today's Ivano-Frankivske), to which the government of the Western Ukrainian Republic had retreated after the Poles had driven it out of Lviv. Stanyslaviv was teeming with refugees from Dnieper Ukraine and the historian kept a low profile and passed almost unnoticed among them. Volodymyr Doroshenko of the SVU recognized Hrushevsky by chance and during a brief meeting asked him about his scholarly work and especially about the completion of his *History of Ukraine-Rus'*. Hrushevsky replied that all of his materials had been destroyed and that under the present circumstances finishing it was impossible. Rather, he would turn his energies toward a major history of Ukrainian literature. Doroshenko noticed that Hrushevsky had still not lost the habit of writing or noting something down in every free moment.[33]

Not all of the historian's chance encounters were pleasant. A more conservative acquaintance from the Poltava area also happened to meet his old hero. Viktor Andriievsky writes:

One beautiful day at the end of March, I ran into Professor Hrushevsky on the streets of Stanyslaviv. My hand automatically went to my cap. Up to now, I had honoured this man as the greatest of my living compatriots. I recall that while I was still a student I had visited him once or twice on business related to our Ukrainian club [*hromada*] and each time I went with liturgical solemnity as if to a holy man or to a prophet. When in 1912 he visited Poltava for the celebrations honoring Kotliarevsky and came to the opening of our Ukrainian Club, I rejoiced in having the great honour of welcoming him to our home in the name of Poltava society . . . His portrait used to hang in a place of honor above my desk . . . But now my hand froze as it was rising: I would not raise my cap before this man! Old Professor Hrushevsky, for whom I had once prayed, the author of the *History of Ukraine-Rus'*, the organizer of the NTSh, the great scholar, the great teacher and leader of the Ukrainian nation, had died in my eyes! I saw before me a member of the '[Russian] Soviet of Workers' and Peasants'

ukrainskoi partii sotsiial-revoliutsioneriv,' *Boritesia-poborete*, no. 4 (Vienna, 1920), and reprinted in *Vybrani pratsi*, pp. 157–69, he plainly states, that during the dissolution of the Kamianets Committee, he feared that 'Directory circles' planned to have him killed.

32 Hrushevsky, 'V pershii delgatsii,' pp. 157–8.

33 Doroshenko, 'Pershyi prezydent vidnovlenoi ukrainskoi derzhavy,' pp. 29–30.

Deputies'! Not the ideologue of the Ukrainian nation, but only of unity and brotherhood with our age-old enemies! . . . Now I had only one desire: to return home and snatch that portrait of comrade Hrushevsky from the wall![34]

The former patriarch of *Ukrainstvo,* the deposed President of the Ukrainian People's Republic, did not remain long in Stanyslaviv. Upon learning that the Socialist International was gathering in Amsterdam, Hrushevsky hurried across Czechoslovakia to Prague, where he arrived on 18 April 1919. There he learned that the meeting had been postponed for a few months and would be held in Lucerne. He spent two months in Prague, arranging for the publication of French-language pamphlets on the Ukrainian revolution and establishing contacts with fellow scholars and various Czech socialists. He also visited his old acquaintance Professor Masaryk, who was now president of the newly created Czechoslovak Republic. 'The discussions I had with him and his Deputy Foreign Minister, [Bedrich] Štěpánek,' Hrushevsky tells us, 'and also with [R.W.] Seton-Watson (Scotus Viator), who was at that time staying at President Masaryk's home – I was also acquainted with him from Lviv where he had come before the war to study Austrian affairs – were very valuable in competently informing me about the political situation.'[35]

From Seton-Watson, Hrushevsky learned that there was no sympathy for an independent Ukraine in either England or France and that the Entente felt duty-bound to stand by the old Russia with whom it had been allied. Neither was there any hope for a wider Slavic or Black Sea federation of states, nor even much for the decentralization of a resurrected Russia.[36] With Masaryk, Hrushevsky discussed both international politics and the question of Carpathian Ukraine, which had been newly annexed to Czechoslovakia. He was assured that the president would strive to secure the native language and the native element in the country (*narodna mova narodnyi eliement*) and oppose outside influences.[37]

34 V. Andriievsky, *Z mynuloho*, vol. II (Berlin, 1923), pp. 236–7. This passage is quoted in full and discussed in D. Solovei, 'U spravi zhyttiepysu M. Hrushevskoho,' *Vilna Ukraina*, no. 17, (1958), 9–22.

35 Hrushevsky, 'V pershii delegatsii,' pp. 159–60. The meeting between Hrushevsky and Seton-Watson seems to be confirmed by a note in the latter's diary. H. Seton-Watson, in a letter of 2 February 1981, informs me of his father's Ukrainian sympathies: 'As to my father as an "English Slavophile" – this is a fairly apt description, and he occasionally used it himself. Of his great interest in the Ukraine, which lasted until the end of his life, there is no doubt at all: he often spoke to me of it.'

36 Hrushevsky, 'V pershii delegatsii,' pp. 160–1.

37 Ibid., pp. 159–62, and M. Hrushevsky, 'Lyst M. Hrushevskoho do Myroslava Sichynskoho z 1919 roku,' *Ukrainskyi istoryk*, nos. 1–3 (1978), 160–2. The adjective *narodna*, of course, has many levels of meaning – native, national, popular – but in the context of Hrushevsky's writings there is no doubt that it is juxtaposed to Russifying influences.

Galician Ukrainians, who were hard pressed by the Poles, talked of some kind of Central European Slavic federation with the Czechs and Slovaks, but Hrushevsky learned that the very real Czech interest in the scheme was circumscribed by the veto of the Western European powers.[38] He was advised to go to the Paris Peace Conference and acquaint himself with the real masters of Europe.

Hrushevsky arrived in Paris on 17 June 1919, and quickly discovered that his Prague informants had not erred. The French wished to make Poland the major power in Eastern Europe and only Lloyd George ventured to restrain them. The American adviser, Professor Robert H. Lord, even repeated to Hrushevsky the old stories that the Germans had created the Ukrainian movement and that Ukrainians were incapable of governing themselves.[39] Meanwhile, conservative White Russian émigrés encouraged such sentiments and published literature in Western languages reminiscent of Shchegolev, Savenko, and Florinsky. Once again, Hrushevsky appears as the inventor of the Ukrainian people and a master of treason and deception:

History was against Ukrainianism? – he wrote a history of it. The idiom spoken by the people living in Little Russia, was too poor to have any literary or artistic pretensions? – he invented a language and called it the Ukrainian language. This language grated upon the ears and wounded aesthetic feelings, but he was not discouraged by so small a thing. He wrote numerous books and brochures and the Germans gave him all the money that he wished so that he could print these falsehoods in millions of copies . . . Mr Grushevsky's jargon, this hodge-podge of local idiom, Polish, and German words drove off the reader . . . Ridicule killed it. Mr Grushevsky the journalist killed Mr Grushevsky the statesman.[40]

This negative propaganda did not stop Hrushevsky completely. Although he quickly saw the hopelessness of lobbying among the Paris diplomatic corps, he did attempt to spread his SR ideas among the Ukrainian delegates in Paris. He began to

38 Hrushevsky, 'V pershii delegatsii,' p. 161: 'The Czechs drew back from a direct connection with the East Slavic world. The Czechs understood the full import that this connection with the "Ruskyi" would have for them and trembled at the thought of losing him – but they had to firmly reply that this was not the will of Entente.' Czech interest in the Ukrainian question is chronicled in K. Lewandowski, *Sprawa ukraińska w polityce zagranicznej Czechoslowacji w latach 1918–1932* (Wrocław, 1974).

39 Hrushevsky, 'V pershii delegatsii,' pp. 162–3.

40 *Le 'Peuple Ukrainien' par un petit-Russien de Kief* (Nancy, 1919), pp. 22–3, 40. Hrushevsky's undeniably ponderous narrative style drew the fire of his Ukrainian rivals as well as the disdain of the sworn enemies of *Ukrainstvo*. On 1 June 1918, Vynnychenko noted in his *Shchodennyk*, p. 286: 'Hrushevsky is counted as a genius among several of our patriots. Of course it is an important thing to write an eight-volume history of Ukraine. But truly, this is not exactly a work of genius, or even talented. It can be read only as a kind of punishment. Although he was not a genius, Kostomarov wrote fourteen volumes and more which can be read with delight.'

study English and met frequently with Osyp Megas, one of two Ukrainian delegates from Canada, where there was a fair-sized Ukrainian immigrant community. Megas probably put him in touch with other sympathizers in Canada and the United States.[41]

Hrushevsky also transferred his attention to the West European socialists who were meeting in Lucerne. While still in Paris, he met with the socialist representatives of other smaller Eastern European nations – of the newly formed republics, as he put it – and especially with the Caucasians, who were at that time seriously threatened by Denikin's White Army. Hrushevsky and a Georgian named Chkheidze became collaborators. Between 22 and 30 June, a common strategy was worked out and plans laid for a journal to be published in both French and English. A 'Committee for an Independent Ukraine' would gather funds from the Ukrainian communities in North America and distribute literature.[42] During the following months Hrushevsky made many personal appeals to these communities and requested material support in the Ukrainian-language press of both Canada and the United States.[43]

The Lucerne meeting was a congress of the Second Socialist International, which was inclined toward democratic socialism and was to firmly oppose the new

---

41 Osyp Megas, *Heroiska Ukraina: iliustrovani spomyny z Ukrainy* (Winnipeg, 1920). Unpaginated. See the section on Hrushevsky.

42 Hrushevsky, 'V pershii delegatsii,' pp. 166–9. Also see Hrushevsky's 'Lyst do Sichynskoho,' pp. 161–2. The new journal *Eastern Europe/L'Europe orientale* was scheduled to appear immediately after the Lucerne socialist congress.

43 See, in particular, Hrushevsky's long letter of 18 December 1919 to the Ukrainian Canadians. It was written in Geneva and first published as a New Year's greeting in the left-leaning but liberal democratic Winnipeg paper *Ukrainskyi holos*, no. 1, 7 January 1920. It is reprinted as 'Lyst prof. Hrushevskoho do kanadskykh ukraintsiv,' *Ukrainskyi istoryk*, nos. 3–4 (1975), 73–7. Hrushevsky's correspondence with the Ukrainians of North America had been initiated not later than September 1907, and began with advice on the educational question among the Galician Ukrainian settlers on the Canadian prairies. It became most frequent in 1919 when the historian went into emigration. As soon as he had left Ukraine, he was invited to visit North America, and, as he assured Sichynsky, 'Lyst,' 'if time will allow me, I would like to do this.' However, the political situation was so fluid that he never left Europe. For an outline of the correspondence with significant quotations see M. Marunchak, 'M. Hrushevsky i Ukraintsi Kanady,' *Vilne slovo* (Toronto), no. 47, 19 November 1966. Occasionally Hrushevsky would send information to the Ukrainian press of North America but ask that his name not be mentioned. See M.H. Marunchak, 'Znaideno dva nevidomi lysty Mykhaila Hrushevskoho,' *Novyi shliakh* (Toronto), no. 48, 28 November 1981, and M.H. Marunchak, 'Mykhailo Hrushevsky's Letters from Geneva to American Ukrainians,' in *New Soil Old Roots: The Ukrainian Experience in Canada*, ed. J. Rozumnyj and others (Winnipeg, 1983), pp. 243–51. There is a very full manuscript collection of Hrushevsky's circular letters to the North American press in the Public Archives of Canada, National Ethnic Archives, Olha Woycenko Collection, vol. XII. See files 39 and 40 for Hrushevsky's detailed descriptions of East European politics in 1919.

Communist International organized in Moscow. General Secretary Camille Huysmans of Belgium sent official invitations to both the UPSR and the USDLP and Hrushevsky led the Ukrainian delegation to Lucerne. During the debates, the French socialist Jean Longuet and the Russian SR Sukhomlin argued in favour of a united Russia, while Hrushevsky and his Baltic and Caucasian allies argued for the right of the new republics to national independence. The latter were victorious and the congress passed resolutions urging the planned League of Nations to recognize the independence of those new states established through the will of free peoples. Armenia, Estonia, Georgia, Latvia, Lithuania, Ukraine, and the Caucasus were specifically mentioned. The Polish occupation of Eastern Galicia was also condemned and Ukraine was to be given two seats on the executive of the International and fifteen votes in any future congress.[44]

Following the Lucerne congress, Hrushevsky returned to Prague and then travelled about Europe reestablishing scholarly contacts, lobbying, and writing on behalf of the Ukrainian cause. He visited Berlin, Geneva, and other cities. By the autumn of 1919, he had begun to organize a Ukrainian Sociological Institute and a companion Society for the Protection of the New Republics of Eastern Europe. Hrushevsky hoped to base these organizations in Geneva, which was expected to be the seat of the League of Nations. Contacts were established with Swiss scholars, journalists, and politicians, and several meetings were held. As Hrushevsky later noted, an important scholarly institution so close to the League of Nations might have had a beneficial influence upon international questions such as the fate of Eastern Galicia. The Ukrainians of North America, however, did not provide sufficient funding. Hrushevsky writes: 'I was compelled to transfer my activities to a country where American dollars went much further, at first to Prague, and then to Vienna.'[45]

After the conclusion of the World War, Vienna very quickly became a major centre of Ukrainian émigré activities. In 1920, in view of the destruction of Ukrainian cultural institutions in Polish-occupied Eastern Galicia, and the general

44 Hrushevsky, 'V pershii delegatsii,' pp. 168–9; Stakhiv, 'Deiaki dokumenty pro diialnist Hrushevskoho na emihratsii,' in *Mykhailo Hrushevsky u 110 rokovyny narodzhennia*, pp. 163–6. Stakhiv quotes the congress resolutions from *Eastern Europe*, no. 2 (1919). Also see the note in Mykyta Shapoval's *Shchodennyk*, 2 vols. (New York, 1958), I, 40.

45 The story of the Ukrainian Sociological Institute is told in Hrushevsky's 'Passionate Appeal for Help to all true Children of Ukraine across the Ocean ...' in M. Antonovych, ed., 'Lysty M. Hrushevskoho do T. Pochynka,' *Ukrainskyi istoryk*, nos. 1–3 (1970), 173–5. About this same time, Hrushevsky wrote to P.H. Woycenko, the manager of Winnipeg's *Ukrainskyi holos*, offering to become a permanent correspondent in Europe in return for a monthly honorarium. Woycenko sent Hrushevsky what he could, but a fire in the newspaper's office had caused extensive damage and Hrushevsky could not be guaranteed a steady wage. See the Public Archives of Canada, National Ethnic Archives, Olha Woycenko Collection, vol. XII, file 40, item 3, and file 42, item 1.

paralysis of Dnieper Ukrainian life under what was euphemistically called 'War Communism,' the Vienna Union of Ukrainian Journalists and Writers undertook the organization of a 'Free Ukrainian University.' The large Ukrainian emigration – workers, former peasant-soldiers, and their officers, as well as visitors from Galicia – would make up the student body. The philologist and former professor of Lviv University, Oleksander Kolessa, initiated the project. Hrushevsky was soon involved in the organization of courses and, together with Dmytro Antonovych, the son of his Kiev mentor, worked out a general plan for the institution. Everyone saw Hrushevsky as the university's natural rector.[46]

Once again, however, political philosophy could not be divorced from academic life. Hrushevsky's plan called for a People's University (*Narodnyi Universytet*) that would not have an obligatory system of lectures or demand formal academic qualifications of all of its professors. This idea was fairly popular among the younger students from Dnieper Ukraine.[47] On the other hand, Kolessa, who had fought for a Ukrainian university in the Vienna parliament before the war, wanted a free, that is non-state, institution that would, however, maintain formal requirements and be organized along the lines of Western European universities. Most of the professors agreed with Kolessa, and he soon replaced Hrushevsky as rector. Shortly afterward, the Czech government offered to fund the institution and it moved to Prague, where it survived until the close of the Second World War.[48]

Hrushevsky's efforts on behalf of a People's University were only a small part of his public work. He continued to lead the Foreign Delegation of the UPSR, and by 1920 had a clear idea of its tasks. By the beginning of the year, it seems, he thought that the situation of the Ukrainian People's Republic was hopeless and that the armed struggle had to come to an end. The next stage, he thought, would be one of reflection. It was necessary to analyse the situation and seek out the causes for the failure of the liberation struggle. The Vienna-based Ukrainian Sociological Institute would become the focal point of this activity. With Hrushevsky's encouragement, Khrystiuk began work on his four-volume history of the Ukrainian revolution and Mykhailo Lozynsky analysed the Polish-Ukrainian

---

46 S. Narizhny, *Ukrainska emigratsiia: kulturna pratsia ukrainskoi emigratsii mizh dvoma svitovymy viinamy* (Prague, 1942), 119–20.

47 Ibid., Marko Antonovych, interview of 16 and 17 April 1983.

48 Narizhny, pp. 119–20; interview with Marko Antonovych. On 16 November 1920, Shapoval noted in his *Shchodennyk*, p. 45: 'Yesterday I had a conversation with Hrushevsky. He told me about the university courses. The logic of our participation: "learning the ropes" as lecturers and attracting a larger mass of young people to our lectures under the neutral flag of the Society of Journalists and Writers. These people would otherwise be afraid to come. I expressed the opinion that it is necessary to learn to lecture and speak in public on our own, without the Dniester gentlefolk [that is, the Galician *pany*].'

conflict in Galicia. All this effort, Hrushevsky joked darkly, was the final 'liquidation' of the revolutionary period that had just ended.[49]

The political mentor of the SRs did not stop at analysis of past mistakes. He was also concerned with their amelioration and rectification. Analysis, he believed, could take place in emigration; rectification, however, had to take place in the homeland. In fact, Hrushevsky told his SR followers that all struggles for social and national liberation must be ultimately based at home and that even under the most oppressive regimes some opportunities for productive work arise. The SRs must return to Ukraine as soon as political conditions would allow.[50]

Hrushevsky made no secret of his general strategy. At the beginning of 1920, he declared his principles in the new journal of the UPSR Foreign Delegation. He had been brought up a populist, he confessed, and from the example of Antonovych had learned to put the people above the state. Like Antonovych, who had done battle against the Russian state some thirty years before, and like the famous 'Tatar people,' those Medieval ancestors of modern Ukrainians who had preferred heathen Tatar rule to that of their own oppressive kings and boyars, the modern Ukrainian who would serve his people must stay at home. The modern boyars – the Skoropadskys and Petliuras – and the modern Tatars – the Bolshevik invaders – would face modern 'Tatar people,' Ukrainian servitors, who would use every opportunity to promote the cause of the Ukrainian working people. The soviet form of rule had to be temporarily accepted, but only as a transitional phase toward a socialist federation of autonomous communes and territories. In the meantime, a Ukraine that had already suffered the vices and enjoyed the virtues of independence could not enter a discredited Russian federation. Hrushevsky pretended to learn from the Bolsheviks and looked forward to a wider European and World Federation that would most certainly – in the communist vocabulary that he used – 'liquidate' the question.[51]

49 Kovalevsky, *Pry dzherelakh borotby*, pp. 597–9.
50 Ibid.
51 M. Hrushevsky, 'Ukrainska partiia sotsiialistiv-revoliutsioneriv ta ii zavdannia,' *Boritesia-poborete!*, no. 1 (Vienna, 1920), 1–54. In this article, Hrushevsky makes some interesting remarks about his attitude toward Ukrainian independence. He confesses: 'In the past I was never a devotee of independence in the transitory, vulgar sense of the term. The Ukrainian populists were never enthusiastic about having an army, police, prisoners, and gallows. In so far as this had to be a part of community life, the Ukrainian populists thought it better to spread these unpleasantries across a larger union, a wider federation ... When the first cries for independence began to sound out from Bachynsky's *Ukraina irredenta* and RUP's *Independent Ukraine*, the Ukrainian populists of the old style reacted with scepticism, fearing that chauvinist reaction and nationalist adventure would be hatched from this egg. And it was true that national exclusiveness and backwardness were integrated into these slogans from the very beginning.' With regard to his role in the revolution and the accusation that the SRs were blind imitators of an ideology developed by Russians, Hrushevsky

While Hrushevsky attempted to establish a dialogue with the Bolsheviks, Petliura continued to parley with the Poles. More conservative Ukrainian factions supported him; Hrushevsky, Shapoval, Vynnychenko, who now headed a tiny 'Foreign Committee' of an independent Ukrainian Communist Party (UKP), and Galicians of all political convictions strongly objected. On 5–9 April 1920, Hrushevsky, Vynnychenko, and Shapoval met to discuss the situation,[52] but by 22 April Petliura had signed the Warsaw Treaty which recognized Polish supremacy in Galicia, made major concessions to the Polish gentry on the right bank, and gave a great deal of power to Pilsudski and his army. Two days later, without warning the SRs, Vynnychenko left for Moscow to initiate direct discussions on the question of an independent communist Ukraine.[53] On 22–4, May Hrushevsky, Shapoval, and Zhukovsky held an UPSR conference in Prague. The conference issued a declaration calling the Polish alliance an 'adventure' and Petliura a 'traitor' who had sold out the Republic to the reactionary European bourgeoisie.[54]

While the Ukrainian political emigration was still trying to gain its bearings, the armies of Pilsudski and Petliura advanced rapidly eastward, and on 7 May captured Kiev. The Polish ascendancy did not last long, however, and soon Pilsudski was in full retreat and hard pressed to defend Warsaw. In the midst of this war of rapid advances and more rapid retreats, Hrushevsky held firm to his original position. Petliura's concessions to the Poles were merely a ploy to get Entente support; they did not have the support of the population. Just as Khmelnytsky had once sold out the Ukrainians to the slave-seeking Crimean Tatars, so Petliura sold them out to the Poles. Denikin's successor, Wrangel, was no better. Only Lenin promised self-determination for Ukraine and spoke against Russian chauvinism. But even he imposed a single-party Russian dictatorship upon the country and backed it up with the Red Army. During the Polish occupation of Kiev, a local SR

writes: 'I saw that only the SRs went the way of the people and if it were not for their dependence on Russian ideology ... this party would have unconsciously become the bearer of the old slogans of the revolutionary populist tradition. The entire Ukrainian intelligentsia, which was radical and populist-oriented, had to go along with it and I felt it my duty to proceed in the closest contact with these "boys," considering it a logical development of all my previous work ... For good or for bad, the SRs led the Ukrainian peasantry into the world socialist revolution ... and by their action they saved the national idea and the nationally conscious Ukrainian intelligentsia from being fully compromised in the eyes of the people ... Thus it is not really important if the UPSR took a few ideas from the Russian SRs.'

52 Shapoval, *Shchodennvk*. I, 43.

53 M. Czajkowski, 'Volodymyr Vynnychenko and His Mission to Moscow and Kharkiv,' *Journal of Ukrainian Graduate Studies*, no. 5 (Toronto, 1978), 3–24.

54 The declaration is printed in *Boritesia-poborete!*, no. 1 (1920), 61–4. There is a brief discussion in Mazepa, *Ukraina v ohni i buri revoliutsii*. III, 33. About this same time, M. Kovalevsky, M. Zalizniak, and V. Kedrovsky were expelled from the party for *Petliurivshchyna*. See Shapoval, 'Narodnytstvo v ukr. vyzvolnomu rukhovi,' p. 111.

party conference had condemned 'socialism by decree,' and so, Hrushevsky concluded, even though it would be easier to come to an agreement with the Bolsheviks than with any other Russian government or party, Ukraine remained caught 'between Moscow and Warsaw.'[55]

Pilsudski's successful defence of Warsaw and the ensuing retreat of the Red Army led to the opening of peace negotiations at Riga. The Soviet Ukrainian government was represented by a delegation which for purposes of propaganda included Vynnychenko; he used the opportunity to escape from the Soviet state, which had greatly disappointed him. By the end of October 1920, he was describing the details of his adventure to a private conference of socialist leaders that included Hrushevsky, Shapoval, and Matvii Stakhiv, who represented the Ukrainian socialist youth in Prague. Vynnychenko described the Bolshevik party dictatorship in great detail and concluded that 'not only is there no independent Soviet Ukrainian state, but neither is there the slightest practical trace of any kind of federal structure.'[56]

Hrushevsky listened to Vynnychenko's account with nervous impatience and, when he had finished, strongly criticized him on several counts: he should never have gone to Moscow or Kharkiv without gaining concrete concessions first; since the Bolsheviks would yield nothing, he should have gone privately and not as a political leader. He should have informed the rest of the emigration, and once there, he should have stayed and worked from within to strengthen the Ukrainian position within the Soviet Ukrainian Republic. At this same meeting, Shapoval, who was generally opposed to any agreement with the Bolsheviks, was much more restrained in his criticism of Vynnychenko. It seemed that Shapoval and Vynnychenko were coming together, while Hrushevsky was on his own.[57]

A few days after the socialist conference, Hrushevsky arrived suspiciously late at a student meeting held to celebrate the November insurrection against the Hetman and so avoided hearing Shapoval's eulogy of this event. In private, Hrushevsky criticized the insurrection as untimely and irresponsible and cited Shapoval as an example of an undisciplined member of the UPSR. In private, Shapoval criticized Hrushevsky for calling the Germans into Ukraine and for

---

55 M. Hrushevsky, 'Mizh Moskvoiu i Varshavoiu,' *Boritesia-poborete!*, no. 2 (1920). 1–18. In this article, Hrushevsky gives a very detailed picture of the corruption by the Bolsheviks of the conciliar/rada/soviet idea and clearly states that 'no competition among communist parties is allowed and so in Ukraine no national communist parties are allowed but only one Communist Party of Bolsheviks of Ukraine [CPbU] which is, in fact, a regional organization of the Russian Communist Party.'

56 See M. Stakhiv, 'Chomu M. Hrushevsky povernuvsia v 1924 rotsi do Kyieva?' in *Mykhailo Hrushevsky u 110 rokovyny narodzhennia*, p. 116.

57 Ibid., pp. 116, 121.

usurping the leadership of the UPSR when he was not even a formal member of the party.[58] During the next months, the personal antagonism between the two men was to deepen steadily. Eventually there was a formal break, which was caused by their different tactics in relation to the problem of Moscow's domination of the Soviet Ukrainian Republic. Shapoval and the 'Prague Group' were opposed to any dealings with the Soviet Ukrainian Rakovsky government; Hrushevsky and the 'Foreign Delegation' wished to carry on the liberation struggle by legal work within Soviet Ukrainian state.[59] In the end, each side accused the other of 'fomenting intrigues' and of undue ambition. Hrushevsky thought Shapoval to be just as much a glory seeker as was Vynnychenko, only lacking Vynnychenko's literary talent. Shapoval and his group accused Hrushevsky of wanting to establish a personal dictatorship over the party, of wanting to be an SR 'pope' and of, as they put it, 'wanting to serve the Chekists.'[60]

At the beginning of 1921, the Soviet Ukrainian delegation at Riga conveyed to Hrushevsky an invitation 'to go to Ukraine for cultural work with his comrades.'[61] The arrest by the Soviets of Holubovsky and the SR leaders who had remained in Ukraine made Hrushevsky hesitate, but by June 1921 M. Chechel, a representative of the Foreign Delegation, was in Kharkiv negotiating with Rakovsky for the legalization of the UPSR. By late summer, Chechel had returned to Vienna with a negative response, but with general expressions of good will and suggestions that Hrushevsky head the Ukrainian Red Cross and organize help from abroad for famine relief in Ukraine. The Soviets also suggested that he organize publication abroad of school, scholarly, and literary production to aid the Ukrainian Education Commissariat, which lacked proper materials because of the continual warfare. Thereafter, further negotiations were carried on with M. Levytsky, who headed

---

58 Ibid., pp. 121–2. Also see Shapoval, *Shchodennyk,* I, 44, which confirms Hrushevsky's late arrival at the student meeting and dates the event 12 November 1920.

59 See Shapoval, *Shchodennyk,* I, 45ff., who claims that by January 1921 he had compelled Hrushevsky to declare 'that he had entered the party and bound its fate with his own' (p.51). In March 1921, Shapoval learned that Zhukovsky had gone to Riga to negotiate with the Bolsheviks. 'On 6 July 1921,' writes Shapoval, 'the Prague group officially broke all ties with the Foreign Delegation.' See his 'Narodnytstvo v ukr. vyzvolnomu rukhovi,' p. 119.

60 For Hrushevsky's opinion of Shapoval see M. Antonovych, ed. 'Lysty M. Hrushevkoho do T. Pochynka,' *Ukrainskyi istoryk,* no. 4 (1969), 78–98, especially 97. Also see Shapoval, *Shchodennyk* I, 45, and N. Hryhoryiv, 'Lyst t. N.Ia. Hryhoryiva do t. P.D. Khrystiuka z pryvodu taktyky M. S. Hrushevskoho ta ynshykh chleniv b. zakord. delegatsii UPSR,' *Vilna spilka,* no. 1 (Lviv, 1921). 112–21.

61 F.P. Shevchenko, 'Chomu Mykhailo Hrushevsky povernuvsia na radiansku Ukrainu?' *Ukrainskyi istorychnyi zhurnal.* no. 2 (Kiev, 1966), 17. This article, which appeared on the centenary of Hrushevsky's birth, was part of a general attempt by Ukrainian scholars living under Soviet rule to 'rehabilitate' the historian. See Appendix c.

the diplomatic mission of Soviet Ukraine to Czechoslovakia, and with Iu. Novakivsky, who headed a Soviet Ukrainian trade mission to the same country.[62]

Hrushevsky understood the nature of the Bolshevik overtures. On the one hand, Rakovsky and the Communists would not legalize or share power with the SRs, but on the other, they were willing to use the famous historian's name and compromise his independent position by coopting him into an administrative position linked to the Soviet bureaucracy. In an open letter to Rakovsky, Hrushevsky thanked the Soviet leader for the hospitality that he had shown Chechel, but pointed out that he (Hrushevsky) had never been a bureaucrat and never intended to be one. The Soviet bureaucracy, like the Imperial Russian one that it had replaced, was hostile to everything outside of its grasp and was cut off from the Ukrainian population. It was, the historian wrote, non-national and even anti-Ukrainian in character. Until some basic changes were made, no agreement could be reached. In the meantime, Hrushevsky assured Rakovsky that he would try to arrange for famine relief and academic supplies through some neutral institution such as the UNT.[63]

In the following months, Hrushevsky was active in a 'Society for the Relief of the Hungry in Ukraine,' and he was successful in collecting a certain amount of money from the Ukrainians of Canada and the United States. It was used for both food and educational supplies and was sent to members of the Ukrainian Academy of Sciences in Kiev. The UNT and, in particular, Hrushevsky's brother Oleksander seem to have been the intermediaries. In secret, Hrushevsky also tried to aid the Ukrainian Autocephalous Orthodox Church, which was cautiously beginning to reassert itself, and which the historian saw as a badly persecuted but promising aspect of the Ukrainian national movement.[64] Thus in his own eyes, at least, the historian managed to carry out his plan and avoid being politically compromised by cooption into the Soviet bureaucracy.[65]

62 Ibid., pp. 17–21.

63 'Vidkrytyi lyst Mykh. Hrushevskoho, zakordonoho deliegata UPSR, holovi rady narodnykh komisariv ukrainskoi sotsiialistychnoi radianskoi respubliky Kh. G. Rakovskomu,' *Boritesia-poborete!*. no. 10 (1921). 1–8. Also see his letter to M. V. Levytsky and Iu. S. Novakivsky on pp. 28–31 in the same volume. In late 1923, Hrushevsky learned that Soviet agents were destroying the books that they had purchased from the Ukrainian Sociological Institute. See M. Andrusiak, 'Mykhailo Hrushevsky iak istoryk, narodnyk, i derzhavnyk,' in *Mykhailo Hrushevsky u 110 rokovyny narodzhennia*, p. 15.

64 See M. Hrushevsky and Iu. Tyshchenko-Siry, 'Spravozdannia Komitetu "Holodnym Ukrainy", ch. 2,' and the letter to the editors of *Ukrainskyi holos* marked 'Dovirochno, ne dlia druku!' The latter concerns the Ukrainian Autocephalous Orthodox Church. Both documents are preserved in the Public Archives of Canada, National Ethnic Archives, Olha Woycenko Collection, vol. XII, file 45, items 9 and 10.

65 Several of Hrushevsky's letters and appeals to the North American Ukrainians are printed in Stakhiv, 'Deiaki dokumenty pro diialnist Hrushevskoho na emihratsii,' pp. 149–59. In a letter of

Social and academic work remained important to Hrushevsky, but with each passing month, the political significance of the Foreign Delegation seemed to diminish. On the one hand, the Ukrainian political emigration was beginning to turn sharply toward the right;[66] on the other hand, Rakovsky did not take up the questions raised by his open letter, and so, in 1922, he quietly retired from open political work and devoted himself exclusively to the publication program of the Ukrainian Sociological Institute. In addition to the work on the revolution by Khrystiuk and Lozynsky, the institute also published Hrushevsky's shorter French-language works on history and literature, his anthropological study on the origins of society, his book on Drahomanov in Geneva, and his history of religious thought in Ukraine.[67] More significantly, however, in 1922, he began serious work on a monumental *History of Ukrainian Literature,* the first three volumes of which he completed at his cottage in Baden on the outskirts of Vienna.[68] To support this publishing activity, Hrushevsky could rely on no government institution and therefore had to keep up a wide correspondence with dedicated Ukrainian activists in North America. At one time or another, simple workmen, a country school teacher, and a protestant town pastor were all busy selling his books and acting as his agents. It was a difficult way to support an ambitious publishing program, and Hrushevsky and his family were just able to survive until the end of 1923.[69]

There were other alternatives. In 1923, Hrushevsky and a few other Ukrainian

24 December 1922, to the Ukrainian Red Cross in Canada, he appeals to the Galician emigrants 'not to forget Great Ukraine,' as Dnieper Ukraine was generally called after 1917, '... because the situation of our brothers living under Bolshevik occupation is incomparably worse and more frightful than in Galicia. This is due to the impossibility of organizing any kind of social relief there.' Also see the general remarks of Marunchak, 'M. Hrushevsky i Ukraintsi Kanady.'

66 A. Motyl, *The Turn to the Right: The Ideological Origins and Development of Ukrainian Nationalism* (New York, 1980).

67 *Anthologie de la littérature ukrainienne jusqu'au milieu du XIX siècle avec une préface de M.A. Meillet* (Paris–Geneva–Prague, 1921); *Pochatky hromadianstva* (Vienna, 1921); *Z pochyniv ukrainskoho sotsiialistychnoho rukhu: Mykhailo Drahomanov i zhenevskyi sotsiialistychnyi hurtok* (Vienna, 1922); *Z istorii religiinoi dumky na Ukraini* (Lviv, 1925). In general, Hrushevsky's works of this period reveal a heightened interest in Drahomanov and a new respect for the humanistic trends which emerged from the Protestant revolution.

68 M. Hrushevsky, *Istoriia ukrainskoi literatury,* 5 vols. (Vienna–Kiev, 1923–7; reprinted New York, 1959–60). The New York edition contains a valuable introductory essay by D. Chyzhevsky, 'Mykhailo Serhiievych Hrushevsky iak istoryk literatury,' pp. i–x. Chyzhevsky stresses the originality of Hrushevsky's contribution to the history of Kievan-Rus' literature and his knowledge of foreign and especially Byzantine sources which throw new light on this literature.

69 See his correspondence with T. Poychynok cited in notes 45 and 60 above. Also see M. Antonovych, ed. 'Lysty M. Hrushevskoho do E. Faryniak,' *Ukrainskyi istoryk,* nos. 1–2 (1977), 118–31, and nos. 3–4, (1977), 106–12. For his attitude toward Protestantism see Lev Bykovsky, *Vasyl Kuziv i Mykhailo Hrushevsky,* (Winnipeg–Detroit, 1968). In Canada, A. Gregorovich of Smoky Lake, Alberta, was one of his principal agents. A series of letters and postcards from

scholars were in correspondence with the School of Slavonic Studies at the University of London, and it was proposed that he teach at Oxford. He was also told that he might be able to teach at Princeton University if he would only come to America. Moreover, he made some inquiries about returning to Lviv in Eastern Galicia. But none of these alternatives proved attractive. Britain and America were too far from the homeland, and Galicia was in the hands of the Poles, whom Hrushevsky had always considered to be far more hostile to the Ukrainian cause than were the Russians. Once again, Hrushevsky believed that the principal Ukrainian leaders were inclined to compromise with the Poles and that he would be completely isolated in Lviv. Hrushevsky remained in Vienna.[70]

While he lived in Vienna, Hrushevsky's contacts with Soviet Ukraine were never completely broken. The attempt to legalize the SRs had failed, but private correspondence continued and certain figures within the Soviet Ukrainian government – especially Hrushevsky's former SR colleagues from the pro-Soviet *Borotbisty* – wanted to see him return. Over the course of 1922, it seems that Hrushevsky slowly accepted the idea of returning to Ukraine as a private citizen. Of course, the Bolsheviks would try to use his return for the purposes of propaganda, but he would be able to continue his cultural and historical work on behalf of the Ukrainian people. He would be one of those modern 'Tatar people' who would resist the conquerors from within.[71]

Throughout 1923, his resolve to return to Ukraine was steadily strengthening. There were inquiries as to whether he would be willing to accept the Chair of

Hrushevsky beginning 27 March 1920 and ending 15 December 1923 has been preserved in the private archive of Andrew Gregorovich, Toronto. Hrushevsky's extensive correspondence with Winnipeg's *Ukrainskyi holos* has also been preserved. See the Public Archives of Canada, National Ethnic Archives, Olha Woycenko Collection, vol. XII, files 43 and 46. All of this correspondence reveals Hrushevsky's difficult material circumstances during the Vienna period.

70 Hrushevsky's contact with the School of Slavonic and East European Studies is mentioned in O. Ohloblyn, 'Ukrainian Historiography 1916–1956,' *Annals of the Ukrainian Academy of Arts and Sciences in the US*, V–VI (1957), 405. Contact was probably made through R.W. Seton-Watson, a central figure in the 'School,' with whom Hrushevsky was in correspondence. (H. Seton-Watson, letter of 2 February 1981 to the author.) The appointment to Oxford and the situation in Galicia is discussed by V. Doroshenko, 'Pershyi prezydent vidnovlenoi ukrainskoi derzhavy,' p. 30. It was the pastor Vasyl Kuziv who tried to arrange for his post at Princeton. See Bykovsky, *Vasyl Kuziv i Mykhailo Hrushevsky*, p. 2, and Shevchenko, 'Chomu Hrushevsky povernuvsia?' p. 26, who quotes the historian as writing that he would only go to America 'if there were no other way to avoid starving to death ... From a moral and national point of view, the present situation would turn the trip into a fiasco.'

71 See Kovalevsky, *Pry dzherelakh borotby,* pp. 599–600, who 'states that Hrushevsky always placed a stress on the long-term effect that environmental and geographic factors would have upon foreigners who come to Ukraine: 'In our conversations, Hrushevsky also said that the cultural-psychological complex of Ukraine has an enormous influence on conquerors and that in the Communist circles which seized power in Ukraine, this same historical process of "Tatar People" will begin and must be utilized.'

Ukrainian History at the Academy of Sciences in Kiev, appeals from Chechel and Khrystiuk, who by the spring were already in Kharkiv, and official announcements concerning a New Economic Policy (NEP) and a New National Policy (*Korenizatsiia*) that would mean extensive 'Ukrainianization' of the Soviet Ukrainian Republic. Hrushevsky accepted this news cautiously, and in his private correspondence discussed its causes, ramifications, and limitations. He believed the threat of a new attack by Pilsudski's Poland to be an important factor in the announcement of a Ukrainianization program, and he thought that there were still powerful forces within the Bolshevik Party which were resisting Lenin's new policies. Nevertheless, the situation in Galicia was even worse, and Hrushevsky thought that, in the event of war, it would be an improvement if the area were to be annexed to Soviet Ukraine. In this case, it would be important that the Soviet political structure in Galicia as well as in the east be primarily manned by Ukrainians and not by unfriendly Poles or Jews. He would stay away from politics and concentrate on purely cultural work, but he would return home.[72]

Rumours of Hrushevsky's final decision spread quickly throughout the emigration. Certainly, it would be a severe blow to the Ukrainian People's Republic and its government-in-exile if the first president of independent Ukraine voluntarily went to live and work in the rival Soviet Republic. In Prague, N. Hryhoriiv, who had recently accused the professor of wanting to be an SR 'pope,' now chaired a conference at which it was decided to offer him well-paid posts at the Free Ukrainian University, the Ukrainian Pedagogical Institute, and the Technical Academy. The Prague community's envoy, M. Stakhiv, travelled to Vienna and tried to convince Hrushevsky that his return would have the effect of legitimizing Soviet rule. The historian replied that he had lost all legal title to the presidency in 1919 at the Toilers' Congress and that he was now returning as a private citizen. He would not enter any political negotiations and thus would make no political statements which might be of use to the Bolsheviks. Finally, he told Stakhiv in confidence that recent revolts against the Communist dictatorship – at Kronstadt, and the Volga region, and in Ukraine – might have been crushed, but that sooner or later a new revolution would come and that, even if it failed,

---

72 See 'Lysty Hrushevskoho do Faryniaka,' pp. 124–130. On 16 December 1923, Hrushevsky informed his correspondent: 'The year before last I had already decided upon my return to Ukraine. They called me there several times, but I did not see favourable conditions for work there, while I could do something here. But with the spring of this year, all possibilities of working here have disappeared – because the books are no longer selling. Meanwhile, over there things have got slightly better. And so in May when the Ukrainian Academy of Sciences in Kiev asked me if I would agree to be elected to the Academy's Chair of Ukrainian History, which it is holding for me, I agreed. (Earlier, in 1918, when the Academy was founded, I did not want to enter it, because the supporters of the Hetman organized it, destroying our Ukrainian plan.)'

international conflicts would bring war and further changes. He was returning to prepare the ground.[73]

At the end of December, 1923, Hrushevsky was formally elected a member of the Ukrainian Academy of Sciences. A Chair of Ukrainian History was reserved for him, and he was assured that he would be able to return to his scholarly work without interference on the part of the authorities. It took two more months to set his affairs in order, obtain financing for his journey home, and get the necessary documents. The Hrushevsky family left Vienna on 2 March 1924, and arrived in Kiev on 7 March.[74] The renowned patriarch of *Ukrainstvo* and hero of the revolution had returned to the city that he considered his ancestral home.

The period which began with Skoropadsky's *coup d'etat* and ended with the return to Kiev was a humiliating and frustrating one for Hrushevsky. With the Central Rada discredited and his very life in danger, the historian retired to the countryside and refused to have anything to do with a German-supported Ukrainian monarchy. When the national intelligentsia overthrew Skoropadsky, its leaders rejected the idea of renewing the Central Rada and unceremoniously brushed Hrushevsky to the side. He replied by calling for popular rule and a temporary acceptance of the conciliar/soviet principle. In Kamianets, he even tried to put this idea into action. But the experiment was a failure and Hrushevsky was compelled to flee to the West. In Prague, Paris, Lucerne, and Vienna, he represented the Ukrainian cause to the outside world but at the same time rejected the policies and questioned the legitimacy of the Ukrainian government. He stood firmly upon the principles of popular rule, but there seemed to be no way to implement these principles and his following continued to diminish.

By 1920, Hrushevsky was already reevaluating the revolutionary period and admitting some mistakes. At this time, he consciously returned to the Proudhonian vision of socialism and federalism that he had inherited from Antonovych and had

73 See M. Stakhiv's detailed memoir, 'Chomu M. Hrushevsky povernuvsia v 1924 rotsi do Kyieva? (Zhmut faktiv i uryvok iz spohadiv),' in *Mykhailo Hrushevsky u 110 rokovyny narodzhennia.* pp. 126–47. A few of Stakhiv's details are confirmed in Hrushevsky's letter of 16 December 1923, to Faryniak. See 'Lysty Hrushevskoho do Faryniaka,' pp. 129–31.

74 His election to the Academy can be dated by comparing his letter of 16 December 1923 to Faryniak ('Lysty Hrushevskoho do Faryniaka') with *Avtobiohrafiia–1926,* p. 88. For the trip to Kiev, during which he caught cold, see his next letter to Faryniak, which was written from Soviet Ukraine. See 'Lysty Hrushevskoho do Faryniaka,' p. 107. Also see Shevchenko, 'Chomu Hrushevsky povernuvsia,' p. 29. According to Lviv's *Dilo,* no. 72, 1 April 1924, Hrushevsky returned by way of Warsaw, where he was greeted at the railway station by a crowd of well-wishers with whom he discussed the impoverishment and need of the Ukrainian emigration in both Czechoslovakia and Poland. The paper stated that Hrushevsky crossed into the Soviet Union at the border town of Zdolbuniv.

publicly espoused in 1905. This plan put the emphasis on autonomous communes and regions; in the quest for federation of the world it minimized the importance of national-state independence. Hrushevsky suggested this model to Rakovsky and urged the legalization of the UPSR. When his advice was ignored, the historian retreated once more to cultural work. Conditions changed, and soon there was more opportunity to carry out this work in Soviet Ukraine than in Vienna. At this point, he reached some sort of agreement with the Soviet authorities and returned home.

By going to work in the Soviet Ukrainian Republic, which he well knew was a front for the dictatorship of the Russian Bolsheviks, Hrushevsky was certain to stir up a great deal of controversy. In later times, Soviet historians would write that the veteran scholar had begged to return home and that 'after several requests to the Soviet Ukrainian government, in which Hrushevsky condemned his counter-revolutionary activity, the VUTsVK [All-Ukrainian Central Executive Committee] allowed him to return to Soviet Ukraine for scholarly work.'[75] But obsequious conduct was hardly one of the historian's faults. On the contrary, Ukrainians living under Soviet rule soon realized that Hrushevsky had important contacts within the Communist Party (Bolsheviks) of Ukraine (CPbU) and was acting according to a well-thought-out strategy. One young admirer, who had an opportunity to discuss these matters with him, testifies:

M.S. Hrushevsky did not do any bending or make any promises to serve the Soviets. On the contrary, he had an official agreement [*ofitsiinyi dohovir*] with the President of the Council of People's Commissars of the Ukrainian Soviet Socialist Republic, V. Ia. Chubar, to the effect that the Soviet government would secure Hrushevsky full personal amnesty and full freedom in his scholarly activity – in exchange, M.S. Hrushevsky promised not to act publicly by word or in print against Soviet power, that is, to refrain from political struggle with it.[76]

Thus the Ukrainian scholar returned to Kiev without making any concessions in

75 See M.A. Rubach's article on Hrushevsky in the *Ukrainska Radianska Entsyklopediia*, vol. III (Kiev, 1979). 202. Some non-Soviet sources also say that Hrushevsky took the initiative in this matter. For example, V. Kedrovsky, writing thirty-five years after the event, described a chance meeting that he had with Hrushevsky shortly before his departure. The historian asked Kedrovsky if he knew 'that he had made a request that he be allowed to return to Ukraine' (*vin podav prokhannia dozvolyty iomu* ... See V. Kedrovsky, 'Povorot M.S. Hrushevskoho na Ukrainy,' *Vilna Ukraina*, no. 51 (1966), 65–6.

76 See V. Dubrovsky's critique of the Rubach/Soviet position in *Ukrainskyi istoryk*, nos. 1–2 (1966), 108–9. N. Polonska-Vasylenko, who was active in the Ukrainian Academy of Sciences and was married to one of its central figures, M.P. Vasylenko, clearly states that the initiative was wholly from the side of the Soviet authorities. See her *Ukrainska Akademiia Nauk*, I, 44.

principle; he merely withdrew from political life and transferred his activities to the cultural arena. For their part, the Communist authorities had introduced a policy of 'Ukrainianization' of the party and state apparatus, but had not altered the principle of the dictatorship of their own party; the SRs would never be legalized. It remained to be seen whether this delicate arrangement would work for any length of time.

9
The All-Ukrainian Academy of Sciences (VUAN) 1924–1927

Hrushevsky's return to Ukraine was immediately condemned by many in the emigration. Shapoval, in particular, disliked the thought of accepting any kind of amnesty from the Soviets, and believed that Hrushevsky's action reflected his lack of political will, his basic dishonesty, and a betrayal of his 'political testament' of 1918. Sociological analysis had shown Shapoval that the Russians still ruled Ukraine, and thus, despite the new government programs, the 'Muscovite occupation' was still intact. He concluded with emphasis: 'Talk about amnesty should not be directed toward us, but rather toward the occupiers. *Our people has not given the occupiers an amnesty and will never do so* . . . This is the order of the Ukrainian people. The emigration executes it.'[1]

Shapoval's analysis of the Soviet power structure was essentially correct. The CPbU was, in fact, still Russian-dominated and divorced from the Ukrainian population. On the other hand, those *Borotbisty* or 'Militants' who had gone over to the Soviets in late 1918 and had later been compelled to forsake the UPSR and join the CPbU were now working hard to ensure that Lenin's new economic and national policies were put into effect. The Kremlin's policy of 'nativization' (*Korenizatsiia*), which the Kharkiv government interpreted as 'Ukrainianization,' was strongly supported by Hrushevsky's former SR followers, Oleksander Shumsky and O. Butsenko. The former was now Kharkiv's commissar of education and the latter was secretary of the All-Ukrainian Central Executive Committee (VUTsVK). The policy was also supported by the commissar of justice, Mykola Skrypnyk, who was an 'old Bolshevik' and one of the few

---

1 M. Shapoval, 'Emigratsiia i Ukraina,' *Nova Ukraina*, nos. 4–6 (Prague, 1925), 1–17. On the other hand, many émigrés, especially from Galicia, where the political and economic climate was extremely unfavourable, approved of Hrushevsky's action. See, for example, 'M. Hrushevsky pro svii povorot,' *Dilo*, no. 67, 26 March 1924, and 'V pereizdi na Batkivshchynu,' *Dilo*, no. 72, 1 April 1924.

Ukrainians to have been personally acquainted with Lenin. Thus the arrival of the former patriarch of *Ukrainstvo* caused a great sensation in Kiev. In private conversations, many enthusiastic Communists claimed that 'even Hrushevsky is with us.'[2]

The claim was not exactly well founded. Neither in his public statements nor in his private correspondence did the historian ever declare himself in support of Communist rule. His early letters to friends abroad, which were certainly read by the political police, contain no praise of the regime and are filled with carefully worded complaints about physical conditions in Soviet Ukraine. Moreover, when Hrushevsky made the required statement to the Kharkiv government press about the reasons for his return, he limited these reasons to his desire to complete his great *History of Ukraine-Rus'* and his *History of Ukrainian Literature* and to organize a range of other scholarly projects. There was no direct word of support for the Soviet regime.[3]

Neither the professor nor his Marxist opponents had any illusions about the political, economic, and cultural struggles that characterized the NEP period. The party had withdrawn significantly from certain spheres of economic and cultural life, it is true, but its distant goal was not abandoned. Meanwhile, those parts of society independent of the state – peasants, the professionals, and the scholars – set about their work without undue regard for Marxist dogma. It was common knowledge that the two sides were building up strength in a competition that was to be resolved some time in the future. Hrushevsky's understanding with Chubar, the head of Soviet Ukrainian government, and his early statements to the Soviet press reflected this half-stated but very real competition.[4]

In the summer of 1924, Hrushevsky went to Kharkiv to confer with various government officials. As capital of the Ukrainian Soviet Socialist Republic, this city was the bureaucratic centre from which the policy of Ukrainianization was being carried out. The conferences with the education commissar, Shumsky, seem to have been constructive, for Hrushevsky very quickly acquired substantial financial support for the series of 'Historical Institutions' that he was in the process of establishing. On the other hand, if the historian conferred with the members of Skrypnyk's group, the meetings were probably more tense, for Skrypnyk's close

2 See V.V. Dubrovsky, 'Velykyi patriot: hromadska diialnist M. Hrushevskoho po povoroti v rad. Ukrainu,' *Na chuzhyni*, no. 1 (28) (Munich?, 1947), 5–7. On Shumsky and his circle see I. Maistrenko, *Borotbisty: A Chapter in the History of Ukrainian Communism* (New York, 1954). More generally, see the relevant chapters of B. Dmytryshyn, *Moscow and the Ukraine 1918–1953* (New York, 1956).

3 Interview with Hrushevsky, *Visti VUTsVK* (Kharkiv), no. 13, 30 March 1924, and partly reprinted in Stakhiv, 'Deiaki dokumenty pro diialnist Hrushevskoho na emihratsii,' pp. 166–7. Also see 'Lysty M. Hrushevskoho do E. Faryniaka,' pp. 106–12.

4 Dubrovsky, 'Velykyi patriot.'

associate, Andrii Richytsky, and the dean of Ukrainian party historians, Matvii Iavorsky, were just then criticizing Hrushevsky's non-Marxist approach to various historical and sociological questions.[5]

These public criticisms did not prevent the Ukrainian intelligentsia of Kharkiv, especially the young, from rejoicing in Hrushevsky's return. Volodymyr Doroshenko, who followed events from the NTSh library in Lviv, later described the ovations with which Hrushevsky was greeted in the official capital of Soviet Ukraine:

The meeting took place at the university. The great hall, which held a thousand people, was filled to overflowing. The entire [nationally] conscious Kharkiv Ukrainian intelligentsia was present. They greeted M. Hrushevsky like the legitimate leader [*zakonnyi providnyk*] of Ukraine in juxtaposition to the Bolshevik authorities.[6]

A contemporary Kharkivite further explains that the national poet, Shevchenko, was a beloved father (*Batko*) for the youth, just as Kotliarevsky had been the same for Shevchenko. 'Hrushevsky was *Batko* Hrushevsky. The hierarchy of human relations went along family, not bureaucratic lines.'[7]

5 M. Iavorsky, 'De shcho pro "krytychnu" krytyku, pro "obiektyvny" historiiu ta shche i pro babusynu spidnytsiu,' *Chervony shliakh*, no. 3 (Karkiv, 1924), 167–82, was directed primarily against Hrushevsky's fellow academician D. Bahalii, who had critically reviewed one of Iavorsky's books. Bahalii replied in a further issue of *Chervonyi shliakh*, hinting that he stood closer to the *narodnyk* Hrushevsky than to the Marxist Iavorsky. Also see A. Richytsky, 'Iak Hrushevsky "vypravliaie" Engelsa,' *Chervonyi shliakh*, no. 3 (1924), 183–90, which criticized Hrushevsky's *Pochatky hromadianstva* (Vienna, 1922). Richytsky later became editor of the first Ukrainian-language edition of Marx's *Capital* (1927–8).
6 Doroshenko, 'Pershyi prezydent vidnovlenoi ukrainskoi derzhavy,' p. 31. Also see V. Dubrovsky, 'M.S. Hrushevsky u Chernihovi,' *Kalendar-Almanakh 'Vidrodzhennia'* (Buenos Aires, 1961), 99–119, which describes a similar meeting in July 1924, in Chernyhiv.
7 Oleksander Semenenko, *Kharkiv Kharviv ...* (Munich, 1976), p. 32. For a similar description of the warmth with which Hrushevsky was greeted in Kharkiv see O[leksii] K[onoval], 'Chy Hrushevsky i Vynnychenko spravdi skapituliuvaly pered bilshovyzmom,' *Novi Dni*, no. 5 (Toronto, 1980), 26–7. Konoval reports that, when asked why he had returned to Ukraine, Hrushevsky paused a moment, and then replied: 'Remember the words of Prince Sviatoslav: "It is better to lay one's bones to rest in one's own land, rather than to find glory in a foreign one."'. Konoval's basic position is that Hrushevsky returned to Ukraine to continue the struggle for national liberation, not to capitulate before Bolshevism. According to Volodymyr Dolenko (b. 1889), a leader of the underground Peasant or *Muzhycha* Party, which was based in the official Ukrainian capital, the idea of Hrushevsky's public address in Kharkiv originated with the former SRs Holubovych, Khrystiuk, and others. Since the SRs had only recently been released from prison or allowed to return home, they turned to their colleagues of the *Muzhycha* Party to carry out the project. After Hrushevsky's official address, says Dolenko, the historian met informally with the *Muzhycha* Party leaders – B. Shcherbanenko, V. Leshchenko, etc. – and discussed the basic question of the tactics to be followed within a police state. All agreed to keep to legal activities. See F. Pigido, 'Mykhailo Hrushevsky ta ioho istorychni ustanovy,' *Ukrainski visti* (Novyi Ulm), nos. 94–5, 1952. On the

Having secured the necessary funding in Kharkiv, Hrushevsky immediately set about reorganizing the historical work of the academy. He soon replaced M.P. Vasylenko in the Chair of Scholarly Research and took over the Archaeographic Commission, which had been inactive since the death of V.S. Ikonnikov in late 1923. He also returned to his place at the head of the UNT Historical Section and renewed the publication of its journal under the title *Ukraina*. Hrushevsky hoped that this autonomous Historical Section would become a link between the VUAN and the general public, and, in fact, after his return its work progressed rapidly.[8] Where other academicians were responsible for only one or two scholarly commissions, Hrushevsky was soon responsible for scores. Each commission had two or three salaried employees and ten to twenty voluntary workers. To staff these ventures the scholar drew his wide circle of acquaintances and even his family into the work.[9] At first, Hrushevsky and his collaborators shared the cold and the cramped conditions that the VUAN veterans had endured since the academy's foundation. Eventually, however, the scholar was able to obtain a separate two-storey building on Korolenko Street, and his old friend, the artist Krychevsky, adorned it with artifacts and the portraits of major Ukrainian cultural figures. Hrushevsky's 'Historical Institutions' soon became a by-word.[10]

Throughout the 1920s, the scholars grouped around Hrushevsky's Historical Institutions produced a great mass of new literature dealing with the history of Ukraine and of Eastern Europe. Political conditions would not allow non-Marxist historians any large degree of generalization, but in its periodization, its terminology, and its subject matter, the new historical literature revealed the influence of Hrushevsky's 'scheme' and reflected his emphasis upon popular social and cultural movements.[11] While the master busied himself with the eighth and ninth volumes of his *History of Ukraine Rus'*, the volumes dealing with the era

Muzhycha Party, which until the arrests of 1927 was active in the cooperative movement and its publishing house *Rukh*, see Dmytro Solovei, *Holhota Ukrainy* (Winnipeg, 1953), pp. 112–17.

8 O. Hrushevsky, 'Ukrainske naukove tovarystvo v Kyivi ta istorychna sektsiia pry VUAN v rr. 1914–1923,' *Ukraina*, no. 4 (Kiev, 1924), 180–8. Also see Polonska-Vasylenko, *Ukrainska akademiia nauk*, I, 44–5.

9 See N. Polonska-Vasylenko, 'Istorychna nauka v Ukraini za sovietskoi doby ta dolia istorykiv,' *Zbirnyk na poshanu ukrainskykh uchenykh znyshchenykh bolshevytskoiu Moskvoiu, ZNTSh*, CLXXIII (Paris, 1962), 12. Hrushevsky was especially proud of his daughter, Kateryna, who was breaking new ground in anthropology, comparative ethnology, and the collection of historical songs. At one point during this period of constant stress, he confided to a friend in America: 'I have one consolation and that is my daughter; her scholarly work is going very nicely and in several fields of scholarly activity she is beginning to replace me quite well.' See 'Lysty M. Hrushevskoho do E. Faryniaka,' p. 112.

10 Polonska-Vasylenko, *Ukrainska akademiia nauk*, I, 45, says that some academicians became alarmed at the extravagance of Krychevsky's renovations.

11 See the general remarks of Borys Krupnytsky, *Ukrainska istorychna nauka pid sovietamy* (Munich, 1957), pp. 10–13.

of Bohdan Khmelnytsky, he set his colleagues to work on various other projects: collective works on the Chernyhiv and Kiev areas, the history of the city of Kiev, and the documentation of the Cossack era. In nineteenth-century studies, his collaborators investigated a number of important problems: Osyp Hermaize, who was of Jewish background and a former USDLP member, worked on the Haidamaky, the Decembrists, Drahomanov, the RUP, and the Ukrainian national movement up to the end of the World War; Serhii Shamrai worked on the Kiev area peasant rebellion of 1855; Fedir Savchenko on the national movement in the 1860s and the 1870s and the Russian bureaucracy's attempt to repress it. Numerous other studies were undertaken and Hrushevsky himself published many new historiographical articles as well as biographical characterizations of the major figures of the nineteenth-century renaissance. New editions of Kostomarov and Antonovych were undertaken, and Hrushevsky helped his brother Oleksander with the monumental *Historical and Geographical Dictionary of Ukraine* which had been started by Antonovych many years before. By 1928, it was almost completed.[12]

This manifold activity had a considerable effect upon Russian as well as Ukrainian historiography. The Russian statist school of Kliuchevsky, which accepted Muscovite genealogical claims to the Kievan heritage and breathed a strongly national tone, was already being attacked by the leading historian of the Communist regime, M.N. Pokrovsky. From his position at the head of the Moscow Institute of Red Professors, Pokrovsky opposed glorification of the old Russian state and revealed a certain sympathy for the various subject and colonized peoples. In the beginning, at least, the dethronement of Kliuchevsky and the new emphasis on the role of the people left a certain degree of room to manoeuvre for populists of Hrushevsky's type.[13] In the 1920s, Kliuchevsky's student, M.K.

12 Borys Krupnytsky, 'Die ukrainische Geschichtswissenschaft in der Sowjetunion 1921–1941,' *Jahrbücher für die Geschichte Osteuropas*, nos. 2–4 (Breslau, 1941), 125–51, is one of the better surveys of the historical literature of this period. Also see his 'Die archäographische Tätigkeit M. Hrušewskyjs,' *Jahrbücher für Kultur und Geschichte der Slaven*, XI, 3–4, (Breslau, 1935), 610–21. On the historical dictionary, which was to have complemented the Dictionary of National Biography being prepared by Serhii Iefremov and his collaborators, see O. Hermaize, 'Die ukrainische Geschichtswissenschaft in der USSR,' *Slavische Rundschau*, no. 1 (Prague, 1929), 363–6. Both of these large-scale projects were cut short by the Stalin purges of the 1930s. Not a single volume was published.

13 Pokrovsky thought that Imperial Russian rule in the Baltic lands, Poland, Ukraine, and the Western borderlands was of a colonial type, though it completely lacked those elements of progress that could be found in Central Asia. He believed that the Russian government exported backwardness to the more advanced 'borderlands' to preserve a reactionary and outdated system in Russian itself. See the introductory essay by the Ukrainian-American historian Roman Szporluk in *Russia in World History: Selected Essays by M.N. Pokrovsky* (Ann Arbor, 1970), especially p. 21. It might be added that Pokrovsky (1868–1923) and Hrushevsky (1866–1934) were almost exact contemporaries.

Liubavsky, who had studied the history of both Lithuania and Muscovy, arrived independently at conclusions similar to those of Hrushevsky, and A.E. Presniakov openly stated his debt to the Ukrainian historian in his major work on the northern Russian rather than Kievan Rus' origins of the Muscovite state.[14] In Belorussia and Lithuania too there was a natural interest in Hrushevsky's work, and another of Antonovych's students, M.V. Dovnar-Zapolsky, and the 'Ukrainophile' V. Picheta were important figures in the Belorussian national revival.[15]

The influence of the Ukrainian historian did not stop at the borders of the Soviet Union. As soon as was possible, Hrushevsky established contacts with the NTSh in Lviv and initiated the election of a number of Galician scholars to the VUAN. The new academicians included his friend and sympathizer Kyrylo Studynsky, who had just been elected the new president of the NTSh, and his old colleague, the ethnographer, Volodymyr Hnatiuk.[16] On another level, Hrushevsky took care to ensure that the new Ukrainian academic literature was sent to major libraries abroad, such as the New York Public Library.[17] He also initiated negotiations for an exchange program with the Institute of Slavic Studies in Paris, which, he hoped, would establish a special Ukrainian section. 'Great was our astonishment,' writes I. Borshchak, one of the historian's Parisian contacts, 'when some months later we learned that Kharkiv was ready to finance the plan. It must be said that Monsieur Rakovsky, who was then ambassador to Paris, supported Hrushevsky's project.'[18] Although an uncertain political situation prevented the exchange program from being carried out, Hrushevsky's friend Antoine Meillet, the French Slavist, was elected a foreign member of the VUAN, and Hrushevsky's daughter,

14 Liubavsky's views were clear as early as 1910, when his major work on the Lithuanian state appeared. His major work on the Great Russian nationality and the formation of Russia was published in 1929. Presniakov's *The Formation of the Great Russian State*, trans. A. Moorhouse (Chicago, 1970), also appeared in 1929. Both works were hailed as landmarks in modern Russian historiography when they first appeared, but fell into official disfavour shortly afterward. For some general remarks, see George Vernadsky, *Russian Historiography: A History* (Belmont, Mass., 1978), pp. 163–6, 287–91, 335–8.

15 Dovnar-Zapolsky (1867–1934) was one of the founders of the Belorussian State University in Minsk (1921). Picheta was born in Poltava, studied in Moscow, and became Rector of the Belorussian State University in 1921. He was noted for his insistence upon the mastery of the Belorussian tongue. See U. Hlybinny, *Vierzig Jahre weissruthenischer Kultur unter den Sowjets* (Munich, 1959), p. 21. More generally, see Anastas'in and Voznesensky, 'Nachalo trekh natsionalnykh akademii,' p. 172ff.

16 Both men were elected to the VUAN in 1924. See Wynar, *Mykhailo Hrushevsky i NTSh*, pp. 72–4.

17 See his letter of 10 March 1925 to Faryniak in 'Lysty M. Hrushevskoho do E. Faryniaka,' p. 112.

18 E. Borschak [I. Borshchak], 'Mikhailo Hruševskij (1866–1934),' *Le monde slave*, no. 1 (Paris, 1935), 32–4. Hrushevsky also seems to have had the support of the education commissar, Mykola Skrypnyk, who in 1927 visited Borshchak in Paris. See Ivan Koshelivets, *Mykola Skrypnyk* (Munich, 1972), pp. 226–7.

Kateryna, did visit Paris, where her lecture on old Ukrainian *Dumy,* or oral epic literature, was very well received.[19]

Hrushevsky's international projects, his publishing ventures, and the very existence of the Historical Institutions were made possible by personal contacts within the Kharkiv government. But these contacts were not without complications. The academy's permanent secretary, Ahatanhel Krymsky, and the other veterans who had been appointed at the time of the Hetman resented Hrushevsky's direct connections with Kharkiv, disliked his independence of the VUAN administration, and feared his dabbling in politics. In November 1924, Krymsky wrote to Dmytro Bahalii in Kharkiv that 'from the time Hrushevsky arrived, the academy has simply breathed intrigues.' The general political situation was already dangerous enough. Krymsky continued: 'For this reason one should always be on guard lest he cause the academy to be politically compromised.'[20]

Hrushevsky and Krymsky would frequently come into conflict at administrative meetings. On occasion Krymsky would even leave the meeting and threaten to resign. Serhii Iefremov would usually side with Krymsky, while the education minister from the Hetman's time, the historian M.P. Vasylenko, would try to mediate the disputes.[21] In general, Hrushevsky claimed that only his arrival had given the academy a truly Ukrainian character, while the VUAN veterans claimed that the historian's emphasis upon the humanities was impeding the institution's proper development. The otherwise dry published *Proceedings* give us a hint of what happened behind the large oaken doors of the academy:

For scientific-scholarly expenses in 1924, 8950 rubles were sent to us. From them, 1530 rubles went to the institutions set up under the Chair of Academician Hrushevsky (that is, more than 17 per cent, a little less than 1/5 of all the money sent us) and 7420 rubles for all the rest of the numerous institutions of our Academy and all their three departments.

Such reports of the Academy do not contain many footnotes, but this matter is footnoted thus:

It must not be assumed that such an inequitable [*nerivnomirnyi*] distribution of funds is due to the administration's giving more weight to history, archaeography, or archaeology, than

19 See Borshchak's note in *Ukraina*, no. 7 (Paris, 1952), 500.
20 Quoted in O. Babyshkin, *Ahatanhel Krymsky* (Kiev, 1967), pp. 28–9. Krymsky continues: 'It is especially necessary to watch closely when Hrushevsky endeavours to elect someone as an Active Member or a Corresponding Member; not only the interests of his parish, but also all the political reminiscences of the times of the Central Rada or emigration bring woe here.'
21 Polonska-Vasylenko, *Ukrainska akademiia nauk*, 1, 46–7, and her 'M.P. Vasylenko i VUAN,' *Ukraina*, no. 5 (Paris, 1951), 337–45, and also her 'Ahatanhel Krymsky,' *Ukraina*, no. 2 (Paris, 1949), 121–8.

to the equipping of laboratories, economic work, etc. Simply, Kharkiv gave the order to reserve a certain sum for the institutions of Academician M.S. Hrushevsky, and the administration cannot turn it to any other purpose.[22]

This type of complaint was common during the entire period of Hrushevsky's presence in the academy. By 1926, the historian's return to Soviet Ukraine and his apparent arrogance, meanness, and 'petty politicking' caused his former friend and admirer Mykhailo Mohyliansky, the Kadet who had once quoted him with approval in *Rech*, to have him symbolically executed in a fictional tale published in the journal of the Commissariat of Education.[23]

On occasion, however, Hrushevsky's politicking was able to do some good. This was the case in 1924 when the academy became involved in its first political trial. M.P. Vasylenko and a number of VUAN collaborators were falsely charged and then convicted of spying for Poland. The trial thoroughly shook the academy, but both Krymsky and Hrushevsky brought all of their influence to bear on the matter. The latter turned to Shumsky and Butsenko, while Vasylenko's wife approached Rakovsky, who had just returned from France, where the affair had received considerable attention. Vasylenko served eight months of a ten-year prison term before he was amnestied. It remains a mystery whether the decisive factor in his release was the press coverage in France, or the appeals of Hrushevsky and his colleagues.[24]

The Vasylenko case was only one example of how deeply political events could affect cultural life. In fact, the actions of Hrushevsky were being monitored and discussed at the highest level, in Moscow, as well as in Kharkiv. About a year after Hrushevsky's arrival, the GPU in Moscow sent the following top-secret circular to its local detachments:

The *History of Ukraine-Rus'* by the ideologue of Ukrainian nationalism, Prof. Hrushevsky, has been designated as a falsely scientific history, dangerous, and harmful to Soviet rule. The question of the banning of this book is now being considered by the government of the USSR and the OGPU in Moscow. Meanwhile, we advise the RR [local police units] to identify all of those who express an interest in the aforementioned book and distribute it among the population. Inform our S/O [secret agents] about this and oblige them to intensify their observation over such persons.[25]

22 *Zvidomlennia VUAN za 1924* (Kiev, 1925), p. 69.
23 M. Mohyliansky, 'Vbyvstvo,' *Chervonyi shliakh*, no. 1 (Kharkiv, 1926), 53–5. By this time, it seems, Shumsky, who had been the founder and the first editor of *Chervonyi shliakh*, was no longer in control of its editorial policy.
24 Polonska-Vasylenko, *Ukrainska akademiia nauk*, I, 49–51.
25 This document, along with others of a similar nature, was removed from Soviet police files during the Second World War. For the Russian text see *Ukrainskyi zbirnyk*, no. 8 (Munich, 1957), 147. It is reprinted in *Vybrani pratsi*, pp. 259–60.

This same year, Krymsky was approached by party or police officials with some kind of request for information about Hrushevsky's activity. In a carefully composed reply, the permanent secretary noted that 'Hrushevsky's psychology, that of a newly arrived immigrant, is quite often completely different from that of all those members of the academy who have worked under Soviet rule during the past six years.' Krymsky reassured his correspondent that, for the veterans of the academy, Soviet rule was not some kind of dread lord to be recognized out of necessity. Science had to be 'in the closest contact with the Communist Party, this revolutionary avant-guard.' Hrushevsky, on the other hand, had only just returned, and 'by this had undoubtedly recognised the power and might of Soviet rule; we have only not yet seen whether he consciously and in a showy way [*iaskravo*] has declared himself for it as an ideal and has freed himself from all émigré sympathies.'[26]

The question of Hrushevsky's relationship with the Soviet state came up at the Ninth Conference of the CPbU held in December 1925. While Solodub, a follower of Shumsky, spoke out in support of the historian, the old Bolshevik Chubar complained that 'unfortunately through the essence of his work, Hrushevsky has never publicly declared that he recognized Soviet rule and that he is content to work together with it.' Chubar added that Hrushevsky was ignoring the advice of those around him and still paying too much attention to émigré opinion:

It appears that the emigration considers him to be an independent scholarly worker and a fighter for socialism, only not by Communist roads. He apparently wishes to preserve this view and by this to say to the emigration that under Soviet rule even such independent people as himself can live. It is good when he says this, but it would be better if he left his independence for our common cause and worked together with us without heeding a small group of émigrés.[27]

It is clear that Chubar, who represented the most powerful faction within the CPbU, was not entirely satisfied with the agreement by which Hrushevsky had returned to Ukraine.

Throughout 1925 and 1926 in his articles in the Historical Section's *Ukraina*, Hrushevsky consistently avoided any statements that could be taken as support for the Communist regime. In fact, both in subject matter and in tone, his writings

26 Quoted in V.H. Sarbei, 'Pershyi neodminyi sekretar ukrainskoi akademii nauk,' *Visnyk AN URSR*, no. 1 (Kiev, 1971), 95–6.
27 'Tov. Chubar pro Tiutiunnyka i Hrushevskoho,' *Visti VUTsVK* (Karkiv), no. 282, 10 December 1925, and reprinted in *Vilna Ukraina*, no. 17 (Detroit, 1958), 21–2. Also see R. Sullivant, *Soviet Politics and the Ukraine 1917–1957* (New York, 1952), pp. 138 and 357, who makes a brief reference to Solodub's address.

stood clearly in the traditions of Ukrainian national scholarship. He penned numerous editorials dealing with purely academic subjects, but he always managed to inject some contemporary relevance. He contributed seminal articles on Shevchenko, Kostomarov, Kulish, Antonovych, Drahomanov, and Franko, and stated that their goals had not yet been achieved. He never openly broached politics, but he occasionally complained about 'technical difficulties.' With the skills of a veteran long used to writing under conditions of censorship, the intrepid historian somehow managed to make every editorial read like an exhortation. From the centre of a Soviet Socialist Ukraine ruled by the Communist Party, Hrushevsky once again raised high the banner of the national poet, Shevchenko, whose *Testament,* as he put it, 'commands us to work for its fulfilment with all our strength, under all conditions, and by every possible avenue.'[28]

In 1926, it was possible for Hrushevsky to speak out so clearly because the party's 'Ukrainianization' campaign was beginning to gather momentum and its strongest opponents had already been removed from the centres of power. Many opportunities for fruitful work, especially in the educational field, seemed to be opening up. The entire question of the future of the academy was discussed on 26 January 1926, at a session of the Main Ukrainian Scientific and Methodology Committee, which was the Soviet organ that directed and controlled almost all scholarly life in Ukraine. At this meeting, Hrushevsky called out strongly for the independence of the Ukrainian Academy in relation to the Russian. He said that much of what was known abroad as 'Russian' science was, in reality, a Ukrainian product and that it was necessary to found a society that would establish intellectual contacts with Western countries, but would do this directly and not go through Moscow. The representative of the Kharkiv government, who was presiding over the session, supported Hrushevsky's position. On 27 February, the historian wrote to Borshchak in Paris that 'the session of the Main Scientific Committee has created a good atmosphere and I hope to bring my personal work as well as that of my collaborators to a good end.[29]

Hrushevsky described the meeting of the Main Scientific Committee in a leading editorial in *Ukraina.* In this article, he protested against the fact that Moscow treated the Russian Academy of Sciences as if it were an All-Union institution, taking its financial support from the All-Union budget which included the Ukrainian Republic. At the same time, it treated the Ukrainian Academy as a

28 M. Hrushevsky, 'V shistdesiat chetverti shevchenkovi rokovyny,' *Ukraina,* no. 1 (Kiev, 1925), 1–5.

29 In Borshchak, 'Mikhailo Hruševskij (1866–1934),' pp. 29–30. In another letter to Borshchak, Hrushevsky said that his speech at the Main Scientific Committee was the event's 'pink carnation' and that it had raised his spirits considerably. See I. Borshchak, ed., 'Dva nevydani lysty M. Hrushevskoho,' *Soborna Ukraina* (Paris), April 1947, 37–8.

provincial affair and gave it nothing from the All-Union budget. Thus Ukrainian taxation supported two academies; Russian, one.[30]

Hrushevsky's public criticism of the USSR government's bureaucratic centralism coincided with a general trend in Ukrainian Communist literature, which, as its leading exponent, Mykola Khylovy, expressed it, was oriented 'Away from Moscow!'[31] It also coincided with a major power struggle within the CPbU. In this struggle, Shumsky's group of Ukrainianizers faced a group of Moscow loyalists beginning to gather around Stalin's man in Ukraine, Lazar Kaganovich. The beginning of 1926 saw Shumsky in Moscow, complaining to Stalin that, because of the stubborn resistance of certain elements within the party, the Ukrainianization program was not proceeding at a suitable pace. March saw Chubar, who still seemed to take an independent position in the struggle between Shumsky and Kaganovich, criticize Hrushevsky's statements at the Main Scientific Committee. As he told a Komsomol gathering:

There was a united session of the plenum with members of the Ukrainian Academy of Sciences, our supposedly red academy . . . Academician Hrushevsky, who was the head of the Central Rada, who arrived here, requesting [*poprosyvshys*] to work under the conditions of Soviet rule in Ukraine, and who supposedly had accepted all these conditions, suggested to us, public figures of the Soviet government, that we are continuing those [same] policies for which he had fought many years ago.

Chubar then explained that the times had changed. The old regime had oppressed the Ukrainian people with Great State Chauvinism, but the October Revolution had proclaimed the self-determination of nations and liberated them:

The academicians of the Hrushevsky type do not understand this and do not want to understand this. Among the scholars who work with us there are those who do not wish to understand that the October Revolution has liberated all of the working people from national oppression. Either they do not understand this, or they understand and they do not show how they understand it.

Chubar concluded by repeating that Hrushevsky had still not publicly declared his loyalty to the Soviet state but that it was absolutely necessary that the academy work together with the regime to fulfil Soviet goals.[32] Shortly afterward, the

30 M. Hrushevsky, 'Perspektyvy i vymohy ukrainskoi nauky,' *Ukraina*, no. 1 (Kiev, 1926), 3–15.
31 See George Luckyj, *Literary Politics in the Soviet Ukraine 1917–1934* (New York, 1956).
32 Chubar's speech is in Stakhiv, 'Deiaki dokumenty pro diialnist Hrushevskoho na emihratsii,' pp. 167–9, who quotes it from *Dilo* (Lviv), 21 March 1926. On the meeting between Shumsky and Stalin, see the works by Dmytryshyn and Sullivant cited in notes 2 and 27 above.

Kharkiv government sent two young Communist activists to do 'graduate work' with Hrushevsky. The historian protested against this imposition, but to no avail.[33]

About this same time, Hrushevsky penned one of his strongest criticisms of Russian chauvinism to be published under Soviet rule. In an article commemorating the Ems Ukaz of 1876, which had banned the printing of books in the Ukrainian language, Hrushevsky criticized both the old regime and its liberal critics, who, like Peter Struve, sought to relegate the Ukrainian language to a regional particularism, saving for Russian alone the role of a window on the world. Hrushevsky suggested that this kind of chauvinism was once again rearing its ugly head and that it did no credit to the socialist state. His arguments are similar to those which he had put to Rakovsky in 1920:

Would not an acceptance of Great Russian culture as the basis of the national cultures of the Soviet Union and the reduction of these national cultures to the role of provincial appendices equally signify the deprivation of this union of its universal character, of its spread throughout the world, and result in its eternal limitation to within the bounds of old Russia? For is it not in this area alone that Great Russian culture would, through the inertia of its old domination, be able to maintain its pan-union significance?

Hrushevsky ended with arguments which reflected the current Communist lexicon but were similar to those which he had once used against the Imperial Russian bureaucracy: national oppression is the cause of any Ukrainian extremism. A wise national policy would eliminate it:

In order to avoid Ukrainian nationalist exaggerations, it is necessary to keep an eye on both fronts: both on Ukrainian chauvinist caprice and also on Great Russian, Polish, Czech and all imperialistic covetousness. Such a struggle on two fronts was the destiny of all those who stood for the wide, healthy, normal development of the Ukrainian people – and it remains a testament for us from the great apostles of a New Ukraine: Shevchenko, Drahomanov, Franko – we remember their legacy today.[34]

This clear statement against imperialist sentiment, as a younger contemporary later recalled, 'made a great impression on all society.'[35]

In October 1926, Hrushevsky celebrated his sixtieth birthday. The Academy

33 Polonska-Vasylenko, *Ukrainska akademiia nauk*, I, 53, sees this government action as one of the first steps toward 'Sovietization' of the VUAN. See the group photograph in *Vybrani pratsi*, p. 219, in which these two Komsomol members pose together with the venerable élite of Ukrainian historical scholarship.

34 M. Hrushevsky, 'Hanebnoi pamiati,' *Ukraina*, no. 4 (Kiev, 1926), 46–57; reprinted in Iu. Lavrinenko, *Rozstriliane vidrodzhennia* (Paris, 1959), pp. 920–30.

35 Lavrinenko, p. 915.

made elaborate preparations, and the principal organizer, Academician Tutkivsky, invited scholars from all over the Soviet Union and from countries beyond its borders. Leading party officials were also to attend. There were to be speeches, a banquet, and preparations for a large three-volume *Festschrift*. 'Kiev had never before seen such a festive occasion, such a celebration of Ukrainian scholarship,' a VUAN worker later wrote.[36]

During the afternoon cermonies, various Ukrainian figures outlined Hrushevsky's important role in the development of modern Ukrainian scholarship. Studynsky spoke of the historian's importance for Galicia, Picheta for Belorussia, and Ioninas for Lithuania. Messages were received from scholars in Western Europe, and from Pokrovsky, Platonov, and Lunacharsky. Finally, the Kiev party officials, and Panas Liubchenko in particular, spoke of the favourable conditions in which Hrushevsky now worked and put the question directly to the historian: on which side of the barricades do you now stand.[37]

In his reply, Hrushevsky thanked the various speakers. He directed special attention toward the representatives from Belorussia and Lithuania and mentioned that they had all worked together in old Russia and during the 1917 Congress of Peoples. Far from praising the Soviet system which the party men claimed had 'made possible' his success, Hrushevsky reminded the audience that the Main Scientific Committee had recently determined that support for Ukrainian scholarship was inadequate. The task of enlightening the village population and building the Ukrainian nationality was still not finished; only when a nationally conscious peasantry moved into the cities would Ukraine become a fully worker-peasant land. Hrushevsky then expressed his solidarity with the tradition of Ukrainian scholarship established in the nineteenth century, called for the unification of all the Ukrainian lands, and declared that, like Franko, he would continue the fight to become 'masters in our own house, lords of our own land.' The hall shook with resounding applause.[38]

Not everyone was so pleased. That evening, when the guests arrived for dinner and the concert, the officials of party and government were conspicuous by their

36 Polonska-Vasylenko, *Ukrainska akademiia nauk*, I, 47. It seems that Krymsky and his circle would have nothing to do with the Hrushevsky jubilee, and therefore the historian's personal friend, Tutkivsky, headed the organizational committee. Tutkivsky was known as a strong Ukrainian patriot. See I. Rozhin, 'Pavlo Tutkivsky (1858–1930),' *Novi dni*, no. 88 (Toronto, 1958), 15–21. Krymsky had earlier complained to Vernadsky about Hrushevsky's 'attempt to bring into the academy people who were little involved in science, but assuredly Ukrainian chauvinists for all that.' In Sarbei, 'Pershyi neodminyi sekretar,' p. 95.

37 Most of these speeches are given in *Vybrani pratsi*, pp. 213–24.

38 Full text in *Vybrani pratsi*, pp. 225–35, ending: 'I hlianesh, iak khaziain domovytyi, / po svoiy khati i po svoim poli. ... '

39 Polonska-Vasylenko, *Ukrainska akademiia nauk*, I, 48.

absence. Sitting alone at the head table, the Hrushevsky family and the organization committee was visibly shaken. 'None of them were able to get hold of themselves,' writes Polonska-Vasylenko, 'and the banquet took on more of a funeral than a festive air.'[39] The patriarch of *Ukrainstvo* had celebrated a great symbolic triumph, but nevertheless, it seems, was not indispensable to the Soviet authorities.

The confrontation at the Hrushevsky jubilee frightened the VUAN veterans. Bahalii's jubilee was approaching and the more conservative academicians were anxious to avoid trouble. In December 1926, Krymsky wrote to the former VUAN president, Vernadsky, that he wanted to stress the connection 'with our Russian Ukraine, and not the Austrian borderlands. Together with the most of the academicians, I have decided to turn this jubilee into the banner of that *former* Academy of Sciences which developed in its first six years under your spiritual guidance.'[40] When the jubilee finally took place, it lacked the public and political character of the earlier event. The government showed its favour by promising to reprint Bahalii's *Collected Works* at state expense. But caution worked no better than confrontation. The promise was never kept.[41]

The real shift in the balance of forces within the CPbU had come as early as April 1926, when Stalin wrote to Kaganovich condemning Khvylovy's orientation away from Moscow and criticizing Shumsky's mistakes in the implementation of the Ukrainianization program.[42] There could be no doubt that this change would affect Hrushevsky. In fact, shortly afterward, during the party's battle against 'Khvylovism,' Kaganovich at one point asked a representative of the Communist Party of Western Ukraine how the Ukrainians living under Poland would react if the Politburo 'gave the order to strike at Hrushevsky.' He was told that this would cause a great commotion.[43]

The struggle between Kaganovich and Shumsky continued throughout 1926. By October, certain of the former *Borotbisty*, such as Liubchenko, seemed to be going over to Kaganovich. After all, the latter did oppose the old anti-Ukrainian 'left' led by Larin, and was allied with Skrypnyk, who was known to be a strong

40 In Sarbei, 'Pershyi neodminyi sekretar,' p. 95. As might have been expected, Iefremov too had a negative attitude toward the Hrushevsky jubilee and in a letter to Chykalenko criticized the historian for lacking tact and not being able to lower himself or be circumspect about his past. See V. Miiakovsky, ed., 'Lysty S.O. Iefremova do Ie. Kh. Chykalenka (prodovzhennia),' *Ukrainskyi istoryk*, nos. 1–2 (1975), 112–19, especially 115.

41 Polonska-Vasylenko, *Ukrainska akademiia nauk*, I, 48.

42 Joseph Stalin, *Works*, vol. VIII (Moscow–Leningrad, 1954), pp. 149–50. See the discussion in Dmytryshyn, pp. 102–4. This move against Shumsky might explain his absence from the Hrushevsky jubilee.

43 Dmytro Solovei, *Holhota Ukrainy* (Winnipeg, 1953), p. 222. Solovei says that Hrushevsky's 'furious' organizational activities had caught the party off guard and were unexpected.

Ukrainian. By December, Shumsky had already lost most of his functions, and by March 1927 was removed from office.[44] About the same time, that is, in December 1926, Liubchenko made what seems to have been the first severe public attack on Hrushevsky. In an article directed largely against Khvylovy, Mykola Zerov, and other Ukrainian writers and critics who stood to the side of the centralizing trends represented by Stalin and Kaganovich, Liubchenko accused Hrushevsky of trying to ignore the victory of the proletariat and Lenin's distinction between the poor, the middle, and the rich peasants. All this, he said, amounted to reactionary theorizing about a Ukrainian nation without a bourgeoisie. He continued:

Under such conditions, what does it mean to declare for an orientation toward the history of the peasant masses and their interest? To speak in favour of an 'orientation' 'toward the history of the peasant mass, toward its interest and its consciousness' as an 'independent class' which could act outside the leadership of the proletariat. This means to speak about bourgeois democracy; this means to bother oneself with petty bourgeois dreams and, in essence prepare the way for a restoration of capitalism.

Liubchenko concluded by darkly suggesting that Hrushevsky's 'peasant orientation' put him in a block with the anti-Soviet nationalists in Galicia.[45]

Liubchenko's criticism of Hrushevsky was symptomatic of the growing pressure on non-Marxist Ukrainian scholarship which followed Shumsky's removal as education commissar. Shumsky's long-time critic, Lenin's follower Mykola Skrypnyk, replaced him. Like Shumsky, Skrypnyk supported the general policy of 'Ukrainianization' and held up the ideal of the new proletarian Ukraine symbolized by the Dnieper hydro-electric station.[46] But he was an 'Old Bolshevik'

44 The fullest treatment of the struggle between Shumsky and Kaganovich is Ivan Maistrenko's *Istoriia Kommunistychnoi partii Ukrainy* (Munich, 1979), pp. 124–31. Also see Sullivant, pp. 140–41.

45 Panas Liubchenko, 'Stari teorii i novi pomylky,' *Zhyttia i revoliutsiia*, no. 12 (Kiev, 1926), and reprinted in Stakhiv, 'Deiaki dokumenty pro diialnist Hrushevskoho na emihratsii,' pp. 169–74. Liubchenko's biography has a certain interest. During the revolution he had joined the UPSR, had been a member of the Central Rada, and, according to Stakhiv, an aide to Hrushevsky. In 1918, he joined Shumsky's group and then entered the ranks of the CPbU together with the other *Borotbisty*. In 1926, he was already gravitating toward the Kaganovich group, and his presence at the Hrushevsky jubilee and his subsequent attacks on the historian may well have been the humiliating *confession de foi* that the regime usually demanded of a new convert. He was later appointed chairman of the Ukrainian government and was to be the last survivor among the former *Borotbisty*. Threatened with arrest and liquidation during the terror of the late 1930s, he shot himself and his wife (30 August 1937) rather than go to certain death in Moscow on Molotov's instructions. He was 'rehabilitated' in the 1960s. See Maistrenko, *Borotbism*, pp. 254–5; and the official Soviet biography by P. Bachynsky, *Panas Petrovych Liubchenko* (Kiev, 1970).

46 See Koshelivets, *Mykola Skrypnyk*, pp. 212–13, who stresses the new education commissar's loyalty to the Ukrainianization program and his efforts to inject some substance into the Ukrainian

with a stronger commitment to Marxism and a stronger sense of party loyalty. He was determined to break the conservative atmosphere that reigned in the Ukrainian Academy and visited the VUAN in person. Shortly afterward, he ordered the dismissal of two academicians on the grounds that they had once been theology professors. He then decreed that in future the election of all academicians would have to be confirmed by the Commissariat of Education. The 'sovietization' of the VUAN had begun.[47]

A similar process was occuring in Leningrad. The Russian Academy had functioned under a constitution that gave it considerably more independence from government than did that of the VUAN, but by June 1927 government pressure had forced the Russian Academy to adopt a new constitution which allowed it to retain its sovereign rights in the election of members, but gave the party a significant say in the nomination procedure.[48] In the growing battle for control of the Russian Academy, Vernadsky, who had moved to Leningrad, and the famous physiologist I.P. Pavlov were to lead resistance to the party's attack. Within the VUAN, Vernadsky's friend Krymsky was to play a similar role.

The disagreements between Krymsky and Hrushevsky were no secret and it was logical that the party would try to exploit them. In fact, it was generally believed that the special status of the Historical Institutions was a deliberate Bolshevik attempt 'to drive a wedge' between the more conservative academicians and their strong-willed colleague.[49] The populist historian was certainly the most left-leaning figure in the academy, and on one occasion had even complimented Skrypnyk in print.[50] Therefore, it appears, the Kharkiv Politburo commissioned Skrypnyk to approach Hrushevsky. According to a contemporary who knew both men what then occurred was a repetition of cultural politics under the short-lived Hetmanate:

When, later on, the Bolsheviks made some attempts to condition Hrushevsky to pronounce the very slightest recognition of Soviet rule from his academic tribune, M. Hrushevsky answered entirely sensibly, although also sarcastically, that he had not promised to enrol in the Komsomol. The pressing demands of M. Skrypnyk, the education commissar, to place

Republic's theoretical sovereignty. Koshelivets claims that Skrypnyk grew to look upon Hrushevsky 'if not favourably, then rather indulgently.'

47 Polonska-Vasylenko, *Ukrainska akademiia nauk*, I, 53. The two dismissed academicians were F.I. Myshchenko and K.V. Kharlampovych, the latter of whom was celebrated for his classic study of Ukrainian religious and cultural influences on Muscovy.

48 L. Graham, *The Soviet Academy of Sciences and the Communist Party 1927–1932* (Princeton, 1967), pp. 82–9.

49 Polonska-Vasylenko, 'Istorychna nauka ... ta dolia istorykiv,' p. 13.

50 In his 1926 article attacking Russian chauvinism, Hrushevsky had said that Skrypnyk defended Ukrainian culture 'clearly and strongly.' See Hrushevsky, 'Hanebnoi pamiati,' p. 929.

M. Hrushevsky in the post of president of the VUAN and, by means of official titles, put him in a block with the Soviet authorities – ended with M. Hrushevsky's categorical rejection of this proposition. This meant that the scholar, that is, the person of free scientific work, M. Hrushevsky, did not wish to bind himself into some kind of adminstrative role under the Soviet regime, even such an honourable, and, in theory, independent one as president of the Academy of Sciences.[51]

Hrushevsky's rejection of the VUAN presidency turned out to be a wise move. He was already quite busy with his research and editorial work, and his great study of Khmelnytsky was in its final stages. Even for a man as ambitious as Hrushevsky, the assumption of the academy's presidency would have been a hollow victory. Krymsky, Iefremov, and his other conservative rivals were already under considerable pressure and the first steps at 'sovietization' of the academy had already been taken. The presidency would have brought the historian no additional power and would only have compromised him politically.

The extent of pressure on Ukrainian scholarship is indicated by the fate of the director of the Ukrainian Historical Museum in Kiev. Danylo Shcherbakivsky, who had spent many years gathering together one of the best collections of *Ukrainica* in the country, had been forced to accept rude police agents on his staff, submit to personal abuse, and see the gradual despoliation of the museum's treasures and their removal to Moscow and Leningrad. Unable to endure such persecution, in June 1927 he named his tormentors and their deeds in a suicide note and killed himself by tying himself to large rock and jumping into the Dnieper. Hrushevsky, Iefremov, and a large number of prominent Ukrainian scholars sent an open letter of protest to the paper *Proletarska pravda,* which in a black frame had announced Shcherbakivsky's death. But the GPU forbade printing of the letter, and, when thousands of mourners came to the funeral, that same night bulldozed the grave so that no sign of it remained. A judicial inquiry was cut short and further mention of Shcherbakivsky's name became dangerous.[52]

The events surrounding Shcherbakivsky's death did not intimidate Hrushevsky. He continued to work and publish in the belief that the struggle between the Bolshevik dictatorship and the general population had not yet come to an end. The work of the 'Tatar people,' it seems, was not yet finished. In fact, only a few weeks

51 Dubrovsky, 'Velykyi patriot,' and 'Mykola Skrypnyk iak ia ioho bachyv,' *Novi dni,* no. 93 (Toronto, 1957), 19–23, 30–2, especially 30. This passage is also quoted in the excellent work by Fedir Pigido, *Ukraina pid bolshevytskoiu okupatsiieiu,* (Munich, 1956), p. 43.

52 H. Kubanska, *Ternystymy shliakhamy* (Winnipeg, 1948), pp. 42–4; Solovei, *Holhota Ukrainy,* pp. 217–18. Also see Vadym Pavlovsky, 'Danylo Shcherbakivsky (1877–1977),' *Ukrainskyi istoryk,* nos. 3–4 (1977), 83–8, who says that Skrypnyk called the scholars' letter demanding a public criminal investigation 'an anti-Soviet impulse.'

after Shcherbakivsky's death, Hrushevsky tried to persuade a Ukrainian-American visitor to remain in Soviet Ukraine and join in the work. The visitor was surprised to find that police agents were continually watching and following Hrushevsky and that the historian accepted it as a matter of course. The visitor returned to America.[53]

Hrushevsky's first years in Soviet Ukraine were ones of great difficulty but also of great success. By making the fullest possible use of the ideological postulates, the theoretical independence, and the Ukrainianization program of the CPbU, Hrushevsky had been able to finance, organize, and carry out a wide range of scholarly activity that had a definite impact on cultural life in the Ukrainian Republic. The untiring historian and his 'Tatar people' were at work in all levels of social and public life: in the academy, in the schools, in the party. Their goal was, in theory, compatable with the objectives of the Communist Party, and Hrushevsky never hesitated to state it. Both in his private correspondence and in his public writings, the historian said that he wished to work for the Ukrainian people within the formal structure of the theoretically independent Soviet state, 'within the Ukrainian Republic that we began to build in 1917.[54] Through the rapid expansion of scholarship and science, Hrushevsky intended to raise the general level of Ukrainian culture and foster the spread of education and national consciousness among the broad population, especially the country folk. When a nationally conscious peasantry moved into the cities, Ukraine could become, in fact, a true 'worker-peasant' state, and all Ukrainians, as he put it, 'masters in our own house.'

There were obstacles to this plan. From the very beginning Hrushevsky's agreement with Chubar had forced him to remain silent on the essential issues of political life. He could never openly criticize the Soviet authorities or their policies, even when he obviously disagreed with them; he was reduced to complaining about 'technical difficulties.' Nevertheless, both in his scholarship and his editorials in the journal *Ukraina*, Hrushevsky set forth his ideals and hoped to influence the general atmosphere in which political events took place. During a particularly critical period, he returned to his old themes and raised his voice against bureaucratic centralization, Russian chauvinism, and the psychological complex that they created in Ukrainian national feeling. He spoke up most strongly in 1926, during the struggle between Shumsky and Kaganovich, and, though his former comrade could not withstand the blows of his Stalinist rival,

53 Bykovsky, *Vasyl Kuziv i Mykhailo Hrushevsky*, pp. 17–18.
54 See M. Antonovych, ed., 'Lysty M. Hrushevskoho do T. Pochynka,' *Ukrainskyi istoryk*, nos. 1–3 (1970), 178–83. Also see the editorial statement in *Ukraina*, no. 4 (Kiev, 1924), 190, which discusses the possibility of fruitful work 'in our own home, in the Ukrainian Republic.'

Hrushevsky's words were not without effect. Even Skrypnyk admitted their contemporary political content.[55]

The conservative VUAN veterans did not like this dabbling in politics and thought that it endangered the academy. As late as 1927, the literary historian V.M. Peretts, Krymsky's sympathizer in Leningrad, warned Hrushevsky not to 'bring bad fortune to the land of Rus'!'[56] But the bold Ukrainian patriarch would not be stopped. His energies would not be confined; his principles would not be compromised.

By the end of 1927, there were already signs that the party would no longer tolerate this kind of half-spoken challenge. The victory of Kaganovich over Shumsky indicated that the interregnum which followed Lenin's death was coming to an end. With a new strongman in Moscow, it was certain that sooner or later bureaucratic control over the Ukrainian Republic would be tightened. At the same time, the party would feel free to bring the remaining non-Marxist institutions and figures into line. This offensive by the Communist Party is the next theme in our story.

55 Koshelivets, *Mykola Skrypnyk*, pp. 212–13 and *passim* paints a benign picture of the former Chekist and justice commissar and quotes him as telling a gathering of Galician Ukrainian Communists that in the journal *Ukraina* 'there are tendentious articles by both Hrushevsky and other contributors in which their political thoughts are expressed in a veiled way.'
56 See Polonska-Vasylenko, *Ukrainska akademiia nauk*, I, 47.

10
The Party Attacks 1928–1930

In December 1927, at the Fifteenth Congress of the Communist Party of the Soviet Union, a two-pronged program of collectivization and rapid industrialization was adopted. At first, the pace of collectivization was not forced. But in the next few years, as the party's general secretary, Joseph Stalin, outmanoeuvred his political rivals, collectivization gained momentum and a social revolution of unprecedented magnitude took place. Scholars all over the Soviet Union were certain to be affected.

At the beginning of 1928, the Moscow Politburo specifically took up the matter of higher education and the reorganization of the Russian Academy of Sciences.[1] As in Ukraine, there had already been some pressure on the Russian Academy to expand its membership and reflect what were called 'the new political realities.' Now the pressure became intense. In March 1928, D.B. Riazanov, the head of the Marx-Engels Institute, publicly asked for the liquidation of the academy; he asserted that academies had been replaced by large institutes as the main centres of research.[2] In April the Moscow government arbitrarily changed the academy's new constitution and ordered a large increase in the number of academicians.[3] The adoption of this tactic suggests that the central authorities had decided that the old academies still contained much that was useful and would not be abolished. Instead, they would be infused with new Communist blood, reorganized, and integrated into the general plan of socialist construction. In spite of their

---

1 Graham, *Soviet Academy of Sciences*, p. 89, citing V.T. Ermakov, *Borba Kommunisticheskoi partii za perestroiku raboty nauchnykh uchrezhdenii v godypervoi piatiletki*, unpublished dissertation for the degree of *Kandidat* (Moscow State University, 1956), p. 133. Ermakov obtained this information from the archives of the Marx-Engels-Lenin-Stalin Institute, as it was then called.

2 Graham, p. 93, citing Ermakov, pp. 133–4.

3 Ibid., p. 90.

theoretical independence in educational matters, this was, in fact, exactly what was to occur in the Belorussian and Ukrainian Republics as well as the RSFSR. The same pattern was followed simultaneously in Leningrad, Kiev, and Minsk.

As this process was first getting under way, the Communist authorities asked the Presidium of the Ukrainian Academy to elect two party men as full members of the VUAN. The Presidium – in fact, Krymsky and Vasylenko – replied that all candidates must follow the rules set out in the constitution: submission of scholarly work for evaluation by specialists, election into the department, and finally, election by the general assembly of academicians. As it turned out, only one of the party candidates was elected, and then only as a corresponding and not a full member. Afterwards, it was rumoured that Kharkiv was very upset and that Skrypnyk himself now wanted to be elected into the VUAN. 'An apprehensive mood gripped the Academy,' a VUAN worker later remarked.[4]

During the course of 1928, the pressure on the VUAN mounted. By government fiat, seven high-ranking government and party leaders were named to the General Assembly. These included Skrypnyk and the chairman of the Kharkiv Central Control Commission, V.P. Zatonsky.[5] At this point, officials from the Main Scientific Committee and the Commissariats of Finance and Education began visiting the academy. Budgets were examined and the details of various projects had to be defined.[6]

The first really open conflict between the academy and the party came during the May 1928 elections to the VUAN Presidium. The academicians had already reluctantly agreed to accept the government candidate for president, the microbiologist D.K. Zabolotny.[7] Skrypnyk and the other government men now participated in the election meeting.

When the ceremonies commenced, one of the academicians proposed that Vernadsky, who had just arrived from Prague, chair the gathering. But quite unexpectedly, one of Hrushevsky's closest associates, P.A. Tutkivsky, suggested that Skrypnyk himself chair the meeting. The retiring president, V.I. Lypsky, put the question to a vote: all the academicians present except for Tutkivsky voted for Vernadsky; only the seven party members and Tutkivsky supported Skrypnyk.

---

4 Polonska-Vasylenko, *Ukrainska akademiia nauk*, I, 53.

5 Ibid. In 1933, Zatonsky would replace Skrypnyk as commissar of education. See Borys Levytsky, *The Stalinist Terror in the Thirties* (Stanford, 1974), pp. 387–8.

6 Polonska-Vasylenko, *Ukrainska akadamiia nauk* I, 53.

7 Polonska-Vasylenko (ibid.) reports that Krymsky and Vasylenko offered to support Zabolotny even though he was the government candidate, if he would promise to resolve all questions in accord with the other academicians. She says that Zabolotny agreed 'with tears in his eyes.' A few months later, that is, in December 1928, Pavlov, the famous Russian physiologist, fiercely attacked Zabolotny's candidacy for the Russian Academy. Zabolotny was known chiefly for his practical work fighting various epidemics in pre-1914 Ukraine. Pavlov was, of course, mainly a theoretician. See Graham, pp. 108–9.

Amidst general applause Vernadsky took the chair. Skrypnyk and his colleagues retired to discuss the matter.

The ballots were cast: Zabolotny was unanimously elected to the presidency while Krymsky was easily reelected as permanent secretary. Then Skrypnyk suddenly rose, declared the meeting closed, and with the party men in tow, walked out. As Polonska-Vasylenko later put it, 'an atmosphere of scandal which promised nothing good' enveloped the room.[8] Afterwards, the Commissariat of Education refused to confirm Krymsky's election. It named O.V. Korchak-Chepurkivsky as 'provisional' secretary and left him at this post till 1939. Several other members were appointed directly to the VUAN Presidium. Hrushevsky's principal VUAN antagonist had lost his base of power, but it would do the historian little good. The 'sovietization' of the academy had begun.

In the following months, the party's growing influence proceeded apace. The new government members began naming new workers to the various commissions; the academic 'Council' began to replace the old General Assembly of Academicians as the main centre of administrative power. As in Polonska-Vasylenko's account of the Academy elections of 1928, so too in the various descriptions of these administrative changes Hrushevsky's name does not appear. He was obviously continuing his old tactic of avoiding all administrative appointments and confining himself to the purely academic world of the Historical Institutes. Thus far he had successfully avoided being compromised by association with the Soviet regime, and, at the same time, had managed to have a significant influence upon the Ukrainian cultural scene. He remained an 'independent scholar,' but the atmosphere was more tense than ever, and the institutions which surrounded him were in a constant state of flux.

Hrushevsky's discipline, history, was one of the first to feel the increasing pressure of the official Marxist ideology. This occurred both at the All-Union and the Republic level. In March 1928, at a first All-Union Conference of Marxist-Leninist Research Institutes, complaints were voiced that Marxist scholarship was too weak outside of Moscow and Leningrad. It was suggested that Moscow and Leningrad scholars be dispatched to the various parts of the Soviet Union. In response, the conference heard from Matvii Iavorsky, who headed the Ukrainian school of party historians. Iavorsky admitted the influence in Ukraine of 'bourgeois and petty bourgeois ideology,' but at the same time complained of pressure from the 'Russian bourgeois school,' which, as he carefully put it, 'could be felt even in Marxist circles.'[9] The strongest attack on the non-Marxists came

8 Polonska-Vasylenko, *Ukrainska akademiia nauk*, I, 55.

9 'Pervaia vsesoiuznaia konferentsiia marksistko-leninskikh nauchno-issledovatelskikh uchrezhdenii,' *Vestik kommunisticheskoi akademii*, no. 26 (1928), 254–5, 271–3, cited in G. Enteen, *The Soviet Scholar Bureaucrat: M.N. Pokrovsky and the Society of Marxist Historians* (Pennsylvania State University Press, 1978), pp. 80–2.

from D.B. Riazanov, the head of the Marx-Engels Institute, who disagreed with the very idea of an academy of sciences. He particularly objected to 'Soviet' money being spent on non-Marxist scholarship.[10] In general, the conference reflected a trend toward more central planning and increased Communist supervision of non-Marxist scholars.

In the summer of 1928, the Soviet Marxist historians had a rare opportunity to display their achievements to the outside world. In the hope of reestablishing contact between historians living under Soviet rule and those in Western Europe, Hrushevsky's old acquaintance, Otto Hoetzsch, had organized and invited a 'Soviet' delegation, including Hrushevsky, to a 'Week for Russian Historians' to be held in Berlin. Hrushevsky had always been interested in promoting direct contacts between Ukraine and the Western world and there can be little doubt that he would have liked to attend. But it was not to be. As Dmytro Doroshenko, the director of the Berlin-based Ukrainian Research Institute, shortly afterward reported to his fellow conservative historian Viacheslav Lypynsky at this historical conference, '"Russian" scholarship, for the most part, represented Ukrainian scholarship as well. Such "Russian scholars" as Hrushevsky himself were supposed to represent Ukraine. But as I was told by a certain official of the Foreign Ministry here, the Bolsheviks would not allow it.'[11] The only representatives of Ukrainian historiography to attend the conference were the Kharkiv Marxists, Iavorsky and V.A. Iurinets. The latter was a former student of Pokrovsky. Platonov, Liubavsky, and Picheta also received permission to attend.[12]

In Berlin, the president of the Norwegian Academy of Sciences invited the Soviet delegation to the Sixth International Congress of Historical Science, which was to be held in Oslo. The Russian Europeanist E.V. Tarle was supposed to represent the Russian Academy of Sciences, and Hrushevsky was supposed to represent the Ukrainian. Both failed to appear. A Soviet delegation did arrive, but it counted only eleven scholars. The most significant event of the meeting was an intense verbal confrontation between Pokrovsky and the émigré archeologist M.I. Rostovtsev.[13] For historians in the Soviet Union, both Russian and Ukrainian, this

10 Ibid.

11 Dmytro Doroshenko, letter of 15 July 1928, in I. Korovytsky, ed., 'Lysty Dmytra Doroshenka do Viacheslava Lypynskoho,' *Viacheslav Lypynsky Arkhiv*, vol. VI (Philadelphia, 1973), pp. 301–4.

12 Enteen, p. 211, note 6. At least one observer claimed that the conference failed to produce the hoped-for collaboration between European and Soviet scholars. See J. Pfitzner, 'Die Geschichtswissenschaft in der Sowjetunion,' in *Bolschewistische Wissenchaft und Kulturpolitik* (Königsberg and Berlin, 1938), pp. 186–7. Shortly afterward, however, Picheta did manage to publish a survey of Soviet Belorussian historical scholarship, and Hermaize a survey of the Ukrainian, in the Prague-based *Slavische Rundschau*, no. 1 (1929). Doroshenko gives a personal assessment of the various speakers in his letter to Lypynsky cited in note 11 above.

13 Enteen, pp. 82–4, 212, note 8; Pfitzner, pp. 186–7; K. Shteppa, *Russian Historians and the Soviet*

fruitless confrontation in Oslo was to be the end of international contacts for many years.

In the second half of 1928, direct attacks on non-Marxist historians became more intense. Elections of new members to the Russian and Ukrainian academies were then just getting under way, and the attacks coincided with them. E.V. Tarle, the historian of antiquity S.A. Zhebelev, and the medievalist D.M. Petrushevsky, who was known as a friend of Hrushevsky, all came under intense criticism.[14] Meanwhile, Pokrovsky congratulated Presniakov, Grekov, and others who, he maintained, had been moving continuously in the direction of Marxism. This orchestrated campaign against the non-Marxists climaxed in December, at the First All-Union Conference of Marxist Historians. It was a meeting that was bound to affect public attitudes toward Hrushevsky and his school.

Pokrovsky set the tone for the six hundred assembled historians with a strong exposé of the inadequacies of non-Marxist scholarship. In a direct reference to his recent conflict with Rostovtsev, he stated that 'if there once were some naive people who used to believe in historical scholarship isolated from politics, then I submit that now, after the congress in Oslo, there cannot be any.' Indeed, if such people exist, they are, as he put it, 'pathological and must be cured.'[15] Such statements did not bode well for 'independent scholars' like Hrushevsky.

Having discussed the inadequacies of non-Marxist scholarship, the conference turned next to the influence of this scholarship in the Union Republics. Marxist historians from Ukraine, Belorussia, Georgia, Armenia, and Central Asia had been accused of 'bourgeois and petty-bourgeois' tendencies. They were now expected to prove their orthodoxy.

The Ukrainian delegation to the conference was a strong one. Iavorsky, in particular, was a member of the conference presidium, and displayed a forcefulness and independence that had a definite impact upon the gathering. In his opening report on the development of Marxist historiography in Ukraine, Iavorsky conceded that conditions in his republic had been less favourable than in the RSFSR. But he also listed a number of important achievements. 'Firstly,' he began, 'I consider it a great achievement that we have created a correct Marxist scheme on the Ukrainian historical process. Here in this room this might not seem like a great achievement, but in our Ukrainian reality, where Hrushevsky's scheme with its "classless" historical process rules in all its power and attracts those who do not understand these questions, the creation of a Marxist scheme of the

State (New Brunswick, NJ, 1962), p. 48, says that Hrushevsky and Tarle were recalled 'at the very last moment,' while Platonov and others had been refused permission beforehand.

14 See Enteen, p. 84 and 88.

15 *Trudy pervoi vsesoiuznoi konferentsii istorikov-marksistov*, second edition, 2 vols. (Moscow, 1930), I, 13; Enteen, p. 93.

Ukrainian historical process has great significance.' He then went on to note that Bahalii, 'under our influence,' as he put it, had recently declared himself for 'historical materialism.' Iavorsky further informed his audience that a new Ukrainian Society of Marxist Historians had been created, that Marxist historical and theoretical journals were being published, that research (especially on the October revolution) was proceeding apace, and that a Ukrainian delegation had participated in the congresses at Berlin and Oslo. All in all, he concluded, the forecast was optimistic for the period of the upcoming Five Year Plan.[16]

In a separate address, Iavorsky dealt with the delicate subject of non-party and non-Marxist historical scholarship in the Ukrainian Republic. He began by contrasting the aristocratic 'estate' approach developed abroad by the émigré Lypynsky with the approach which, he believed, Hrushevsky had derived from Kostomarov and Drahomanov.[17] The latter approach, according to Iavorsky, was essentially 'anarcho-federalist' and based on a peasantry which Hrushevsky described as a classless category. The ideological difference between the two men, said Iavorsky, was also reflected in politics. In 1917 and 1918, Hrushevsky had headed the Central Rada, while Lypynsky supported the Skoropadsky monarchy. At present, Iavorsky continued, some of the more right-wing elements surviving in Soviet Ukraine such as Vasylenko and the juridical school are moving leftward and accepting Hrushevsky's older views. Meanwhile, Hrushevsky himself stands on the left flank of the scholars who actively oppose the Marxist front. Hrushevsky makes use of the terminology of class struggle, but does not hide his sympathy for his old anarcho-federalist theory. His influence is pervasive and his school is large. Moreover, Iavorsky continued, Drahomanov study circles are not uncommon among our youth. These circles often discuss 'toiling society,' but they do this more in the spirit of the Toilers' Congress of 1919, or of the émigré Shapoval, than as a true adoption of our program. At his 1926 jubilee, said Iavorsky, Hrushevsky seemed to adopt the slogan of our revolution; but in fact this was not so. He believes that proletarian Ukraine will exist only when the workers are consciously Ukrainian. Hrushevsky talks about various sociologists, but not about Marx. The old Ukrainian historian does not even acknowledge the lawfulness of the historical process, and says that to accept it, as do Marx and Engels, is to reduce all to a mechanical investigation. In sum, concluded Iavorsky . . .

In spite of the fact that at his jubilee Hrushevsky declared that he would adhere to the slogan of our proletarian revolution, I consider that his declaration must be understood in the same

16 M. Iavorsky, 'Doklad o rabote marksistskikh istoricheskikh uchrezhdenii na Ukraine,' *Trudy*, I, 36–40.
17 Doroshenko (see note 11 above) had earlier written that at the Berlin conference Iavorsky had given an accurate assessment of Lypynsky's views.

way as the declaration of Bismarck, who, I believe, in the 1870s said that he was ready to endure anything, even revolution, to save Prussia. Hrushevsky is also ready to adhere to the slogans of our revolution, but only in so far as, in his view, it will save the independence of the Ukrainian people. As one of our contemporaries has said, he acknowledges [our slogans] as a fact of life, but not as truth.

Having exposed Hrushevsky's non-Marxist position and revealed his independence of the party's agenda for historians, Iavorsky then proceeded to criticize those whom he labelled 'national Marxists'; that is, the historians who made some use of Marxist methodology but in his opinion were not true Marxists. According to Iavorsky, these included the historian Ohloblyn, the economist Volobuev, Ravych-Cherkassky, who was the author of a major history of the CPbU and Hrushevsky's associate Hermaize, the student of social and political movements.[18]

Other members of the Ukrainian delegation developed Iavorsky's points. N.L. Rubinshtein, who was later to publish a synthesis of Russian historiography, made some cursory observations. Then Zynovii Hurevych reopened the attack on Hrushevsky, and even went so far as to criticize Iavorsky for the mildness of his critique of the Ukrainian historian. Hurevych would have put the old master more firmly in a block with Russian Kadets and the Ukrainian bourgeoisie, who, he claimed, in 1905 dreamed of creating their own internal market through regional autonomy. In the opinion of Hurevych, Hrushevsky's talk of a worker-peasant Ukraine was a bourgeois-populist, counter-revolutionary Trojan horse by which he got back onto the territory of Soviet Ukraine.

And so, comrades, we must state that Hrushevsky has not made single concession in principle. I now speak, in fact, of concessions in principle and not in tactics. For Hrushevsky has made very many tactical concessions. In this area he has gone through a colossal evolution, while not making a single concession in principle to our Marxist scientific historical theory. And in this lies the irreconcilability in principles, and the tactical opportunism which is the strength of Hrushevsky, who, in essence, leads the forces on the historical front which are hostile to us.

Like Iavorsky, Hurevych then went on to criticize Hermaize for his alleged pseudo-Marxism. He ended with a few words of criticism for the Russian historian M.V. Nechkina, who, it seems, had ignored Ukrainian factors in her recent work on the Decembrists.[19] In sum, Hurevych's heavy artillery was directed against

18 M. Iavorsky, 'Sovremennye antimarksistskie techeniia v ukrainskoi istoricheskoi nauke,' *Trudy*, I, 426–35.
19 *Trudy*, I, 437ff.

Hrushevsky and the Ukrainian historians who stood to the side of party historiography. The criticism of Nechkina was no more than a parting shot in the opposite direction.

Both Hermaize and Nechkina took the floor to defend themselves. They confined themselves to specific points of fact. Hermaize said a few cautious words in defence of Hrushevsky, while Nechkina suggested that the idea of a Ukrainian theme in the Decembrist story had originated with Bahalii, Hrushevsky, and other non-Marxist scholars. She conceded, however, that Ukrainian matters were generally ignored in the Russian journals.[20] In fact, a certain degree of balance seemed to be emerging from the discussion. This fragile balance was upset by the next speaker.

Pokrovsky's associate P.O. Gorin, the secretary of the Moscow-based Society of Marxist Historians, was the next to take the floor. With greater passion and less politeness, he repeated all the criticisms of Hrushevsky uttered by previous speakers. Furthermore, he accused Iavorsky and his school of exaggerating the role played in the 1917 revolution by what he called 'the Ukrainian bourgeois and kulak classes.' Gorin claimed that Iavorsky and his followers had idealized the non-Bolshevik socialist parties and had minimized the importance of the proletariat in Ukraine. They had yielded to Hrushevsky too often and had made too much of his ideas. Of course, being a Moscow academic administrator, Gorin did not discuss the problem of persistent Russian chauvinism which the Ukrainian speakers had briefly but unmistakably dealt with under the euphemism of 'great powerism' (*velikoderzhavnost*).[21]

One more member of the Ukrainian delegation presented his views. M.A. Rubach [M.A. Rubanovych], who had recently graduated from Pokrovsky's Moscow-based Institute of Red Professors, explained Hermaize's inconsistencies as being due to his physical proximity to Hrushevsky in Kiev. Rubach said a few words in favour of Iavorsky and Hurevych and explained that, like other populist historians, Hrushevsky had exercised some progressive functions in the past. The present, however, is the time for true Marxism. Rubach concluded that the struggle against pseudo-Marxism and open idealism was joined.[22]

As principal organizer of the Marxist historical conference, Pokrovsky made the final comments on Iavorsky's paper. He began by asserting that, as he put it, 'reaction and counterrevolution in the fields of the history of the RSFSR and Ukraine take one and the same position.' The latest position of the Russian liberal historian Paul Miliukov is peasant revolution; the latest position of Hrushevsky is peasant-worker revolution. The Ukrainian historian had come to these conclu-

20 Ibid., pp. 441–8.
21 Ibid., pp. 448–52.
22 Ibid., pp. 452–5.

sions, said Pokrovsky, because of his memories of the past weakness of the Ukrainian proletariat. He then jibed: 'But Hrushevsky is an old man, one year older than myself, if not more; so naturally he lives by his memories.'[23]

Pokrovsky then returned to the question of Miliukov and his advocacy of a peasant revolution. He said that, unlike Hrushevsky, Miliukov's non-Marxist attitudes could not be forgiven, for he had lived in the midst of the vigorous Russian proletariat. Miliukov even hopes to use a peasant revolution against Soviet rule, and this has become the common program of all 'White émigrés,' whether they speak Russian or Ukrainian. Pokrovsky then indicated the necessity for countering this common émigré program; he suggested a united front of Russian and Ukrainian Marxist historians and concluded that it might be beneficial, as he put it, 'to set aside, for a time, what are called the Ukrainian, Belorussian, and Great Russian traditions.'[24] On this note the session ended.

The First Conference of Marxist Historians was a landmark in Soviet historical science. It indicated the rising influence of Marxist scholarship in general, and within this scholarship, pointed toward the predominence of Pokrovsky's school. Non-Marxist scholars were censured, and non-party and quasi-Marxist historians were told to mend their ways. In the new definitions of Marxist interpretations of history that were being developed, the general centralizing tendency was clear. When Hermaize returned to the VUAN in Kiev, he had little good news for Hrushevsky and his colleagues. Even such a left-leaning populist figure as Hrushevsky could no longer expect any indulgence from the representatives of the party. The pressure was mounting.[25]

While the Marxist historians were holding their conference, elections to the Russian and Ukrainian Academies of Sciences were taking place. Under a new government order the membership in the Russian Academy was to be nearly doubled. New chairs in socio-economics and related disciplines were to be created and six new historians to be elected.[26] A new procedure with wide 'public' and

23 Ibid., pp. 455–9. In a brief discussion of these remarks and those of other commentators, Iavorsky explained Hrushevsky's position more clearly: 'Among other things, comrade Hurevych misinformed us here, and later M.N. Pokrovsky repeated the mistake. It was said that Hrushevsky has raised the banner of a peasant-worker Ukraine. This is not so. Hrushevsky says: to the present day Ukraine is only peasant, but in the future it will be peasant-worker ... so, despite the fact that, as Comrade Hurevych has pointed out, Hrushevsky has joined in the slogans of October, and has adhered to the socialist revolution, even today he is on the other side of our revolution, on the other side of its program.' See ibid., pp. 464–5.

24 Ibid.

25 Other left-leaning, but non-Bolshevik, historians, such as Petrushevsky and Tarle, came under attack at this same time. See John Barber, *Soviet Historians in Crisis 1928–1932* (London, 1981), pp. 31–46.

26 Graham, pp. 89–91.

party participation was also announced. Workers' committees and party institutions took part and the candidacies were discussed in the government press. Only the final secret ballot in the General Assembly of Academicians was left entirely to the Academy.[27]

The plan worked well. As a result of these measures, Pokrovsky, Riazanov, Bukharin, and several other party favourites were elected to the Russian Academy. On the other hand, the academicians still tried to elect candidates who they felt had earned membership by dint of scholarly achievement. In fact, for a time, three prominent party men were refused admission, while both Hrushevsky, who was being severely criticized by party historians, and Liubavsky, who was fiercely attacked in the party press, were elected.[28]

At this same time, parallel elections were taking place at the Ukrainian Academy in Kiev. Party and trade organizations, various committees, and newspapers nominated and discussed candidates and, on 29 July 1929, thirty-four new academicians were elected. In Kiev, unlike Leningrad, government representatives participated in the final balloting, which was by show of hands and thus not secret.[29] Once again, many party bureaucrats with dubious qualifications in the world of scholarship were elected. These included Skrypnyk, Zatonsky and others. A few party men, like the historian Iavorsky, were somewhat better qualified. Nevertheless, even with the lack of a secret ballot, many genuine scholars were named to the VUAN. These included the Odessa historian Mykhailo Slabchenko and the Cossack enthusiast Dmytro Iavornytsky. Mykhailo Vozniak and Vasyl Shchurat, the literary historians from Western Ukraine, were also elected.[30]

The election of a significant number of Communist Party members into the VUAN, together with the steady tightening of bureaucratic controls, brought stronger demands that the academy take a more direct part in what the authorities called 'socialist construction.' The academicians were now expected to tie their work to the newly announced Five Year Plan of industrialization and collectivization. In spite of any private reservations that he may have had, Hrushevsky too was conscripted into this work. According to the official accounts, in 1929 Hrushevsky participated in the work of the new Popularization Commission, which was to

27 Ibid., pp. 91–2. According to Graham, the selection commissions which received the nominations would contain not only members of the Russian Academy itself but also representatives of each Union Republic. The intention was, as Graham writes, 'to demonstrate the "All-Union" character of the Russian Academy, and, simultaneously, to counter the academy's opposition to party candidates.'

28 Ibid., p. 95ff.

29 Polonska-Vasylenko, *Ukrainska akademiia nauk*, I, 63.

30 Ibid.

bring the VUAN's work to the attention of the general press.[31] In the same year, both Hrushevsky and Vasylenko were chosen to work on a Commission for the Revision of the VUAN Constitution.[32] There is no doubt that the authorities intended to use the new constitution to bring the academicians under the control of both party and government. The 'sovietization' of the VUAN continued.

Before 1930, scholars living in the Soviet Union had still been able to make occasional contributions to scholarly publications abroad. But by the end of 1928, about the same time that the Conference of Marxist Historians was held, the prominent Russian historian of antiquity S.A. Zhebelev was attacked for a few indiscreet words in a Prague scholarly publication.[33] Simultaneously, a parallel case occured in Ukraine. Serhii Iefremov, who had never been particularly well regarded by the authorities, came under severe criticism for a polemic that he had published in the Lviv *Dilo*. The polemic was directed against Hrushevsky's associate Kyrylo Studynsky, the VUAN member from Western Ukraine. In the West Studynsky was considered to be a 'Sovietophile,' and the authorities chose to view Iefremov's article as a general criticism of Soviet rule. A campaign to discredit Iefremov followed.[34]

The press campaigns against Zhebelev and Iefremov resulted in the immediate reduction of scholarly contacts with the outside world. International projects, like those of Hrushevsky, which had once enjoyed the support of such party bureaucrats as Rakovsky and Skrypnyk, now became next to impossible. Moreover, such vitriolic criticism tended to weaken the resistance of both the Russian and Ukrainian academies; in particular, they weakened the Historical-Philological Sections in the midst of the general elections that were then taking place.[35] The attacks on Zhebelev and Iefremov, like the attacks on Hrushevsky and other 'bourgeois' historians, or upon non-party Marxists like Hermaize, were all part of a general trend toward increased party influence over scholarly life. At this

31 *Visti VUAN za 1929*, nos. 5–6 (Kiev, 1929), 45, 60.

32 Ibid., no. 2, p. 39.

33 In a contribution to the *Seminarium kondakovianum* on Byzantine art and archaeology, Zhebelev made a brief reference to 'the hard years' which had already begun in 1918. The party press took this to be a political reference and the attack began. See Graham, pp. 105–9; T. Epstein, 'Die marxistische Geschichtswissenschaft in der Sowjetunion seit 1927,' *Jahrbücher für Kultur und Geschichte der Slaven*, VI (Breslau, 1930), 78–203, especially 133–40.

34 See Polonska-Vasylenko, *Ukrainska akademiia nauk*, I, 68; Graham, p. 171. Iefremov's hostility to Hrushevsky is reflected in his criticism of Studynsky, who he, in fact, thought was a downright 'lackey.' See his letter of 21 December 1926 to Chykalenko, in V. Miiakovsky, ed., 'Lysty S.O. Iefremova do Ie. Kh. Chykalenka,' *Ukrainskyi istoryk*, nos. 3–4 (1975), 112–19, especially 116. The campaign against Iefremov was quickly noted by his friends in the West. See Korovytsky, 'Lysty Doroshenka do Lypynskoho,' pp. 320–1.

35 Graham, p. 171; Polonska-Vasylenko, *Ukrainska akademiia nauk*, I, 68.

point, the sovietization process left 'independent scholars' like Hrushevsky with very little room in which to manoeuvre.

In Ukraine, the sovietization process was compounded by the national question. The CPbU had always had a strong Russian component, and even during the period when the Ukrainianization program was most intense, the influence of the Moscow loyalists could be felt. During the course of 1928, for example, Mykhailo Volobuev, a Ukrainian economist influenced by Hrushevsky and encouraged by Skrypnyk's circle, suggested that the Ukrainian Republic should have control over its own economy. This was seen by all as a protest against Russian 'colonialism' in Ukraine. It caused an instant storm of denunciations within the CPbU and Volobuev was immediately forced to recant. The Kharkiv bureaucrats Skrypnyk, Zatonsky, and Richytsky, all of whom had resisted Moscow's encroachments, were now compelled to say that 'the flooded bell of Great Power nationalism no longer tolls' because 'October has broken it to pieces. Pieces cannot toll.' This was an attack both on Volobuev and on Hrushevsky, who in his 1926 article on Russian chauvinism wrote that the 'flooded bell' of Russian Great Powerism was still sounding out from under the water.[36]

By 1929, it was clear that Hrushevsky would not be able to repeat his 1926 comments on Russian nationalism. On the official level, of course, the party's Ukrainianization program had not yet ended, but by the same token, the Kharkiv bureaucrats had suffered repeated setbacks and there were disturbing signs that Moscow's attitude toward Russian history was beginning to change. For example, in 1929, the authorities allowed the publication of Alexei Tolstoi's historical novel *Peter the First*. The book was given a very wide circulation and the government publishing houses of the Union Republics were induced to translate and print it in local languages. Tolstoi's work was generally seen 'as a clear apology for the conquests of the first Russian emperor.'[37] In this same year, the Russian historian B.D. Grekov, who was opposed to Hrushevsky's revision of Russian history, published his first general work on Kiev Rus'. Grekov would eventually become one of the most influential historians in the Soviet Union.[38]

36 For Hrushevsky's protest against Russian chauvinism, see chapter 9 above. On the Volobuev controversy see Maistrenko, *Istoriia komunistychnoi partii Ukrainy*, pp. 136–7, and the brief remarks of Stakhiv, 'Deiaki materiialy pro bolshevytskyi nastup na Hrushevskoho,' in *Mykhailo Hrushevsky u 110 rokovyny narodzhennia*, pp. 194–6.

37 Ivan Maistrenko, *Natsionalnaia politika KPSS* (Munich, 1978), p. 118.

38 Maistrenko, who was not a professional historian, says that Grekov 'was known as an apologist for the empire and also as an opponent of the historical school of Hrushevsky who maintained the originality of the history of the Ukrainian people' (ibid.). In many ways, Grekov was a fitting successor to Karamzin-Soloviev-Kliuchevsky. He cast aside the statist or juridical theory of the origins of serfdom in Muscovy, preferring to extend Kliuchevsky's socio-economic approach. But

The appearance of the books by Tolstoi and Grekov coincided with a mounting attack on Iavorsky and the Kharkiv school of party historians. When Gorin, the secretary of the Russian Society of Marxist Historians, declared Iavorsky guilty of using a 'class national method' akin to that of Hrushevsky, his accusations appeared not only in the published proceedings of the Marxist conference but also in Moscow's official ideological journal, *Bolshevik*, and in *Pravda*. At first, Iavorsky, who seems to have enjoyed the support of Skrypnyk, fought back, but weakened by the desertion of Rubach, and under strong 'administrative' pressure, he finally conceded defeat. At the same time, he displayed a new vigour in his opposition to non-Marxist Ukrainian historiography. Hrushevsky was obviously his prime target.[39]

The appearance of Communists in the ranks of the VUAN led to immediate changes in the conduct and direction of scholarship. In the Historical Section, Iavorsky led the attack an Hrushevsky and his school. At the end of November, 1929, the Academic Council of the VUAN, which was by this time dominated by party bureaucrats, decided to liquidate some of Hrushevsky's commissions. These included the Commission for Left Bank Ukraine and the Commission on Modern Ukrainian History. Bahalii was to take over the responsibilities for Left Bank history; Iavorsky for modern history. The Commission for Southern Ukraine was to be given to the new academician from Odessa, M.E. Slabchenko. In reply, Hrushevsky protested strongly against these moves. He suggested alternate methods of organization; he objected to the speed with which the changes were rammed through, and he protested that the work of many members of the former commissions would be lost if these people were not transferred to the new teams and given an opportunity to complete their tasks. Hrushevsky's objections were overuled. On 22 December, another of his commissions, one on Old Ukraine, was give over to Slabchenko. Once again Hrushevsky protested; again in vain.[40] The Archaeographic Commission too was taken away from the beleaguered scholar, and, as a formal organization, the Historical Section, which dated back to the UNT

he was also (like Hrushevsky) a strong anti-Normanist who thought that Kiev had developed a complex agricultural system and (unlike Hrushevsky) stressed that both Lithuania and Muscovy had inherited the traditions of Kiev. Thus Ukrainians, Belorussians, and especially Russians shared this common heritage. Under Stalin, Grekov's theory became sacrosanct. For a summary see A. Mazour, *The Writing of History in the Soviet Union* (Stanford, 1971), pp. 54–6.

39 For Gorin's attacks on Iavorsky, see *Pravda* (Moscow), 4 January 1929 and 10 February 1929, and also 'O roli proletariata v revoliutsionnom dvizhenii Ukrainy,' *Bolshevik*, VII, no. I (Moscow, 1930), 43–52, which is summarized in Krupnytsky, *Ukrainska istorychna nauka pid sovietamy*, pp. 23–7. Also see Barber, *Soviet Historians in Crisis*, pp. 44–6, and Sullivant, *passim*.

40 See Hrushevsky's report in *Ukraina*, nos. 3–4 (Kiev, 1930), 187–98, and the summary in Krupnytsky's introduction to the New York edition of *Istoriia Ukrainy-Rusy*, I, xvi.

of pre-revolutionary days, ceased to exist. In early 1930, when the last issue of *Ukraina* appeared, the famous Historical Institutions were no more.[41]

The halls and committee rooms of the Kievan VUAN were not the only battleground on which Hrushevsky defended Ukrainian cultural independence. When, on 12 January 1929, along with Liubavsky, Petrushevsky, Bukharin, Riazanov, and many other prominent personalities, Hrushevsky had been elected to the Russian Academy of Sciences, this institution was just beginning its transformation from a purely Russian, but independent, centre of thought into a new All-Union Academy of Sciences responsive to the demands of party and government. The rapid expansion and infusion of aggressive new Communist members brought about considerable disorientation, but also offered some hope that certain earlier problems might be solved. Three years before, Hrushevsky had complained about the financial support that the Ukrainians were required to give to the Russian Academy, while at the same time maintaining their own without any outside help. In 1929, events developed in a way that caused the new Union Academy also to continue as the academy of the Russian people. Hrushevsky, however, in keeping with his ideas about mutual respect between the Russian and Ukrainian people, would have liked to see the parallel existence of a Union Academy and a separate Academy of Sciences for Russia proper. Thus the Russians, Ukrainians, and Belorussians would all be placed on an equal level and the opportunity for cultural imperialism on the part of the Russians would be reduced. Unfortunately, however, this plan proved difficult to implement, and as an interim measure, Hrushevsky suggested the creation of three major institutes within the union Academy: an Institute of Russian History, an Institute of Ukrainian History, and an Institute of Belorussian History. Hrushevsky's idea was favourably received, and on 21 April 1929 it was decided to begin with the creation of an Institute of Ukrainian History that would act as a liaison with the still independent Ukrainian Academy. When he returned to Kiev, Hrushevsky reported to the Ukrainians that his presence in the Russian Academy 'had served as a means of bringing special attention to the activities and importance of the VUAN.'[42]

Hrushevsky also spoke up on other issues that touched upon Ukrainian interests within the Union Academy. Foremost among these was the matter of national terminology. After 1917, the terms 'Belorussian' and 'Ukrainian' were officially

41 *Visti VUAN za 1929*, nos. 8–9 (Kiev, 1929), 4; Polonska-Vasylenko, 'Istorychna nauka ... ta dolia istorykiv,' p. 17. In 1929, Panas Liubchenko's first public attack on Hrushevsky, which had originally appeared in 1926 as a reply to the historian's famous jubilee speech, was reprinted in *Budivnytstvo radianskoi Ukrainy*, part I (Kharkiv, 1929), p. 86ff.

42 M. Hrushevsky, 'Zvidomlenniia z uchasty y kvitnevii sesii akademii nauk URSR,' *Visti VUAN za 1929*, nos. 5–6 (Kiev, 1929), 20–3. Also see Krupnytsky's remarks in *Istoriia Ukrainy-Rusy*, I, xvi–xvii.

accepted names used in both colloquial speech and in works of literature. However, the older term *Russkii* was still often used and there was considerable confusion as to its meaning. Hrushevsky suggested that, to avoid confusion, it would make more sense to talk about the 'Eastern Slavs,' or about Great Russians, Belorussians, and Ukrainians. This had immediate practical consequences, for it was still an open question whether the Ukrainian and Belorussian languages would be dealt with inside the Russian Department of the Philological Section, or within a section devoted to 'other Slavic languages and literatures,' as Hrushevsky preferred.[43]

On almost all counts the Ukrainian historian was defeated. The nebulous term *Russkii* remained in use alongside 'Belorussian' and 'Ukrainian'; only 'Great Russian' was definitely dropped, while the term 'Eastern Slavs' was to be used primarily among linguists and philologists. Hrushevsky's organizational suggestions were not followed, and even those which had already been accepted, such as the liaison Institute of Ukrainian History, were eventually discarded as the Soviet Union's Academy of Sciences underwent further changes. The independence of Ukrainian institutions of scholarship was not to be preserved. In the end, the All-Ukrainian Academy of Sciences (VUAN) was liquidated; its place was taken by the Academy of Sciences of the Ukrainian SSR, which was, in fact, merely a branch of the Union Academy.[44]

The destruction of Hrushevsky's Historical Institutions did not yield anything constructive in return. The Communist Party attack on Iavorsky continued, and, finally, in February 1930, in spite of his willingness to confess his mistakes, the Ukrainian Communist historian was expelled from the CPbU and the Marxist Institute in Kharkiv was dissolved. Iavorsky eventually found himself in the Gulag along with so many other victims of Stalin's new 'general line.'[45] The surviving members of Iavorsky's school were compelled to follow the approach laid down

---

43 See 'Dopovid M. Hrushevskoho pro zasidannia soiuznoi akademii u kvitni 1929 r.' *Ukraina*, no. 34 (Kiev, 1929), 167–9; Krypnytsky, pp. xvi–xvii.

44 Krupnytsky, pp. xvi–xvii.

45 For Iavorsky's expulsion see Krupnytsky, 'Die Ukrainische Geschichtswissenschaft in der Sowjetunion 1921–1941,' p. 146, and also his *Ukrainska istorychna nauka pid sovietamy*, pp. 23–7. Iavorsky was arrested in March 1933 (at the same time as Shumsky, Solodub, and other 'national communists') and charged with belonging to an alleged Ukrainian underground military organization. Polonska-Vasylenko, *Ukrainska akademiia nauk*, I, 65–6; H. Kostiuk, *Stalinist Rule in the Ukraine: A Study of the Decade of Mass Terror (1929–1939)* (London–New York, 1960), p. 51. He was sent to the Solovki Islands penal colony, where his spirit remained unbroken to the end. To a questionnaire asking his party affiliation, he answered that 'he had the misfortune to belong to the most wretched Communist Party in the world and considered this as his greatest crime.' See the moving account of his fellow prisoner Semen Pidhainy, *Ukrainska inteligentsiia na Solovkakh* (Neu Ulm, 1947), pp. 57–60.

by Pokrovsky in Moscow. Under Pokrovsky's direction, Rubach codified his views about what he called Hrushevsky's anarcho-federalist ideology and his nationalistic bourgeois scheme of Ukrainian history; he set the stage for the legend of Hrushevsky's 'ideological capitulation' and humble request to return to Soviet Ukraine, and labelled him 'one of the ideologues of the nationalistic movement and its Western, German, orientation.' In spite of its highly polemical tone, Rubach's brief 1930 essay is the most serious work on Hrushevsky ever to appear in the Soviet Union; it is cited as a basic reference to the present day.[46]

Criticism of Hrushevsky was to be expected, but the attack on Iavorsky and the Ukrainian Marxist scholars surprised the older Ukrainian intelligentsia. These veterans of the national movement were generally liberal and democratic and did not expect any mercy from the new regime. It came as a shock to see the new order begin its latest assault by 'devouring its own.' The democratic intelligentsia trembled, knowing that its turn would come next.[47]

The influence of party administrators upon the VUAN was growing and had already had some effect. The public attack upon Iefremov had begun in 1928. By February of 1929, the party members within the academy were strong enough to demand his dismissal.[48] President Zabolotny was unable to support M.P. Vasylenko's plea for a united front behind Iefremov. By December, Zabolotny himself was dead. He received official honours, but his untimely death looked very suspicious to contemporaries abroad.[49]

The biggest single blow to the VUAN was the announcement by the GPU of their discovery of a vast plot of academics, teachers, and members of the Ukrainian Autocephalous Orthodox Church, who were trying to overthrow the Soviet regime. The alleged conspiracy aimed to establish an independent democratic Ukraine on the Western European model and it was charged that Iefremov was its central figure. He was arrested along with the historians Slabchenko and Hermaize. In addition, several hundred of the academy's scholarly staff were suddenly arrested and an attempt was made to implicate Academician Krymsky. The organization was called the 'League for the Liberation of Ukraine' (*Spilka vyzvolennia Ukrainy* or simply SVU) and was

46 M.A. Rubach, 'Federalisticheskie teorii v istorii Rossii,' *Russkaia istoricheskaia literatura v klassovom osveshchenii,* ed. M.N. Pokrovsky, 2 vols. (Moscow, 1930), II, 77–107. Rubach himself was arrested, disgraced, and exiled at the height of the Stalinist terror (1937), but was later 'rehabilitated' and wrote encyclopaedia articles on Hrushevsky until his death in the 1980s. For an assessment of his character see Dubrovsky's note in *Ukrainskyi istoryk,* nos. 1–2 (1966), 107–11.
47 Polonska-Vasylenko, *Ukrainska akademiia nauk,* I, *passim,* and Krupnytsky, *Ukrainska istorychna nauka pid sovietamy.*
48 Polonska-Vasylenko, *Ukrainska akademiia nauk,* I, 68–9.
49 Ibid., I, 66; Michael Antonowytsch, 'Das Schicksal der ukrainischen Gelehrten in der Sowjetukraine,' in *Bolschewistische Wissenschaft und Kulturpolitik,* pp. 45–8, especially p. 47.

supposed to involve thousands of people from the academicians in Kiev to ordinary workers and countryfolk. An atmosphere of terror fell upon the academy as day by day more arrests were made; many workers from Hrushevsky's Historical Institutions suddenly disappeared.[50]

Hrushevsky himself was not arrested. His personal disagreements with Iefremov and Krymsky were too well known for the GPU to simply lump them together in a single conspiracy. This kind of thing would come later. Rather, there was a general press campaign against the SVU and an attempt was made to draw Hrushevsky into it. The party journalists, who tried to coax Hrushevsky into condemning his colleagues, got nowhere. The historian simply refused to comment; he would say nothing to condemn the accused and nothing against the regime. Finally, the party detailed a certain Mishchenko, a Communist activist from the Arsenal, to get some kind of firm statement from Hrushevsky.

One evening in the winter of 1929–30 Mishchenko and some workers from the Arsenal called on Hrushevsky, who still lived in a small reconstructed wing of his old house on Pankivsky Street. Some eight workers, Mishchenko, and a stenographer, who was to note Hrushevsky's every word, crowded into the professor's tiny study, where there was not room for all to sit. At the end of a lengthy discussion concerning the power of the Soviet Union and the nature of the SVU conspiracy, the group could get no sign of disloyalty out of Hrushevsky. Suddenly, the historian smiled and motioned to the stenographer: 'You, comrade stenographer, please come and sit here on the desk and relax. We don't really need you.' Shortly afterward, the delegation left, Mishchenko concluding that 'this Hrushevsky certainly is a cunning fellow!'[51]

In April 1930, the attention of all Ukraine was riveted on the State Opera House in Kharkiv, where the tragicomedy of the SVU trial was being acted out. Before a tribunal appointed by the All-Ukrainian Central Executive Committee, some forty-five defendants faced that same Panas Liubchenko who had been rebuffed at Hrushevsky's jubilee and was now acting as prosecutor. The trial was broadcast by the State Radio and attracted international attention. Setting a new precedent for

---

50 Polonska-Vasylenko, *Ukrainska akademiia nauk*, I, 67–76 and 'Istorychna nauka ... ta dolia istorykiv,' pp. 17–19.

51 Polonska-Vasylenko, 'Z moikh spohadiv pro M. Hrushevskoho,' *Ukraina*, no. 9 (Paris, 1953), 744–7, describes a chance encounter with Mishchenko in 1930 in a hospital where her husband was recovering from a nervous condition that was fast becoming the epidemic disease of the era. L. Ivchenko, 'Faktychni dovidky,' *Novi dni*, nos. 126–7 (Toronto, 1960), 21–4, recalls the inspiration that this very unusual Hrushevsky interview produced when, amidst cries of 'Punish them,' 'Condemn them,' the historian was quoted in the newspaper as saying nothing more than: 'Whatever I know about the SVU affair is only from the communiqué of the GPU. I can say nothing about it until I find out the facts.'

Stalinist Russia, Iefremov, Hermaize and their co-defendants openly confessed their crimes and were sentenced accordingly.[52]

About the same time, the party press revealed that the authorities had discovered certain 'secret archives' in the Ukrainian Academy. These papers, it was said, had been hidden from government officials. In the 'archives scandal' that followed, there were many parallels to a similar archives scandal and uproar against the Russian Academy, which had occurred a month or two earlier and was designed to weaken the resistance of the Leningrad scholars.[53] Throughout the summer of 1930, the atmosphere of terror increased. Party activists and factory workers joined together in special tribunals which set out to purge the VUAN of unsatisfactory members. Private inquests weeded out some 120 to 150 men, who faced public inquisition and humiliation at a series of four consecutive open meetings. The inquisitions were not held in the academy buildings but at various public places in Kiev. The atmosphere was partly that of a carnival , partly that of a horror show. Most of the historians were dealt with at the second meeting held at the ironworkers hall. Selected workers and party activists sat in judgment over senior students and history researchers. Many dedicated scholars fell victim to the ignorant and arbitrary judgments of the makeshift court. The elderly translator S.O. Buda, who was completely innocuous and had dedicated his life to the academy, was relieved of his work on Iefremov's Commission for the History of Social Movements, and on the great Dictionary of National Biography. Kateryna Lazarevsky, daughter of the historian Oleksander Lazarevsky and already a respected scholar in her own right, was plainly told that the court was not interested in what she or her father had written, but only, in the phrase of the presiding Communist official, in 'how your [landowning] family has spilled peasant blood.'[54] The inquisitors and ironworkers were shocked at the testimony of two young researchers from the Historical Institutions, Evfymovsky and Kravtsov, whom Hrushevsky had dispatched to Moscow to identify and copy documents for

---

52 Perhaps because of the international attention, the official sentences were surprisingly light, amounting to several years incarceration. In actual fact, almost none of the accused were to escape the Gulag alive. Of the hundreds of scholars and thousands of simple folk who just disappeared, little is known. The whole affair caused a storm of protest in the Western Ukrainian lands. See M. Kovalevsky, *Opozytsiini rukhy v Ukraini i natsionalna polityka SSSR (1920–1954)* (Munich, 1955), pp. 34–64; Solovei, *Holhota Ukrainy*, pp. 119–24.

53 See Graham, p. 127, who details the Leningrad affair and mentions its Ukrainian counterpart.

54 Polonska-Vasylenko, *Ukrainska akademiia nauk,* I, 106; 'Istorychna nauka ... ta dolia istorykiv,' p. 23. Buda was sixty-four years old when he was thus dismissed; he later managed to find work at the State Publishing House, where all of his articles went unsigned. Kateryna Lazarevsky was one of the best palaeographers in Ukraine and was scholarly secretary of the Archaeographic Commission under Hrushevsky. Though severely shaken by the inquest, she was not officially expelled from the academy until 1933.

the *History of Ukraine-Rus'*. In Moscow, the two lived in quarters rented by the VUAN for the convenience of visiting scholars. In the eyes of the inquisitors, however, this was clearly a case of the exploitation of 'proletarians' by the bourgeois Hrushevsky. The court sought to convince the researchers that the archival documents in question were fully their own property, and not that of master Hrushevsky.[55] In a similar vein the inquisitors examined many other members of the Historical Institutions. But Hrushevsky himself was not yet touched.

The VUAN and Hrushevsky's Historical Institutions were not the only centres of non-Russian scholarly activity to suffer such heavy blows. Events of striking similarity were also occurring in Belorussia, where the 'sovietization' process was again compounded by the national question, and again had equally tragic consequences. At the Belorussian Academy of Sciences, arrests began in the spring of 1930, and continued throughout the summer. Once again, the historians were very hard hit. Some three hundred people – writers, teachers, students – were arrested in connection with an alleged 'League for the Liberation of Belorussia.' These included Hrushevsky's friend Picheta and many others. The GPU made an attempt to link this fictitious organization with its namesake in Ukraine and thus build up the image of a vast conspiracy extending over the borders of the Union Republics, uniting them with émigrés and foreign powers, and directing everything against Soviet Russia. Once again, there was an unsuccessful attempt to implicate Hrushevsky.[56] The Belorussian Academy of Sciences was almost physically liquidated. The academy's president, the Communist V.M. Ignatovsky, committed suicide in February 1931, and the famous cultural figure Academician Ianko Kupala made a similar attempt.[57] In Belorussia, as in Ukraine, the sovietization process was significantly fiercer than

55 Polanska-Vasylenko, 'Istorychna nauka ... ta dolia istorykiv,' p. 22. According to O. Pritsak, a student of Krymsky, Hrushevsky's reputation for exploitation of his students' work dated back to his days in Galicia before 1914. Hrushevsky would seldom allow students and researchers working for him to publish their results before they had been incorporated into the *History of Ukraine-Rus'*. Pritsak claims to know of at least one major work which was lost because of this. (Interview with O. Pritsak, March 1981.)

56 Polanska-Vasylenko, ibid., p. 59, note 34, states that, some time afterward, Picheta himself told her that the investigator had specifically asked him about his relations with Hrushevsky after the latter's jubilee celebrations in 1926. Picheta suffered detention and exile but was one of the few Belorussian scholars to survive the 1930s. Like Krymsky (see appendix B), he began to enjoy official favour with the partition of Poland in 1939, and he received the Order of the Toiling Red Banner on his deathbed in 1946. See I.O. Hurzhii, *Vydatni radianski istoryky* (Kiev, 1969), pp. 162–4.

57 H. Niamiha, 'The Belorussian Academy of Sciences, Oct. 13, 1928–July 7, 1936,' *Belorussian Review*, no. 6 (Munich, 1958), 5–29. More generally, see Anastas'in and Voznesensky, 'Nachalo trekh natsionalnykh akademii,' p. 178ff.

in the Russian Republic. But in general, the winter of 1930–1 was sufficiently dangerous for scholars everywhere in the Soviet Union.

Both in Moscow and in Leningrad, Hrushevsky's professional colleagues, rivals, and friends did not weather the storm without injury. On 14 November 1930 some fifteen workers from the Russian Academy of Sciences were arrested; the group included the famous historian of the Russian national school, S.F. Platonov. At the end of January 1931, Tarle was arrested; on 5 February, the historian of iconography N.P. Likhachev was arrested, and then so too was Hrushevsky's intellectual ally M.K. Liubavsky. All of these arrests were closely bound up with the 'sovietization' of the Russian Academy and the establishment of a clear line on what party historians called the 'historical front.'[58] Hrushevsky's case was more complicated.

Hrushevsky was a leading non-Marxist historian; thus he was certain to be affected by the sovietization process. But since he was the foremost Ukrainian scholar of his time, Hrushevsky was also closely identified with the party's Ukrainianization policy. Though there were signs that this policy had already seen its best days, it was, at least on the official level, not yet ended. Hrushevsky's prestige was still enormous. On still another level the old scholar was a former political leader with academic connections and a reputation that reached as far as Western Europe and North America. He had long symbolized the national unity of Western and Eastern Ukraine. Thus at least three divergent factors were at work helping to determine his fate: first, the 'sovietization' process, which was occurring all over the Soviet Union; second, the 'Ukrainianization' policy, which was not yet officially abandoned; and third, relations with the outside Communist and non-Communist world, where Hrushevsky was well known both as a scholar and as a political figure. As the months passed, the purges continued, the terror intensified, and Ukrainian academic life ground to a halt. Still Hrushevsky continued to write and to teach; he gave no sign of surrender to the new 'Marxist-Leninist methodology' or to the precepts of its most definitive interpreter, Joseph Stalin. In the end, the old pillar of *Ukrainstvo* stood almost alone amidst the ruins of the Ukrainian Academy.

---

58 Graham, p. 129. Liubavsky was sent to Ufa, where he died; Likhachev to Astrakhan, and Tarle to Alma-Ata, whence he returned two years later with a far greater appreciation of the wisdom of Karl Marx. According to Graham: 'The large number of historians who were given severe punishments can be partially explained as a result of the dictatorship of the Marxist historian M.N. Pokrovsky.' Professor George Vernadsky, whom Graham interviewed, believed that Platonov might have returned from exile also had he not died before the discrediting of Pokrovsky. Barber, *Soviet Historians in Crisis*, pp. 140–1, points out the irony that while Pokrovsky and his closest followers were to fall from grace in the middle 1930s, the former non-Marxists – Druzhinin, Grekov, Petrushevsky, Picheta, and Tarle – 'all returned to positions of honour and influence.'

Last Years and Death 1931–1934

Between 1928 and 1931, Hrushevsky was often the target of criticism at historical conferences and in the press. He was accused of standing to the side of the program of socialist construction and of being the main Ukrainian opponent of Marxist historical science. His work was labeled 'petty bourgeois' and his Historical Institutions were dissolved. The beginning of 1931 saw the arrest of many historians throughout the Soviet Union, and, given the past criticism of Hrushevsky, there was little reason to think that he would escape unscathed. In fact, he did not.

At an administrative meeting held during the January 1931 session of the VUAN, the recently elected Bolshevik academician V.P. Zatonsky initiated a direct attack upon Hrushevsky's political record and historical work. This criticism was fiercer than anything that had gone before and turned out to be the signal for a whole wave of public attacks upon Hrushevsky. Some of the points that Zatonsky made in his speech became major themes in the party's campaign against Hrushevsky's interpretation of East Slavic history; others were clear indications of serious political accusations which were to be made later on.

Zatonsky began with a general declaration that Bolsheviks only want to preserve selected elements from the past and object to the idea of continuity in Ukrainian history and to the 'fetish' of separatism. He then described Hrushevsky's political career and claimed that the Bolsheviks were fully aware of the motivation for his return to Soviet Ukraine. 'Professor Hrushevsky,' wrote Zatonsky, who had once faced the historian at the 1917 All-Ukrainian Congress of Soviets, 'is very well known to us.'

We knew that in the past he went from a position close to the Kadets and from limited cultural autonomy, to full separation 'from the Bolshevik torrent' [as was said] and an orientation on Western Europe as represented by German imperialism. We knew that he was one of the most important ideologues of the German occupation of 1918. We knew that in 1917 his unexpected 'left' position – his leadership of the Ukrainian SRs – was a tactical maoeuvre that he took in order to keep the erupting peasant classes on a road determined by the bourgeoisie. We knew that, as was the case with other theorists of bourgeois nationalism, his theory that the Ukrainian nation was without a bourgeoisie, and that the entire peasantry including the better-off villagers [*kurkuly*] could be taken together as 'the toiling peasantry,' was also not an objective conclusion by a research historian, but rather was called forth by the bourgeois elements of the Ukrainian nation in order to create by force a 'single national front' against the proletarian revolution. All the same, Soviet power allowed him and continues to allow. him every opportunity to do his scholarly work.

With great indignation, Zatonsky then explained that, in spite of this indulgence on the part of the Soviet authorities, Hrushevsky had not altered his basic position and was still continuing his old ways. He was still concentrating on the continuity of Ukrainian national life and, as for example in his 1926 Jubilee speech, was still praising Kostomarov and Antonovych, whom he considered to be the founders of modern Ukrainian scholarship. In a 1928 article on Antonovych, he had even admitted that this mentor of his would rather go through hell with the Ukrainians than be in heaven with the Russians or the Poles. Thus, continued Zatonsky, under the conditions of the world socialist revolution Hrushevsky was using every legal avenue to enflame the most brutal kind of nationalism; that is, the nationalism that sets one nation against another. He blames the Russian proletarian and peasant for the crimes of the Russian tsar, and if this be logic, we would have to blame the Ukrainian collective farmer because Hrushevsky and Vynnychenko sold out Ukraine to the German capitalists. Moreover, in his historical work, Hrushevsky is trying to 'rehabilitate' the Cossack officer class which made up the landowning class of old Ukraine. He engages in emotional hyperbole and draws fanciful and idealized pictures of the past. After all these years Hrushevsky is still continuing his old line: from the peasantry, he is trying to construct a nationally conscious Ukrainian working class, which would complete the formation of the Ukrainian nationality. 'Academician Hrushevsky,' Zatonsky concluded darkly, 'is trying to realize his own program of manorhouse [*khutorianskyi*] kulak culture. He does this consciously and he has not been alone. [Until recently] there were many like him in the Academy.[1]

Zatonsky's provocative speech, his threatening tone, and, in the final passage,

1 V.P. Zatonsky, *Natsionalno-kulturne budivnytstvo i borotba proty natsionalizmu: dopovid ta zakliuchne slovo na sichnevii sesii VUAN* (Kiev, 1934), and largely reprinted in M. Stakhiv, 'Deiaki materiialy pro Bolshevytskyi nastup na Hrushevskoho,' *Mykhailo Hrushevsky u 110 rokovyny narodzhennia*, pp. 175–8. Stakhiv dates this document not by publication date but by the censor's *cum permissu*, 3 March 1931.

his direct reference to the purges of 1930 had the desired effect. It is an indication of the fundamental changes that had occured at the VUAN that the speech was greeted with what the official record called 'clamorous, prolonged aplause.' In the same vein, the meeting endorsed a resolution addressed to 'all scientific workers of Soviet Ukraine.' The resolution discussed socialist construction and relations between the brotherly republics of the Soviet Union. It linked those who used the old Ukrainian terminology of 'national liberation' to spying for Germany and Poland. Ukrainian nationalists, conservative monarchists, democrats, and communists were all indiscriminately lumped together as enemies of the Soviet regime. 'The counter-revoluntionary nationalists,' read the resolution, 'the irreconcilable enemies of the working class and the toiling peasantry, this whole united front from the Petliuras, Vynnychenkos, Hrushevskys, Levytskys, Konovaletses, Skoropadskys, Badans, Shumskys, and Solodubs, are all trying to put the yoke of the landlord and capitalist upon the Ukrainian toiling masses.' The resolution then explained that these negative elements were trying to infiltrate the Ukrainian Academy, but that the academy had responded and was calling upon all the scientific workers of the country to repel them. The document ends with an accolade:

This meeting of the All-Ukrainian Academy warmly greets the tested leaders of the Bolsheviks of Ukraine: Comrades Kosior and Postyshev.

Long live the great party of Lenin-Stalin, the organizer of victory!

Long live the beloved guide of all progressive humanity, Comrade Stalin![2]

The 'sovietization' of the Ukrainian Academy, it seems, was complete.

The first months of 1931 saw the arrest of those among Hrushevsky's friends and former political adherents who still remained at large. Most of the arrested men, like their political mentor, had returned to the homeland during the mid-1920s and had played a significant role in the reconstruction and Ukrainianization campaigns of this period. From Hrushevsky's former SR circle in Vienna, there was Mykola Shrah, who had been busy publishing popular-style pamphlets on geography and history; Pavlo Khrystiuk, who had been engaged in educational work; and M.F. Chechel, who had been teaching engineering and architecture in Kharkiv and whose major work on building mechanics was published anonymously after his arrest. Finally, although he was not an SR, Hryhory Kossak, who had commanded the Galician Ukrainian army during the battle for Lviv and later followed Hrushevsky's example and moved to Soviet Ukraine, where he taught at the Red Officer Training School in Kharkiv, was also arrested. Hrushevsky

2 In Stakhiv, ibid., pp. 178–81.

however, was not yet touched; instead, GPU surveillance over him was tightened and he was privately urged to leave Ukraine.[3]

On 6 March 1931, Hrushevsky told his remaining students that he was leaving for Moscow. The next day he gathered together his papers, and said: 'Goodbye, learn to live without me!' He went out, but returned a moment later, looked around one last time and then, in the words of one of these students, 'left, never to return to these quiet rooms, which he had furnished with so much love and taste.'[4]

Immediately after Hrushevsky had left Kiev, the party began an intensive propaganda campaign against him. Disparaging articles appeared in the papers, and a series of public 'disputes' was held criticizing his scholarly work.[5] The major public 'dispute' on Hrushevsky lasted three days and was followed by similar treatments of other surviving scholars: K.H. Vobly, L.M. Iasnopolsky, and O.P Ohloblyn. The 'dispute' or public judgment of Hrushevsky and his school was held on three consecutive evenings. It took place, in turn, at the old Pedagogical Museum (which had housed the Central Rada), the VUAN Conference Hall, and the Kiev Opera House. The halls were overflowing. The atmosphere was excited, tense, even stifling. Various party officials headed by Skrypnyk's associate A. Richytsky, who had often criticized Hrushevsky in the past, repeated all the now-standard criticisms of the historian's work. It was condemned as being unscholarly, without worth, and the result of backward social views which could not stand the test of what was called 'modern' criticism. Richytsky and the other officials claimed that Hrushevsky's 'views' were positively harmful and had to be eliminated. 'But what was more disturbing, and harder to endure,' recalls an eyewitness from the VUAN, 'was the testimony of [Hrushevsky's] beloved pupils and collaborators, who one after the other confessed their errors and laid the blame for them upon their leader. From the entire grand collective, only a handful were able to display civil courage and not join in this chorus.'[6]

3 O.M. [O. Stepanyshyna], 'Ostanni roky zhyttia Mykhaila Hrushevskoho,' *Nashi dni*, no. 3 (Lviv, 1943), 4–5, reprinted in *Ukrainskyi istoryk*, nos. 1–4 (1981), 174–9, and summarized in H. Kostiuk, 'The Last Days of M. Hrushevsky,' *Ukrainian Review*, v (Munich, 1957), 73–93, and M. Halii, 'Iak Moskva znyshchyla M. Hrushevskoho,' *Vilna Ukraina*, no. 52 (1966), 20–4.

4 See Stepanyshyna's memoir.

5 Stakhiv, 'Deiaki dokumenty pro bolshevytskyi nastup na Hrushevskoho,' p. 181, suggests that the party had commissioned a reluctant Zatonsky to lead the public campaign to discredit Hrushevsky, but that Zatonsky feared a face-to-face debate with the historian and thus arranged for his exile. Kostiuk, 'Last Days,' p. 78, believes that such an important move could not have been made without the consent of Stalin himself. Kostiuk thinks that Hrushevsky's removal interfered with the plans of the local police officials.

6 Polonska-Vasylenko, *Ukrainska akademiia nauk*, II, 16, 32, note 44; 'Istorychna nauka ... ta dolia istorykiv,' pp. 24–5. Three years later Richytsky himself was under attack for trying to 'proletarianize' Shevchenko. He was arrested shortly after the death of Skrypnyk and executed in 1937. See *Entsyklopediia ukrainoznavstva*, vol. VII (Paris–New York, 1973), 2530.

At the end of March, in the official ideological journal of the CPbU, another of Skrypnyk's associates, A. Khvylia, denounced Hrushevsky's scholarly independence and condemned him as a 'bourgeois-nationalist tribune' who was hostile to the Russian people. The scholar was also criticized for his silence in the League for the Liberation of Ukraine affair.[7] In April, M.A. Rubach, the graduate of Pokrovsky's Institute of Red Professors who had fiercely criticized Hermaize's alleged psuedo-Marxism at the First All-Union Conference of Marxist Historians, delivered a stinging attack on Hrushevsky at a session of the Ukrainian Society of Marxist Historians. On 23 May, he repeated his speech before a plenum of the Philosophical-Sociological Section of the Ukrainian Academy. Rubach argued that Hrushevsky was a 'bourgeois-kulak nationalist ideologue' who rejected class warfare in favour of 'a united national front,' who continued to maintain that the Ukrainian people was without a real bourgeoise, and who, under the mask of supporting socialism, Soviet power, and world revolution, in actual fact was against the dictatorship of the proletariat, against industrialization, and against the city itself. Rubach compared Hrushevsky's pre-revolutionary 'moderate liberalism' with his 1926 jubilee speech and declared him an unrepentant reactionary.[8] In June, the Central Committee of the CPbU published more precise instructions for historians. They had been formulated at a meeting held on 15 March.[9] In the same year, *Proletarska Pravda* and *Komunist* repeated the allegations raised by Liubchenko, Richytsky, and Khvylia: Hrushevsky defended the 'national-democratic theory' that the Ukrainian nation did not have a bourgeoisie and he put too much stress on the European cultural influences on Ukrainian history. 'The conscious lie of Lord Hrushevsky,' screamed the party press, 'was intended to strengthen the counter-revolutionary theory of the Ukrainian people without a bourgeoisie. The hero of the yellow and blue romance has been unmasked.'[10]

While the Kievan party press revelled in its victory, Hrushevsky was faced with the difficulties of his second exile in Moscow. Upon his arrival on 9 March, he fell ill. Then he was arrested by the GPU and taken back to the Ukrainian Republic, to Kharkiv, for questioning. Several days later this investigation was unexpectedly and suddenly discontinued and Hrushevsky was returned to Moscow. He was released and the police actually apologized for having troubled him. Meanwhile,

---

7 Sullivant, p. 184, citing A. Khvylia, 'Burzhuazno-natsionalistychna trybuna,' *Bilshovyk Ukrainy*, no. 6 (Kharkiv, 1931) 46–58.
8 Rubach's speech was later printed as 'Burzhuazno-kurkulska natsionalistychna ideologiia pid mashkaroiu demokratii "Trudovoho narodu": sotsiialno-politychni pohliady M.S. Hrushevskoho,' *Chervonyi shliakh* (Kharkiv, 1932), nos. 5–6, 115–35, nos. 7–8, 118–26, nos. 11–12, 127–36.
9 Sullivant, p. 184, citing M. Redin, 'Za bilshovytskyi povorot u vykladanni istorii,' *Bilshovyk Ukrainy*, no. 11 (Kharkiv, 1931) 66–94.
10 In Halii, p. 20.

his illness had developed into a slight attack of pneumonia. Under medical care, however, he quickly recovered. Several weeks later, Hrushevsky received a letter from the GPU in which he was invited to call on the official in charge of his case. Thereafter, he was required to appear regularly, at appointed times, for registration and sometimes interviews at the GPU.[11]

For the next few years, in spite of the close police supervision, Hrushevsky continued to live with his wife and daughter, to do scholarly research, and to write profusely. The Hrushevsky family lived in a single cold, damp poorly lit room rented by the VUAN. Aided by his daughter, Kateryna, and now almost blind, the tireless historian continued his work in the rich Moscow archives. 'Yet hard though the conditions in which he lived were, both materially and morally,' writes one of Hrushevsky's last students, 'he never changed his daily routine: he got up at four o'clock in the morning, perhaps even earlier (his family, at any rate, when waking up, always noticed that he had already begun work); at ten o'clock he left for the archives or the library, and came home for dinner at five P.M. After dinner he would work at home until late at night. It is unknown when and how long Mykhailo Serhiiovych rested.'[12]

By keeping to this rigorous schedule, which he had followed for so many years, Hrushevsky continued to be amazingly productive. During this last Moscow exile, he wrote a series of minor treatises on the history of Ukrainian literature and the development of public opinion in the eighteenth century. The studies contributed to the existing knowledge of the sources and outlined the beginnings of the national awakening of the nineteenth century. At the same time, Hrushevsky completed the seventh, eighth, and in part the ninth volumes of his monumental *History of Ukrainian Literature,* which had been begun in Vienna many years before; he also gathered material for further volumes of his *History of Ukraine-Rus',* and he wrote, but did not complete, a novel based on the life of Ivan Kotliarevsky.[13] Though he was not allowed to publish in the Ukrainian language, Hrushevsky

11 This registration and reporting was compulsory for all those who for political reasons were in so-called 'voluntary exile.' See Kostiuk, 'Last Days,' p. 74, citing the Stepanyshyna memoir. Hrushevsky's family told Polonska-Vasylenko ('Z moikh spohadiv,' p. 745) that after his return from the interrogation in Kharkiv, 'Hrushevsky could not be recognized and looked as if he had aged twenty years.'

12 Stepanyshyna.

13 Stepanyshyna; Kostiuk, 'Last Days,' p. 75. Volume VI of his *History of Ukrainian Literature* had been ready for press before March 1931. O. Ohloblyn, 'Pro deiaki zahubleni pratsi i vydannia VUAN u Kyievi,' *Naukovyi zbirnyk II,* Ukrainian Academy of Sciences in the USA (New York, 1953) p. 197, says that both volumes VI and VII were ready for press, but never saw publication. Polonska-Vasylenko, *Ukrainska akademiia nauk,* II, 196, adds that a typescript survived, and that Kateryna preserved it and submitted it for publication in 1937. Kateryna, however, suffered punitive exile and the fate of the work is not known.

nevertheless managed to print two significant historiographical studies in two different Russian-language organs of the Academy of Sciences of the USSR.[14] All this was accomplished under severe physical conditions and under constant police supervision.

Hrushevsky had few visitors from Kiev; it had become too dangerous. Nevertheless, he often saw his fellow historian D.M. Petrushevsky, who was an old friend from student days in Kiev. Like Hrushevsky, Petrushevsky had a long-standing inclination toward populism, had tried to make use of the new Communist institutions of learning, and had been severely attacked at the 1928 First Conference of Marxist Historians. In spite of strong party pressure, he had also been elected to the Russian Academy in the famous elections of 1929.[15] Petrushevsky often wrote to friends in Kiev informing them of Hrushevsky's fortune.[16]

Hrushevsky continued to receive his salary as a member of both the Union and the Ukrainian academies. On one occasion a party boss in Kiev tried to have it cut off, but under pressure from the academy's president, O.O. Bohomolets, who threatened to take the matter all the way to the education commissar, the salary was restored. Hrushevsky remained a full member until his death.[17] Once when Bohomolets visited Moscow, Hrushevsky asked if he could return home yet. 'No, no,' replied Bohomolets, 'wait a while and do not work yourself up. Everything will be all right.'[18] This was the last time the two men met.

In Kiev things went from bad to worse. The public campaign against Hrushevsky continued. The academy went through successive purges and two of its three Sections were closed down completely.[19] Arrests continued. In 1932, after a ten-month interlude, the journal *Ukraina* appeared once again. But it bore no resemblance to the prestigious periodical once edited by Hrushevsky. It was now the organ of the Socio-economic Section, and in its opening editorial the new journal plainly declared itself for what it called 'Marx-Lenin-Stalin science.' The leading article was a reprint of a contribution by Stalin to the history of

14 'Samovidets ruiny i ego pozdneishie otrazheniia,' *Trudy Instituta Slavianovedeniia AN SSSR*, no. 1 (1932); 'Ob Ukrainskoi istoriografii XVIII v. Neskolko soobrazhenii,' *Izvestiia AN SSSR*, no. 3 (1934). His last Ukrainian-language publication (on Ukrainian educational traditions), 'Try akademii,' appeared in *Kyievskyi naukovyi zbirnyk*, vol. 1 (Kiev, 1931). His English-language article on 'M.P. Drahomanov' appeared in the *Encyclopedia of the Social Sciences*, vol. V (New York, 1931), but had certainly been sent abroad prior to this exile.
15 See chapter 10 above.
16 Polonska-Vasylenko, 'Spohady,' p. 745.
17 Ibid., p. 746, and her *Ukrainska akademiia nauk*, II, 28. Skrypnyk was education commisar until his suicide on 7 July 1933.
18 Stepanyshyna; Halii, p. 21.
19 Polonska-Vasylenko, *Ukrainska akademiia nauk*, II, *passim*.

Bolshevism; it revealed Lenin as the unchanging epitome of Bolshevism from cradle to grave. The other articles were critiques of the former historians of the VUAN. For example, there was a lengthy article attacking the historian of law M.P. Vasylenko. Vasylenko's work was labelled an example of backward, liberal-bourgeois historiography. The volume also dealt with the historiography of the Decembrist revolt and repeated the criticisms of Hrushevsky and other Ukrainian historians that were made at the First Conference of Marxist Historians. Among the reviews, too, there was direct criticism of Hrushevsky's work. Oleska Baranovych, who had produced some good work in the 1920s, and had even contributed to Hrushevsky's jubilee volume, was now compelled to review the great scholar's work in the harshest terms. Baranovych attacked Hrushevsky's plans for the reorganization of the Academy of Sciences of the USSR and observed that the Ukrainian historian did not recognize the Marxist categories of feudal, bourgeois, and proletarian science, but instead erroneously stressed the continuity of various national traditions of scholarship. Baranovych concluded that Hrushevsky would only succeed in solving historical questions 'when he stands on an expressly proletarian position.'[20]

The renewed *Ukraina*'s major attack on Hrushevsky and his historical school was by the legal historian Lev Okynshevych, who had been an associate of Vasylenko and had also worked with Hrushevsky for a while. In an article titled 'The National-Democratic Conception of the History of Ukrainian Law in the Works of Academician M. Hrushevsky,' Okynshevych attempted to prove that Hrushevsky was a true 'nationalist' who was trying to build a sovereign Ukrainian nation-state on the West European model. The whole article was constructed around two basic criticisms: first, Hrushevsky does not accept the Marxist scheme of history or use Marxist terminology; second, Hrushevsky writes as a national democratic partisan of statehood, and therefore is a bourgeois nationalist.

Okynshevych began by claiming that Hrushevsky had previously gone almost uncriticized. However, he continued, with the disputes of the spring of 1931, Marxist-Leninist historical science and the directives set forth by Comrade Stalin had 'ideologically liquidated' Hrushevsky's school. It only remained to remove its last traces. It appears that, since Okynshevych was primarily a legal historian, he was set the task of exposing Hrushevsky's supposed misconceptions in the area of legal-administrative history. The unfortunate Okynshevych had to prove that the leading Ukrainian historian did not concern himself primarily with the struggles of the people, but only with the construction of a national state. Of

20 O. Baranovych, 'Kyivsky zbirnyky istorii ... ' *Ukraina*, nos. 1–2 (Kiev, 1932), 182–9. Baranovych survived the purges of the 1930s and during the 1950s began publishing Russian-language studies of Ukrainian history. For a discussion of Stalin's 'intervention' in the historical debate on Bolshevik history, see Graham, *Soviet Historians in Crisis*, pp. 126–36.

course, this was a rather difficult task, for Hrushevsky was universally known as a major populist historian and a leader of the former UPSR. Nevertheless, Okynshevych claimed to see Hrushevsky's statist bias in his periodization (Kievan state; Lithuanian-Polish state; Cossackdom and the national renaissance), his use of what the Soviets called the 'backward concepts' of aristocratic historiography, his neglect of class oppression with, at the same time, a stress on the struggle for statehood, his portrayal of ecclesiastical history as simply a part of the national movement, and his detailed treatment of the 1654 Treaty of Pereiaslav. At the same time, Okynshevych pointed out, Hrushevsky shows little respect for Marxist historical axioms. He rejects the scheme: slave-holding society, feudalism, capitalism. He thinks of feudalism as primarily a military phenomenon and will not even admit that it existed in old Rus'! Rather, he claims that hereditary land tenure and a 'commercial patriarchate' already existed. In his treatment of Khmelnytsky, the peasant war disappears in the great detail of diplomatics, letters, and civil documents. Thus, claimed Okynshevych, Hrushevsky is not a populist at all, but rather a true 'national democrat' and partisan of statehood. In fact, Okynshevych suggested to what must have been a dumbfounded public, Hrushevsky is not so very far removed from the émigré supporter of the Hetman, Viacheslav Lypynsky, who is really no conservative, but rather 'a national fascist.' Okynshevych triumphantly concluded that the struggle of the Ukrainian bourgeois historians against various Russian historians, who falsely claim to be populists, is nothing more than a 'paper war.' All of them are hostile to the proletarian state.[21]

Okynshevych's brutal and mendacious attack on Hrushevsky reveals the extent to which the party had gone in order to discredit the most respected of Ukrainian historians. Though confused, self-contradictory, and certainly more the work of the censor than of the supposed author, the article did achieve its major purpose: it openly labelled Hrushevsky a 'nationalist,' and lumped him together with every variety of Ukrainian oppositionist from the communist left to the fascist right. The criticism was especially shameful in so far as it seemed to come from one of Hrushevsky's own collaborators, who had previously accepted his general scheme. The tragedy did not go unnoticed abroad, where one acute observer compared the campaign against Hrushevsky with the celebrated order in which Tsar Peter I commanded the Orthodox Churches of the Russian Empire, even those

---

21 L. Okynshevych, 'Natsionalno-demokratychni kontseptsii istorii prava Ukrainy v pratsiakh M. Hrushevskoho,' *Ukraina*, nos. 1–2 (Kiev, 1932), 93–109. On Okynshevych, who escaped to the West during the confusion of the Second World War, see Iaroslav Padokh, 'Lev Okinshevych: vydatnyi istoryk derzhavnoho prava Ukrainy-Hetmanschyny XVII–XVIII st., 1898–1980,' *Ukrainskyi istoryk*, nos. 1–4 (1981), 105–17.

founded by the Ukrainian Hetman, Ivan Mazepa, to curse their rebel patron, that is, Mazepa himself, at the end of the solemn liturgy.[22]

While the party intensified its press campaign against Hrushevsky, arrests continued. The professor's collaborators and family were among those who suffered. In 1932, the archaeologist S.V. Shamrai was arrested; he was the son of Hrushevsky's sister Hanna.[23] The following year, Hrushevsky's brother, Oleksander, was relieved of his duties in the Academy.[24] In fact, not just the intelligentsia, but all Ukraine was to suffer tragically through the fateful winter of 1932–3.

As collectivization was completed and the requisitioning of grain gathered force, millions of Ukrainian peasants starved to death. Stalin's envoy, Pavel Postyshev, became virtual dictator of Ukraine. Terror paralyzed the intelligentsia, and made itself felt within the Communist Party. Vigilance was the theme. The party was turning sharply against the Ukrainians. The Kharkiv Agricultural Commissariat, formerly a focal point of Ukrainian activity, suffered a devastating purge. On 13 May 1933, Khvylovy shot himself. Thereafter, the poet Hirniak took poison, and Havryliv, director of the Kharkiv Pedagogical Institute, shot himself. Finally, on 7 July 1933, just as Postyshev was about to turn on him, M.O. Skrypnyk, the people's commissar of education and most prestigious of all Ukrainian Communists, shot himself with a revolver that he had kept in his desk from the days of the civil war.[25] Hrushevsky's last possible protector from within the party was gone.

In November 1933, the overtly centralistic policies, which had been gathering force for some time, were formally approved by the Central Committee of the CPbU. In official pronouncements by Postyshev and Kosior, the harsh agricultural policies and a reevaluation of nationality policy were tied to the supposed discovery of an oppositional grouping that the authorities called the 'Ukrainian National Centre.'[26] This secret organization, the Bolshevik leaders claimed, was headed by Hrushevsky and was discovered early in 1931; that is, shortly after the destruction of the first group of the democratic intelligentsia in the SVU affair.[27] In fact, arrests had been proceeding for some time. According to the few survivors, a

22 S. Siropolko, 'Vidnovlena "Ukraina" ta ii vystup proty akad. M. Hrushevskoho,' *Tryzub*, no. 8 (Paris, 1933), 3–6.
23 Polonska-Vasylenko, 'Istorychna nauka ... ta dolia istorykiv,' pp. 28–9. Shamrai was sentenced to five years in a Siberian labour camp. He returned to Kiev in 1937, but within a year was again arrested and sent to the Gulag. His further fate is unknown.
24 Ibid., p. 64.
25 Kostiuk, *Stalinist Rule in the Ukraine*, pp. 47–9, 62–5.
26 See the speeches by Postyshev (*Pravda*, 24 November 1933 and Kosior (*Pravda*, 2 December 1933) cited and analysed by Kostiuk, 'Last Days,' p. 75.
27 Ibid.

large number of suspects were told that they were members of a counter-revolutionary network headed by Hrushevsky and were systematically tortured to extract suitable confessions.[28] The Ukrainian National Centre was supposed to contain all kinds of oppositional elements united under the leadership of the former Ukrainian patriarch. According to the official speeches of Postyshev and Kosior, these elements ranged from the former *Borotbisty* and those who were called 'national communists' like Shumsky to right-wing nationalist groups with contacts in Galicia. At the same time, the Ukrainian National Centre was said to have contacts with Shapoval's émigré socialists and to be 'a militant national fascist organization.'[29] Simultaneously, Hrushevsky was accused of being the central figure in a certain Organization of Ukrainian Socialist Revolutionaries, which espoused foreign intervention, insurrection, and cooperation with Russian Kadets, Georgian Mensheviks, and Belorussian nationalists. By April/May of 1934, the organ of the Central Committee of the CPbU was calling Hrushevsky a falsifier of the entire historical process who used zoological categories to set Ukrainian against Russian and unite Ukraine with Germany.[30] The historian could expect to be arrested at any time.

The arrest did not come. Instead, Hrushevsky, who was by this time more than half blind, was summoned to appear at the GPU more frequently, and, at the same time, the interrogations became more prolonged. In September 1934, Hrushevsky was required to report to the office of the Central Committee of the All-Union Communist Party of Bolsheviks, which was represented by Shumsky's old foe and Stalin's tool in Ukraine, Lazar Kaganovich. What these talks were about is not known. It is only known that after each of the conversations at the Central Committee, Hrushevsky was in a state of depression. According to Stepanyshyna, during the Moscow exile Hrushevsky was patronized by a certain G.I. Lomov, a high official with access to Stalin, who was related to Hrushevsky. Stepanyshyna writes:

Sometime in September, 1934, Mykhailo Serhiiovych was summoned to Kaganovich and requested to make a statement. Mykhailo Serhiiovych refused. Two days later, a relative of Lomov's called on Hrushevsky and told him that Lomov had sent him the following message: if Mykhailo Serhiiovych refused to make a statement, then he, Lomov, could not

28 O. Buzhansky, 'Za gratamy GPU-NKVD,' *Svoboda* (New York), nos. 288–300, December 1950, cited by Solovei, *Holhota Ukrainy*, pp. 125–9.
29 See the discussion in Kostiuk, 'Last Days,' p. 79.
30 On the Organization of USRs see ibid., pp. 80–2. The Central Committee's *Bilshovyk Ukrainy* for the early months of 1934 is analysed by Stakhiv, 'Deiaki materiialy pro bolshevytskyi nastup na Hrushevskoho,' pp. 189–94, who reprints the relevant passages.

vouch for Mykhailo Serhiiovych's safety. 'Well, so that's that,' said Mykhailo Serhiiovych calmly, and nothing more was said on the subject.[31]

The historian was not summoned to speak to Kaganovich again.

In the summer of 1932 and 1933, Hrushevsky had received permission for a brief visit to the spa for scholars at Kislovodsk in the Caucasus. In 1934, Mariia Sylvestrivna feared that this would no longer be possible and that the GPU/NKVD would refuse a new application. But surprisingly enough, permission came, and by 15 October the Hrushevsky family was in Kislovodsk. For the first week or so, Hrushevsky seemed to be in good health, and he enjoyed listening to a friend play the violin. But by the beginning of November, he had got an infection which developed into a carbuncle or swelling on his upper spine. An operation was necessary and a reluctant Hrushevsky was taken to a town hospital that was situated nearby. Conditions in the hospital were poor and Mariia Sylvestrivna asked that a family friend, who was a medical man and happened to be in the area, be permitted to perform the operation. The presiding physician, a man by the name of Khurgin, would not allow it, and performed the operation himself. Instead of getting better, Hrushevsky's condition deteriorated. Khurgin admitted that he had done the operation too soon.

Feeling that he was near death, the historian gave some final instructions to his wife and daughter. These concerned arranging and completing the subsequent volume of the *History of Ukraine Rus'*, and also the personal safety of his family. Turning to his wife, he said: 'If something should happen to me, go to Galicia. Do not stay with the Bolsheviks.'

Khurgin performed another operation. Hrushevsky's condition only got worse. Stepanyshyna describes what then occured:

At this time the famous surgeon Butsenko was resting in Kislovodsk. But Mariia Sylvestrivna did not know it. The physicians at the spa asked him to go see Mykhailo Serhiiovych but only on 24 November. Entering the hospital, Butsenko did not wish to see the patient without Khurgin. But Khurgin had suddenly disappeared and did not turn up for quite a while. Finally, the renowed surgeon went in to see Mykhailo Serhiiovych. Coming out into the reception room, Butsenko was very worked up: 'Why did you call me to see a dying person?' he exclaimed.

At this very time Mariia Sylvestrivna arrived – to unexpectedly hear such a judgment.

31 According to Stepanyshyna, it was Lomov who intervened with Stalin on Hrushevsky's behalf in 1931 as well. Kostiuk, however, doubts that Stalin would have stopped Hrushevsky's interrogation and ordered his release merely on Lomov's suggestion. Kostiuk believes that Stalin had reasons of his own, possibly the fabrication of another major conspiracy, for Hrushevsky's Moscow detention.

Mykhailo Serhiiovych did not despair, but faced his situation boldly, quietly, and there was no talk of death among those close to him . . .

On this same day, 24 November, at five in the evening, Mykhailo Serhiiovych died. He died at sixty-eight years of age, his creative vigour still full, with great scholarly plans and ideas.[32]

The death made a deep impression upon the scholars at Kislovodsk. Flowers arrived, and mourning music was played and delegations received. From Kislovodsk, the funeral cortège, accompanied by Mariia Sylvestrivna, went on to Kiev. Hrushevsky was given a state funeral. His body lay in state in the great hall of the Ukrainian Academy of Sciences, and those who had dared not visit him in life now paid their respects. 'In his honour the scholarly workers stood in rows like motionless statues,' writes an eyewitness. 'From its place to the side, Kiev's best orchestra played Chopin's funeral march. In the half-lit hall a great stream of people quietly circled the casket. They came without end. It seemed that all Kiev passed through the room. Alone, entirely by themselves, sat M.S. Hrushevska, the daughter, brother, and his wife. No one approached them.'[33]

On the next day, the funeral procession wound its way up to Baikovsky Cemetery through crowded streets lined with mounted militiamen. At the cemetery Hrushevsky's old foe V.P.Zatonsky, now Skrypnyk's replacement in the dangerous job of commissar of education, had the difficult task of giving the funeral oration. 'It is with great sadness,' he began, 'that today we honour Mykhailo Serhiiovych Hrushevsky.' Zatonsky then went on to say that Hrushevsky was a renowned historian, the author of many fundamental works, a member of both the Ukrainian and the Union Academies; he was considered to be the founder of Ukrainian bourgeois historiography. Zatonsky continued:

Hrushevsky was the recognized leader of the bourgeois national liberation movement, which in its time had helped to destroy the hateful 'prison of nations' – the Russian Empire. The tsarist government persecuted Mykhailo Serhiiovych for this, and it compelled him to emigrate. Only the revolution of 1905 had enabled him to return to Kiev. In 1917, as a politician, Hrushevsky took a position hostile to the proletarian revolution. Heading the Central Rada, M.S. Hrushevsky carried on armed struggle against worker-peasant Ukraine. But after the victory of the socialist revolution, while he was still in exile, Hrushevsky did not hold to a position that was hostile to the socialist revolution . . . The experience of life showed historian Hrushevsky that the proletarian revolution had finally destroyed the

---

32 On the basis of press reports and official announcements, Kostiuk corrects the date, establishing the day of Hrushevsky's death as 25 November 1934.
33 Polonska-Vasylenko, 'Spohady,' p. 446.

'prison of nations' and had freed such previously enslaved countries as Ukraine from their colonial status. It had shown him that Soviet rule had created all the conditions for the free development of Soviet Ukraine.

Zatonsky next pointed out that when Hrushevsky returned in 1924, the nationalists – Mohyliansky and others – had attacked him for his loyalty to the Soviets, and although he had many hesitations and doubts, 'the facts of life were most convincing for historian Hrushevsky.' He witnessed the collapse of bourgeois civilization and recognized the victory of socialism; he sought and found his place among the scholars of the Soviet land. Zatonsky concluded: 'We honour M.S. Hrushevsky as an extraordinary scholar. The academician of Soviet Ukraine, M.S. Hrushevsky, has found his last resting place here, in the capital of Soviet Ukraine, in Red Kiev.'[34]

In the crowd at the conclusion of the speeches, a confused young Communist, a secretary from the academy, turned to the person next to her and said: 'Tell me, how are we to understand what has happened? Yesterday it was forbidden to read Hrushevsky's works and he was declared an enemy of the people, but today there was a pompous ceremony and speeches?' A chill passed over the second person and she replied curtly: 'Dialectics.' She then turned away, wishing to end the dangerous conversation as quickly as possible.[35]

These were the last official honours that the Soviet government was to confer upon the celebrated historian who had known such fame and endured such abuse. During the week of the funeral, all of the newspapers carried Zatonsky's speech. But 'dialectics' seemed to be turning into a way of life in the Soviet Union, and shortly afterward the authorities confiscated the entire run of an academy serial which attempted to reprint Zatonsky's cautious words.[36] Thereafter for many years to come, Hrushevsky's name could never be mentioned in print without an accompanying series of opprobrious adjectives.

The last period of Hrushevsky's life, the period of his second Moscow exile, was at the same time both tragic and heroic. On the one hand, his historical work was officially discredited, his school dissolved, his followers and colleagues in fear for

34 'Promova narkoma osvity USRR Akad. V.P. Zatonskoho na pokhoronakh Akad. M.S. Hrushevskoho,' *Visti VUAN*, nos. 6–7 (Kiev, 1934), 36–9. This issue also contained a brief biographical outline of Hrushevsky's career and the resolutions of the Ukrainian government which honoured him with a state funeral, burial in Kiev, and a pension of 500 *karbovantsi* (rubles) monthly to his immediate family. The very next number of *Visti VUAN*, nos. 8–9 (1934), contained a spectacular obituary of Kirov (believed to be Stalin's rival), who was assassinated on 1 December 1934; that is, six days after Hrushevsky's death.
35 Polonska-Vasylenko, 'Spohady,' pp. 446–7.
36 Ibid.

their lives, and his family isolated in the small damp Moscow room which was the unwilling historian's final home. He was closely watched by the political police, and, like his nineteenth-century predecessor Mykola Kostomarov, was almost completely blind by the time of his death. On the other hand, Hrushevsky never ceased to work for the cause to which he had devoted his entire life. He continued to rise early and work as he always had, and the list of his published and unpublished works continued to grow. Just as cold, hunger, and blindness did not put an end to his scholarly activities, so too the destruction of the principal institutions of Ukrainian academic life did not stop him from publishing. He reluctantly transferred his compositions to Russian-language publishing houses in Moscow and Leningrad, but he continued to appear in print.

The period which followed Hrushevsky's departure from Kiev is filled with mysteries. His sudden arrest in Moscow, interrogation in Kharkiv, and unexpected release remain unexplained. The degree to which his fate depended upon the general sovietization process and the degree to which it was influenced by the end of the Ukrainianization policy are uncertain. However, it must be noted that while Hrushevsky's professional counterparts in Russia were being arrested and sent to the Gulag, the Ukrainian historian walked the streets of Moscow; and after the death of Pokrovsky in 1932, while the chastened non-party Russian historians returned from their places of exile, Hrushevsky was ever more severely attacked in the party press and endured exhausting interviews with the bane of the Ukrainian Communists, Lazar Kaganovich. Hrushevsky's final years are thus not typical of the non-party Russian historians who lived under Soviet rule, and the difference is probably explicable only in terms of the national question. One year after the great Ukrainian famine of 1933, and only a short while before the historian's death, the party finally felt strong enough to move the capital of the Ukrainian Republic back to the spiritual heartland of the old Ukrainian intelligentsia, Hrushevsky's true home, the City of Kiev. It was a symbolic act that reflected the beginning of a new era in Soviet history.[37]

Mystery also clouds the circumstances and reasons for Hrushevsky's death. Why did Khurgin not allow Mariia Sylvestrivna's friend to perform the necessary operation and thus escape the responsibility for a critical medical procedure for which, as Khurgin later admitted, he was unprepared? Did the surgeon's knife purposely slip in accordance with an order from above? It is possible that the

37 At this very same time, Stalin was 'rehabilitating' love for the homeland and announcing the new concept of 'Soviet patriotism' in a massive publicity campaign connected with the rescue by air of the crew of the steamship *Cheluskin*, which had got stuck in the ice during a polar expedition. The Soviet flyers became the first official 'heroes of the Soviet Union.' See 'Za rodinu,' *Pravda* (Moscow), no. 157, 9 June 1934, and the discussion in E. Oberländer, *Sowjet-patriotismus und Geschichte* (Cologne, 1967), pp. 15–16.

archives of the Soviet political police contain a firm answer to this intriguing question. On the other hand, it is possible that the full truth will never be known with certainty. What was clear to contemporaries, however, and what must be fully stated by any biographer of the Ukrainian historian, is that the Soviet authorities persecuted and harried Hrushevsky throughout his last years, so that an illness such as the one which appears to have killed him was almost unavoidable. Cold, malnutrition, and physical exhaustion were the immediate causes of his fatal condition; its certain cure – physical and psychological rest, shelter, and proper nourishment – was beyond his reach. The Soviet government, and most probably Stalin himself, destroyed the diminutive historian. The only question is whether it was done directly through the surgeon's knife or indirectly through public denunciation and private persecution.

Both Hrushevsky's historical work and his identification with his native land survived the onslaught. The fact that he was only allowed to return to Kiev when he was safely dead and that he was accorded official honours in a state funeral testifies to the continued power of the old scholar's name. The Soviet state, which was committed to the materialist conception of history, could physically annihilate the venerable partriarch of *Ukrainstvo*, but as late as 1934 it could not exorcise his ghost. The memory of the man whom Zatonsky was compelled to acknowledge as the long-time leader of the 'national liberation movement' would not be destroyed so easily.

Conclusion

From the time of his youth, when he first began corresponding with Nechui-Levytsky on various literary questions, to the time of his last exile in Moscow, when he penned his final contributions to Ukrainian historiography, Hrushevsky had devoted himself to the Ukrainian national cause. He was a central figure in the Ukrainian cultural flowering of the turn of the century, a teacher and an adviser to pre-revolutionary Ukrainian political representatives in Vienna and in Saint Petersburg, a national martyr during the First World War, and a symbol of national aspirations during the revolution that followed. Hrushevsky shared in the victories of the Ukrainian intelligentsia during the 1920s and shared in its defeats during the 1930s. As early as 1905, contemporaries listed him with Shevchenko and Drahomanov as one of the three greatest Ukrainians of modern times. As a cultural force, a political figure, and a national awakener, he was compared with the Czech Palacký and the Russian Karamzin, and he has stood the comparison well. Among Ukrainians in the West, his fame has long surpassed that of Drahomanov, and he is a cult figure in the same class as Shevchenko and Franko.

For non-Ukrainians too, Hrushevsky's career has been of considerable significance. He was the most celebrated federalist and the most vilified 'separatist' in the Russian Empire. His plans for the decentralization of the Russian state were adopted by a significant number of deputies to the Russian State Duma, and in 1917, his projects were even put into action so that all the world could see. In the realm of scholarship, he documented the history of his people through many centuries, supervised the creation of a new body of historical literature, and, very significantly, oversaw his nation's final adoption of the term 'Ukrainian.'

If, during his own day, Hrushevsky was compared with his predecessors Palacky and Karamzin, more recent observers might well put him in a class with his contemporary awakeners, the Czech scholar Tomáš Masaryk, the Jewish historian Simon Dubnow, or the Romanian historian Nicholae Iorga. Hrushevsky shared certain ideas about federalism and democracy with Masaryk, symbolized in his person the unification of the divided territories of a weaker nationality, as did Iorga, and thought of the nation in secular sociological terms and autonomous political forms, as did Dubnow. Iorga and Dubnow died tragically in the hands of the fascists; Hrushevsky, somewhat more mysteriously, in the hands of the Communists, but all four men played a definite role in the formation of the national identities of their respective peoples.

As in the case of Masaryk, Dubnow, and Iorga, Hrushevsky's role as a national figure is fairly clear. When his career is viewed as a whole, one is struck by the remarkable energy, creativity, and consistency of his endeavour. He never abandoned the ideals of the national awakening that he had first adopted during his youth, and, from his 1894 inaugural lecture in Lviv to his 1920 reflections on the revolution, he reiterated these ideals before many a different audience. Hrushevsky was thoroughly committed to the cause of the common people, and in 1917, when the time for state-building finally arrived, his early ideas about popular rule and mutual respect among peoples were reflected in the emerging state structure. In fact, Hrushevsky was almost dogmatic in his devotion to democratic forms, his condemnation of imperialism, and his abhorrence of extreme nationalism. As early as 1905, he had announced a project for the complete reorganization of the Russian Empire, and in his project stressed popular rule, decentralization, and the full national development of all peoples. However, he did not go so far as the idealization of a sovereign national state. His was not, as was said, a 'blood and iron' vision of nationalism, but rather a humanitarian, universal one. In 1917, he reiterated his project in greater detail and tried to put it into practice. The experiment failed, but in 1920, he still claimed to be faithful to his old beliefs and was still citing his old populist-SR ideals; he was still condemning both imperialism and nationalist extremism and daring to correct the Soviets. In spite of enormous pressure, at his 1926 jubilee, Hrushevsky did not renounce the goals for which he had struggled throughout his life. He never became a servile Communist apparatchik, and he never became a 'nationalist' partisan of national sovereignty.

There are, of course, some important exceptions to this general pattern. In 1899, Hrushevsky was a central figure in the foundation of the Ukrainian National Democratic Party, and at that time he signed a declaration espousing national unity and full political independence. Thus, in spite of Hrushevsky's abhorrence of the term, the modern historian might well be tempted to call him a 'nationalist.' It must be remembered, however, that Franko, not Hrushevsky, was the real author of this document, and that neither man remained long within the National Democratic Party. Even more significant, perhaps, is the fact that this party was an Austrian-Galician institution, and that Hrushevsky was always very pessimistic about the future prospects of the Habsburg monarchy. The party program also contained a clause that stipulated cooperation with federalists within the Russian Empire.

The second major exception to the general pattern of populism and federalism occurs in 1918, when the Bolsheviks were attacking the Ukrainian People's Republic and the Central Rada was compelled to issue the Fourth Universal, which declared the full independence of the Ukrainian state. During this same period, Hrushevsky wrote a number of political tracts announcing the end of the 'Muscovite orientation' and a general renewal of the country. At this time, he admitted that his traditional Russian orientation had been a mistake, and he began to look elsewhere for political friends.

This exception, though occurring at a particularly critical moment, did not affect Hrushevsky's ultimate vision of some kind of future world federation of nations. Though the Russian orientation had to be abandoned, and independence was declared, Hrushevsky continued to talk and write about economic and political ties with other countries, especially with the new republics of other emerging peoples. This was the period of Hrushevsky's 'Black Sea orientation' and of his orientation towards the West.

In general, Hrushevsky was not greatly concerned about the possible tension between the ideal of the complete independence of a Ukrainian national state and the ideal of a regional, European, and ultimately world federation of free nations. He was working toward the enlightenment and strengthening of the Ukrainian people and he most certainly believed that there was so much to be done in this regard that the question of a conflict between the partisans of national statehood and the partisans of international federalism would be an unnecessary and a negative phenomenon.

Though he strenuously defended the dignity and national rights of the Ukrainian people, Hrushevsky was generally indifferent to the advantages of the legal concept of national sovereignty. In fact, for Hrushevsky, 'sovereignty' may well have been a term that had more disadvantages than advantages. Its frequent use could very well send otherwise indifferent neighbours into the enemy camp. Moreover, Hrushevsky was always most concerned with what he considered to be the real needs of the Ukrainian people, not with what he thought to be the legal fictions of international diplomacy. Thus, while he would often write about popular enlightenment, national development, autonomous statehood, and even the cultural, economic, and political independence of the Ukrainian people, Hrushevsky almost never used the term 'sovereignty.' His vision was of a popular-national and decentralized state that would naturally enter into political relations with other peoples. Unlike his Russian nationalist critics, who had labelled him as the 'heresiarch' of Mazepist separatism, or his Ukrainian nationalist critics, who thought him out of date and too idealistic, Hrushevsky had no use for what he considered to be a bureaucratic-legal national sovereignty based either upon monarchical-historical principles or, alternatively, upon extreme nationalism and 'blood and iron.' In the end, this master of Ukrainian historians always tied the full national development of his people to international human progress. In spite of his uncompromising commitment to the principles of nationality and popular rule, Hrushevsky was neither a narrow nationalist nor a demagogue. He was, rather, a humanist and a believer in the universal progress of all mankind.

The espousal of such lofty ideals did not mean that Hrushevsky was entirely without personal prejudices or political faults. On the religious and national levels, for example, his criticism of Catholicism focused solely on the conservative traditions of the Western Church and ignored all modernizing and ecumenical openings that took place during his lifetime. In fact, he always retained far more Eastern Orthodox preconceptions than he ever cared to admit. Moreover, his criticism of the Poles was strikingly inflexible, concentrating solely on the gentry traditions of Polish culture and ignoring the compromises occasionally promoted by more moderate Polish socialists or democrats with whom he should have been able to cooperate.

The same thing is true within the arena of power politics. At the dawn of the new century, Hrushevsky's rapid departure from the Ukrainian National Democratic Party indicated his lack of patience for party politics while, eighteen years later, his dogmatic parliamentarianism and insistent populism made inevitable a clash with the Central Rada's conservative German protectors.

Such weaknesses were also present on the personal level and did not make Hrushevsky an easy person to live with. He was, in fact, intolerant of criticism, very insensitive to the personal weaknesses of his closest colleagues, and jealous of contributions to the national cause in which he had taken no part. He was a demanding editor, a stingy publisher, a tortuous writer, and a boring lecturer. His manner was authoritarian and his personality abrasive. His academic and social peers could barely tolerate his nervous irritability. One after another, they abandoned his politics and fled his company. This was true for Shukhevych, Pavlyk, Hrinchenko, Iefremov, Tomashivsky, Franko, Vynnychenko, Doroshenko, Chykalenko, Shapoval, Hryhoriiv, Krymsky, and Ohloblyn. Hrushevsky may well have been a 'heresiarch' and a martyr for the national cause, but he was certainly no saint.

On the other hand, he had personal qualities that turned out to be of immense importance when put in the service of the national movement. He had a clear sense of mission and a self-confidence that inspired others with the justice and eventual victory of his cause. He was brave in the face of personal danger, as even his political rivals like Skoropadsky readily acknowledged. He was spontaneous, unassuming, and accessible, and always able to inspire the youth. His ability to work was simply phenomenal; his ability to organize legendary. It was not without reason that outsiders and enemies saw 'the magical hand of Hrushevsky' in almost every manifestation of Ukrainian national feeling to occur at the turn of the century. If we were to believe these distraught critics, Hrushevsky was the head Mazepist; Hrushevsky had invented the Ukrainian language; Hrushevsky had dreamed up the Ukrainian people; Hrushevsky had betrayed the Provisional Government and caused the downfall of Russia; Hrushevsky had drawn up a false scheme of Russian and Ukrainian history; Hrushevsky was the ringmaster of an international anti-Soviet conspiracy of academics, peasants, and soldiers, democrats, nationalists, communists, and fascists, Russians, Belorussians, Georgians, and Ukrainians. Hrushevsky had done it all.

In a distorted and warped sort of way, all these allegations were a grudging acknowledgment of the greatness of the conscientious historian who had done so much for the creation of the modern Ukrainian nation. They were matched by the awe in which his own people held him. In the eyes of his compatriots, Hrushevsky would always be the author of the monumental *History of Ukraine-Rus'*, the miracle-worker who had almost single-handedly organized an unoffical national Academy of Sciences in Lviv, and the first president of the short-lived but precedent-setting independent Ukrainian state. During his long and eventful life, Hrushevsky had often known criticism, failure, and tragedy, but he had also known praise, achievement, and victory. The criticism and the praise did not end with his mysterious death at Kislovodsk. They continue today, and the legend of the diminutive historian, whose real stature has hardly been grasped, lives on.

The Fate of the Hrushevsky Family

It seems that the Hrushevsky family did, in fact, receive the pension awarded it by the Soviet state. According to a memoir by Roman Chubaty, Mariia Sylvestrivna received the pension, and she also received a message of consolation from representatives sent by Stalin. Chubaty's 'Spohady pro Prof. Mykhaila Hrushevskoho, ta podorozh i vidvidyny Kyieva v 1941 r.' is summarized by Pavlo Klymenko, who wrote a conservative criticism of Hrushevsky, in 'Ne khovaty pravdy vid ukrainskoho narodu,' *Kanadiiskyi farmer* (Winnipeg) no. 47, 26 November 1966. Mariia Sylvestrivna and Kateryna seem to have lived in Kiev after Hrushevsky's death. Kateryna gave up her own scholarly work for the sake of publishing her father's numerous manuscripts. It was she who saw the fifth volume of the *History of Ukrainian Literature* and the tenth volume of the *History of Ukraine-Rus'* to press. She was invited to work in the Institute of Literature in the now reorganized Academy of Sciences of the Ukrainian SSR (AN URSR). But 1937 was a year of renewed terror (now generally referred to as the *Iezhovshchyna*, after another of Stalin's infamous police chiefs). Kateryna was arrested and all of the remaining Hrushevsky manuscripts were confiscated. Polonska-Vasylenko, 'Istorychna nauka ... ta dolia istorykiv,' p. 45, writes: 'In prison she endured unspeakable tortures. They carried her out from the interrogations unconscious and beaten. She was exiled to one of the most frightening concentration camps, Nogaiska Bukhta. In 1941, her mother, Mariia Sylvestrivna, received information that Kateryna was in Moscow and would soon arrive in Kiev. War broke off further communications. Information has been received by private means that both Hrushevsky women – mother and daughter – died in 1953. We do not have exact information whether they lived together or lived apart from each other at the time ... According to rumours current in the USA, it might be concluded that K.M. Hrushevska was accused by the NKVD of "espionage" on behalf of, of all countries, Japan.' Also see Marta Kalytovska, 'Pamiati Marii i Katri Hrushev-skykh,' *Ukrainska literaturna hazeta* (Munich), no. 5, November 1955.

Hrushevsky's brother, Oleksander Serhiiovych, was arrested at the same time as was Kateryna. He was sent to a camp in the Urals. Thus after 1937, of the Hrushevsky family, only three women, Mariia Sylvestrivna, H.S. Shamrai, (the sister of the Hrushevskys), and Oleksander's wife, remained in Kiev. See Polonska-Vasylenko, *Ukrainska akademiia nauk,* II, 75, and also her 'Svitlii pamiati Marii ta Kateryny Hrushevskykh,' *Nashe zhyttia*, no. 4 (Philadelphia, 1956), 9–10.

The Fate of Hrushevsky's School and of His Colleagues from the Ukrainian Academy (Some Examples)

Of Hrushevsky's closest collaborators, none survived the purges of the 1930s. Almost all suffered either exile, prison, or death. (See the lists compiled by Polonska-Vasylenko, 'Istorychna nauka ... ta dolia istorykiv,' pp. 63–9.) About most of them, very little is known; about others more. F. Ia. Savchenko (1892–?) seems to have been fairly typical. After the revolution, he had lived in Paris, where he was the head of the Ukrainian Society and also worked in the fields of West European literature and history. (He discovered some previously unknown Bossuet manuscripts.) He was active in both cultural life and in émigré politics and under Hrushevsky's influence cooperated with the UPSR. In 1924, Hrushevsky made vigorous appeals to various Communist Party institutions in order to permit his return. After his return to Kiev in 1925, Savchenko became Hrushevsky's principal aide and his secretary. He helped in publishing matters, dealt with the State Publishing House in Kharkiv, and travelled to the capital of Soviet Ukraine on Hrushevsky's behalf. He was a member of many academic commissions, wrote numerous articles, and was the author of the masterly *Zaborona Ukrainstva v 1876* (Kiev, 1930; reprinted Munich–Cambridge, Mass., 1970). In 1934, Savchenko was arrested, and he disappeared forever into the Siberian Gulag. Soon afterward, his wife, who was related to Mariia Sylvestrivna, was also arrested. See Polonska-Vasylenko, 'Istorychna nauka ... ta dolia istorykiv,' pp. 31 and 68, and Omeljan Pritsak's brief biography in the introduction to the new edition of *Zaborona Ukrainstva*.

A similar profile can be sketched for Iosyf [Osyp] Hermaize (1892–?), who, in spite of his Marxism, was one of Hrushevsky's closest collaborators, and, according to a fellow prisoner, shared the historian's views about a 'popular-legal, non-dictatorial, independent Ukrainian State.' Hermaize's pioneering history of the RUP had come under severe attack at the First All-Union Conference of Marxist Historians, and in 1929 he was excluded from the ranks of the Society of

Marxist Historians. He was extremely popular among the university youth and, according to S. Pidhainy, a fellow historian and victim of the GPU, 'the student youth gathered about him and his seminar, and his extra-curricular student groups were, in fact, the organization of the SVU.' But then came the purges and the famous SVU trial. Some of these students were executed outright; others faced the tribunal. Pidhainy writes: 'With its tortures the GPU broke Hermaize and at the trial it was hard to recognize the one-time fiery and decisive anti-Bolshevik ideologue, the committed defender of the idea of Ukrainian democracy, the tribune and professor.' Hermaize was sentenced to eight years in the Solovki Islands penal colony, high in the Soviet Arctic. There he was put in the 'isolator,' as were Professor Slabchenko and some others. According to the testimony of another prisoner, he was still alive in 1937. His further fate is unknown. See the methodical and moving account of Semen Pidhainy, *Ukrainska inteligentsiia na Solovkakh*, pp. 64–6, and the biographical outline in the *Entsyklopediia ukrainoznavstva*, vol. VII (Paris–New York, 1973), 2684.

Though Ahatanhel Krymsky (1871– ?) was not, strictly speaking, a member of Hrushevsky's 'historical school,' his later career is worthy of a brief discussion. After his 1928 forced retirement from the job of permanent secretary of the VUAN, Krymsky kept a very low profile and managed to escape arrest during the worst repressions of the 1930s. He lived in the uncertainties of official disfavour and saw his personal secretary arrested. In 1939, however, Stalin annexed the Western Ukrainian lands under Poland as a part of his bargain with Hitler, and felt it necessary to make some concessions to the newly united Ukrainians. Krymsky became the hero of the hour and, in January 1941, on the occasion of his seventieth birthday, received the 'Order of the Toiling Red Banner.' Before an overflowing hall, he piously kissed the medal, and in his speech exclaimed dramatically:

Oh Holy Party!	O Partiia Sviataia!
Whose heart does not pound	kakoe serdtse ne drozhit,
When thinking of you!	tebia vospominaia!

The double meaning was clear. Nevertheless, the next day, in the privacy of Polonska-Vasylenko's home, he explained: 'If I had said less, "our own people" would have believed in my sincerity, but in this way it is clear to all that it is not sincere, and "those people" in the same way will not believe it.' A few months later, Hitler invaded the Soviet Union and Krymsky's observation was proved correct. While the other academy personnel were evacuated to Ufa in Bashkiria, an NKVD car took the famous orientalist away and he was never heard from again. It appears that he was incarcerated or held in detention somewhere in Central Asia. In the 1960s, he was partially rehabilitated and a Soviet scholar described his fortune in the following terms: 'When the Great Patriotic War came A. Krymsky was old and weak. His fate was tragic. In the storm of the war he was taken deep into the interior. He died in Kazakhstan on 25 January 1942, and was buried there in a fraternal grave.' See O. Babyshkin, *Ahatanhel Krymsky* (Kiev, 1967), p. 30. More generally, see Polonska-Vasylenko, 'Ahatanhel Krymsky,' *passim*.

The Hrushevsky Legend in the Soviet Union 1934 to the Present

Between 1934 and 1939, the charges against Hrushevsky that had been voiced during his lifetime and had reached a kind of climax just before his death remained unchanged. Unlike Krymsky or Picheta, in 1939 Hrushevsky was not rehabilitated or used to advantage by the Soviet authorities. His reputation as an advocate of the unity of the western and the eastern parts of Ukraine was passed over in silence and he remained a posthumous *persona non grata* within all territory controlled by the Soviets. In a history textbook published in 1940, it was charged that Hrushevsky and other 'bourgeois nationalists' had tried to use the 'Leninist-Stalinist policy of Bolshevik Ukrainianization' to strengthen the position of the bourgeoisie, tear Ukraine out of the USSR, restore the rule of landlords and capitalists, and turn the country into a colony of the imperialist states. The book, *Istoriia Ukrainy: korotkyi narys* (Kiev, 1940), continues in a familiar vein: 'In 1931, a counter-revolutionary organization called the "Ukrainian National Centre" was discovered by the GUP. Hrushevsky stood at its head. Once he had returned to Soviet Ukraine "for honourable work," M. Hrushevsky came to an agreement with the Russian Kadets and SRs, Georgian Mensheviks, and Belorussian nationalists. They agreed upon common action to overthrow Soviet rule and transfer Ukraine into the bondage of the Polish gentry.' See the discussion and long quotations in Stakhiv, 'Deiaki materiialy pro bolshevytskyi nastup na Hrushevskoho,' pp. 182–6.

When the Germans launched their surprise attack against the Soviet Union, they did not make any significant concessions to Ukrainian national sentiment. This allowed the Soviet regime to pose as the sole defender of Ukrainian culture, and, during the 'Ufa period,' the surviving historians of the Ukrainian Academy were allowed some room for the expression of patriotic feelings. The Ufa academicians were, in fact, careful to adhere to the directives of the party, but they were somewhat less dogmatic in their periodization and they did not make a point of criticizing the work of Hrushevsky.

The Soviet victory and the annexation of Galicia and the other western Ukrainian lands changed all of this. During the summer of 1946, party organs criticized the work of Krypiakevych, Korduba, and other Lviv professors – now Soviet citizens – who had once been students of Hrushevsky. Mykola Petrovsky, who was the most prominent historian of the Ufa period, was compelled to publish a self-criticism and demand the 'exposure' of Hrushevsky and his school. In the immediate aftermath of the war, he once again labelled Hrushevsky a Germanophile who had been an enemy of Russia. Moreover, Nikita S. Khrushchev, who was at that time first secretary of the CPbU, reported to Moscow that there had been 'attempts to revive the bourgeois-nationalist conceptions of the historian Hrushevsky and his school' (*Pravda*, 23 August 1946). A series of repressions followed and the attacks on the most prominent of Hrushevsky's Galician students, Professor Krypiakevych, continued until 1951. See Danylo Lobai, *Neperemozhna Ukraina* (Winnipeg, 1950), pp. 43–58, who gives long quotations from Khrushchev's speech and from various Soviet periodicals. Also see Jaroslaw Pelenski, 'Soviet Ukrainian Historiography after World War II,' *Jahrbücher für Geschichte Osteuropas*, XII, 3 (Munich, 1964), 376–8. On Krypiakevych, see Omeljan Pritsak, 'Ivan Krypiakevych (1886–1967),' *Ukrainskyi istoryk*, nos. 1–4 (1968), 82–6, and Volodymyr Kubiiovych, 'Moi pryiateli, spivrobitnyky, kolegy,' *Suchasnist*, no. 12, (Munich, 1983), 106–21, especially 119–21, who explains that Krypiakevych was planning on fleeing to the West upon the approach of the red army, but decided against doing so for family reasons.

The death of Stalin and Khrushchev's subsequent de-Stalinization campaign led to a certain amelioration of the conditions under which Soviet Ukrainian historians worked. In 1958, Krypiakevych was elected a full member of the Ukrainian Academy. New historical journals were founded and Soviet Ukrainian historiography, though still formally bound by the precepts of Marxist-Leninist 'science,' began to grow in volume and acquire a serious factual base. There was considerable interest in Hrushevsky among the young, and in the late 1950s and early 1960s, in spite of three decades of negative propaganda, every spring saw fresh white chrysanthemums placed on his grave. See *Suchasnist*, no. 9 (Munich, 1980), 42.

Nevertheless, Hrushevsky remained a target of official criticism and could only be cited as an authority by Russian authors who could not be accused of Ukrainian nationalism. In 1963, an anti-Semitic booklet, put out by a prominent Ukrainian publishing house on orders from Moscow, ridiculed Hrushevsky's positive reputation among Ukrainian Jewry and tried to create hostility between Ukrainians and Jews. See the caricature of Hrushevsky as Moses pulling the Jew by the nose through the desert, in T.K. Krychko, *Iudaizm bez prykras* (Kiev, 1963); reprinted and analysed in John Kolasky, *Two Years in Soviet Ukraine* (Toronto, 1970), pp.

98–103, especially p. 100. Hrushevsky remained a taboo subject and, in Ukrainian-language publications, it was necessary to refer to him always as the 'inveterate enemy of the Ukrainian people' (ibid., p. 149).

It was only in 1966, on the occasion of the hundredth anniversary of Hrushevsky's birth, that there was a serious attempt to change this situation. In that year, Ivan Boiko and Ievhen Kyryliuk published a long article devoted to Hrushevsky in the cultural newspaper *Literaturna Ukraina* (Kiev), no. 77 (2361), 30 September 1966. The article had a cautiously positive tone and argued in favour of the use of factual materials from Hrushevsky's works. Simultaneously, F.P. Shevchenko, the principal editor of Kiev's *Ukrainskyi istorychnyi zhurnal*, published an article in this periodical (no. 11, 1966), which tried to show that Hrushevsky stood on the left wing of UPSR and had returned to Soviet Ukraine, not as an enemy who wished to organize an insurrection, but rather as a sensible man who realized the enormous importance that Soviet rule had for the Ukrainian population whom he wished to serve. (Shevchenko intended to discuss Hrushevsky's contributions to Soviet Ukrainian historigraphy in a following issue of the same publication.) At this same time, the Warsaw-based *Ukrainskyi kalendar*, which was the only Ukrainian-language almanac allowed by the government of the People's Republic of Poland, published a brief biographical commemorative article on Hrushevsky and quoted the *Bolshaia sovietskaia entsiklopediia*, vol. XIX (Moscow, 1930), and several prominent Polish Scholars, including A. Brückner, M. Jakobiec, and Z. Wójcik, on the importance and quality of Hrushevsky's work. See A.V., 'Mykhailo Hrushevsky (29.IX.1866–24.XI.1934), '*Ukrainskyi kalendar* (Warsaw, 1966), pp. 152–3. A similar article also appeared in Czechoslovakia, where the Ukrainian minority in Eastern Slovakia had somewhat more cultural autonomy than did the community in Poland. Accordingly, in addition to a factual biographical outline, the Ukrainians of Czechoslovakia saw the publication of a brief memoir by a Czech scholar who had corresponded with Hrushevsky in the 1920s. This article called Hrushevsky 'one of the greatest figures not only of Ukrainian, but of world scholarship.' See F. Tikhyi, 'Ukrainskyi istoryk ta Chekhy,' *Druzhno vpered*, no. 10 (Bratislava, 1966), 8. Meanwhile, the literary review *Duklia*, which was published in Priashiv (Prešov) and was the most prestigious voice of the Ukrainian intelligentsia in Eastern Slovakia, called for the rehabilitation of a whole series of Ukrainian personalities who had suffered disgrace during the Stalin purges, and managed to print a cautious article on Hrushevsky himself. See I. Shelepets' and I. Bacha, 'Nevzhe zabudetsia (Do 100 – richchia z dnia narodzhennia M. Hrushevskoho),' *Duklia*, no. 4 (Priashiv, 1966), 56–7. It was rumoured that the historians in Kiev were even preparing a new and carefully selected edition of Hrushevsky's *Collected Works*.

This general effort to rehabilitate Hrushevsky did not pass unnoticed by Ukrainian scholars living in the West. As early as 1964, Jaroslaw Pelenski ('Soviet Ukrainian Historiography,' p. 414) had noticed a slight amelioration in the previously virulent Soviet invectives against Hrushevsky. In 1966, Lubomyr Wynar noted the appearance of the articles in *Ukrainskyi istorychnyi zhurnal* and *Literaturna Ukraina*, criticized Shevchenko's presentation of Hrushevsky's supposedly positive attitude toward Engels's anthropology, and complained that these two articles were a very meagre tribute to so great a scholar. See the notes in *Ukrainskyi istoryk*, nos. 3–4 (1966), 121, and nos. 1–2 (1967), 124. Panas Fedenko, a veteran of the socialist movement living in West Germany, also noted the efforts at rehabilitation, but thought that if Moscow would not even allow the rehabilitation of a Communist novelist like Khvylovy, who had only dreamed about an independent socialist Ukraine, then there was no way that it would ever allow the rehabilitation of the historian who had actually presided over the creation of such a state and had urged his people to defend it against Russian aggression. See P. Fedenko, 'M. Hrushevsky v nautsi i polytytsi,' pp. 12–13.

Events proved Fedenko right. Unlike the pre-revolutionary Russian historians Solovev and Kliuchevsky, whose politics were much more conservative than those of their discomforting Ukrainian critic, Hrushevsky was not rehabilitated and his works were never reprinted. In fact, Shevchenko seems to have been severely reprimanded for his efforts on Hrushevsky's behalf. His plans for the publication of further materials on Hrushevsky were not carried out and in 1972 he lost his influential position as chief editor of *Ukrainskyi istorychnyi zhurnal*. Moreover, by 1972, the first secretary of the CPU, Petro Shelest – the man who is generally assumed to have been the protector of the fragile Ukrainian cultural flowering of the 1960s – was dismissed from his post, and a series of purges and arrests occurred throughout the Ukrainian Republic. Several Ukrainian historical periodicals – including *Istorychni dzherela ta ikh vykorystannia* (Kiev, 1964–72), and *Istoriohrafichni doslidzhennia v ukrainskii RSR* (Kiev, 1968–72) – were closed down, and dreary articles on the history of the party filled the pages of the surviving *Ukrainskyi istorychnyi zhurnal*. This situation continued through the early 1980s. On the fall of Shelest and its consequences see, for example, Y. Bilinsky, 'Mykola Skrypnyk and Petro Shelest: An Essay on the Persistence and Limits of Ukrainian National Communism,' in *Soviet Nationality Policies and Practices*, ed. J. Azrael (New York, 1978), 105–43, who gives further references.

In spite of the repressions of the early 1970s, there are indications that the Ukrainian intelligentsia has still not forgotten its greatest historian. Though official attitudes toward Hrushevsky remain unchanged, the appearance of a new unauthorized Ukrainian literature (*samvydav*) has provided a new forum in which the renowned scholar's historical role might be discussed. In fact, Hrushevsky's name is occasionally mentioned in this literature, and, in one of the most significant documents to find its way to the outside world, the literary critic and historian Iurii Badzo speaks out against the automatic labelling of any Ukrainian sentiment as 'Ukrainian bourgeois nationalism' (UBN, as he prefers to abbreviate this magic formula of the authorities). He also speaks out against the irresponsible labelling of Hrushevsky as an enemy of the Ukrainian and Russian peoples. 'At the end of the nineteenth century and the beginning of the twentieth century,' concludes Badzo, 'our great historian M.S. Hrushevsky did very much for Russian-Ukrainian mutual understanding.' It is almost certain that other manuscripts with similar conclusions lie unpublished among the papers of contemporary Soviet Ukrainian intellectuals. Written 'for the drawer,' as they say, any such papers will most certainly be made public upon a change in the rules of censorship. The Western scholar must patiently await such a development before any true history of 'the Hrushevsky legend in the Soviet Union' can be written. For Iurii Badzo's comment on Hrushevsky, see his 'Znyshchennia i rusyfikatsiia ukrainskoi istorychnoi nauky v sovietskii Ukraini: vidkrytyi lyst do rosiiskykh ta ukrainskykh istorykiv,' *Ukrainskyi istoryk*, nos. 1–4 (1981), 83–97, and nos. 1–2 (1982), 54–64, especially 62.

Bibliography

The following bibliography is selective, with an emphasis upon titles of interest to the student of Hrushevsky's public life. The lists below contain only titles that I have seen in the original. A few other titles of significance, which I have only seen in the form of excerpts, long quotations, or summaries, or which appeared too late to be used in the present work, are also included, but are marked with an asterisk (*). Additional information on publishing histories may be found in the notes. The bibliography is organized as follows:

I Reference Aids and Serials

A BIBLIOGRAPHIES

B JOURNALS AND NEWSPAPERS

C HISTORIOGRAPHICAL STUDIES

II Primary Materials

A ARCHIVAL MATERIALS

   1 / *Public Archives of Canada, National Ethnic Archives, Ottawa*

   2 / *Andrew Gregorovich Papers, Private Archives, Toronto*

   3 / *Author's Archive, Toronto*

B HRUSHEVSKY'S WRITINGS

   1 / *Autobiographical Essays*

   2 / *Histories*

   3 / *Other Works*

  i Collections of Articles

  ii Pamphlets, Essays, Letters, Speeches

C CORRESPONDENCE, DIARIES

D GOVERNMENT DOCUMENTS, MEMORANDA, OFFICIAL PUBLICATIONS

E CONTEMPORARY PRESS REPORTS AND POLEMICS

F MEMOIRS RELATING DIRECTLY TO HRUSHEVSKY

G ORAL HISTORY

III Secondary Materials

A COLLECTIVE WORKS, ENCYCLOPAEDIAS

B MONOGRAPHS, ARTICLES, MEMOIRS OF A GENERAL NATURE

I Reference Aids and Serials

A BIBLIOGRAPHIES

For a general discussion of the problems facing the Hrushevsky bibliographer, see L. Wynar's 'Potribna bibliohrafiia tvoriv Mykhaila Hrushevskoho,' *Suchasnist*, no. 7 (Munich, 1966), 228–35, which gives an evaluation of previous bibliographies. The most comprehensive Hrushevsky bibliography, which includes most works by him, and also a list of works about him, is Lubomyr Wynar, ed., *Mykhailo Hrushevs'kyi 1866–1934: Bibliographic Sources* (New York–Munich–Toronto: Ukrainian Historical Association, 1985). Earlier bibliographies of Hrushevsky's works compiled by I.E. Levytsky (1906) and D. Balyka (1929) are reprinted in the Wynar compendium. Also see N. Polonska-Vasylenko, 'Istorychna nauka ... ta dolia istorykiv.' (Full reference below.)

On Franko, see M.O. Moroz, *Ivan Franko: bibliohrafiia tvoriv 1874–1964* (Kiev, 1966). On the Ukrainian movement on the eve of and during the revolution, see Oleh and Olexandra Pidhainy, *The Ukrainian Republic in the Great East European Revolution*, vol. VI in 2 parts (Toronto–New York, 1971–5). Part I deals with the pre-revolutionary era and part II deals with the period from 1917 to 1920.

B FREQUENTLY CITED JOURNALS AND NEWSPAPERS

Note: Abbreviations are given in square brackets.

Dilo	(Lviv, 1880–1939). Organ of the 'populists' or *narodovtsi*, and then of the Ukrainian National Democratic Party.
*Kievlianin	(Kiev, 1864–1919). Monarchist paper closely affiliated with the Russian Nationalist Club.
[*LNV*]	*Literaturno-naukovyi vistnyk* (Lviv–Kiev, 1898–).
Rech	(Saint Petersburg, 1906–14; Petrograd, 1914–17). Organ of the Kadet Party.
Vilna Ukraina	(Detroit–New York, 1953–). A democratic socialist Ukrainian-language quarterly.
Ukrainskyi istoryk	(Munich–New York–Toronto, 1963–).
[*ZNTSh*]	*Zapysky Naukovoho Tovarystva im. Shevchenka* (Lviv, 1892–). After 1945, further volumes have appeared in Munich, Paris, and New York.
[*ZUNT*]	*Zapysky Ukrainskoho Naukovoho Tovarystva* (Kiev, 1908–14).

C HISTORIOGRAPHICAL STUDIES

Budurovych, B. 'Mykhailo Hrushevsky v otsintsi zakhidno-evropeiskoi i amerykanskoi istoriohrafii,' *Vyzvolnyi shliakh*, xx (London, 1967), 171–81.

Doroshenko, Dmytro 'A Survey of Ukrainian Historiography,' *Annals of the Ukrainian Academy of Arts and Sciences in the US*, v–vi (New York, 1957), 13–286.

Enteen, G. *The Soviet Scholar Bureaucrat: M.N. Pokrovsky and the Society of Marxist Historians* (Philadelphia, 1978).

Epstein, T. 'Die marxistische Geschichtswissenschaft in der Sowjetunion seit 1927,' *Jahrbücher für Kultur und Geschichte der Slaven*, vi (Breslau, 1930) 78–203.

Grothusen, K. *Die historische Rechtsschule Russlands* (Giessen, 1962). Thorough treatment of Hrushevsky's scholarly opponents.

– 'Die russische Geschichtswissenschaft des 19 Jahrhunderts als Forschungsaufgabe,' *Jahrbücher für Geschichte Osteuropas*, viii (Munich, 1960), 32–61.

Hermaize, [Iosef] Osyp 'Die ukrainische Geschichtswissenschaft in der USSR,' *Slavische Rundschau*, no. 1 (Prague, 1929), 363–6.

Krupnytsky, Borys 'M. Hrushevsky i ioho istorychna pratsia,' in *Istoriia Ukrainy-Rusy*, I, 1–29. (See 'Hrushevsky's writings' II, B, 2 below.)

– *Ukrainska istorychna nauka pid sovietamy* (Munich, 1957).

– 'Die archaographische Tätigkeit M. Hruševskyijs,' *Jahrbücher für Kultur und Geschichte der Slaven*, xi (Breslau, 1935), 610–21.

– 'Die ukrainische Geschichtswissenschaft in der Sowjetunion 1921–1941,' *Jahrbücher für die Geschichte Osteuropas*, nos. 2–4 (Breslau, 1941), 125–51.

Mazour, A. *The Writing of History in the Soviet Union* (Stanford, 1971).

Oberländer, E. *Sowjetpatriotismus und Geschichte* (Cologne, 1967). Deals with events after 1934.

Ohloblyn, Oleksander 'Pro deiaki zahubleni pratsi i vydannia Vse-ukrainskoi Akademii Nauk u Kyievi,' *Naukovyi zbirnyk II, Ukrainska Vilna Akademiia Nauk u SShA* (New York, 1953), pp. 196–8.

– 'Ukrainian Historiography 1917–1956,' *Annals of the Ukrainian Academy of Arts and Sciences in the US*, v–vi (New York, 1957), 307–436.

Pelenski, Jaroslaw 'Soviet Ukrainian Historiography after World War II,' *Jahrbücher für Geschichte Osteuropas*, xii, 3 (Munich, 1964), 375–418.

Polonska-Vasylenko, N. *Two Conceptions of the History of Ukraine and Russia* (London, 1968).

– 'Istorychna nauka v Ukraini za sovietskoi doby ta dolia istorykiv,' *Zbirnyk na poshanu ukrainskykh uchenykh znyshchenykh bolshevytskoiu Moskvoiu*, ZNTSh, CLXXIII (Paris, 1962), pp. 7–110.

Vernadsky, George, *Russian Historiography: A History* (Belmont, Mass., 1978).

II Primary Materials

A ARCHIVAL MATERIALS

Note: The principal collections of unpublished materials by and about Hrushevsky are located in the Soviet Union. In 1981, I visited Soviet Ukraine in the hope of using materials stored in the Central State Historical Archive of the Ukrainian SSR, Kiev, but found this to be impossible. In the West, archival materials on Hrushevsky are very scattered and deal principally with the period from 1919 to 1923, when Hrushevsky lived in emigration. A few such collections of archival matter were used in the present study.

1 / *Public Archives of Canada, National Ethnic Archives, Ottawa*

Julian Stechishin Collection, uncatalogued, containing Stechishin's book-length essay 'Pohliad Kanadiiskoho Ukraintsia na Kontroversiiu pro Hrushevskoho.' 273 pp. Written c. 1965.

Olha Woycenko Collection, vol. XII, containing Hrushevsky's correspondence with *Ukrainskyi holos* of Winnipeg, Canada, 1919–23, a large manuscript collection of his circular letters to the Ukrainians of North America, report of the famine relief committee (1922), and secret letter on aid for the Ukrainian Autocephalous Orthodox Church (1922).

Andrii Zhuk Collection, vol. XV, file 24, containing two versions of Zhuk's essay 'Prof. M. Hrushevsky i Soiuz Vyzvolennia Ukrainy v rokakh pershoi svitovoi viiny,' and two postcards (one dated 1923, and the other undated) from Hrushevsky to Zhuk.

2 / *Andrew Gregorovich Papers, Private Archive, Toronto*

Letters from Hrushevsky to A. Gregorovich of Smoky Lake, Alberta, dated 27 March 1920 to 15 December 1923.

Newspaper clippings, leaflets, and correspondence concerning Hrushevsky.

3 / *Author's Archive, Toronto*

Stakhiv, Matvii 'Concerning the Author of this work [i.e. *The History of Ukraine-Rus'* by] Mykhailo Hrushevsky,' ed. Paul Yuzyk, 119 pp. This essay was written for the NTSh as an introduction to its planned English language edition of Hrushevsky's multi-volume *History of Ukraine-Rus'*.

Correspondence with Ivan L. Rudnytsky, H. Seton-Watson, Lubomyr Wynar, and others.

B HRUSHEVSKY'S WRITINGS

1 / *Autobiographical Essays*

001 [*Avtobiohrafiia-1906*] *Avtobiohrafiia* (Lviv, 1906; reprinted with an afterword by Andrew Gregorovich, Toronto, 1965).

002 [*Avtobiohrafiia–1926*] *Avtobiohrafiia* (Kiev, 1926). This work is reprinted with notes by L. Wynar in *Ukrainskyi istoryk*, nos. 1–4 (1979), 79–87, and nos. 1–4 (1980), 71–88. It is also reprinted together with notes, an analytic essay by Wynar, and other materials under the title *Avtobiohrafiia Mykhaila Hrushevskoho z 1926 roku* (New York–Munich–Toronto, 1981). All references in the present work are to the *Ukrainskyi istoryk* edition.

003 [*Avtobiohrafiia–1914–1919*] 'Z zhyttia prof. M. Hrushevskoho,' *Ukrainskyi holos* (Winnipeg), no. 16, 21 April 1920; reprinted in *Ukrainskyi istoryk*, nos. 1–2 (1966), 98–101.

004 'Iak ia buv kolys beletrystom,' preface to *Pid zoriamy*; reprinted in Hrushevsky's *Vybrani pratsi*, ed. M. Halii, pp. 170–7, in *Ukrainskyi istoryk*, nos. 1–4 (1980), 89–94, and in *Avtobiohrafiia Mykhaila Hrushevskoho z 1926 roku*, pp. 42–7. All references in the present work are to the Halii edition.

005 'Iak mene sprovadzheno do Lvova. Lyst do Khv. Redaktsii *Dila*,' *Dilo*, no. 137, 1898; reprinted in *Ukrainskyi istoryk*, nos. 1–4 (1984), 230–7.

2 / *Histories*

006 *Istoriia Ukrainy-Rusy*, 10 vols. (Lviv–Kiev, 1898–1936; reprinted New York, 1954–8). The New York edition is reprinted from the third revised edition of vol. I (Kiev, 1913), the second revised edition of vols. II–IV (Lviv–Kiev, 1905–7), and the first edition of the remaining volumes.

007 *Istoriia ukrainskoi literatury*, 5 vols. (Vienna–Kiev, 1923–7; reprinted New York, 1959–60.)

008 *Iliustrovana istoriia Ukrainy* (Kiev–Lviv, 1911; reprinted Winnipeg, 1919?).

009 *A History of Ukraine* (New Haven, 1941). This a translation of the preceding entry.

010 *Ocherk istorii ukrainskogo naroda* (Saint Petersburg, 1912).

011 *The Historical Evolution of the Ukrainian Problem* (London, 1915; reprinted Cleveland: John T. Zubal, 1981).

012 *Ocherk istorii kievskoi zemli ot smerti Iaroslava do kontsa XIV veka* (Kiev, 1891).

013 *Pereiaslavska umova Ukrainy z Moskvoiu 1965 roku* (Kiev, 1917).

014 *Pro batka kozatskoho Bohdana Khmelnytskoho* (Kiev, 1909; reprinted New York, 1918).

015 *Kulturno-natsionalnyi rukh na Ukraini XVI–XVIIv.* (Kiev–Lviv, 1912).

015a *Pro stari chasy na Ukraini. Korotka istoriia Ukrainy*, 6th edition (1919). The title page states that this book was printed in Kiev, but it actually appeared in Vienna.

016 'Hromadskyi rukh na Ukraini-Rusy v xiii vitsi,' *ZNTSh*, I (1892), 1–28.

017 'Iuzhnorusskie gospodarskie zamki v polovine xvi veka,' *Universitetskie izvestiia*, no. 2 (Kiev, 1890), 1–33.

018 'Vstupnyi vyklad z davnoi istorii Rusy vyholoshenyi u lvivskim universyteti 30 veresnia 1894,' *ZNTSh*, iv (1894), 140–50.

019 'Zvychaina skhema "russkoi" istorii i sprava ratsionalnoho ukladu istorii skhidnoho Slovianstva,' in *Stati po slavianovedeniiu*, part 1, ed. V.I. Lamansky (Saint Petersburg, 1904), pp. 298–304; reprinted by Andrew Gregorovich, n.p., n.d.

020 *The Traditional Scheme of 'Russian' History and the Problem of a Rational Organization of the History of the East Slavs*, ed. and trans. A. Gregorovich (Winnipeg, 1965).

021 *'Spirni pytannia staroruskoi etnografii,' in *Stati po slavianovedeniiu*, and separately (Saint Petersburg, 1904).

022 'Some Debatable Questions in Old Russian Ethnography,' in *On the Historical Beginnings of Eastern Slavic Europe*, ed. and trans. Nicholas Chirovsky (New York: Shevchenko Scientific Society, 1976), pp. 13–38.

023 *'Etnografichni katagorii i kulturno-arkheologichni typy v suchasnykh studyiakh skhidnoi Evropy,' in *Stati po slavianovedeniiu*, and separately (Saint Petersburg, 1904).

024 'Ethnographic Catagories and Cultural-Archaeological Groups in Contemporary Studies of Eastern Europe,' in *On the Historical Beginnings of Eastern Slavic Europe*, pp. 39–52.

025 'Samovidets ruiny i ego pozdneishie otrazheniia,' *Trudy instituta slavianovedeniia AN SSSR*, no. 1 (Moscow, 1932).

026 'M.P. Drahomanov,' *Encyclopedia of the Social Sciences*, vol. v (New York, 1931), 233.

3 / Other Works

i Collections of Articles

027 *Pid zoriamy* (Kiev, 1928).

028 *Z bizhuchoi khvyli: stati i zamitky na temu dnia 1905–1906* (Kiev, 1906).

029 *Osvobozhdenie Rossii i Ukrainskii Vopros* (Saint Petersburg, 1907).

030 *Ukrainskii Vopros* (Saint Petersburg, 1907).

031 *Nasha polityka* (Lviv, 1911).

032 *Pro ukrainsku movu i ukrainsku shkolu* (Kiev, 1912).

033 *Z polituchnoho zhytia staroi Ukrainy: rozvidky stati promovy* (Kiev, 1917).

034 *Vilna Ukraina* (Kiev, 1917; reprinted New York, 1918).

035 *Na porozi novoi Ukrainy* (Kiev, 1918).

036 *Vybrani pratsi*, ed. M. Halii (New York, 1960).

ii Pamphlets, Essays, Letters, Speeches

037 'Bekh al-Dzhugur,' in *Pid zoriamy*, pp. 21–38.

038 'Ukrainska partiia sotsiialistiv-revoliutsioneriv ta ii zavdannia,' *Boritesia-poborete*, no. 1 (Vienna, 1920), 1–54.

039 'Z sotsiialno-natsionalnykh kontseptsii Antonovycha,' *Ukraina*, no. 5 (Kiev, 1928), 3–16. Reprinted in *Ukrainskyi Istoryk*, nos. 1–4 (1984), 200–18.

040 'Volodymyr Antonovych: osnovni idei ioho tvorchosty i diialnosty,' *ZUNT*, no. 3 (1909), 5–13. Reprinted in *Ukrainskyi Istoryk*, nos. 1–4 (1984), 193–9.

041 'Apostolovi pratsi,' *Ukraina*, no. 6 (Kiev, 1926), 3–20.

042 'Dlia iuvileiu Ivana Kotliarevskoho,' *ZNTSh*, II (1893), 146–61.

043 *Iz polsko-ukrainskikh otnoshenii Galitsii* (Saint Petersburg, 1907).

044 'Vstupne slovo,' *Peterburska Akademiia Nauk v spravi znesenia zaborony ukrainskoho slova* (Lviv, 1905; reprinted Scranton, Pa., 1916, and also in Munich, 1976).

045 'Sviate Pysmo,' *LNV*, I (1905), 96.

046 'Sviate Pysmo na ukrainskoi movi,' *LNV*, I (1905), 201.

047 'Ukrainstvo i pytannia dnia v Rosii,' in *Z bizhuchoi khvyli*, pp. 5–15. Very important.

048 'Na konstytutsionnyia temy,' in *Osvobozhdenie Rossii i Ukrainskii Vopros*, pp. 121–31.

049 'Na ruinakh,' in *Z bizhuchoi khvyli*, pp. 33–43.

050 'Pershi kroky,' in *Z bizhuchoi khvyli*, pp. 46–53.

051 'Bezhluzda natsionalna polityka Rosii,' *Dilo*, no. 100, 18 May 1905.

052 'U ukrainskykh posliv rosyiskoi dumy,' in *Z bizhuchoi khvyli*, pp. 79–84.

053 'Z derzhavnoi dumy,' in *Z bizhuchoi khvyli*, pp. 85–92.

054 'Vopros dnia (Agrarnyia perspektivy),' *Osvobozhdenie Rossii i Ukrainskii Vopros*, pp. 141–5.

055 'Natsionalnye momenty v agrarnom voprose,' in *Osvobozhdenie Rossii i Ukrainskii Vopros*, pp. 141–5.

056 'Konets getto!' in *Osvobozhdenie Rossii i Ukrainskii Vopros*, pp. 146–8.

057 'Duma i natsionalne pytannie,' in *Z bizhuchoi khvyli*, pp. 93–9.

058 'Natsionalnyi vopros i avtonomiia,' in *Osvobozhdenie Rossii i Ukrainskii Vopros*, pp. 68–80.

059 'Persha richnytsia rosyiskoi konstytutsii,' in *Z bizhuchoi khvyli*, pp. 112–16.

060 'Pislia dumy,' in *Z bizhuchoi khvyli*, pp. 106–11.

061 'Halychyna i Ukraina,' in *Z bizhuchoi khvyli*, pp. 117–26.

062 'Do nashykh chytachiv v Rosii,' *LNV*, VII (1907), 1–6.

063 *Vopros ob ukrainskikh kafedrakh i nuzhdy ukrainskoi nauki* (Saint Petersburg, 1907).
064 'Na ukrainski temy: "O liubvi k otechestvu i narodnoi gordosti,"' *LNV*, VII (1907), 495–505; VIII (1907), 111–24.
065 'Na ukrainski temy: kriachut vorony … ' *LNV*, VII (1907), 318–29.
066 'Neduha d-ra Ivana Franka,' *LNV*, XLII (1908), 405–6.
067 'Na ukrainski temy: nedotsiniuvannie,' *LNV*, LV (1911), 81–8.
068 'Ukrainske Naukove Tovarystvo v Kyivi i ioho naukove vydavnytstvo,' *ZUNT*, I (1908), 4–5.
069 'Na ukrainski temy: hymn vdiachnosty,' *LNV*, L (1910), 46–51.
070 'Na ukrainski temy: v velykyi chetver,' *LNV*, L (1910), 337–41.
077 'Na ukrainski temy: fabrykatsiia separatyzma,' *LNV*, LIV (1911), 128–34.
078 'Na ukrainski temy: slovo na malodushnykh,' *LNV*, XLIX (1910), 330–4.
079 'Na ukrainski temy: hrikhy nashi,' *LNV*, VIII (1907), 324–30.
080 'Na ukrainski temy: hrim – ta ne z tuchi … ' *LNV*, IX (1907), 385–91.
081 'Na ukrainski temy: mazepynstvo i bohdanivstvo,' *LNV*, LVII (1912), 94–102.
082 'Antrakt,' *LNV*, XLI (1908), 116–21.
083 'Na ukrainski temy: ne pora,' *LNV*, XLII (1908), 130–40.
084 'Iuvylei Mykoly Hoholia,' *LNV*, XLV (1909), 606–10.
085 'Na ukrainski temy: za mist novorichnoi,' *LNV*, LIII (1911), 57–65.
086 'Na ukrainski temy: ische pro nashe kulturne zhytie,' *LNV*, LIII (1911), 392–403.
087 'Na ukrainski temy: po koshmari,' *LNV*, LXIV (1913), 268–71.
088 'Nad svizhoiu mohyloiu,' *LNV*, LI (1910), 157–9.
089 'Shcho zh dali,' *LNV*, XXIX (1905), 1–5.
090 'V spravi ruskykh shkil i ruskoho teatru,' *LNV*, XXIX (1905), 11–19.
091 'Het z rutenstvom!' *Dilo*, no. 129, 27 June 1907.
092 'Na ukrainski temy: "Konets rutenstva!"' *LNV*, XL (1907), 135–47.
093 'Kinets polskoi yntryhy,' *Dilo*, no. 131, 1908.
094 'Krov,' *LNV*, XLII (1908), 380–5.
095 'Na ukrainski temy: ukrainstvo i vseslovianstvo,' *LNV*, XLII (1908), 540–7.
096 'Na ukrainski temy: na novyi rik,' *LNV*, XLV, (1909), 115–26.
097 'Ukraine, Weisrussland, Litauen,' *Ukrainische Rundschau*, no. 2 (Vienna, 1909), 49–52.
098 'Na ukrainski temy: pokhorony unii,' *LNV*, LI (1910), 289–98.
099 'Na ukrainski temy: v slavianskykh obiimakh,' *LNV*, LVI (1911), 394–409.
100 'Realna polityka na halytskim grunti,' in *Nasha polityka*, pp. 40–57.
101 'Dva roky halytskoi polityky,' in *Nasha polityka*, pp. 17–39.
102 'Mali dila,' in *Nasha polityka*, pp. 58–70.
103 'Na ukrainski temy: vidluchenie Kholmshchyny,' *LNV*, LIX (1912), 3–12.
104 *'Nova Duma i Ukraintsi,' *Rada* (Kiev), no. 38, 1907.

105 'Na natsionalnyia temy: k vopros o natsionalno-territorialnoi avtonomii,' *Russkoe bogatstvo*, no. 1 (Saint Petersburg, 1913), 225–43.

106 *Ukrainstvo v Rossii: ego zaprosy i nuzhdy* (Saint Petersburg 1906). This is a reprint of the concluding chapter of his *Ocherk istorii ukrainskogo naroda*.

107 'Na ukrainski temy: ukrainska debata,' *LNV*, LXIII (1913), 153–61.

108 'Na ukrainski temy: nova khvylia,' *LNV*, LXV (1914), 22–30.

109 'Na ukrainski temy: siianie vitra,' *LNV*, LXV (1914), 24–31.

110 'Novye lozungi,' *Ukrainskaia zhizn*, no. 1 (Moscow, 1914), 5–10.

111 'Pislia balkanskoi viiny,' *LNV*, LXIV (1913), 321–32.

112 'Saraievska tragediia,' *LNV*, LXV (1914), 424–31.

113 'Vetkhii prakh,' *Ukrainskaia zhizn*, no. 10 (Moscow, 1915), 85–92; also in *Rech* (Saint Petersburg), no. 281, 1915.

114 'Neskolko slov ob ukrainstve,' *Rech* (Saint Petersburg), no. 156, 1916.

115 'V godovshchinu voiny,' *Ukrainskaia zhizn*, no. 7 (Moscow, 1915), 5–8.

116 'Novyi god,' *Ukrainskaia zhizn*, no. 1 (Moscow, 1916), 5–9.

117 'Edinstvo ili raspadenie?' in *Osvobozhdenie Rossii i Ukrainskii vopros*, pp. 55–67.

118 'Z nedavnoho mynuloho,' *Pysmo z Prosvity* (Lviv), nos. 7–8, 1922.

119 'Velyka khvylia,' in *Vybrani pratsi*, pp. 113–16.

120 *Khto taki Ukraintsi i choho vony khochut* (Kiev, 1917).

121 *Iakoi my khochemo avtonomii i federatsii* (Kiev, 1917).

122 'Povorotu nema,' in *Vybrani pratsi*, pp. 117–20.

123 'Vid slova do dila,' in *Vybrani pratsi*, pp. 121–5.

124 'Narodnostiam Ukrainy,' in *Vybrani pratsi*, pp. 126–9.

125 'Chy Ukraina tilky dlia Ukraintsiv?' in *Vybrani pratsi*, pp. 130–2.

126 **Ukraina i Rosiia* (Kiev, 1917).

127 **'Promova Prof. Hrushevskoho (na z'izdi narodiv v Kyievi),' Ukrainske slovo* (Lviv), no. 248, 1917.

128 'The Congress of the Allogenian [sic!] Peoples of Russia,' *Eastern Europe*, vol. I, no. 5 (Paris, 1919).

129 'Promova Hrushevskoho (20.XI.1917 pered oholoshenniam universalu tsentralnoi rady,' *Ukrainske slovo* (Lviv), no. 291, 1918.

130 'Na Ukraini ide pokhodom vorozhe viisko. Promova Prof. Hrushevskoho do vse-ukrainskoho z'izdu rad robitnychykh, selianskykh i soldatskykh deputativ,' *Dilo*, no. 307, 1917.

131 'Velykyi oboviazok,' in *Vybrani pratsi*, pp. 35–7.

132 'Ukrainska samostiinist i ii istorychna neobkhidnist,' in *Vybrani pratsi*, pp. 37–40.

133 'Promova pid tsentralnoiu radoiu na pokhoroni sichovykiv studentskoho kurenia 19 Bereznia 1918 roku,' in *Vilna Ukraina*, nos. 55–6 (1967), 16–17.

134 'Na perelomi,' in *Vybrani pratsi*, pp. 51–6.

135 'Ochyshchennia ohnem,' in *Vybrani pratsi*, pp. 40–3.

136 'Myr zemli nashii!' in *Vybrani pratsi*, pp. 47–8.

137 'Choho pryishly nimtsi na Ukrainu,' in *Vilna Ukraina*, no. 52 (1966), 27–8.

138 'Provorotu ne bude!' in *Vybrani pratsi*, pp. 49–50.

139 'Na perelomi,' in *Vybrani pratsi*, pp. 51–6.

140 'Kinets moskovskoi oriientatsii,' in *Vybrani pratsi*, pp. 57–60.

141 'Nasha zakhidnia oriientatsiia,' in *Vybrani pratsi*, pp. 61–4.

142 'Orientatsiia chornomorska,' in *Vybrani pratsi*, pp. 65–8.

143 'Novi perspektyvy,' in *Vybrani pratsi*, pp. 69–76.

144 'Kultura krasy i kultura zhyttia,' in *Vybrani pratsi*, pp. 77–83.

145 'Velyka Ukraina,' in *Vybrani pratsi*, pp. 84–9.

146 'Pidstavy velykoi Ukrainy,' *Vybrani pratsi*, pp. 90–4.

147 'Tryzub-ukrainskyi herb,' *Vilna Ukraina*, nos. 59–60 (1969), 91.

148 'Stara istoriia,' *Vilna Ukraina*, no. 57 (1968), 4–6.

149 *La lutte sociale et politique en Ukraine* 1917 1918 1919 (Prague, 1920).

150 'V pershii delegatsii ukrainskoi partii sotsiialistiv-revoliutioneriv,' in *Vybrani pratsi*, pp. 157–69.

151 :Lyst M. Hrushevskoho do Myroslava Sichynskoho z 1919 roku,' *Ukrainskyi istoryk*, nos. 1–3 (1978), 160–2.

152 'Lyst prof. Hrushevskoho do kanadskykh ukraintsiv,' *Ukrainskyi istoryk*, nos. 3–4 (1975), 73–7.

153 M. Antonvoych, ed., 'Lysty M. Hrushevskoho do T. Pochynka,' *Ukrainskyi istoryk*, no. 4 (1969); nos. 1–3 (1970), 168–83.

154 'Mizh Moskvoiu i Varshavoiu,' *Boritesia-poborete!*, no. 2 (Vienna, 1920), 1–18.

155 'Vidkrytyi lyst Mykh. Hrushevskoho, zakordonnoho deliegata UPSR holovi rady narodnikh komisariv ukrainskoi sotsiialistychnoi radianskoi respubliky Kh. G. Rakovskomy,' *Boritesia-poborete!*, no. 10 (Vienna, 1921), 1–8.

156 M. Antonvoych, ed., 'Lysty M. Hrushevskoho do E. Faryniaka,' *Ukrainskyi istoryk*, nos. 1–2 (1977), 118–31; nos. 3–4 (1977), 106–12.

157 'V shistdesiat chetverti shevchenkovi rokovyny,' *Ukraina*, no. 1 (Kiev, 1925), 1–5.

158 I. Borshchak, ed., 'Dva nevydani lysty M. Hrushevskoho,' *Soborna Ukraina* (Paris), April 1947, 37–8.

159 'Perspektyvy i vymohy ukrainskoi nauky,' *Ukraina*, no. 1 (Kiev, 1926), 3–15.

160 'Hanebnii pamiati,' *Ukraina*, no. 4 (Kiev, 1926), 46–57.

161 1926 Jubilee Speech, in *Vybrani pratsi*, pp. 225–35.

162 'Zvidomlenniia z uchasty v kvitnevii sesii akademii nauk URSR,' *Visti VUAN*, nos. 5–6 (Kiev, 1929), 20–3.

163 'Dopovid M. Hrushevskoho pro zasidannia soiuznoi akademii u Kvitni 1929 r.,' *Ukraina*, no. 34 (Kiev, 1929), 167–9.

C CORRESPONDENCE, DIARIES

Chykalenko, Ievhen *Shchodennyk (1907–1917)* (Lviv, 1931). Very important.
Doroshenko, Dmytro 'Lysty Dmytra Doroshenka do Viacheslava Lypynskoho,' *Viacheslav Lypynsky Arkhiv*, vol. VI, ed. I. Korovytsky (Philadelphia, 1973).
Franko, Ivan *Tvory v dvadtsiaty tomakh*, vol. XX (Kiev, 1956). Contains Franko's correspondence.
– *Literaturna spadshchyna Ivana Franka*, vol. I (Kiev, 1956).
– *Lystuvannia I. Franka i M. Drahomanova*, ed. M. Vozniak (Kiev, 1928).
Hryhoriiv, N. 'Lyst t. N.Ia. Hryhoryiva do t. P.D. Khrystiuka z pryvodu taktyky M.S. Hrushevskoho ta ynshykh chleniv b. zakord. delegatsii UPSR,' *Vilna spilka*, no. I (Lviv, 1921), 112–21.
Iefremov, Serhii 'Lysty S.O. Iefremova do Ie. Kh. Chykalenka,' ed. V. Miiakovsky, *Ukrainskyi istoryk*, nos. 3–4 (1975), 112–19.
Kobylianska, Olha *Tvory v piaty tomakh*, vol. V (Kiev, 1963). Contains her correspondence.
Kosach-Kryvuniuk, Olha *Lesia-Ukrainka: khronolohiia zhytiia i tvorchosty* (New York, 1970). Mostly correspondence.
Krymsky, Ahtanhel *Tvory v p'iaty tomakh*, vol. V, part I (Kiev, 1973). Contains Krymsky's letters.
Nechui-Levytsky, I.S. *Nechui-Levytsky, I.S. Zibrannia tvoriv u desiaty tomakh*, vol. X (Kiev, 1968). Contains his letters.
Shapoval, Mykyta *Shchodennyk*, 2 vols. (New York, 1958).
Vynnychenko, Volodymyr *Shchodennyk*, vol. I (Edmonton, 1980).

D GOVERNMENT DOCUMENTS, MEMORANDA, OFFICIAL PUBLICATIONS

*Antonovych, Marko 'Sprava Hrushevskoho,' *Ukrainskyi istoryk*, nos. 1–4 (1984), 262–7. Austrian government documents, 1914– .
Browder, R.P., and Alexander Kerensky *The Russian Provisional Government 1917 Documents*, vol. I (Stanford, 1961).
Franko, Ivan *Ivan Franko: dokumenty i materiialy* (Kiev, 1966).
Gerych, Iu. 'Do biohrafii M. Hrushevskoho,' *Ukrainskyi istoryk*, nos. 1–2 (1972), 66–84.
Hornykiewicz, Theophil *Ereignisse in der Ukraine 1914–1922*, vol. I (Philadelphia, 1966). A collection of Austrian documents.
Khrystiuk, Pavlo *Zamitky i materiialy do istorii ukrainskoi revoliutsii*, 4 vols. in I (New York, 1969). A basic collection of documents on the Ukrainian revolution compiled by a leading SR under the direction of Hrushevsky.

Visti VUAN za 1929 (Kiev).
Visti VUAN za 1934 (Kiev).
Zvidomlennia VUAN za 1924 (Kiev, 1925).

E CONTEMPORARY PRESS REPORTS AND POLEMICS

Baranovych, O. 'Kyivski zbirnyky istorii ... ' *Ukraina*, nos. 1–2 (Kiev, 1932), 182–9.
Doroshenko, Volodymyr *Ukrainstvo v Rosii* (Vienna, 1916).
Frankiewicz, Czeslaw [Dr Czef.] *Poglądy historyczne Prof. M. Hruszewskiego w kwestji ukrainskiej w świetle krytyki naukowej* (Lublin, 1916).
Franko, Ivan *Zibrannia tvoriv u piatdesiaty tomakh*, vol. xxvii (Kiev, 1980).
– 'Za chto starika obideli?' *LNV*, xiii (1901), 39–41.
– *Moloda Ukraina* (Lviv, 1912).
– 'Mykhailo Pavlyk: zamist iuvileinoi sylvetky,' in *Ivan Franko pro sotsiializm i marksysm* (New York, 1966) 191–233.
– *Beiträge zur Geschichte und Kultur der Ukraine*, ed. E. Winter (Berlin, 1963). Franko's German-language corpus.
Iavorsky, Matvii 'De shcho pro "krytychnu krytyku" pro "obiektyvnu" historiiu ta schche i pro babysynu spidnytsiu,' *Chervonyi shliakh*, no. 3 (Kharkiv, 1924), 167–82.
– 'Doklad o rabote marksistskikh istoricheskikh uchrezhdenii na Ukraine,' in *Trudy pervoi vsesoiuznoi konferentsii istorikov-marksistov*, second edition, 2 vols. (Moscow, 1930), pp. 36–40.
– 'Sovremennye antimarksistskie techeniia v ukrainskoi istoricheskoi nauke,' in *Trudy*, i, 426–35.
Iefremov, Serhii, and H. Semeshko 'Prof. M. Hrushevsky,' *Kalendar Kanadyiskoho Rusyna na rik 1917* (Winnipeg).
Kulczycki, Ludwik *Ugoda polsko-ruska* (Lviv, 1912). The Ukrainian question as seen by a Polish socialist.
Lenin, V.I. 'Cadets on the Question of the Ukraine,' in *Collected Works*, vol. xix (Moscow, 1963), pp. 266–7.
– Marginalia on Hrushevsky's *Ukrainstvo v Rossii*, in *Leninskii sbornik*, vol. xxx (Moscow–Leningrad, 1937), 18, 25–6.
Levynsky, Volodymyr *Tsarska Rosiia i ukrainska sprava* (Montreal, 1917).
Lototsky, Oleksander [A. Bilousenko] 'Ukrainskie dni v Gosudarstvennoi Dumy,' *Ukrainskaia zhizn*, no. 3 (Moscow, 1914), 7–18.
Lozynsky, M. 'Mykhailo Hrushevsky,' *Dilo*, 28 June 1910.
Makovei, O. 'Iuvylei 25-litnoi literaturnoi diialnosty Ivana Franka,' *LNV*, iv (1898), 115ff.
Mohyliansky, M. '"Vseukrainskii" s"ezd studenchestva,' *Rech* (Saint Petersburg), no. 174, 29 June 1913.

- 'Vbyvstvo' *Chervonyi shliakh*, no. 1 (Kharkiv, 1926), 53–5.
Okynshevych, Lev 'Natsionalno-demokratychni kontseptsii istorii prava Ukrainy v pratsiakh M. Hrushevskoho,' *Ukraina*, nos. 1–2 (Kiev, 1932), 93–109.
Petliura, Symon 'Skorochene vykryvannia Ukrainstva panom Shchegolevym,' in *Symon Petliura: stati lysty dokumenty*, vol. II (New York, 1979), pp. 262–73.
Le 'Peuple Ukrainien' par un petit-Russien de Kief (Nancy, 1919).
Porsh, Mykola 'Pro "moderne moskvofilstvo" (z nahody broshury D. Dontsova *Moderne moskvofilstvo*),' *LNV*, LXIV (1913), 360–71.
Prykhylnyk 'Erupivtsiv' 'Ne kydaite biseru,' *LNV*, XXXII (1905), 61–5.
Richytsky, A. 'Iak Hrushevsky "vypravliaie" Engelsa,' *Chervonyi shliakh*, no. 3 (Kharkiv, 1924), 183–90.
Rubach, M.A. 'Federalisticheskie teorii v istorii Rossii,' in *Russkaia istoricheskaia literatura v klassovom osveshchenii*, 2 vols., ed. M.N. Pokrovsky (Moscow, 1930), II, 2–120.
- 'Burzhuazno-kurkulska natsionalistychna ideologiia pid mashkaroiu demokratii "Trudovoho narodu,"' *Chervonyi shliakh* (Kharkiv, 1932), nos. 5–6, 115–135, nos. 7–8, 118–26, nos. 11–12, 127–36.
Shapoval, Mykyta 'Narodnytstvo v ukr. vyzvolnomu rukhovi,' *Vilna spilka*, no. 3 (Prague, 1927–9), 95–128.
- 'Emigratsiia i Ukraina,' *Nova Ukraina*, nos. 4–6 (Prague, 1925), 1–17.
Shchegolev, S.N. *Ukrainskoe dvizhenie kak sovremennyi etap iuzhnorusskago separatizma* (Kiev, 1912). An important contemporary work known as a 'police handbook' on the Ukrainian movement.
Shumytsky, M. 'Ukrainskyi arkhitekturnyi styl ... ' *Iliustrovana Ukraina*, no. 8 (Lviv, 1913), 8–9.
Siropolko, S. 'Vidnovlena *Ukraina* ta ii vystup proty akad. M. Hrushevskoho,' *Tryzub*, no. 8 (Paris, 1933), 3–6.
Stalin, Joseph *Works*, vol. VIII (Moscow–Leningrad, 1954).
Steed, Henry Wickham *The Habsburg Monarchy* (London, 1913).
Svistun, F. 'Kto bolshii: M. Grushevsky ili A. Petrushevich?' *Galichanin* (Lviv), nos. 216–18 (1900).
Ukraine's Claim to Freedom, ed. E. Björkman *et al.* (New York, 1915).
Zatonsky, V.P. 'Promova narkoma osvity USRR Akad. V.P. Zatonskoho na pokhoronakh Akad. M.S. Hrushevskoho,' *Visti VUAN*, nos. 6–7 (Kiev, 1934), 36–9.

F MEMOIRS RELATING DIRECTLY TO HRUSHEVSKY

Bachynsky, L. 'Malyi spomyn,' *Zhinocha dolia*, nos. 15–16 (Kolomyia, 1935), 12–13.
Berehulka, A. 'Liutyi 1918 roku v Kyievi,' *Biuleten soiuzu buvshykh ukrainskykh voiakiv u Kanadi*, no. 10 (Toronto, 1962), 13–16.

Chubaty, Mykola 'Dodatkovi spomyny pro Mykhaila Hrushevskoho z 1912–1914 rokiv,' *Ukrainskyi istoryk*, nos. 3–4 (1975) 78–9.

Dubrovsky, V.V. 'Velykyi patriot: hromadska diialnist M. Hrushevskoho po povoroti v rad. Ukrainu,' *Na chuzhyni*, no. 1 (28) (Munich?, 1947), 5–7.

– 'M.S. Hrushevsky u Chernyhovi,' *Kalendar-Almanakh 'Vidrodzhennia'* (Buenos Aires, 1961), 99–119.

Hoetzsch, Otto 'Michael Hruševskyj,' *Zeitschrift für osteuropaische Geschichte*, IX (Berlin, 1935), 161–4.

Ilnytsky, A. 'Rozhin tsentralnoi rady,' *Vilna Ukraina*, no. 52 (1966), 24–6.

Ivchenko, L. 'Faktychni dovidky,' *Novi dni*, nos. 126–7 (Toronto, 1980), 21–4.

Kachura, S. 'Perebuvannia uriadu ukrainskoi respublyky v Sarnakh (spohady),' *Ukrainski visti* (Munich) no. 28 (1968), 3–7.

Kedrovsky, Volodymyr 'Povorot M.S. Hrushevskoho na Ukrainu,' *Vilna Ukraina*, no. 51 (1966), 65–6.

Korduba, M. 'Pryizd prof. M. Hrushevskoho do Lvova,' *Vistnyk Soiuza vyzvolenia Ukrainy*, no. 128 (Vienna, 1916), 795.

*Kostiuk Hryhorii, 'Triiumf: Iuvilei akad. M. Hrushevskoho 1926 roku (Urivok iz knyhy spohadiv),' *Novi dni*, nos. 413–14, (Toronto, 1984), 9–13, no. 415, 5–7.

Kovalevsky, Mykola 'Iak proholosheno IV universal: pamiat Mykhaila Hrushevskoho,' *Vilna Ukraina*, no. 52 (1966), 17–19.

Krychevska, Ievhenia 'Pozhezha budynku Mykhaila Hrushevskoho,' *Novi dni*, no. 105 (Toronto, 1958), 13–20.

Krypiakevych, Ivan *Mykhailo Hrushevsky: zhyttia i diialnist* (Lviv, 1935). A brief popular-style biography published upon Hrushevsky's death by the most celebrated of his students.

Marinen, M. 'Dvi zustrichi z Prof. Hrushevskym,' *Lysty do pryiateliv*, no. 4 (New York, 1960), 7–10.

Martos, B. 'M.S. Hrushevsky iakym ia ioho znav,' *Ukrainskyi istoryk*, nos. 1–2 (1966), 73–81.

*Mirshuk, Danylo 'Akademik Mykhailo Hrushevsky,' *Ukrainskyi holos* (Winnipeg) no. 9, 4 March 1985.

Polonska-Vasylenko, N. 'Z moikh spohadiv pro M. Hrushevskoho,' *Ukraina*, no. 9 (Paris, 1953), 744–7.

– 'Svitlii pamiati Marii ta Kateryny Hrushevskykh,' *Nashe zhyttia*, no. 4 (Philadelphia, 1956), 9–10.

Rakovsky, I. 'Prof. M. Hrushevsky u Lvovi,' *Almanakh UNS na 1952 rik* (Jersey City).

Sevriuk, O. 'Beresteiskyi myr: uryvky zi spomyniv,' in *Bereteistkyi Myr*, ed. I. Kedryn (Lviv–Kiev, 1928), pp. 143–66.

Shulhyn, Oleksander [Alexander Choulguine] 'Mykhailo Serhiiovych Hrushevsky: iak polityk i liudyna,' in *Zbirnyk na poshanu Oleskandra Shulhyna* (1889–1960), *ZNTSh*, vol. CLXXXVI (Paris–Munich, 1969), 143–55.

Stepanyshyna, O. [O.M.] 'Ostanni roky zhyttia Mykhaila Hrushevskoho,' *Nashi dni* (Lviv), no. 3 (1943), 4–5; reprinted in *Ukrainskyi istoryk*, nos. 1–4 (1981), 174–9.

Siry, Iuryi [Iuryi Tyshchenko] 'Veleten ukrainskoi nauky: urivok zi spohadiv pro M.S. Hrushevskoho,' *Ukraina*, no. 2 (Paris, 1949), 78–84.

Zerkal, Sava 'Do statti "Iak proholosheno IV universal,"' *Vilna Ukraina*, no. 54 (1967), 64.

G ORAL HISTORY

Interviews with

Marko Antonovych, son of Dmytro and grandson of Volodymyr Antonovych, Toronto, 16 and 17 April 1983. Concerning the Antonovych family and its relations with M. Hrushevsky; also concerning the relationship between Franko and Hrushevsky.

Vasyl Lev, active for many years in the *Naukove Tovarystvo im. Shevchenka* (NTSh), New York, March 1981. Concerning NTSh traditions and Hrushevsky's ideas about language.

Omeljan Pritsak, student of Ahatanhel Krymsky, Cambridge, Mass., March 1981. Concerning the relations between Krymsky and Hrushevsky, Hrushevsky's personality, and his ideas about history.

III Secondary Material

A COLLECTIVE WORKS, ENCYCLOPAEDIAS

Bolschewistische Wissenschaft und Kulturpolitik, ed. B. von Richthofen (Königsberg–Berlin, 1938).

Encyclopedia of Ukraine, vol. I (Toronto, 1984).

Entsyklopediia ukrainoznavstva: slovnykova chastyna, many volumes (Paris–New York, 1955–).

Mykhailo Hrushevsky u 110 rokovyny narodzhennia, *ZNTSh*, CXCVII, ed. M. Stakhiv (New York–Paris–Sydney–Toronto, 1978).

Radianska entsyklopediia istorii Ukrainy, 4 vols. (Kiev, 1969–72).

The Ukraine 1917–1921: A Study in Revolution, ed. T. Hunczak (Cambridge, Mass., 1977).

Ukrainska radianska entsyklopediia, second edition, many vols. (Kiev, 1978–).

Wasilewski, L., and others *Spohady, Pratsi Ukrainskoho Naukovoho Instytutu*, vol. VII (Warsaw, 1932).

Zbirnyk 'Ukrainskoi literaturnoi hazety' 1956 (Munich).

B MONOGRAPHS, ARTICLES, MEMOIRS OF A GENERAL NATURE

Anastas'in, D., and I. Voznesensky 'Nachalo trekh natsionalnykh akademii,' *Pamiat':
istoricheskii sbornik*, vol. V (Moscow–Paris, 1981–2), 165–225. A detailed and fairly
reliable *samizdat* essay later published in the West.

Andriievsky, V. *Z mynuloho*, vol. II (Berlin, 1923).

Andrusiak, Mykola [Nicholas] *Narysy z istorii halytskoho moskvofilstva* (Lviv, 1935).

– 'Dumky Hrushevskoho pro potrebu ukrainskoi armii,' *Litopys chervonoi kalyny*, VII
(Lviv, 1935), 7–8.

– 'Mykhailo Hrushevsky iak istoryk narodnyk i derzhavnyk,' in *Mykhailo Hrushevsky u
110 rokovyny narodzhennia*, pp. 7–20.

Antonovych, Marko 'Do vzaiemyn M.S. Hrushevskoho z S.O. Iefremovom,' *Ukrainskyi
istoryk*, nos. 1–2 (1975), 91–9.

– 'O. Konysky i M. Hrushevsky,' *Ukrainskyi istoryk*, nos. 1–4 (1984), 48–63.

Antonowytsch, Michael 'Das Schicksal der ukrainischen Gelehrten in der Sowjetukraine,' in *Bolschevistische Wissenschaft und Kulturpolitik*, pp. 45–8.

Babyshkin, Oleh *Ahatanhel Krymsky* (Kiev, 1967).

Bacha, Iuryi, and I. Shelepets 'Nevzhe zabudetsia?' *Duklia*, no. 4 (Priashiv, 1966), 56–7.

Bachynsky, P. *Panas Petrovych Liubchenko* (Kiev, 1970).

Barber, John *Soviet Historians in Crisis 1928–1932* (London, 1981).

Bass, I.I. *Ivan Franko Biohrafiia* (Kiev, 1966).

Bilas, L. 'Geschichtsphilosophische und ideologische Voraussetzungen der geschichtli-
chen und politischen Konzeption M. Hrušveskyjs,' *Jahrbücher für Geschichte Osteuropas*, IV (Munich, 1956), 262–92. Linguistic and content analysis of Hrushevsky's
major works.

Bohachevsky-Chomiak, M. 'The Directory of the Ukrainian National Republic,' in *The
Ukraine 1917–1912: A Study in Revolution*, pp. 82–103.

Bohatsky, Pavlo *Ukrainska khata ... spohady*, ed. Sava Zerkal (New York, 1955).

Boiko, Ivan, and Ievhen Kyryliuk 'Mykhailo Hrushevsky: z nahody 100-richchia vid dnia
narodzhennia,' *Literaturna Ukraina* (Kiev), no. 77, 30 September 1966.

Borowsky, Peter *Deutsche Ukrainepolitik 1918* (Lubeck–Hamburg, 1968).

Borshchak, I. [E. Borschak] 'Le movement national ukrainien au XIXe siècle,' *Le monde
slave*, no. 12 (Paris, 1930), 375–83.

– 'La paix ukrainienne de Brest-Litovsk,' *Le monde slave*, nos. 4–8 (Paris, 1929) II,
33–62, III, 63–84, 199–225.

– 'Mikhailo Hruševśkij (1866–1934),' *Le monde slave*, no. 1 (Paris, 1935), 12–35.

– 'Masaryk et l'Ukraine,' *Le monde slave*, no. 2 (Paris, 1930), 467–80.

Borys, Jurij *The Sovietization of Ukraine 1917–1923* (Edmonton, 1980).

Bykovsky, Lev *Vasyl Kuziv i Mykhailo Hrushevsky* (Winnipeg–Detroit, 1968).

Chirovsky, Nicholas *On the Historical Beginnings of Eastern Slavic Europe* (New York, 1976).

Chykalenko, Ie. *Uruvok z moikh spomyniv za 1917* (Prague, 1932).

– *Spohady (1861–1907)* (New York, 1955). Important.

Conquest, Robert *The Great Terror* (New York, 1973).

Czajkowski M. 'Volodymyr Vynnychenko and His Mission to Moscow and Kharkiv,' *Journal of Ukrainian Graduate Studies*, no. 5 (Toronto, 1978), 3–24.

Dibert, Vasyl 'Studentska demonstratsiia 1914 r. v Kyievi,' *Vilna Ukraina*, no. 45 (1965), 47–52.

Dmytryshyn, B. *Moscow and the Ukraine 1918–1953* (New York 1956).

Dombrovsky, Oleksander 'Do pytannia anhliiskoho perekladu istorii Ukrainy-Rusy M. Hrushevskoho,' *Ukrainskyi istoryk*, nos. 1–4 (1968), 138–41.

– 'Do pytannia ukrainskoi istorychnoi shkoly v diiaspori,' *Ukrainskyi istoryk*, no. 4 (1974), 74–84. A critique of the claim of O. Pritsak, who maintains that the Ukrainian institute at Harvard is the principal heir and successor to Hrushevsky's school of history. (See below.)

*Dontsov, Dmytro *Dukh nashoi davnyny* (Prague, 1944).

*– *Moderne moskvofilstvo* (Lviv, 1913).

Doroshenko, Dmytro *Istoriia Ukrainy 1917–1923*, 2 vols. (New York, 1954).

– *Moi spomyny pro davnie-mynule 1901–1914* (Winnipeg, 1949).

– *Moi spomyny pro nedavne-mynule (1914–1920)* (Munich, 1969).

– *Volodymyr Antonovych* (Prague, 1942).

Doroshenko, Volodymyr 'Ivan Franko i Mykhailo Hrushevsky,' *Suchasnist, no.* 1 (Munich, 1962), 16–36. Important.

– 'Literaturno-naukovyi vistnyk,' *LNV*, no. 1 (Regensburg, 1948), 47–55.

– 'M. Hrushevsky: hromadskyi diiach, polityk i publitsyst,' *Ovyd*, no. 6 (Chicago, 1957), 15–19; no. 10 (1957) 23–6; no. 11 (1957), 18–19.

– 'Pershyi prezydent vidnovlenoi ukrainskoi derzhavy,' *Ovyd*, no. 1 (Chicago, 1957), 25–6; nos. 2–3 (1957), 27–32.

– 'Zasluhy M. Hrushevskoho dlia ukrainskoi kultury,' *Ovyd*, no. 5 (Chicago, 1957), 18–22.

– 'Zhyttia i diialnist Mykhaila Hrushevskoho,' in *Vybrani pratsi*, pp. 11–30.

Dubrovsky, V.V. 'Mykola Skrypnyk iak ia ioho bachyv,' *Novi dni*, no. 93 (Toronto, 1957), 19–22, 30–2.

Edelman, R. *Gentry Politics on the Eve of the Russian Revolution: The Nationalist Party* (New Brunswick, NJ, 1980). Ignores the Ukrainian question.

Fedenko, Panas 'Mykhailo Hrushevsky v nautsi i politytsi,' *Vilna Ukraina*, no. 52 (1966), 1–17.

– 'Na stulecie Mychaily Hruszewskiego,' *Kultura*, no. 12 (Paris, 1967), 111–22.

Fedyshyn, O.S. *Germany's Drive to the East and the Ukrainian Revolution 1917–1918* (Newark, NJ 1971).

Franko-Kliuchko, Anna *Ivan Franko, i ioho rodyna: spomyny* (Toronto, 1956).

Goldenveizer, A.A. 'Iz Kievskikh vospominanii,' in *Revoliutsiia na Ukraine po memuaram Belykh*, ed. S.A. Alekseev (Moscow–Leningrad, 1930), pp. 1–63.

Graham, L. *The Soviet Academy of Sciences and the Copmmunist Party 1927–1932* (Princeton, 1967).

Grebing, H. 'Osterreich-Ungarn und die Ukrainische Aktion,' *Jahrbücher für Geschichte Osteuropas*, VII (Munich, 1959), 270–96.

Halii, M. 'M. Hrushevsky i "Ukrainska radianska entsyklopediia,"' *Vilna Ukraina*, no. 42 (1964), 29–38.

– 'Iak Moskva znyshchyla M. Hrushevskoho,' *Vilna Ukraina*, no. 52 (1966), 20–4.

Havryliuk, I. 'Chertvertyi universal: spohady,' *LNV*, XCV (1928), 16–24.

Himka, John Paul 'Ukrainskyi sotsiializm u Halychyni,' *Journal of Ukrainian Graduate Studies*, no. 7 (Toronto, 1979), 33–51.

Hlybinny, U. *Vierzig Jahre weissruthenischer Kultur unter den Sowjets* (Munich, 1959).

Hnatiuk, Volodymyr 'Naukove tovarystvo im. Shevchenko u Lvovi,' *LNV*, LXXXVI (1925), 1–11, 173–81, 263–72, 367–74; reprinted in book form by the Ukrainian Free University, Munich-Paris, 1984.

– 'Uvahy na suchasni temy: sprava ukrainsko-ruskoho universytetu u Lvovi,' *LNV*, XVII (1902), 49–72.

Horak, S. 'Michael Hrushevsky: Portrait of an Historian,' *Canadian Slavonic Papers*, X (Ottawa, 1968), 341–56.

– 'The Shevchenko Scientific Society (1873–1973): Contributor to the Birth of a Nation,' *East European Quarterly*, VI (Boulder, 1973), 249–64.

Hryhoriiv, N. *Spohady 'Ruinnyka': iak my ruinuvaly tiurmu narodiv a iak my buduvaly svoiu khatu* (Lviv, 1938).

Hunczak, Taras 'The Ukraine under Hetman Pavlo Skoropadskyi,' in *The Ukraine 1917–1921: A Study in Revolution*, pp. 61–81.

Hurzhii, I.A., and V.S. Petrenko *Vydatni radianski istoryky* (Kiev, 1969). A biographical dictionary of Soviet historians which appeared during the relatively tolerant 'Shelest' period. There is no entry on Hrushevsky.

Ieremiiv, M. 'Za lashtunkamy tsentralnoi rady (storinky zi spohadiv),' *Ukrainskyi istoryk*, nos. 1–4 (1968), 94–104.

Ivanys, V. *Symon Petliura: prezydent Ukrainy* (Toronto, 1952).

Kaluski, Marian 'O wielkosci Hruszewskiego,' *Kultura*, no. 6 (Paris, 1968), 182–6.

Kalytovska, Marta 'Pamiati Marii i Katri Hrushevskykh,' *Ukrainska liternaturna hazeta* (Munich), no. 5, November 1955.

*Kamenetsky, Ihor 'Hrushevsky and Ukrainian Foreign Policy 1917–1918,' *Ukrainskyi istoryk*, nos. 1–4 (1984), 82–102.

Katrenko, A.M., and T.D. Suslo 'Ukrainske naukove tovarystvo v Kyievi,' *Ukrainskyi istorychnyi zhurnal*, no. 5 (Kiev, 1967), 130–3.

Kedrovsky, Volodymyr *1917 rik. Spohady* (Winnipeg, 1967).

Kerensky, Alexander [Oleksander] 'Chy rosiiskyi tymchasovyi uriad buv rozpochav sudove slidstvo proty tsentralnoi rady?' *Ukraina*, no. 9 (Paris, 1953), 795–6.

Klymenko, Pavlo 'Ne khovaty pravdy vid ukrainskoho narodu,' *Kanadiiskyi farmer* (Winnipeg), no. 47, 26 November 1966).

Klymkevych, Roman O. 'Diialnist M. Hrushevskoho v tsaryni ukrainskoi heraldyky i sfrahistyky,' *Ukrainskyi istoryk*, nos. 1–2 (1966), 82–90.

Kohn, Hans *Panslavism: Its History and Ideology* (New York, 1960).

Konoval, Oleksii 'Chy Hrushevsky i Vynnychenko spravdi skapituliuvaly pered bilshovyzmom?' *Novi dni*, no. 5 (Toronto, 1980), 26–7.

Konovalets, Ievhen *Prychyky do istorii ukrainskoi revoliutsii*, second edition (n.p., 1948).

*Korduba, Myron 'Mykhailo Hrushevsky, iak uchenyi,' *Ukrainskyi istoryk*, nos. 1–4 (1984), 33–47.

Koshelivets, Ivan *Mykola Skrypnyk* (Munich, 1972).

Kostiuk, H. 'The Last Days of M. Hrushevsky,' *Ukrainian Review*, no. 5 (Munich, 1957), 73–83.

– *Stalinist Rule in the Ukraine: A Study of the Decade of Mass Terror (1929–1939)* (London–New York, 1960).

Kovalevsky, Mykola *Pry dzherelakh borotby* (Innsbruck, 1960).

– *Opozytsiini rukhy v Ukraini i natsionalna polityka SSSR (1920–1954)* (Munich, 1955).

Kovaliv, Panteleimon 'Mykhailo Hrushevsky u borotbi za ukrainsku movu,' in *Mykhailo Hrushevsky u 110 rokovyny narodzhennia*, pp. 42–55.

Kubanska, H. *Ternystymy shliakhamy* (Winnipeg, 1948). A memoir.

Kubiiovych, Volodymyr 'Moi pryiateli, spivrobitnyky, kolegy,' *Suchasnist*, no. 12 (Munich, 1983), 106–21.

Lapteva, L.P. 'S"ezd russkykh slavistov 1903 g.' in *Issledovanniia po istoriografii slavianovedeniia i balkanistiki* (Moscow, 1981), pp. 261–78.

Lavrinenko, Iurii 'Deshcho do evoliutsii svitohliadu i politychnoi dumky Ivana Franka,' in *Zbirnyk 'Ukrainskoi literaturnoi hazety'* (1956), pp. 3–28.

– *Rozstriliane vidrodzhennia* (Paris, 1959). On the central figures of the Ukrainian 'renaissance' of the 1920s who were destroyed in the Stalin purges. There is a chapter on Hrushevsky.

Levytsky, Borys *The Stalinist Terror in the Thirties* (Stanford, 1974).

Levytsky, Kost *Istoriia politychnoi dumky halytskykh Ukraintsiv*, in 2 parts (Lviv, 1926).

Lewandowski, K. *Sprawa ukraińska w polityce zagranicznej Czechoslowacji w latach 1918–1932* (Wrocław, 1974).

Lobai, Danylo *Neperemozhna Ukraina* (Winnipeg, 1950).

Lototsky, Oleksander *Storinky mynuloho*, 4 vols. (Warsaw, 1932–9; reprinted in the USA, 1966). Important.

Lozynsky, M. *Mykhailo Pavlyk: ioho zhyttia i diialnist* (Vienna, 1917; reprinted Irvington, USA, 1974).

– *Notes sur les relations ukraino-polonaises en Galicie pendant les 25 dernières années* (Paris, 1919).

Luciw, L. *Borets za natsionalnu i sotsiialnu spravedlyvist* (New York, 1968).

Luckyj, George *Literary Politics in the Soviet Ukraine 1917–1934* (New York, 1956).

Lyzhnytsky, H. 'Ivan Franko pro zavdannia i tsili teatru,' *Kyiv*, IV (Philadelphia, 1956), 156–63.

Mace, James E. *Communism and the Dilemmas of National Liberation: National Communism in Soviet Ukraine 1918–1933* (Cambridge, Mass., 1983). Well-documented synthesis.

– 'Politics and History in Soviet Ukraine, 1921–1933,' *Nationalities Papers*, X, 2 (1982), 157–79.

Magocsi, Paul 'Nationalism and National Bibliography: Ivan E. Levyts'kyi and Nineteenth-Century Galicia,' *Harvard Library Bulletin*, XXVIII (Cambridge, Mass., 1980), 81–109.

– *National Cultures and University Chairs* (Toronto, 1980). A lecture containing a brief discussion of Hrushevsky's appointment to the Chair of Ukrainian History in Lviv.

– 'Old Ruthenianism and Russophilism: A New Conceptual Framework for Analyzing National Ideologies in Late Nineteenth-Century Eastern Galicia,' *American Contributions to the Ninth International Congress of Slavists Kiev 1983*, vol. II (Columbus, Ohio, 1983), pp. 305–24.

Maistrenko, I. *Borotbisty: A Chapter in the History of Ukrainian Communism* (New York, 1954).

– *Istoriia Kommunistychnoi partii Ukrainy* (Munich, 1979).

– *Natsionalnaia politika KPSS* (Munich, 1978).

Makukh, Ivan *Na narodnii sluzhbi* (Detroit, 1958).

Mandryka, M.I. 'Deshcho za roky 1917 ta 1918 (prodovzhennia),' *Ukrainskyi istoryk*, nos. 3–4 (1977), 75–82.

Manning, C. 'Ukrainians and the United States in the First World War,' *Ukrainian Quarterly*, XIII (New York, 1957), 346–54.

Margolin, Arnold *Ukraina i politika Antanty: zapiski evreia i grazhdanina* (Berlin, n.d.).

Marunchak, M. 'M. Hrushevsky i Ukraintsi Kanady,' *Vilne Slovo* (Toronto), no. 47, 19 November 1966.

– 'Znaideno dva nevidomi lysty Mykhaila Hrushevskoho,' *Novyi shliakh* (Toronto), no. 48, 28 November 1981.

- 'Mykhailo Hrushevsky's Letters to American Ukrainians,' in *New Soil – Old Roots: The Ukrainian Experience in Canada* (Winnipeg, 1983), pp. 243–51.

Martos, Borys 'Pershi kroky tsentalnoi rady,' *Ukrainskyi istoryk*, nos. 3–4 (1973), 99–112.

- 'Pershyi vseukrainskyi selianskyi z'izd,' *Journal of Ukrainian Studies*, no. 6 (Toronto, 1979), 20–8.

- *The First Universal of the Ukrainian Central Rada* (New York, 1968).

Megas, Osyp *Heroiska Ukraina: iliustrovani spomyny z Ukrainy* (Winnipeg, 1920).

Miiakovsky, V. 'Do biohrafii M. Hrushevskoho,' *Krakivski visti* (Cracow), nos. 69–70 (1944); reprinted in *Ukrainskyi istoryk*, nos. 1–4 (1976), 114–20.

Miliukov, P.L. *Istoriia vtoroi russkoi revoliutsii. Tom pervyi*, in 3 parts (Sophia, 1924).

- *Political memoirs 1905–1917*, ed. A.P. Mendel (Ann Arbor, 1967).

Mirchuk, Petro *Ukrainska derzhavnist 1917–1920* (Philadelphia, 1967).

Mlynovetsky, P. *Narysy z istorii ukrainskykh vyzvolnykh zmahan 1917–1918* (Toronto, 1970).

- 'Do tak zvanoho "Polubotkivskoho perevorotu,"' in *Almanakh Kalendar Homonu Ukrainy na rik 1962* (Toronto), pp. 159–66.

Mochulsky, M., 'Z ostannikh desiatylit zhyttia Franka 1896–1916,' *Za sto lit*, III (Kiev, 1928), 226–84.

Modrych-Verhan, V. 'Mykhailo Hrushevsky iak publitsyst,' in *Mykhailo Hrushevsky u 110 rokovyny narodzhennia*, pp. 56–98.

Motyl, A. *The Turn to the Right: The Ideological Origins and Development of Ukrainian Nationalism 1919–1929* (New York, 1980).

Mukhin, Mykhailo 'Prof. M. Hrushevsky (1866–1934),' *Vistnyk* nos. 2–4 (Lviv, 1936), 102–15, 194–202, 268–77.

Mykytas, V.L. *Ideolohichna borotba navkolo spadshchyny Ivana Franka* (Kiev, 1978).

Narizhny, S. *Ukrainska emigratsiia: kulturna pratsia ukrainskoi emigratsii mizh dvoma svitovymy viinamy* (Prague, 1942).

Niamiha, H. 'The Belorussian Academy of Sciences: October 13, 1928–July 7, 1936,' *Belorussian Review*, no. 6 (Munich, 1958), 5–29.

Ohloblyn, O. 'Mykhailo Hrushevsky i ukrainske natsionalne vidrodzhennia,' *Ukrainskyi istoryk*, nos. 2–3 (1964), 1–6. An important synthetic essay.

- 'Mykhailo Serhiievych Hrushevsky 1866–1934,' *Ukrainskyi istoryk*, nos. 1–2 (1966), 6–14; and also available in a somewhat inferior English translation as:

- 'Michael Hrushevsky: Foremost Ukrainian Historian,' *Ukrainian Quarterly*, XXII (New York, 1966), 322–33.

Omelchenkova, Mariia *T.G. Masaryk (1850–1930)* (Prague, 1931).

Onatsky, Ievhen 'M. Hrushevsky: chestnist z narodom,' in his *Portrety v profil* (Chicago, 1965), pp. 285–97.

Padoch, Iaroslav 'Lev Okinshevych: vydatnyi istoryk Hetmanskoi Ukrainy,' *Ukrainskyi istoryk*, nos. 1–4 (1981), 105–17.

Pankivsky, K. 'Spohady pro NTSh,' *Ukrainskyi istoryk*, no. 4 (1978), 94–9.

Pavlovsky, Vadym 'Danylo Shcherbakivsky (1877–1977),' *Ukrainskyi istoryk*, nos. 3–4 (1977), 83–8.

Pelenski, Jaroslaw 'Der ukrainische Nationalgedanke im Lichte der Werke M. Hruševskyjs und V. Lipinskys,' PH D thesis, Ludwig-Maximilians Universität (Munich, 1956).

Petriv, Vsevolod *Spomyny z chasiv ukrainskoi revoliutsii (1917–1921)*, part 1 (Lviv, 1927).

Pfitzner, J. 'Die Geschichtswissenschaft in der Sowjetunion,' in *Bolschwistische Wissenschaft und Kulturpolitik*, pp. 163–218.

Pidhainy, Oleh *The Formation of the Ukrainian Republic* (Toronto, 1966).

Pidhainy, Semen *Ukrainska inteligentsiia na Solovkakh* (Neu Ulm, 1947).

Pidigo, F. *Ukraina pid bolshevytskoiu okupatsiieiu* (Munich, 1956). Good synthesis.

– 'Mykhailo Hrushevsky ta ioho istorychni ustanovy,' *Ukrainski visti* (Neu Ulm), nos. 94–5 (1952). Contains information not included in his book.

Pipes, Richard 'Peter Struve and Ukrainian Nationalism,' *Harvard Ukrainian Studies*, III–IV (Cambridge, Mass., 1979–80), 675–83.

– *The Formation of the Soviet Union* (New York, 1974).

Polonska-Vasylenko, N. *Istoriia Ukrainy*, 2 vols. (Munich, 1972–6).

– 'M.P. Vasylenko i VUAN,' *Ukraina*, no. 5 (Paris, 1951), 337–45.

– 'Ahatanhel Krymsky,' *Ukraina*, no. 2 (Paris, 1949), 121–8.

– *Ukrainska Akademiia Nauk (narys istorii)*, 2 vols. (Munich, 1955–8).

Presniakov, A.E. *The Formation of the Great Russian State*, trans. A. Moorehouse (Chicago, 1970).

Pritsak, Omeljan 'U stolittia narodyn M. Hrushevskoho,' in *Idei i liudy vyzvolnykh zmahan* (New York, 1968), pp. 187–230.

– 'Harvardskyi tsentr ukrainskykh studii i shkola Hrushevskoho,' in his *Chomu katedry ukrainoznavstva v Harvardi?* (Cambridge, Mass.–New York, 1973), pp. 91–107. Pritsak maintains that the traditions of Hrushevsky's 'historical school' are being continued at Harvard.

Prymak, Thomas M. 'The First All-Ukrainian Congress of Soviets and Its Antecedents,' *Journal of Ukrainian Graduate Studies*, no. 6 (Toronto, 1979), 3–19.

– 'Herzen on Poland and Ukraine,' *Journal of Ukrainian Studies*, no. 12 (Toronto, 1982), 31–40.

– 'Hrushevsky's Constitutional Project of 1905,' *Canadian Slavonic Papers*, forthcoming.

– 'Konstytutsiinyi proiekt M. Hrushevskoho z 1905 roku,' *Ukrainskyi istoryk*, nos. 1–4 (1985), 34–45.

– 'Mykhailo Hrushevsky: Populist or Statist?' *Journal of Ukrainian Studies*, no. 10 (Toronto, 1981), 65–78.

- 'Mysterious Historian: The Life of Volodymyr Antonovych,' *Forum*, no. 51 (Scranton, Pa., 1982), 26–7.

Rakhmanny, Roman, [Olynyk] 'Budivnychyi pershoi ukrainskoi narodnoi respubliky,' *Suchasnist*, no. 1 (Munich, 1966), 59–86.

Reshetar, John *The Ukrainian Revolution 1917–1920* (Princeton, 1952).

Riha, Thomas *A Russian European: Paul Miliukov in Russian Politics* (Notre Dame–London, 1969).

Rozhin, I. 'Pavlo Tutkivsky (1858–1930),' *Novi dni*, no. 88 (Toronto, 1958), 15–21.

Rudnytsky, I.L. 'The Ukrainians in Galicia under Austrian Rule,' in *Nation-building and the Politics of Nationalism: Essays on Austrian Galicia*, ed. A.S. Markovits and F.E. Sysyn, (Cambridge, Mass., 1982), pp. 23–67.

Rubach, M.A. 'Hrushevsky, M.S.,' *Ukrainska Radianska Entsyklopediia*, vol. III (Kiev, 1979), 202.

Sarbei, V.H. 'Pershyi neodminyi sekretar ukrainskoi akademii nauk,' *Visnyk AN URSR*, no. 1 (Kiev, 1971), 92–6.

Semenenko, Oleksander *Kharkiv Kharkiv* ... (Munich, 1976).

Seton-Watson, Hugh and Christopher *The Making of a New Europe: R.W. Seton-Watson and the Last Years of Austria-Hungary* (London, 1981).

Shcherbakivsky, Vadym *Pamiati Vasylia Hryhorovycha Krychevskoho* (London, 1954).

Shevchenko, F.P. 'Chomu Mykhailo Hrushevsky povernuvsia na radiansku Ukrainu?' *Ukrainskyi istorychnyi zhurnal*, no. 2 (Kiev, 1966), 13–30.

Shteppa, K. *Russian Historians and the Soviet State* (New Brunswick, NJ, 1962).

Shulhyn, Oleksander [Alexandre Choulguine] *L'Ukraine contre Moscou (1917)* (Paris, 1935).

Siry, Iuryi [Iuryi Tyshchenko] 'Kyiv (uryvok z spomyniv),' *Literaturno-naukovyi zbirnyk*, 1 (Hanover, 1946), 45–77.

- 'Z moikh zustrichiv,' *Literaturno-naukovyi zbirnyk*, III (Hanover–Kiel, 1948), 55–69.

- *Pershi naddniprianski ukrainski masovi politychni hazety* (New York, 1952).

- *Iz spohadiv pro ukrainski vydavnytstva* (Augsburg, 1949).

Solovei, Dmytro 'U spravi zhyttiepysu M.S. Hrushevskoho,' *Vilna Ukraina*, no. 17 (1958), 9–21.

- *Holhota Ukrainy* (Winnipeg, 1953).

Sosnovsky, M. *Dmytro Dontsov: poliychnyi portret* (New York–Toronto, 1974). A full political biography containing a discussion of Dontsov's break with the humanitarian-autonomist tradition represented by Hrushevsky.

Stakhiv, Matvii *Proty khvyl: istorychnyi rozvytok ukrainskoho sotsiialistychnoho rukhu na zakhidnykh ukrainskykh zemliakh* (Lviv, 1934).

- 'Chomu M. Hrushevsky povernuvsia v 1924 rotsi do Kyieva? (zhmut faktiv i uryvok zi spohadiv),' in *Mykhailo Hrushevsky u 110 rokovyny narodzhennia*, pp. 109–47.

- 'Deiaki dokumenty pro diialnist Hrushevskoho na emihratsii,' in *Mykhailo Hrushevsky u 110 rokovyny narodzhennia*, pp. 148–76.
- 'Deiaki materiialy pro bolshevytskyi nastup na Hrushevskoho,' in *Mykhailo Hrushevsky u 110 rokovyny narodzhennia*, pp. 175–220.
- 'Deiaki materiialy pro svitohliad Hrushevskoho,' in *Mykhailo Hrushevsky u 110 rokovyny narodzhennia*, pp. 221–36.
- *Ukraina v dobi dyrektorii UNR*, 6 vols. (Scranton, Pa., 1962–5).
- 'A Scientist and Social Leader as President of a State. Professor M. Hrushevsky, leader of the Ukrainian National Republic,' *Ukrainian Quarterly*, XIII (New York, 1957), 329–36. Hagiographical tone.

Stercho, Petro 'Vydannia velykoi istorii Ukrainy Mykhaila Hrushevskoho nevidkladne zavdannia ukrainskoi vilnoi nauky i usoho hromadianstva,' *Samostiina Ukraina*, nos. 5–6 (Chicago, 1977), 15–22.

Stoiko, Volodymyr 'Z'izd narodiv u Kyievi 1917 roku,' *Ukrainskyi istoryk*, nos. 3–4 (1977), 14–25.

Sullivant, R. *Soviet Politics and the Ukraine 1917–1957* (New York, 1962).

Sydorenko, A. 'Ukraine at Brest-Litovsk,' *Ukrainian Quarterly*, XXIV (New York, 1968), 117–28.

Szporluk, Roman, ed. *Russia in World History. Selected Essays by M.N. Pokrovsky* (Ann Arbor, 1970).

Tabouis, General 'Comment je devins Commissare de la Republique Française en Ukraine,' in *Spohady, Pratsi Ukrainskoho Naukovoho Institutu*, vol. VII (Warsaw, 1932), pp. 142–64.

Tikhy, F. [František Tichý] 'Ukrainskyi istoryk ta Chekhy,' *Druzhno vpered*, no. 10 (Priashiv, 1966), 8.

Topchybashy, A.M.B. 'Soiuz avtonomystiv: z spomyniv pro pershu derzhavnu dumu v b. Rosii,' in *Spohady, Pratsi Ukrainskoho Naukovoho Instytutu*, vol. VII (Warsaw, 1932), pp. 133–41.

Trylovsky, K. 'Ivan Franko iak poet-hromadianyn,' *LNV*, XCI (1926), 33–44.

Tsereteli, I.G. *Vospominaniia o fevralskoi revoliutsii*, 2 vols. (Paris–The Hague, 1963).

Dr. K.U. *Pershyi napad Rosii na Lviv (1914) v 40-littia kontr-napadu ukraintsiv na Peterburh (25.II.1917–25.II.1957)* (New York, 1957).

A.V., 'Mykhailo Hrushevsky (29.II.1866–24.XI.1934),' *Ukrainskyi Kalendar* (Warsaw, 1966), 152–3.

Vernadsky, Vladimir 'The First Year of the Ukrainian Academy of Sciences (1918–1919),' *Annals of the Ukrainian Academy of Arts and Science in the US*, XI (New York, 1964–8), 3–31.

Veryha, V. 'Naukove tovarystvo im. Shevchenka v dobi Hrushevskoho,' in *Iuvileinyi zbirnyk naukovykh prats v 100-richia NTSh* (Toronto, 1977), pp. 15–32.

Voinarenko, Ostap *Pro samostiinist UNR: de koly i iak vona proholoshuvalas ta iakyi buv ii zmist* (Winnipeg, 1966).

Vorob"eva, Iu.S. 'Russkaia vysshaia shkola obshchestvennykh nauk v Parizhe,' in *Istoricheskie zapiski*, vol. CVII (Moscow, 1982), 333–44.

Voskobiynyk, Michael 'The Nationalities Question in Russia in 1905–1907: A study in the Origin of Modern Nationalism, with Special Reference to the Ukrainians,' PH D thesis, University of Pennsylvania (Philadelphia, 1972).

Vozniak, M. 'Ivan Franko v dobi radykalizmu,' *Ukraina*, no. 6 (Kiev, 1926), 113–63.

Vynnychenko, Volodymyr *Vidrodzheniia natsii*, 3 vols. (Vienna, 1920).

Vytanovych, I. 'Uvahy do metodolohii i istoriohrafii M. Hrushevskoho,' *Ukrainskyi istoryk*, nos. 1–2 (1966), 32–51.

Wasilewski, Leon *Kresy wschodnie* (Warsaw–Cracow, 1915).

– 'Moje wspomnienia ukraińskie,' in *Spohady, Pratsi Ukrainskoho Naukovoho Instytutu*, vol. VII (Warsaw, 1932), pp. 5–35.

– *Ukraina i sprawa ukraińska* (Cracow, n.d.).

Wynar, Lubomyr [Liubomyr Vynar] 'Avtobiohrafiia Mykhaila Hrushevskoho z 1906 i 1926 rokiv iak dzherelo dlia vyvchennia ioho zhyttia i tvorochosty,' *Ukrainskyi istoryk*, nos. 1–3 (1974), 103–35.

– 'Chomu Mykhailo Hrushevsky povernuvsia na Ukrainu v 1914 rotsi?' *Ukrainskyi istoryk*, nos. 3–4 (1967), 103–8.

*– 'Dumky z pryvodu p'iatdesiatykh rokovyn smerty M. Hrusheuskoho,' *Ukrainskyi istoryk*, nos. 1–4 (1984), 7–20.

– 'Halytska doba Mykhaila Hrushevskoho,' *Ukrainskyi istoryk*, nos. 1–2 (1967), 5–22.

– 'Istorychni pratsi Ivana Franka,' in *Zbirnyk 'Ukrainskoi literaturnoi hazety' 1956*, pp. 48–63.

– 'Materiialy do biohrafii Mykhaila Hrushevskoho,' *Ukrainskyi istoryk*, nos. 1–2 (1982), 65–75.

– *Molodist Mykhaila Hrushevskoho*, (Munich–New York, 1967). Contains much the same material as 'Zhyttia i naukova ... '.

– *Mykhailo Hrushevsky i Naukove Tovarystvo im. Tarasa Shevchenka 1892–1930* (Munich, 1970).

*– 'Mykhailo Hrushevsky i zahalni zbory NTSh v 1913 rotsi,' *Ukrainskyi istoryk*, nos. 1–4 (1984), 64–81.

*– 'Naivydatnishyi istoryk Ukrainy Mykhailo Hrushevsky (U 50-littia smerty: 1934–1984),' *Suchasnist*, no. 11 (New York, 1984), 895–95, no. 1 (1985), 56–70, no. 2, 73–92, no. 3, 54–78, no. 4, 91–112.

– 'Ranni istorychni pratsi Mykhaila Hrushevskoho i Kyivska istorychna shkola V. Antonovycha,' *Ukrainskyi istoryk*, nos. 3–4 (1966) 26–32.

– 'Ukrainian-Russian Confrontation in Historiography,' *Ukrainian Quarterly*, XXX (New York, 1974), 13–25.

- 'Zamitky do statti Iu. Gerycha: "Do biohrafii M. Hrushevskoho,"' *Ukrainskyi istoryk*, nos. 1–2 (1972), 85–90.
- 'Zhyttia i naukova diialnist Mykhaila Hrushevskoho,' *Ukrainskyi istoryk*, nos. 1–2 (1966), 15–31. On Hrushevsky's childhood and youth.

Yurkevych, Myroslav 'A Forerunner of National Communism: Lev Iurkevych (1885–1918),' *Journal of Ukrainian Studies*, no. 12 (Toronto, 1982), 50–6.

Zozulia, Iakiv *Velyka ukrainska revoliutsiia ... Kalendar istorychnykh podii za liutyi 1917 roku – berezen 1918 roku* (New York, 1967).
- 'Druhyi universal ukrainskoi tsentralnoi rady ta ioho pravno-istorychna vartist,' *Vilna Ukraina*, nos. 55–56 (1967), 10–16.
- 'Obloha Kyieva, vidstup ukrainskoi armii na Volyn,' *Za derzhavnist*, XI (Toronto, 1966), 42–64.

Index